CW00921349

Detail in Contemporary Glass Architecture

Published in 2011 by
Laurence King Publishing Ltd
361–373 City Road
London
EC1V 1LR
e-mail: enquiries@laurenceking.com
www.laurenceking.com

A catalogue record for this book is
available from the British Library

ISBN: 978 1 85669 740 8

Designed by Hamish Muir
Illustrations by Advanced Illustrations
Limited
Picture Research by Sophia Gibb

Printed in China

Detail in Contemporary Glass Architecture

Virginia McLeod

Laurence King Publishing

Contents

Glass is one of the most remarkable materials ever discovered by man. Made from the melting and cooling of one of the planet's most abundant minerals, silica, it has allowed the creation of a substance that is not only rock hard and stable, but transparent. In its 4,000 year history it has been used in almost every aspect of human endeavour including lens making, durable containers, even fabric, and of course in architecture, where its potential for the creation of transparent enclosures has changed the way we live and interact with our surroundings, particularly over the past thousand years. Without glass we would all be living in dimly lit enclosures with little contact with the outside world. Glass used in architectural contexts has, over the centuries, allowed us access to daylight and views from our living environments, not to mention iconic architectural feats over the centuries including wondrous Gothic cathedrals and the sheer exuberance of Victorian glasshouses, each of which represent an enormous breakthrough in glass technology and its astonishing capabilities in architectural environments.

The history of glass in architecture is inextricable from the twin, and often conflicting, needs to create enclosure and shelter for reasons of security and protection from the weather, while at the same time to admit light or provide illumination and access to views. The search for a material that would be sufficiently strong, stable and transparent for use in buildings finally led to the accidental discovery of glass. Silica, or common sand, could be heated to melting point then cooled carefully to avoid crystallization, resulting in an extraordinarily adaptable building material. However, the journey from the discovery of silicate as the raw material needed to create glass and the production of glass for use in buildings was a long and difficult one. The high temperatures and skill needed to create glass were difficult to come by, not to mention the techniques required to control the shape of the molten material as it slowly cooled from a fluid, through a viscous state and finally to a clear vitrified solid. Two thousand years passed between the initial discovery and the development of blown glass which made it possible to create thin transparent sheets that were strong enough for windows. This made it possible to explore new expressions in architecture beyond the necessity for shelter and security. Now the creation of conceptual and technical masterpieces was possible and has continued to lead to some of the most visionary works of architecture today.

This book attempts to demonstrate how contemporary architects from all over the world have used glass in an exemplary way to create outstanding architecture with glass being central to the concept of the design. In some of the buildings presented here, either a special glass has been designed, or a new glass technique has been developed to serve the design concept. For example, FAM Arquitectura developed a new system of curved-ended

glass blocks connected with transparent adhesive to create the stunning memorial to the victims of the terrorist attacks in Madrid. By contrast Steven Holl has used glass planks, usually reserved for more prosaic uses, to create a beautiful series of galleries for the Nelson-Atkins Museum in Missouri. Here, the translucent glass is used for the entirety of the building's volume, creating what appear to be glowing blocks of ice in the landscape.

Elsewhere, architects have used glass as a medium for artistic expression. Both Foreign Office Architects (John Lewis Department Store, UK) and Erick van Egeraat (INHolland University, The Netherlands) have taken advantage of glazed facades on which to print complex screen-printed patterns that express ideas about the history of the site (in the former) and the context of the landscape (in the latter). By contrast, other architects have exploited the sheer transparency and negligible presence of glass to create architectural works of superlative elegance. For example, Toyo Ito's Funeral Hall in Japan features a lightweight concrete wave-like roof which, thanks to full height panes of glass that have been cut to fit the shape of the curved ceiling above, allow the sculptural roof to appear to float effortlessly above the landscape. Similarly, it is the controlled and rigorous application of glazed walls in Thomas Phifer's Brochstein Pavilion in Houston that makes the steel and aluminium trellis roof appear so light and elegant. These examples, and all 50 projects featured in the book, demonstrate that technical understanding and prowess in the use of glass leads to architecture of great beauty.

This book illustrates how construction details are as vital a part of glass architecture as its external form and interior layout. Whether so subtle as to be invisible, or revealed as extraordinarily complex, details determine the quality and character of a building. Good detailing entails exercising the utmost care and attention at the junctions between materials, between the different elements of a building and where a material changes direction. Through details, the myriad parts that make up a building come together to form a whole – joints, connections, seams, openings and surfaces are transformed via a combination of technology and invention into a building.

We are accustomed to being presented with photographic representations of architecture in books, magazines and on-line, with the inspiring image continuing to be the focus of the two-dimensional representation of architecture. Increasingly these images are now often accompanied by floor plans to provide a better understanding of the way a building works. The availability of floor plans is, of course, of enormous assistance in helping us to understand the spatial sequences, the extent and scale of a building. However it is not inherent in the purpose of a plan or a photograph, even if accompanied by a section, to reveal the individual elements – literally the nuts and bolts – that go together to make up a wall, a floor, a roof, a window, a staircase, a kitchen, and so on. Construction details, however, do just this, and this book unites the photograph, the plan and section, as well as the details to bring to the reader a comprehensive insight into the true workings of the building.

Architects draw details specifically to reveal the inner workings of a building – primarily, of course, they are used by the builder in order to construct the building. Readers of architectural publications, however, are all too rarely given the opportunity to examine the details – the 'real' representation of how a building is put together. This book aims to remedy that and provides a guide to the inner workings of 50 of the most inspiring examples of contemporary glass architecture. This book brings to the reader what has previously been hidden behind the facade, what had previously remained invisible. These details reveal not only an 'x-ray' of the houses presented, but an insight into the cognitive processes of the architects who brought the houses into being.

Architectural details make up to 95 per cent of the sometimes hundreds of drawings produced to describe the way a building is put together. They act as the means by which architects communicate their intent to builders, engineers and other participants in the building process. They also act as one of the most challenging intellectual and technical exercises for any architect, producing as they must, a series of what are essentially graphic representations of every single junction and connection in a building. Almost exclusively made up of two-dimensional representations (plans and sectional drawings), the challenge resides in the architect's ability to imagine the most complex of junctions, assemblies and components in three dimensions – as they will actually be built on site – and transfer them on to paper, or on to a screen, into two dimensions, into the conventional drawn representations that have been used in the construction industry for decades, even centuries.

While the selection of details presented for each of the buildings in this book is necessarily limited by space, they nonetheless go a long way towards deconstructing the image of the finished building. They not only inspire, they also help us to understand the thought that went into the making of the building and perhaps the technical problems that were solved along the way.

The last decade has seen a burgeoning of outstanding glass architecture, as is evident from the buildings featured here. It is my hope that these 50 projects, in their diversity, experimental spirit and architectural excellence, illustrate this most alluring of building materials.

Virginia McLeod

Notes

US and Metric Measurements
Dimensions have been provided by the architects in metric and converted to US measurements, except in the case of projects in the US, where dimensions have been converted to metric.

Terminology
An attempt has been made to standardize terminology to aid understanding across readerships, for example 'wood' is generally referred to as 'timber' and 'aluminum' as 'aluminium'. However materials or processes that are peculiar to a country, region or architectural practice that have no direct correspondence are presented in the original.

Floor Plans
Throughout the book, the following convention of hierarchy has been used – ground floor, first floor, second floor, and so on. In certain contexts, terms such as basement level or upper level have been used for clarity.

Scale
All floor plans, sections and elevations are presented at conventional architectural metric scales, typically 1:50, 1:100 or 1:200 as appropriate. An accurate graphic scale is included on the second page near the floor plans of every project to aid in the understanding of scale. Details are also presented at conventional architectural scales, typically 1:1, 1:5 and 1:10.

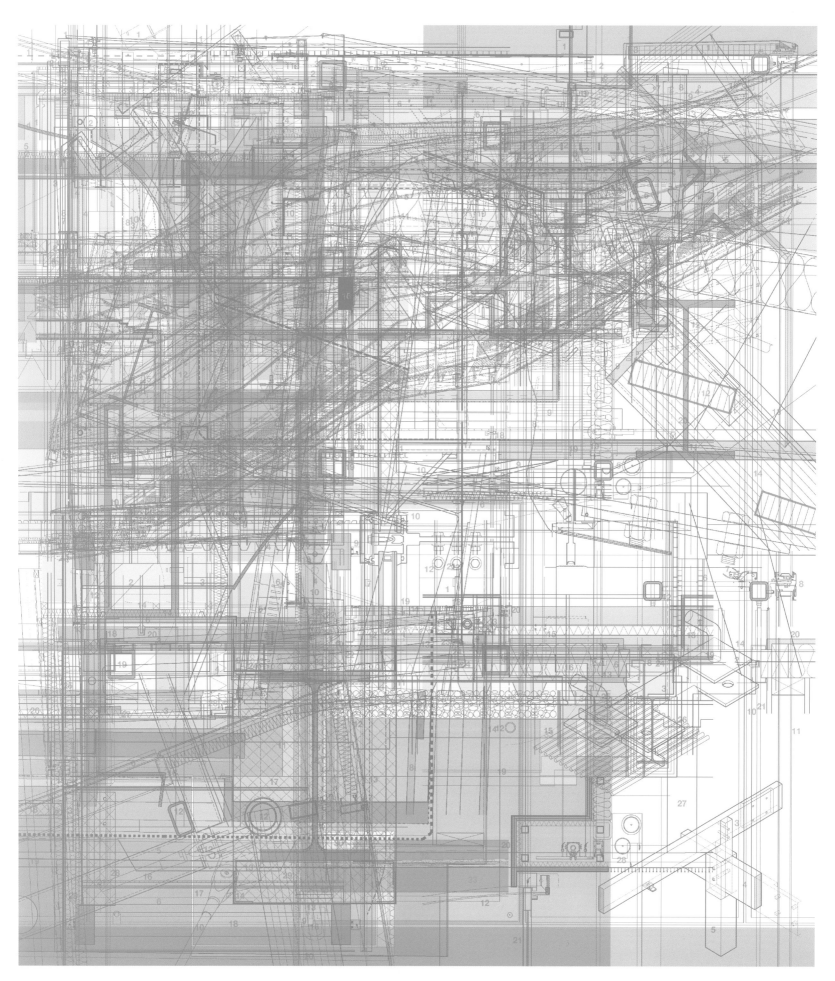

8

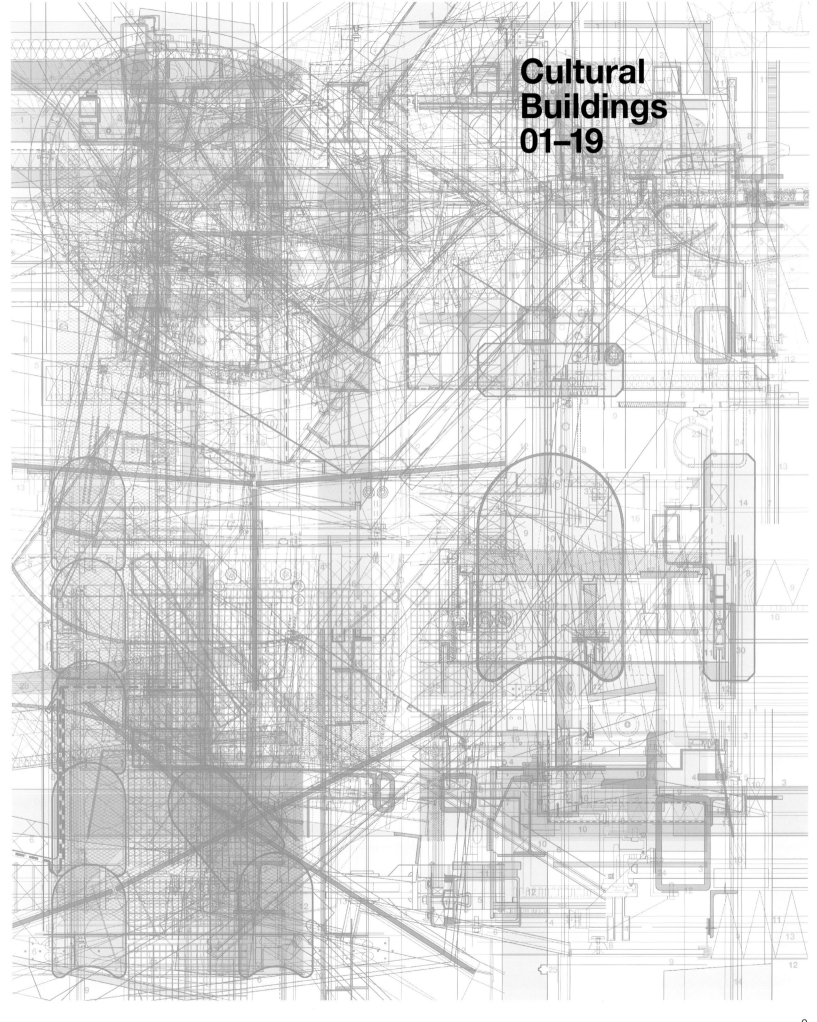

Cultural
Buildings
01–19

01
Lluís Clotet Ballús, Ignacio Paricio Ansuatégui, Abeba arquitectes

**Alicia Foundation
Barcelona, Spain**

Project Team
Javier Baqueró Rodríguez, Queralt Simó Faneca, Cristina Ferrer Sabaté

Structural Engineer
Jesús Jiménez Cañas

Services Engineer
Josep V. Martí Estelles - Miquel Camps

Quantity Surveyor
Santiago Loperena Jené

The new building that houses the Alicia Foundation, a project promoted by the celebrated chef Ferràn Adrià, is dedicated exclusively to investigations into gastronomy. It is situated near the Monastery of Sant Benet de Bages, in central Catalonia on a bend of the river Llobregat. Rather than compete with the ancient monastery and the rural landscape, the new building aims to bring to the user the experience of being surrounded by nature. As a result, the vertical plane that separates the interior from the exterior is made entirely from glass, making the built volume virtually disappear in certain light conditions and in others, acting as a mirror that reflects its surroundings. The geometry also avoids the orthogonal nature of the neighbouring structures and as a consequence it respects the historic walls, fences and paths as well as established trees.

The control of natural light and heat is fundamental to ensure interior comfort. To protect the glazed structure, the building is surrounded by walls, some of them old, others new, many opaque and others with large windows, but all at the height of the glass openings and at a distance that varies between 3 and 14 metres (10 and 46 feet). This intermediate space, interrupted only by the entrance, is treated as an open facade where the planting and the steel pergola ensure quality of light and protection from the sun. This interstitial space allows the interior to be extended into the landscape to create a tranquil, private garden. To achieve an open plan layout, perimeter structural supports have been placed just inside the glass perimeter wall at every metre. Service cores made from concrete walls stabilize each one of the arms of the building.

1 The ancient stone walls that traverse the landscape are reflected in the glazed perimeter wall of the new building.
2 The free polyhedral form and a column-free interior ensure working environments that flow easily through the building.
3 A steel framed pergola creates opportunities for climbing plants as well as creating a sense of enclosure to parts of the interstitial outdoor space that surrounds the building.
4 The free form of the plan allows open courtyards to infiltrate the building, creating intimate outdoor spaces.
5 A series of north facing skylights (left) ensure even lighting conditions throughout the day.

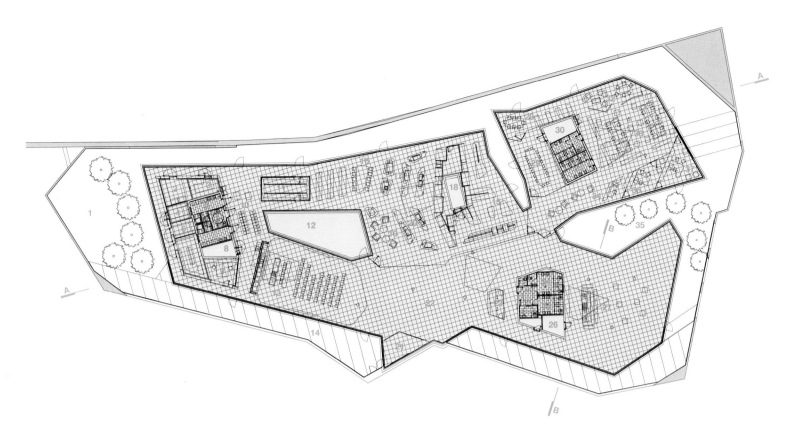

01.01
Ground Floor Plan
1:500

1 Courtyard	10 Auditorium lobby
2 Storage	11 Black box
3 Storage	12 Courtyard
4 Storage	13 Auditorium
5 WCs	14 Courtyard
6 Storage	15 Scientific research
7 Locker room	area
8 Technical room	16 Kitchen laboratory
9 Office	meeting area
	17 Kitchen laboratory
	18 Technical room
	19 Kitchen laboratory

seating	31 WCs
20 Kitchen laboratory	32 Informal meeting
21 Entrance	area
22 Foyer	33 Theoretical work
23 Reception	area
24 Male WC	34 Administration
25 Female WC	reception
26 Technical room	35 Courtyard
27 Children's kitchen	36 Administration
28 Meeting room	37 Director's office
29 Conference room	
30 Technical room	

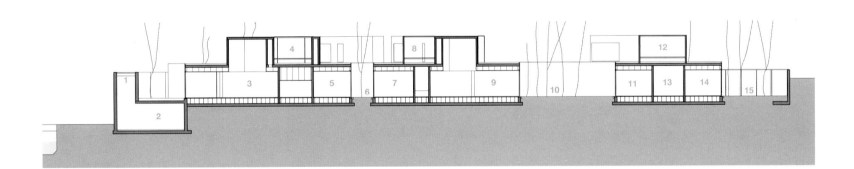

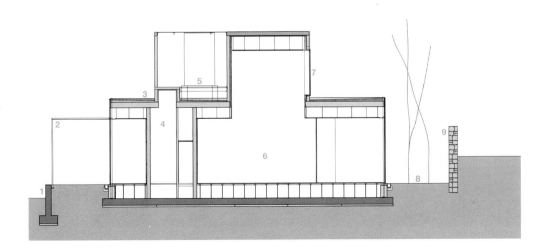

01.02
Section A–A
1:500

1 Courtyard
2 Technical room
3 Locker room
4 Technical room
5 Auditorium lobby
6 Courtyard
7 Kitchen laboratory
8 Technical room
9 Scientific research
area
10 Courtyard
11 Conference room
12 Technical room
13 WCs
14 Theoretical work
area
15 Courtyard

01.03
Section B–B
1:200

1 New retaining wall
2 Steel pergola
3 Flat roof
4 Technical space
5 Technical room
6 Children's kitchen
7 Clerestory window
8 Courtyard
9 Existing stone wall

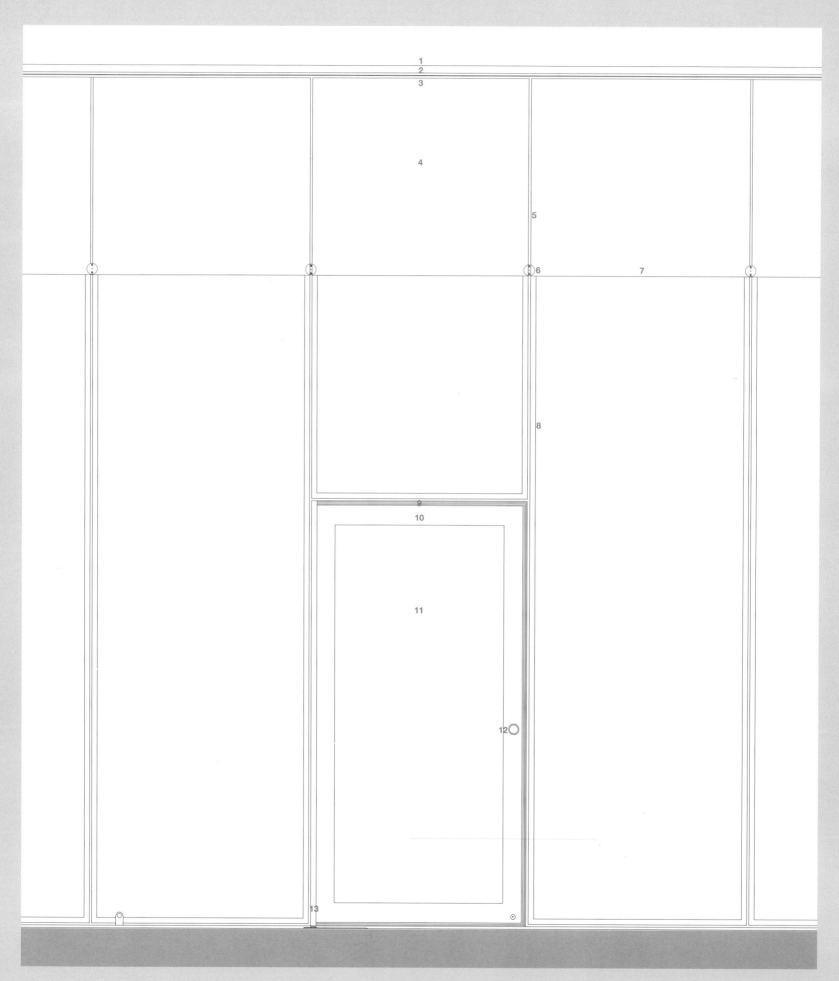

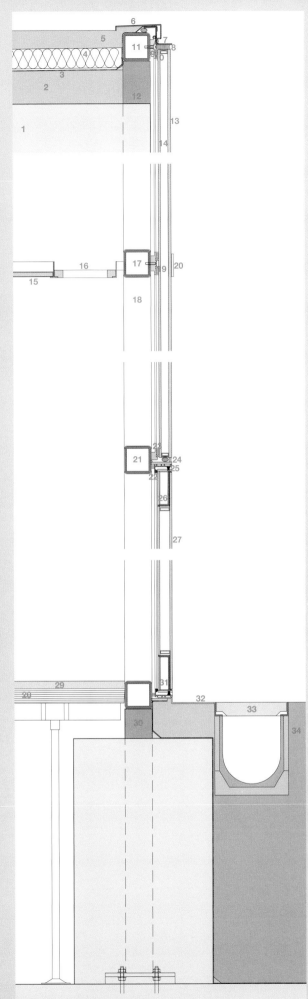

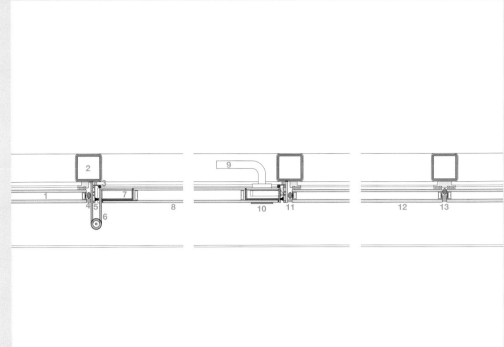

01.04
Glass Facade Elevation Detail
1:20

1 1.5 mm ($1/16$ inch) stainless steel sheet parapet capping
2 3 mm ($1/8$ inch) stainless steel folded plate
3 Neutral silicone seal
4 Double glazing comprised of 8 mm ($1/3$ inch) exterior colourless toughened glass with opaque zone of silk-screened pattern, 20 mm ($3/4$ inch) cavity and 6mm ($1/4$ inch) interior toughened glass with low emissivity coating
5 Structural silicone fixing
6 5 mm ($1/5$ inch) steel disc to mechanical glass fixing system
7 Metal sheet flashing
8 70 x 70 mm ($23/4$ x $23/4$ inch) vertical square steel tube with intumescent paint fire protection
9 Aluminium perimeter profile door
10 Opaque area of silk screened glass to door
11 Double glazing comprised of 8 mm ($1/3$ inch) exterior colourless toughened glass with opaque zone of silk-screened pattern, 20 mm ($3/4$ inch) cavity and 6mm ($1/4$ inch) interior toughened glass with low emissivity coating
12 Stainless steel door handle
13 Continuous vertical hinge from 6 mm ($1/4$ inch) steel sheet with low pivot

01.05
Glass Facade Section Detail
1:10

1 300 mm ($114/5$ inch) reinforced concrete roof slab
2 Lightweight concrete screed to create slopes for drainage
3 Waterproof membrane coated with emulsion epoxy resin
4 Extruded polystyrene thermal insulation
5 Gravel bed
6 1.5 mm ($1/16$ inch) stainless steel sheet parapet capping
7 3 mm ($1/8$ inch) stainless steel folded plate
8 Neutral silicone seal
9 Anodized aluminium extruded profile with stainless steel screw fixings
10 Black structural silicone fixing
11 70 x 70 mm ($23/4$ x $23/4$ inch) square steel tube with intumescent paint fire protection
12 Brick partition
13 Double glazing comprised of 8 mm ($1/3$ inch) exterior colourless toughened glass with opaque zone of silk-screened pattern, 20 mm ($3/4$ inch) cavity and 6mm ($1/4$ inch) interior toughened glass with low emissivity coating
14 Opaque area of silk-screened glass
15 Perforated plasterboard false ceiling with acoustic absorption
16 Painted timber perimeter panel with grooves for climate system return
17 70 x 70 mm ($23/4$ x $23/4$ inch) horizontal square steel tube with intumescent paint fire protection
18 70 x 70 mm ($23/4$ x $23/4$ inch) vertical square steel tube with intumescent paint fire

protection
19 Adhesive joint
20 5 mm ($1/5$ inch) steel disc to mechanical glass fixing system
21 70 x 70 mm ($23/4$ x $23/4$ inch) horizontal square steel tube with intumescent paint fire protection
22 Anodized aluminium extruded profile with stainless steel screw fixings
23 Black structural silicone fixing
24 Neutral silicone seal
25 Aluminium perimeter profile door
26 Opaque area of silk-screened glass to door
27 Double glazing comprised of 6 mm ($1/4$ inch) exterior colourless toughened glass with opaque zone of silk-screened pattern, 27 mm ($11/8$ inch) cavity and 6mm ($1/4$ inch) interior toughened glass with low emissivity coating
28 600 x 600 mm ($232/3$ x $232/3$ inch) raised floor supported on substructure
29 Clay tiles
30 Brick partition
31 Continuous vertical hinge from 6 mm ($1/4$ inch) steel sheet with low pivot
32 3 mm ($1/8$ inch) stainless steel sheet
33 Perimeter drain and agricultural drain
34 Natural ground

01.06
Glass Facade and Door Plan Detail
1:10

1 Double glazing comprised of 8 mm ($1/3$ inch) exterior colourless toughened glass with opaque zone of silk-screened pattern, 20 mm ($3/4$ inch) cavity and 6mm ($1/4$ inch) interior toughened glass with low emissivity coating
2 70 x 70 mm ($23/4$ x $23/4$ inch) vertical square steel tube with intumescent paint fire protection
3 Neutral silicone seal
4 Neutral silicone seal
5 Aluminium perimeter door frame
6 6 mm ($1/4$ inch) steel sheet hinge cover
7 Opaque area of silk screened glass to door
8 Double glazing comprised of 6 mm ($1/4$ inch) exterior colourless toughened glass with opaque zone of silk-screened pattern, 27 mm ($11/8$ inch) cavity and 6mm ($1/4$ inch) interior toughened glass with low emissivity coating
9 Stainless steel door handle
10 5 mm ($1/5$ inch) steel disc to mechanical glass fixing system
11 Neutral silicone seal
12 Double glazing comprised of 8 mm ($1/3$ inch) exterior colourless toughened glass with opaque zone of silk-screened pattern, 20 mm ($3/4$ inch) cavity and 6mm ($1/4$ inch) interior toughened glass with low emissivity coating
13 Adhesive joint

Peter Elliott Architecture + Urban Design

Latrobe University Visual Arts Centre
Bendigo, Victoria, Australia

Client
Latrobe University

Project Team
Peter Elliott, Des Cullen, Justin Mallia, Penny Webster, Rob Trinca

Structural Engineer
Clive Steele Partners

Facade Artist
Robyn Burgess

The Latrobe University Visual Arts Centre gives the university an off-campus presence within central Bendigo for the promotion of its visual arts programme. This includes a small public gallery and lecture theatre as well as postgraduate artist studios, a print workshop and an artist-in-residence apartment. The new building acts as an infill in a section of established streetscape. The View Street facade is composed of two floating glass screens which act as a veil to the main structure beyond. The artist Robyn Burgess has produced a shimmering image titled 'Future Cities', which fills the entire facade and brings art to the street in a very dramatic way. The glazed frontage is the prominent point of address and as such the design of the facade becomes the identity and image for the new facility. The art screen is backlit to create a glowing night effect to give prominence to the street.

Inside, the spaces are arranged around a series of interlinked courtyards strung along a central circulation spine. Every internal space has a companion outdoor space, which produces a dynamic and fluid spatial arrangement. The courtyards provide access to daylight, ventilation, visual relief and usable outdoor work and display spaces. The plan is organized into two principal zones – the front of house gallery, lecture theatre and print workshop, and the back of house artist-in-residence apartment, postgraduate studios and shared amenities. The building's structure is conventional reinforced in-situ concrete slab and edge beams with a structural steel framing and infill walls throughout. The selection of materials and finishes has been kept to a simple robust palette, given the public nature of the building.

1 The facade is composed of two unequally sized floating glass screens that act as veils to the main structure beyond.
2 Detail view of the glazed facade by artist Robyn Burgess.
3 The site is located on an established urban block containing a mixture of uses including retail businesses, residences, a church and a pub. Directly opposite the site are the Bendigo Art Gallery and the Capital Theatre, which form part of the Bendigo arts precinct.
4 Every internal space has a companion outdoor space, which produces a very dynamic and fluid spatial arrangement as one journeys through the building.

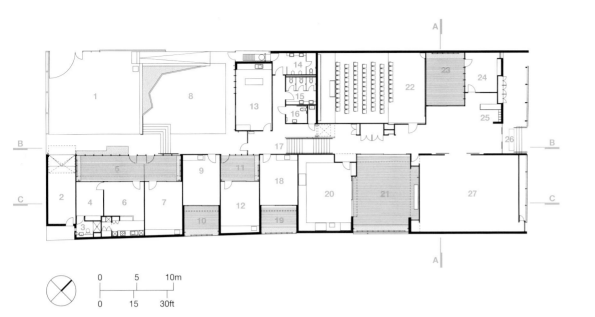

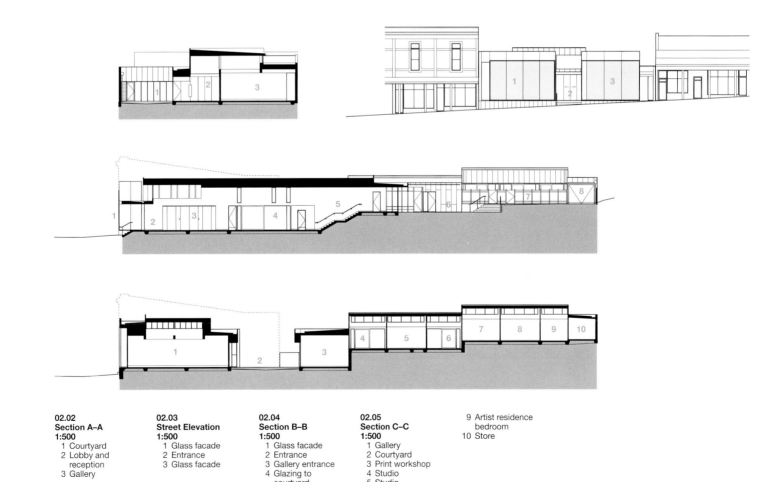

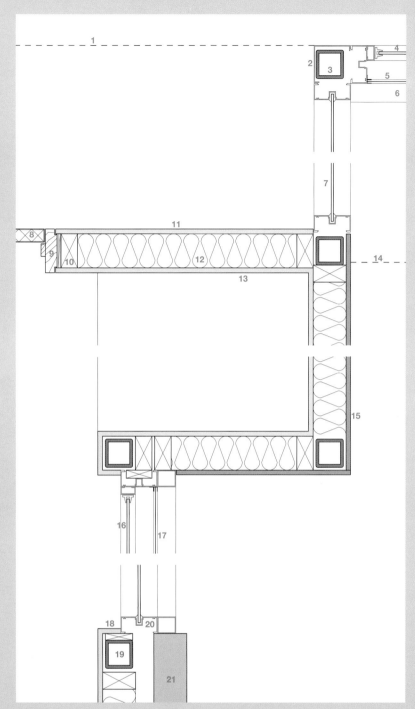

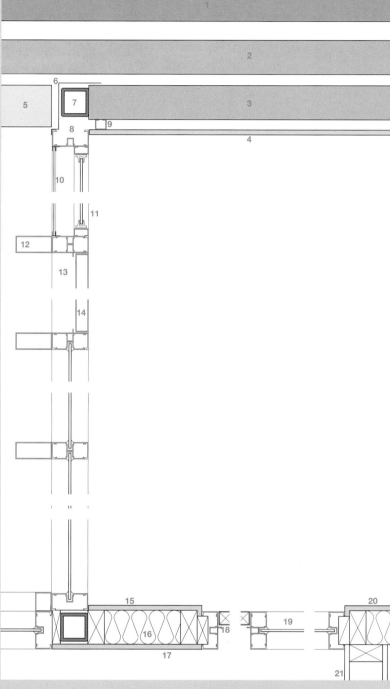

02.06
Sliding Glass Door Detail
1:10
1 Line of wall over shown dotted
2 Folded aluminium coverpiece to conceal fixed metal square hollow section post
3 Fixed metal square hollow section post
4 Powder-coated louvre window with Pilkington ComforTone green tinted annealed glass and aluminium frame
5 Aluminium insect screen
6 Aluminium window sill
7 Powder-coated aluminium window frame with fixed Pilkington ComforTone

laminated glass
8 Flush panel MDF solid core door
9 Kiln dried hardwood door jamb
10 90 x 45 mm (3 1/2 x 1 3/4 inch) pine timber stud framing
11 Painted plasterboard wall lining
12 Insulation
13 Painted plasterboard wall lining
14 Line of canopy over shown dotted
15 Plywood external wall lining
16 Powder-coated louvre window with Pilkington ComforTone green tinted annealed glass and aluminium frame
17 Aluminium insect screen
18 Painted

plasterboard wall lining
19 Fixed metal square hollow section post
20 Powder-coated aluminium window frame with fixed Pilkington ComforTone laminated glass
21 110 mm (4 3/8 inch) brickwork

02.07
Wall Plan Detail to Office
1:10
1 Adjoining building
2 90 mm (3 1/2 inch) outer leaf of blockwork cavity wall
3 90 mm (3 1/2 inch) inner leaf of blockwork cavity wall
4 Painted plasterboard interior wall lining
5 110 mm (4 3/8 inch) inner leaf of brickwork to cavity wall
6 Aluminium flashing
7 Fixed metal square hollow section post
8 30 mm (1 1/5 inch) cavity between stud frame and brick wall
9 25 mm (1 inch) metal firring channel
10 Aluminium insect

screen
11 Powder-coated louvre window with Pilkington ComforTone green tinted annealed glass and aluminium frame
12 Aluminium window frame with 100 x 44 mm (4 x 1 3/4 inch) box section fixed externally to mullion
13 Door sill infill piece below
14 Aluminium framed glazed door
15 Painted plasterboard wall lining
16 Insulation
17 Painted plasterboard wall lining
18 Flush panel solid core door with aluminium door jamb
19 Powder-coated aluminium frame and

sashless double hung windows with safety laminated glass
20 Painted plasterboard wall lining
21 Painted plasterboard wall lining

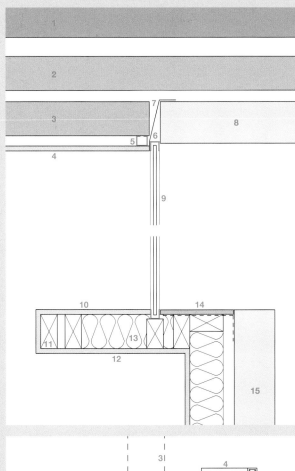

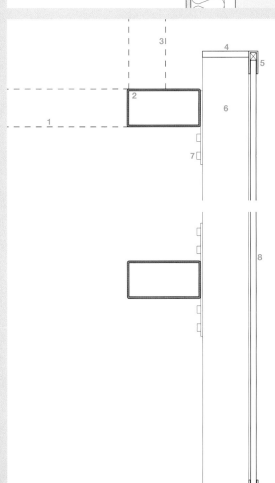

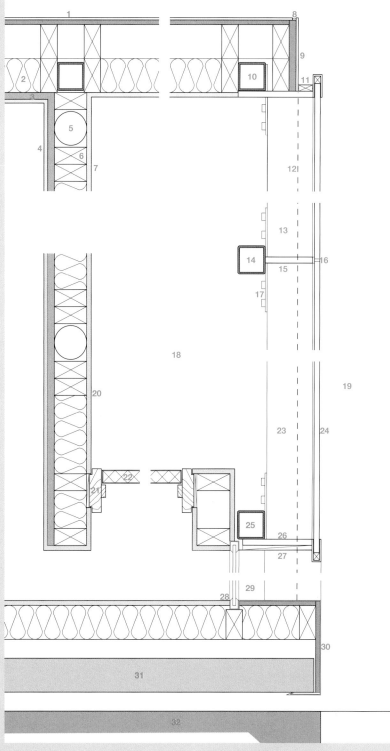

02.08
Window Plan Detail
1:10
1 Adjoining building
2 90 mm (3¹/2 inch)
outer leaf of blockwork
cavity wall
3 90 mm (3¹/2 inch)
inner leaf of blockwork
cavity wall
4 Painted
plasterboard wall lining
5 25 mm (1 inch)
firring channel
6 25 x 25 mm (1 x 1
inch) recessed
aluminium glazing
channel
7 Aluminium flashing
8 110 mm (4³/8 inch)
inner leaf of brickwork
to cavity wall
9 Laminated safety
glass window
10 Painted
plasterboard wall lining
11 Timber stud framing
12 Painted
plasterboard wall lining
13 Insulation
14 Junction between
brickwork and
plywood sealed with
galvanized flashing
15 110 mm (4³/8 inch)
brickwork

02.09
**Glazed Facade Plan
Detail**
1:10
1 Line of steel beams
above shown dotted
2 200 x 100 (8 x 4
inch) rectangular
hollow section column
3 Line of steel beams
above shown dotted
4 16 mm (⁵/8 inch)
thick continuous steel
glazing support plate
welded to preformed
channel top and
bottom rail
5 65 x 25 mm (2¹/2 x
1 inch) perimeter
stainless steel frame
fixed on all sides to
preformed channel
6 125 mm (5 inch)
preformed channel
bottom rail bolt-fixed
to cleats and welded
to 200 x 100 mm (8 x 4
inch) rectangular
hollow section
columns
7 Bolt fixings
8 Glass facade

02.10
**Glazed Facade
Section Detail**
1:10
1 Glass with ply
backing on stud wall
frame
2 Insulation
3 MDF wall lining
backing
4 Painted
plasterboard wall lining
5 Downpipe
6 Timber stud framing
7 Painted
plasterboard wall lining
8 Silicone bead joint
9 Glass with ply
backing on stud wall
frame backing
10 75 x 75 mm (3 x 3
inch) square hollow
section
11 Folded stainless
steel sheet cover piece
to conceal steel plate

fixing
12 Line of parapet
glazing over
13 125 mm (5 inch)
preformed channel
below
14 75 x 75 mm (3 x 3
inch) square hollow
section
15 Steel plate welded
to square hollow
section column
16 6 mm (¹/4 inch)
silicone bead joint
17 Bolt fixings and
welded cleats for fixing
of preformed channel
top and bottom rails
18 Facade access
space
19 Footpath
20 Painted
plasterboard wall lining
21 Timber door frame
22 MDF door to
access space

23 125 mm (5 inch)
preformed channel
bottom rail below
24 Glass facade
25 75 x 75 mm (3 x 3
inch) square hollow
section
26 Continuous steel
glazing support plate
welded to square
hollow section column
27 Lining packed off
steel glazing support
plate
28 25 x 25 mm (1 x 1
inch) aluminium
glazing channels
recessed flush with
wall linings
29 Stainless steel sill
flashing below
30 Folded stainless
steel sheet cover piece
on 15 mm (⁵/8 inch)
structural plywood
31 90 mm (3¹/2 inch)

blockwork
32 Existing adjoining
building

**Jewish Museum Glass Courtyard
Berlin, Germany**

Client
Jewish Museum Berlin

Project Team
Daniel Libeskind, Arnault Biou,
Gerhard Brun

Structural Engineer
GSE Ingenieur-Gesellschaft

Facade Engineer
Arup

Joint Venture Partner
Reese Architekten

The new Glass Courtyard at the Jewish Museum Berlin will provide the museum with a space in which to hold events such as educational workshops, concerts, theatrical performances, and receptions for up to 500 people. The building ensemble in Lindenstrasse, consisting of the iconic Libeskind building with its shiny silver facade and the Old Building, is a successful synthesis of old and new. This combination is strengthened by the addition of the Glass Courtyard. While the original Libeskind building's zigzag form is a metaphorical reference to the tensions and fractures in German-Jewish history, the theme of 'Sukkah' (Hebrew for tabernacle and therefore a meeting place) informs the new glass roof, which covers the U-shaped courtyard of the baroque Old Building.

The roof is supported by four freestanding bundles of tree-like steel pillars that extend into the roof to form a steel network. Integrating the Glass Courtyard with the existing Old Building posed an architectonic challenge. The glass construction avoids overwhelming the Old Building through the use of a self-supporting glazed structure, rather like a freestanding table on four legs. The four branching steel bundles each consist of three tree-thick steel pillars. The pillars were first individually welded from steel plate and were delivered to site completely prefabricated. Striking convolutions lend the glass facade a distinctive appearance. Nine types of glass pane are used, fitted so that each one is reflected twice, mirroring the Libeskind building and the trees in the Museum Garden. A highly transparent white glass with an anti-glare coating on the inside was selected which has resulted is a light-flooded room full of reflections.

1 The Glass Courtyard was designed to be easily recognizable as a later addition to the baroque Old Building, which was the wish of the authorities responsible for the preservation of historical monuments.
2 The expressive and asymmetrical geometry of Libeskind's design presented the steel fabricators, the structural engineers and the facade planners with considerable challenges.
3 The lightness and transparency of the courtyard building reinforce the impression of a free-standing building in the courtyard.
4 The new glass structure is located just a few steps away from the main entrance of the Jewish Museum and its existing infrastructure including cloakrooms, cash desks and the museum restaurant.

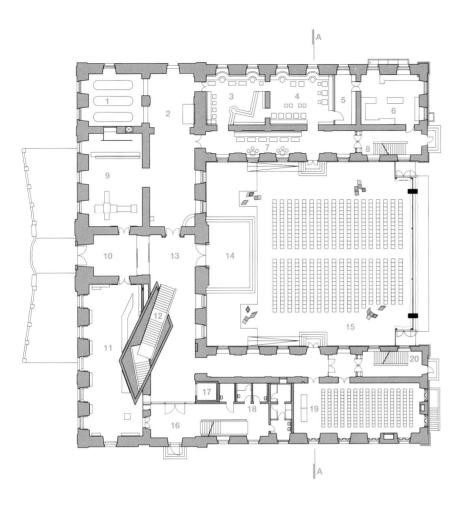

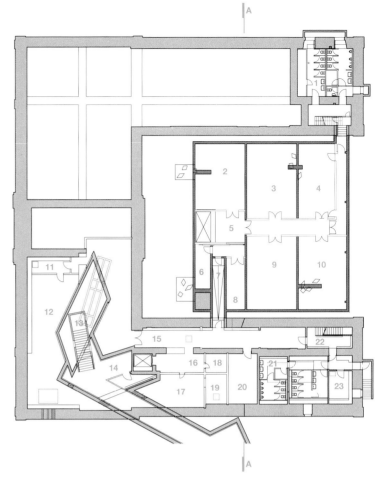

| 0 | 5 | 10m |
| 0 | 15 | 30ft |

03.01
Ground Floor Plan
1:500
1 Coat room
2 Restaurant lobby
3 Restaurant
4 Restaurant
5 Restaurant service
6 Kitchen
7 Restaurant
8 Stair
9 Ticket office
10 Entrance
11 Book shop
12 Main stair
13 Hallway
14 Glass Courtyard
   entrance
15 Glass Courtyard
16 Lobby
17 Lift
18 Toilets
19 Theatre
20 Stair

03.02
Basement Plan
1:500
1 Toilets
2 Storage space
3 Restaurant store
4 Restaurant store
5 Corridor
6 Mechanical and
   electrical services
7 Corridor
8 Mechanical and
   electrical services
9 Mechanical and
   electrical services
10 Mechanical and
   electrical services
11 Corridor
12 Storage
13 Main circulation
   stair
14 Lift lobby
15 Corridor
16 Corridor
17 Mechanical and
   electrical services
18 Storage
19 Mechanical and
   electrical services
20 Mechanical and

electrical services
21 Toilets
22 Stair
23 Mechanical and
   electrical services

03.03
Section A–A
1:500
1 Changing
   exhibition area
2 Hallway
3 Lecture theatre
4 Hallway
5 Steel columns
6 New roof structure
7 Plaster facade of
   existing building
8 Steel columns
9 Hallway
10 Changing
   exhibition area
11 Hallway
12 Changing
   exhibition area
13 New basement
   area

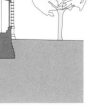

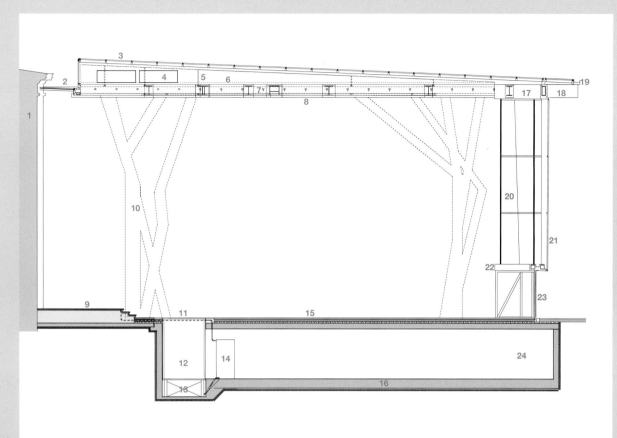

03.04
Detail Section Through Glass Courtyard
1:200
1 Existing building
2 Glazed joint
3 Roof glazing
4 Ventilation flaps
5 Steel structure
6 Mechanical and electrical track on top of beams
7 Double I-beams with cladding
8 Base line of cladding
9 Existing historical stairs incorporated into new building
10 Primary steel columns
11 Top of transport platform lift from basement
12 Transport platform void
13 Transport platform mechanical area
14 Distribution box
15 New concrete floor slab
16 Watertight concrete raft foundation

17 Upper part of horizontal beam cladding seen in elevation
18 Cladding to structural steel double I-beam
19 Gutter
20 Structural glazed cladding seen in elevation
21 Structural glazing
22 Lower horizontal beam seen in elevation
23 Glazed sliding door assembly
24 New basement

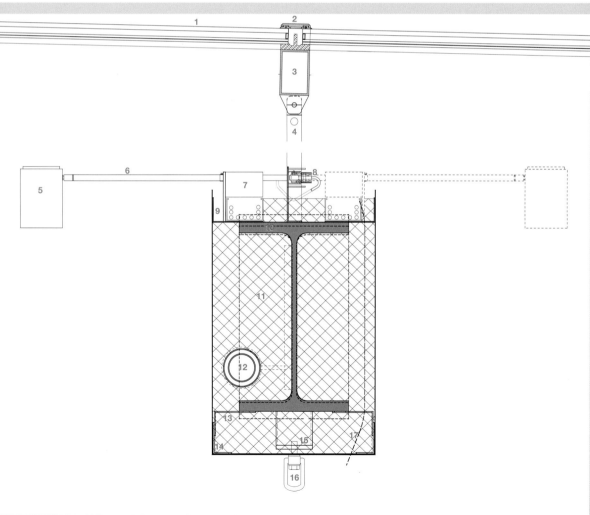

03.05
Roof Glazing and Steel Beam Detail
1:10
1 Double glazing
2 Aluminium glazing bead
3 120 x 80 x 4.5 mm (4³/4 x 1³/5 x ¹/8 inch) steel profile
4 40 x 40 mm (1³/5 x 1³/5 inch) support pin
5 Light fixture
6 Light fixture support
7 Ballast
8 Busbar power distribution
9 Upper support for perforated metal sheet cladding
10 Double I-beam
11 Mineral wool fill acoustic absorber
12 Rainwater pipe
13 Lower cladding support
14 Lower cladding support
15 Load hook support
16 Load hook
17 Wiring conduit

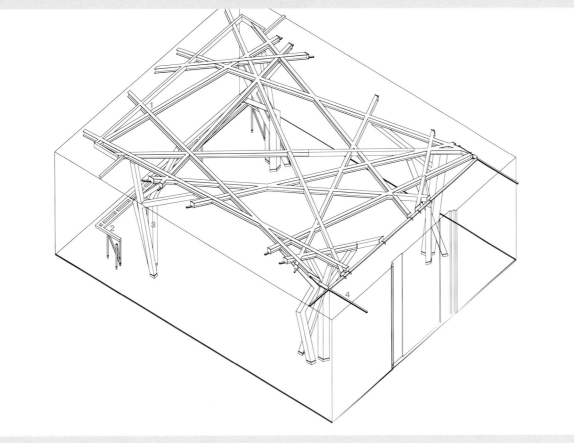

03.06
Steel Structure Detail
Not to Scale
1 Main roof structure
2 Lower horizontal
beam support
3 Welded main steel
columns
4 Horizontal anchor
profile

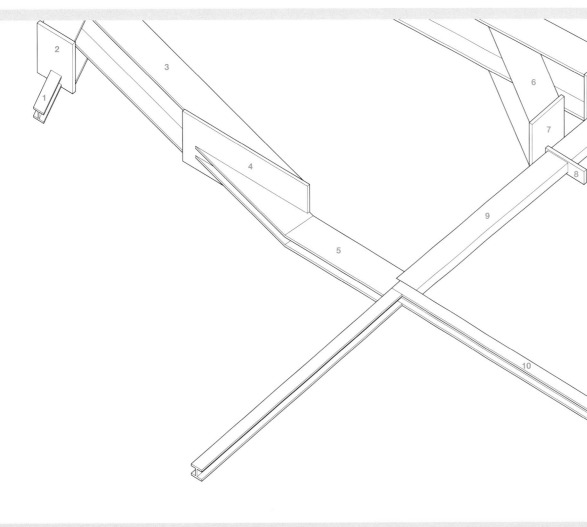

03.07
Steel Roof Structure
Detail
Not to Scale
1 Rainwater gutter
support
2 Welded steel face
plate
3 Main roof profile
steel structure
4 Welded steel face
plate
5 300 x 120 x 20 mm
(11^4/5 x 4^3/4 x ^{3}/4 inch)
welded steel profile
6 Main roof profile
steel structure
7 Welded steel face
plate
8 Rainwater gutter
support
9 Steel edge beam
10 Steel anchor profile

VISUAL and the George Bernard Shaw Theatre Carlow, Ireland

Client
Carlow County Council

Project Team
Terry Pawson, Jeremy Browne, Gustav Ader, Justyna Pollak, Natalie Galland, Andy Summers, Andy Gowing, Sebastian Reinehr

Structural Engineer
Arup

Main Contractor
BAM

VISUAL and the George Bernard Shaw Theatre provides Ireland with a significant new arts space to showcase contemporary visual arts and theatre of national and international importance. The new building formally closes a grassed quadrangle shared by Carlow College and the town's nineteenth-century cathedral. The building presents itself as an assembly of different sized volumes clad in opaque glass raised on a concrete plinth, with the largest gallery at its centre. The muteness of the opaque glass harmonizes with the neutral grey of the town's local limestone and provides a blank canvas to absorb natural light in the day and project more dynamic low-level lighting at night.

During the day natural light filters into the main galleries creating a calm introspective environment conducive to the production and appreciation of visual art. At night the facade is illuminated, projecting a more exuberant glowing presence for the theatre and performance space. The entrance, located on the south elevation, opens into a foyer of cast concrete and dark timber which leads up a short flight of stairs to the galleries, or left to the George Bernard Shaw Theatre. There is a clear procession through the galleries; a Link Gallery with its exposed cast concrete walls, louvred concrete ceiling and polished concrete floor, leads to the Studio Gallery used by artists in residence, and wraps around the Main Gallery which has been designed to accommodate large-scale sculpture. From the Main Gallery, stairs ascend to the black box gallery on the first floor, designed to accommodate video art and installation.

1 The 3,726 square metre (40,106 square foot), three storey building occupies a much larger footprint than the original competition proposal. The larger site affords sufficient space for the gallery and theatre to be expressed and unified within one coherent form.
2 View of the east elevation with the raised planted promenade alongside the reeded pond.
3 The entrance, located on the south elevation, opens into a foyer of cast concrete and dark timber.
4 The Main Gallery asserts itself externally as the tallest form in the building's composition. The interior is a pure white box with backlit clerestory windows that flood the space with ethereal light.

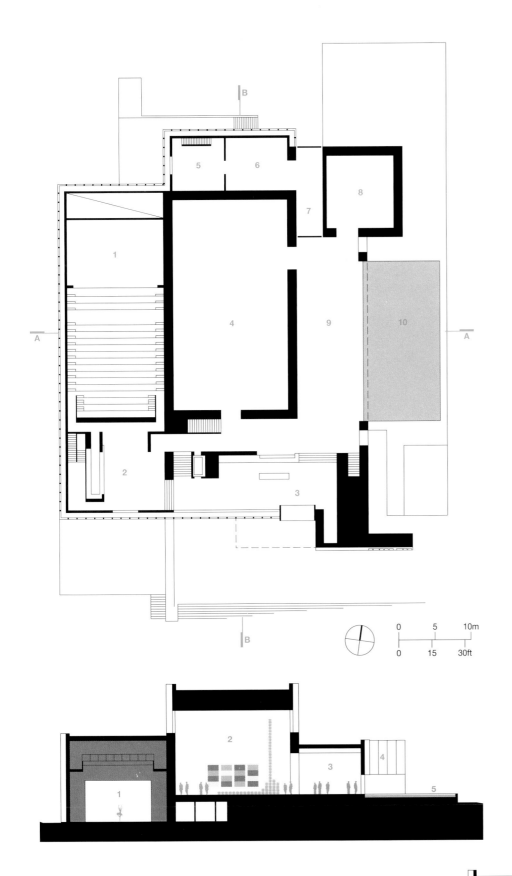

04.01
Ground Floor Plan
1:500
 1 George Bernard
   Shaw Theatre
 2 Bar
 3 Entrance
 4 Main Gallery
 5 Technical room
 6 Storage
 7 Goods entrance
 8 Studio Gallery
 9 Link Gallery
10 Pool

04.02
Section A–A
1:500
 1 George Bernard
   Shaw Theatre
 2 Main Gallery
 3 Link Gallery
 4 Studio Gallery
   beyond
 5 Pool

04.03
Section B–B
1:500
 1 Entrance
 2 Foyer
 3 Digital Gallery
 4 Main Gallery
 5 Plant room
 6 Storage
 7 Kitchen
 8 Toilets
 9 Changing rooms
10 Choir

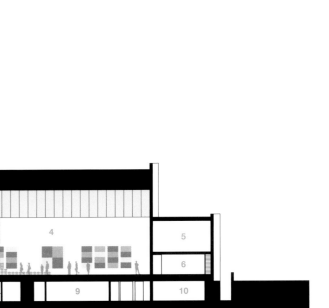

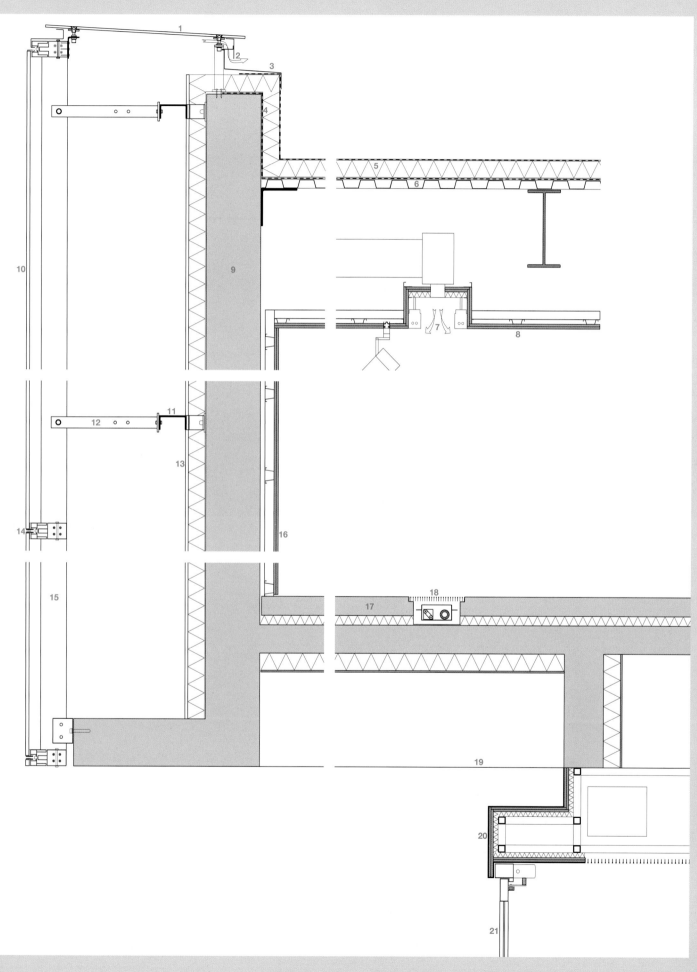

04.04
Detail Section Through Digital Gallery and Entrance
1:20

1 Glazed parapet
2 Ventilation openings covered with perforated metal
3 Parapet flashing
4 Single ply roofing membrane
5 Tapered roof insulation over vapour barrier
6 Corrugated steel deck
7 Recessed lighting and ventilation slot
8 Two layers of 12.5 mm (1/2 inch) plasterboard ceiling, skimmed and painted
9 300 mm (11 3/4 inch) reinforced cast in-situ concrete wall
10 18 mm (7/10 inch) thick laminated glazing element comprised of two layers of 9 mm (1/3 inch) low-iron glass with white Polyvinyl Butyral film layer
11 Horizontal steel spanning between structural column
12 Bracing system
13 Insulation
14 Transom carrier frame for curtain wall with structural sealant glazing
15 Mullion carrier frame for curtain wall with structural sealant glazing
16 Two layers of 12 mm (1/2 inch) medium density fibreboard wall lining on metal firrings
17 100 mm (4 inch) power-floated concrete floor slab
18 Floor service box cast in concrete floor
19 Ribbed reinforced concrete ceiling slab
20 Polyester powder-coated aluminium clad entrance door enclosure
21 Polyester powder-coated aluminium double glazed entrance doors

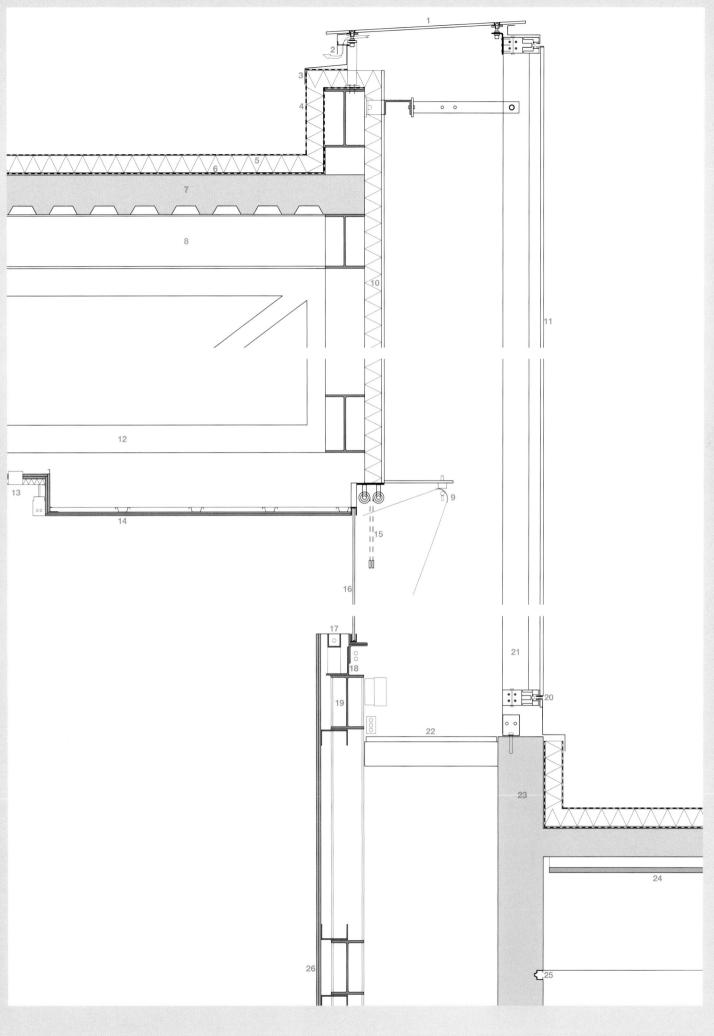

1 Glazed parapet
2 Ventilation openings covered with perforated metal
3 Parapet flashing
4 Single ply roofing membrane
5 Tapered roof insulation
6 Vapour barrier
7 Concrete roof cast in corrugated steel decking
8 Steel truss
9 Gallery luminaire suspended from steel support bracket
10 Insulation
11 18 mm (3/4 inch) laminated glazing element comprised of two layers of 9 mm (1/3 inch) white low-iron glass with Polyvinyl Butyral film layer
12 Structural steel roof truss
13 Recessed lighting and ventilation slot
14 Two layers of 12.5 mm (1/2 inch) plasterboard ceiling, skimmed and painted
15 Motorized blackout blinds
16 Clerestory gallery glazing
17 Low level perimeter heating element
18 Service run for gallery glazing heaters
19 Secondary steel gallery support wall
20 Transom carrier frame for curtain wall with structural sealant glazing
21 Mullion carrier frame for curtain wall with structural sealant glazing
22 Service void walkway
23 215 mm (8 1/2 inch) reinforced cast in-situ concrete
24 Sound absorbent board to ceiling coffers
25 Track fitting cast in concrete for art handling and hanging
26 Two layers of 12 mm (1/2 inch) medium density fibreboard wall lining on metal firrings

**Christchurch Art Gallery
Christchurch, New Zealand**

Client
Christchurch City Council

Project Team
David Cole, Roland Fretwell, David Forbes, Harvey Male, Raylene McEwan, Iain Mather

Structural Engineer
Holmes Consulting Group

Facade Engineer
JML

The new Christchurch Art Gallery contains the largest permanent art collection in New Zealand. The building is sited on the city's principal cultural axis of Worcester Boulevard, and features three main street frontages and a major public sculpture garden. The main entrance is located in the heart of the sculpture garden, facing the historic Christchurch Arts Centre. The principal western facade is angled obliquely to face the northwest in order to admit sunlight into the sculpture garden and the main entrance. The building has been designed as a 'duality' of ordered rectangular masonry elements for the exhibition spaces, juxtaposed against a composition of monumentally scaled organic, light and flowing glazed forms for the main entrance and foyer.

The glazed public face of the gallery building, known as the Sculpture Wall, is the building's iconic grand urban gesture. The Sculpture Wall's multiple glazed facets reflect the infinite variations of the sky, morning to evening, season to season. The wall is comprised of a series of upright and inverted conical sections, which intersect, overlap and interplay. It is a giant urban mosaic of some 16 different clear glass tones in a range of reflective coatings, e-coatings and glass thicknesses. The curved planes of glass are held at arm's length from elliptical shaped columns by means of delicate cast aluminium arms. The exhibition spaces, the heart of the building, have been designed for clarity, calm, delight and surprise, and are intended to foster a sense of journey and discovery.

1 The glazed public face of the gallery building – the Sculpture Wall – expresses a unique presence in Christchurch's distinct formal street grid.

2 As well as admitting natural light into the public spaces of the building, the facade acts as both a reflector and transmitter of light according to the time of day or night.

3 The apparently fragile sheets of glass are supported on white elliptical masts that are themselves expressed as the primary vertical element in the composition.

4 The foyer is a grand indoor–outdoor space, its floor bathed in the shifting complex shadow patterns of the skeletal frame of the glazed sculpture wall.

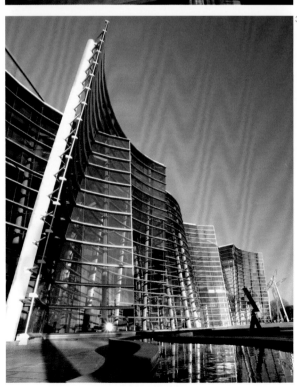

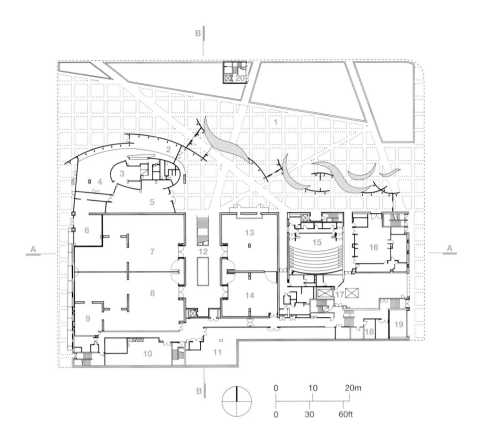

05.01
Ground Floor Plan
1:1000
1 The Community Trust Sculpture Garden
2 Entrance
3 Cafe service areas
4 Cafe
5 Gallery shop
6 Form gallery
7 Touring galleries
8 Touring galleries
9 Borg Henry Gallery
10 Workshop
11 Collection handling area
12 Courtyard
13 William A. Sutton Gallery
14 Ravenscar Gallery for New Zealand Art
15 Philip Carter Family Auditorium
16 Sir Neil and Lady Isaac Education Centre
17 Vertical circulation
18 Shipping and receiving office
19 Entrance to basement car park
20 Car park lift and stair egress

05.02
Section A–A
1:500
1 Terrace
2 Sir Neil and Lady Isaac Education Centre
3 Stout Trust Conservation Laboratories
4 Staff room
5 Education work rooms
6 Car park lift lobby
7 Margaret Austin photography studio
8 Meeting room
9 Female WC
10 Male WC
11 Auditorium
12 Temporary exhibitions
13 Temporary exhibitions
14 Balcony
15 Grand stair
16 Service walkway
17 Permanent collection
18 Temporary travelling exhibitions
19 Temporary travelling exhibitions

05.03
Section B–B
1:500
1 Car park lift and stair egress
2 Glazed entry doors through sculpture wall
3 Foyer
4 Basement car park
5 Smoke exhaust
6 Bridge
7 Stair
8 Balcony
9 Lift lobby
10 Plant room
11 Collection store
12 Collection store
13 Collection handling

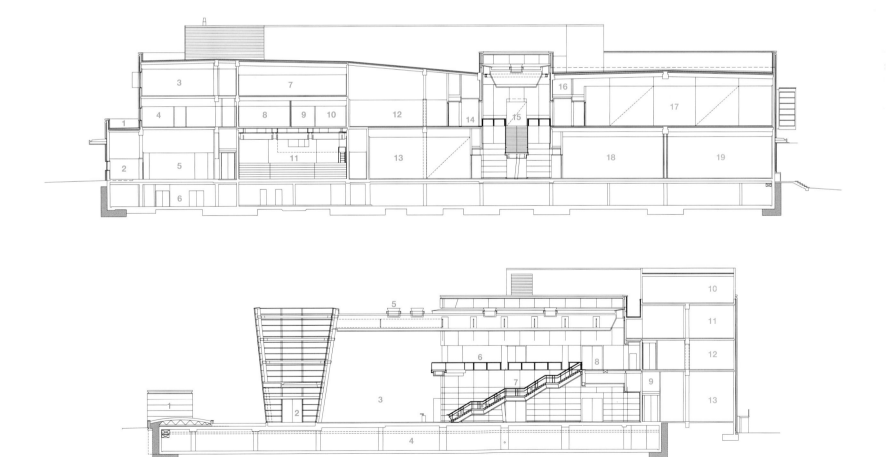

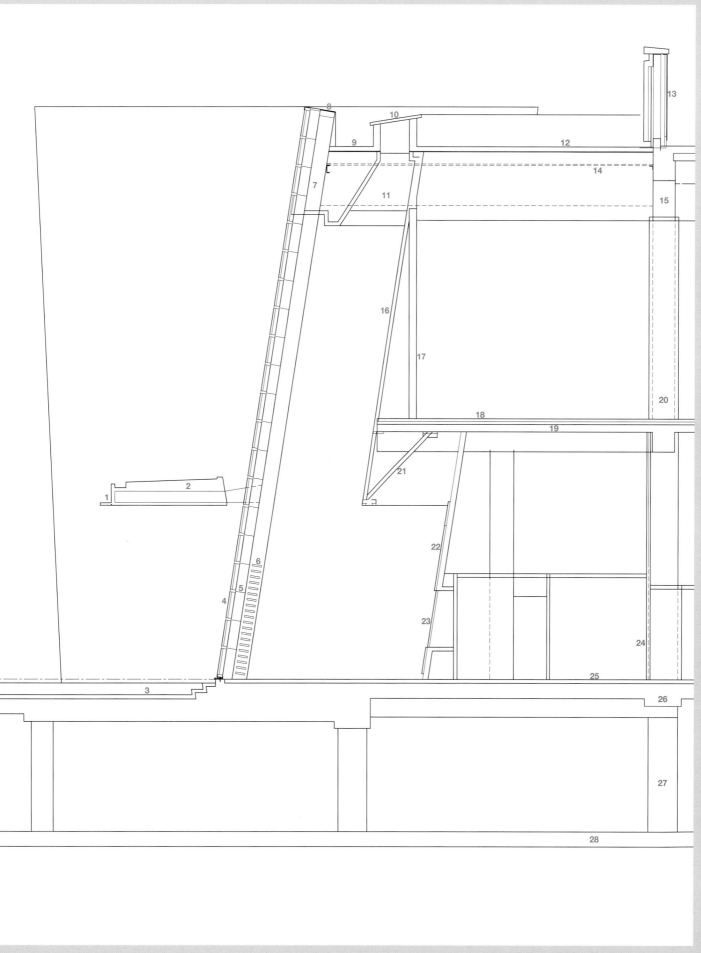

05.04
Detailed Section
Through Glazed
Sculpture Wall
1:100
1 Aluminium canopy fascia
2 Canopy steel deck roofing
3 Water feature
4 Glazed sculpture wall
5 Cast aluminium connection arms
6 Air supply incisions in steel column
7 Steel column
8 Capping
9 Box gutter
10 Skylight
11 Steel beam tying Sculpture Wall columns to sheer wall structure
12 Metal deck roofing
13 Compressed cement sheet internal parapet lining on steel parapet support frame
14 Ceiling
15 Earthquake shear wall
16 Curved plaster wall
17 Plastered wall to Contemporary art gallery
18 Pre-cast concrete floor system
19 Reinforced concrete floor slab
20 Structural column
21 Bulkhead structure
22 Curved timber cladding to cafe wall
23 Bar
24 Timber wall cladding
25 Pre-cast concrete floor system
26 Basement band beams
27 Basement concrete columns
28 In-situ reinforced concrete slab on grade

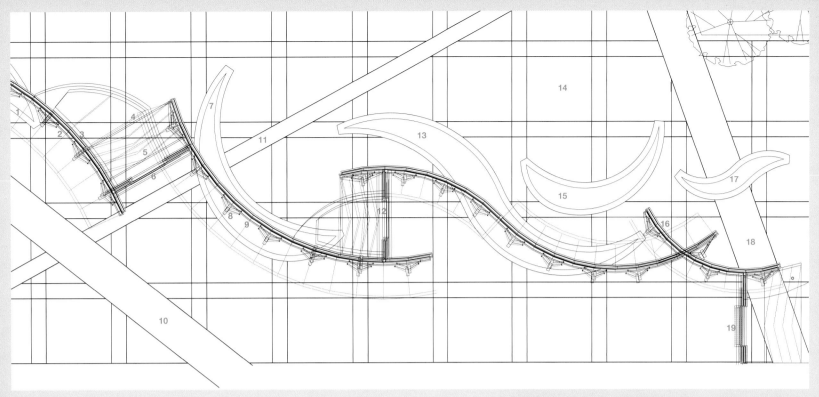

05.05
**Glazed Sculptural
Wall Detail Plan
1:200**
 1 Water feature
 2 Internal transoms to glazed Sculpture Wall
 3 External transoms to glazed Sculpture Wall
 4 Aluminium canopy
 5 Inclined glazed wall section
 6 Glazed entry doors
 7 Internal water feature
 8 Cast aluminium connection arms
 9 Internal water feature
 10 Interior granite paving band
 11 Exterior granite paving band
 12 Glazed entry doors
 13 External water feature
 14 Exterior granite paving
 15 External water feature
 16 Glazed Sculpture Wall
 17 External water feature
 18 Exterior granite paving band
 19 Glazed entry doors

05.06
**Ground Level Glazed
Wall Plan Detail 1
1:10**
 1 Projecting external aluminium transom
 2 Glazing seal to aluminium transom
 3 Internal aluminium transom
 4 Flexible cast aluminium joint element
 5 Cast aluminium connection arm
 6 Head of cast aluminium element
 7 Cast transom jointing piece with fin plates inside transom
 8 Glazing gasket
 9 Interior cast aluminium transom
 10 Single glazing to side lights on transom

05.07
**Ground Level Glazed
Wall Plan Detail 2
1:10**
 1 Structural transom
 2 Glazing seal to aluminium transom
 3 Projecting external aluminium transom
 4 External transom joint
 5 Silicone sealed joint either side of glass
 6 Internal aluminium transom
 7 Cast transom jointing piece with fin plates inside transom
 8 Internal aluminium transom
 9 Flexible cast aluminium joint element
 10 Head of cast aluminium joint element
 11 Cast aluminium connection arm

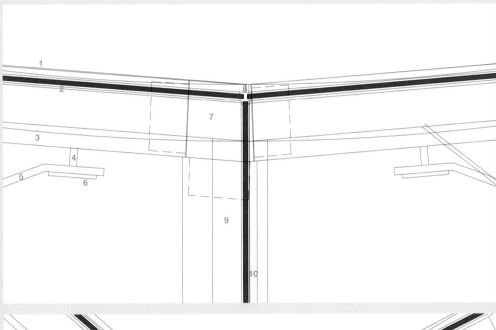

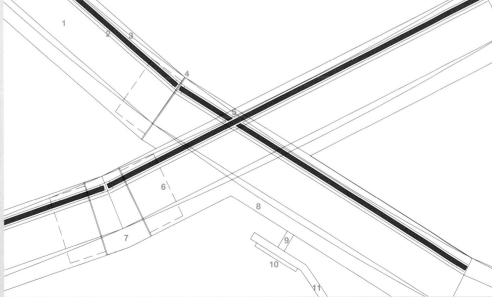

29

**Sport and Culture Centre
Copenhagen, Denmark**

Client
Copenhagen Municipality and LOA
(Danish Foundation for Culture and
Sports Facilities)

Project Team
Dorte Mandrup, Anders Brink, Lars
Lindeberg, Jesper Henriksson, Arno
Brandlhuber, Asterios Agkathidis,
Markus Emde, Jochen Kremer, Martin
Kraushaar, Sarah Breidert

Structural Engineer
Jørgen Nielsen Rådgivende

Main Contractor
NH Hansen & Søn

This sport and culture centre is
situated in a residential area in an
eastern suburb of Copenhagen
predominately made up of housing
blocks from the turn of the century.
The site is long and narrow – on one
side bordering a busy road and a
recreational area on the other. The
heart of this project lies in making a
new crossover building typology that
combines a traditional indoor sports
arena and an outdoor sports field. The
new building is physically connected
to four existing housing blocks,
providing a continuation of the built
fabric of the neighbourhood.

The complex mixed-use programme
was developed in consultation with
local communities and individual
users, adults as well as children. To
express the complexity of the
programme under one roof, the
building is shaped to fit the site with a
form that brings together recreation
and leisure uses in three connected
'houses' that, in effect, reinterpret the
surrounding villas. The exterior of the
building is enveloped in a translucent
polycarbonate skin that brings an
abundance of evenly distributed
natural light into the interior. The
warmth of the light is further enhanced
by the use of wood as part of the
visible structure. The building will be
used for a variety of daily sport and
cultural activities such as concerts
and theatre performances. The
dynamic landscape inside allows for
various activities to take place on
different levels and in visual contact
with each other.

1 The building has
been architecturally
grafted onto the
gabled ends of four
adjacent existing villas.
The form of the
structure then
transforms into
monoform to
accommodate the
multifunctional
programme.
2 The polycarbonate
skin which is used
throughout for the roof
and walls, brings
evenly distributed
natural light into the
heart of the centre.
3 In low light, the
building glows like a
beacon in its
residential
neighbourhood.
4 The green sports
surface extends onto
the tiered seating and
circulation areas
surrounding the courts
to create a three
dimensional ground
plane.

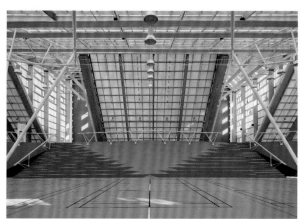

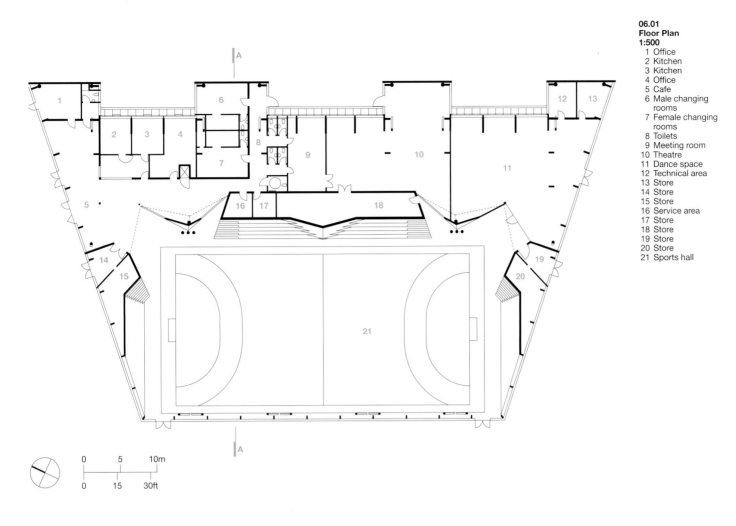

06.01
Floor Plan
1:500
1 Office
2 Kitchen
3 Kitchen
4 Office
5 Cafe
6 Male changing rooms
7 Female changing rooms
8 Toilets
9 Meeting room
10 Theatre
11 Dance space
12 Technical area
13 Store
14 Store
15 Store
16 Service area
17 Store
18 Store
19 Store
20 Store
21 Sports hall

06.02
Section A–A
1:200
1 Sports hall playing surface
2 Sports hall seating
3 Cafe
4 Female changing rooms
5 Male changing rooms

0   5   10m

0   15   30ft

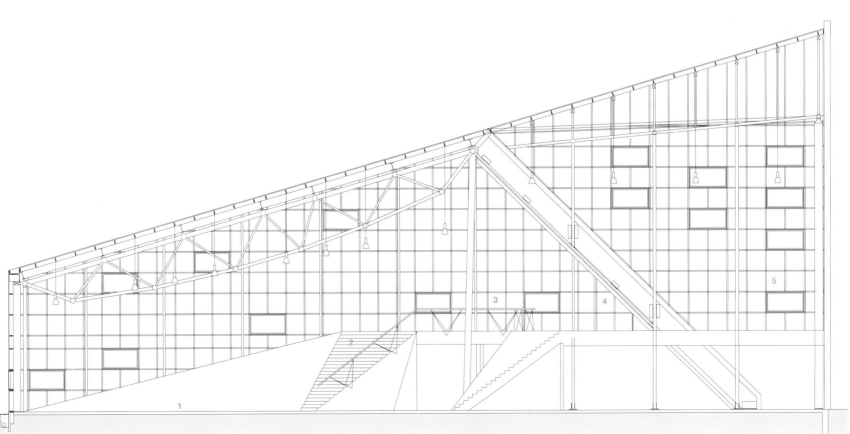

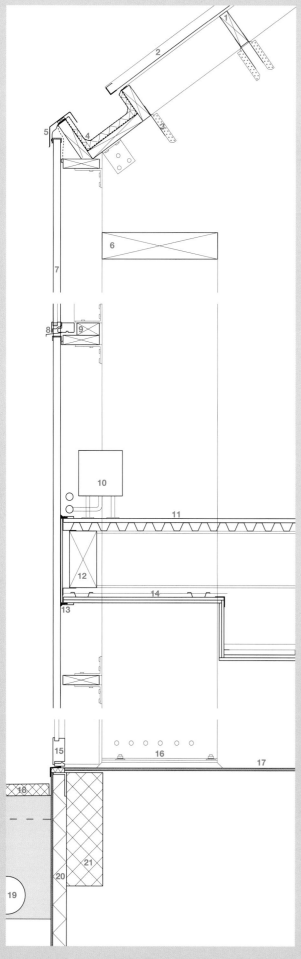

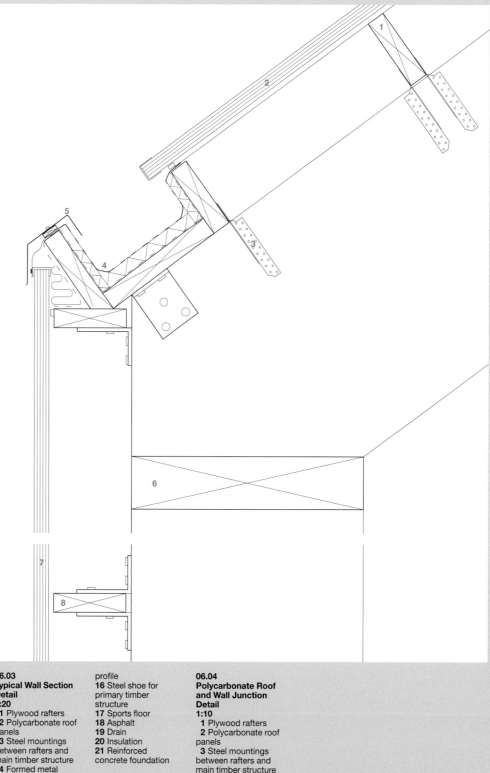

06.03
Typical Wall Section Detail
1:20
1 Plywood rafters
2 Polycarbonate roof panels
3 Steel mountings between rafters and main timber structure
4 Formed metal gutter
5 Aluminium flashing
6 Primary timber structure
7 Polycarbonate wall panels
8 Aluminium base profile
9 Secondary timber profile
10 Radiator
11 Sports floor
12 Secondary timber structure
13 Steel flashing
14 Aluminium base profile
15 Aluminium base

profile
16 Steel shoe for primary timber structure
17 Sports floor
18 Asphalt
19 Drain
20 Insulation
21 Reinforced concrete foundation

06.04
Polycarbonate Roof and Wall Junction Detail
1:10
1 Plywood rafters
2 Polycarbonate roof panels
3 Steel mountings between rafters and main timber structure
4 Formed metal gutter
5 Aluminium flashing
6 Primary timber structure
7 Polycarbonate wall panels
8 Timber wall structure braced by steel L-angles bolt-fixed to primary timber structure

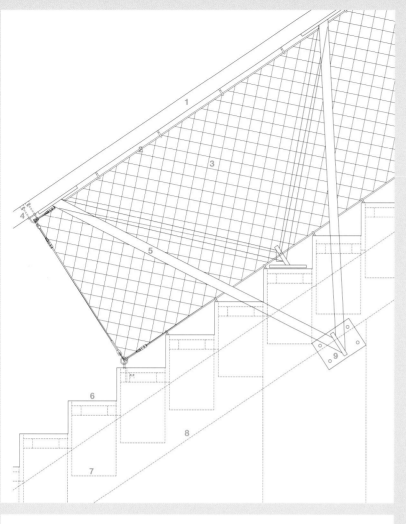

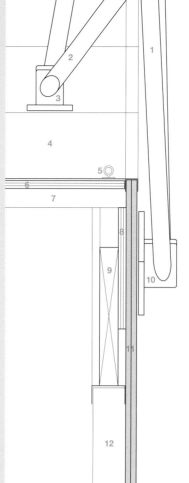

06.05
Stair Railing
Elevation Detail
1:20
1 Timber handrail
2 Steel wire
tensioning strip to steel
netting balustrade
edge
3 Steel netting
4 Steel fastener
5 Steel connector
between stringer and
balustrade
6 Timber step with
coated surface
7 Timber step
concealed
construction
8 Timber stringer
9 Steel mounting
bracket

06.06
Stair Railing Section
Detail
1:10
1 Steel connector
between stringer and
balustrade
2 Steel connector
3 Steel mounting
assembly
4 Stair riser with
coated surface
5 Steel fitting for steel
netting balustrade
panel
6 Step with coated
surface
7 Timber floor panel
8 Timber filler strip
9 Timber structure
10 Steel mounting
assembly
11 Painted
plasterboard wall panel
12 Timber wall
construction

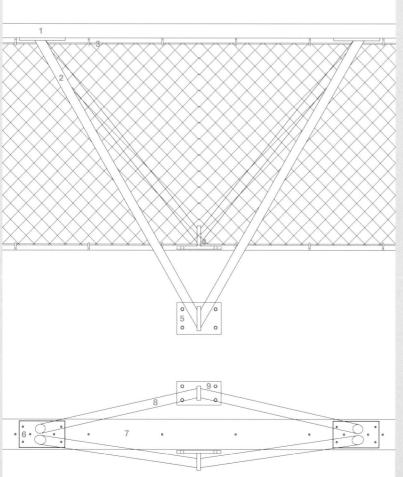

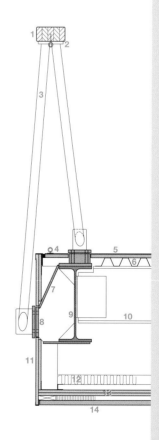

06.07
Mezzanine
Balustrade Elevation
and Plan Detail
1:20
1 Timber handrail
2 Steel rail post
3 Steel wire
tensioning strip to steel
netting balustrade
edge
4 Steel mounting
bracket
5 Steel mounting
bracket
6 Steel mounting
bracket
7 Timber construction
8 Steel rail post
9 Steel mounting

06.08
Mezzanine
Balustrade Section
Detail
1:20
1 Timber handrail
2 Steel plate structure
to timber handrail
3 Steel rail post
4 Steel fittings for
steel netting
balustrade panel
5 Gypsum board
flooring
6 Steel profile floor
construction
7 Steel plate stiffener
8 Steel plate edge
structure
9 Steel beam
10 Steel floor structure
11 Painted
plasterboard wall panel
12 Sound insulation
material
13 Plasterboard
14 Painted
plasterboard ceiling
panel

Brochstein Pavilion and Central Quadrangle, Rice University Houston, Texas, USA

Client
Rice University and Raymond and Susan Brochstein

Project Team
Thomas Phifer, Donald Cox, Eric Richey, Len Lopate, Katie Bennett, Ryan Indovina, Kerim Demirkan

Structural Engineer
Haynes Whaley Associates

Main Contractor
Linbeck

Centrally located on the Rice University campus, the Raymond and Susan Brochstein Pavilion was conceived as a destination for students and faculty to interact and share ideas in a relaxed environment. The Pavilion project includes the landscape design for the Central Quadrangle and a large, shaded seating terrace. The pavilion is capped by a steel and aluminium trellis structure which protects the building and extends in all directions to cover and shade the surrounding seating terrace. The trellis, consisting of an array of small aluminium tubes, effectively reduces solar gain by an average of 70 per cent. This extensive shade protection reduces the requirement for mechanical cooling and allows the structure to be naturally ventilated through much of the year.

A series of wide glass double doors connect the interior seating areas with the surrounding terrace, opening the pavilion to the landscape. The openness of the glass curtain wall system establishes a strong connection to the landscape, encouraging activities within the Pavilion to flow out into the Quadrangle. At the roof, daylight is carefully filtered through skylights by perforated aluminium diffusers on the exterior and by a perforated metal ceiling system on the interior, infusing the space with carefully controlled, natural light. The interior of the pavilion features vibrant, casual seating groups and a seamless circular Corian snack and coffee kiosk. The floor plan is flexible and designed to accommodate small impromptu gatherings as well as large public functions such as concerts which are planned for the Central Quadrangle.

1 The full height glazed walls of the Pavilion are protected from the strong Texas sun by a delicate shade structure constructed from aluminium tubes.
2 The Pavilion project included the design of the surrounding landscape which integrates the Pavilion into the campus landscape.
3 + 4 Expansive seating terraces surround the pavilion, creating multifarious opportunities for students and staff to meet and socialize.
5 The interior is washed with filtered natural light that enters the building via the glazed walls and the ceiling diffusers.

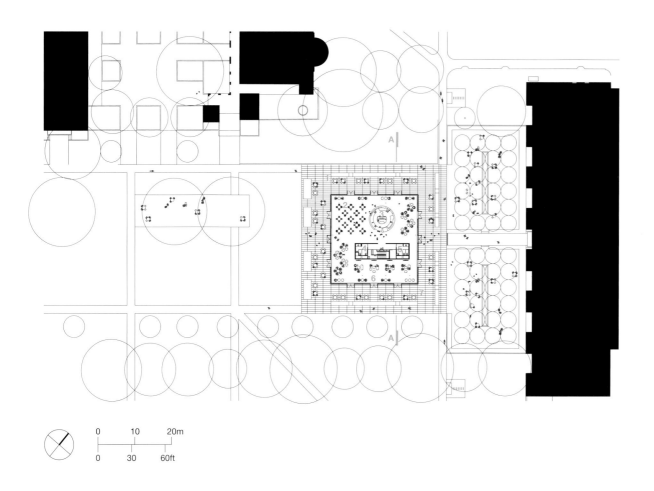

07.01
Ground Floor Plan
1:1000
1 Terrace seating
2 Interior seating
3 Snack and coffee
   kiosk
4 Men's toilets
5 Women's toilets
6 Interior seating
7 Terrace seating

0   10   20m
0   30   60ft

07.02
Section A–A
1:200
1 Planting
2 Aluminium tube
   shade structure
3 Lighting fixture
4 Terrace seating
5 Shade structure
   over skylight
6 Skylight
7 Perforated metal
   ceiling diffusers
8 Interior seating
   area
9 Lobby to WC
   facilities
10 Staff and kitchen
   areas
11 Glazed double
   doors
12 Fixed glazing
13 Mechanical duct
   trench
14 Terrace seating

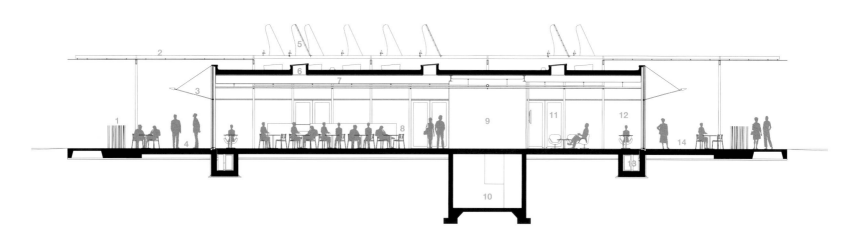

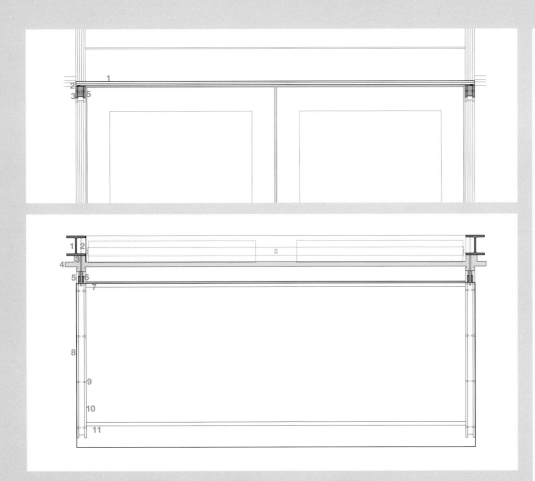

07.03
Glazed Double Doors
Elevation Detail
1:20
 1 Laminated glass
with ground and
polished edges
 2 Structural silicone
and glazing tape
 3 Painted aluminium
cover over 17 mm (^{3}/$_8$
inch) stainless steel
plate
 4 32 mm (1^3/$_{16}$ inch)
stainless steel framing
 5 17 mm (^{3}/$_8$ inch)
stainless steel plate

07.04
Glazed Double Doors
Plan Detail
1:20
 1 Steel column
 2 Steel plate stiffener
 3 Aluminium framing
 4 Face of glass
 5 Snap cover cap
 6 Stainless steel
outrigger
 7 Stainless steel
angle framing
 8 Laminated glass
with ground and
polished edges
 9 32 mm (1^3/$_{16}$ inch)
stainless steel framing
10 17 mm (^{3}/$_8$ inch)
stainless steel plate
11 Stainless steel
angle framing

07.05
Glazed Double Doors
Section Detail
1:20
 1 Stainless steel
glazing frame
 2 Glazed wall
 3 Stainless steel
outrigger
 4 Painted aluminium
break metal
 5 Concealed
mechanical connection
 6 Stainless steel
angle framing with
weather seal, structural
silicone, backer rod
and glazing tape
 7 Countersunk
mechanical fasteners
 8 Stainless steel
outrigger
 9 32 mm (1^3/$_{16}$ inch)
stainless steel framing
10 Stainless steel
angle framing with
structural silicone and
glazing tape
11 19 mm (^{3}/$_4$ inch)
laminated glass with
ground and polished
edges

07.06
Aluminium Canopy
and Steel
Substructure Detail
1:20
 1 12 x 50 mm (^{1}/$_2$ x 2
inch) aluminium purlin
 2 19 mm (^{3}/$_4$ inch)
diameter aluminium
rod
 3 38 x 152 mm (1^1/$_2$ x
6 inch) steel rafter
 4 50 x 203 mm (2 x 8
inch) steel beam
 5 114 x 114 mm (4^1/$_2$
x 4^1/$_2$ inch) steel
column

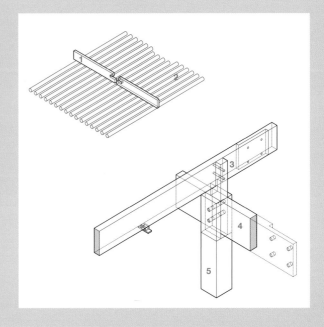

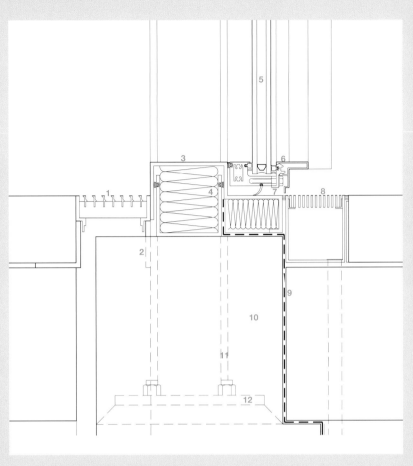

07.07
Detail at Outermost Point of Glass Curtain Wall
1:5
 1 Painted aluminium linear diffuser grill
 2 Continuous angle and plate framing
 3 Painted aluminium extrusion coped to column flange beyond
 4 Insulation
 5 Insulated glass unit with high performance low-E coating
 6 Painted aluminium framing
 7 Painted aluminium framing
 8 Continuous curtain wall drain with stainless steel grill
 9 Waterproofing
 10 Concrete foundation wall
 11 Line of mechanical blockout beyond
 12 Base plate beyond

07.08
Perforated Ceiling System Detail
1:5
 1 Minimum depth of steel beam, painted white, shown dotted
 2 Maximum depth of steel beam, painted white
 3 Aluminium bracket mechanically fastened to beam above, painted white
 4 Intermittent junction box location, shown dotted
 5 7 mm (5/16 inch) threaded hanger pipe, painted white
 6 Sprinkler system, painted white
 7 Sprinkler pipework
 8 3 mm (1/8 inch) thick continuous aluminium extrusion, painted white
 9 Two sided ceiling panel supported on aluminium extrusion at each beam
 10 Perforated aluminium ceiling panel, painted white with limited combustible material laid above

07.09
Typical Plan Detail at Corner
1:5
 1 Painted aluminium mechanical grill
 2 25 mm (1 inch) steel plates welded to form 89 mm (3 1/2 inch) legs
 3 Insulated glass unit with high performance low-E coating
 4 Painted aluminium cap
 5 Stainless steel curtain wall drain

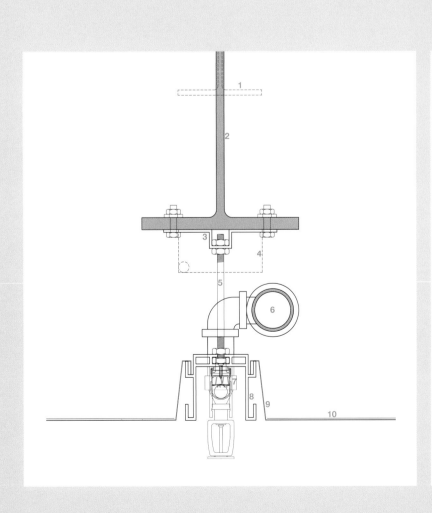

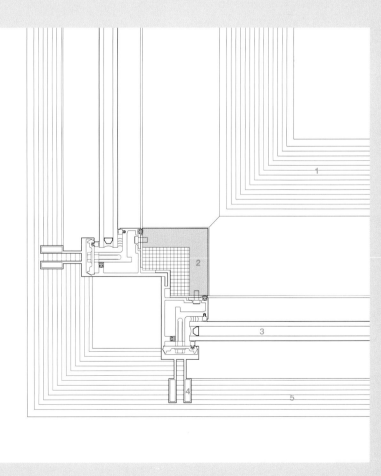

**Municipal Funeral Hall
Kakamigahara, Gifu, Japan**

Client
Kakamigahara City

Structural Engineer
Sasaki Structural Consultants

Lighting Design
Lightdesign

Main Contractor
Toda, Ichikawa,Tenryu

Mechanical Engineers
Kankyo Engineering

Landscape Design
Professor Mikiko Ishikawa

The project has involved the reconstruction of an old crematorium in Kakamigahara in central Japan, which has been designed to integrate into the surrounding park cemetery on the site. The site is peaceful, facing a pond that stretches out to the north and nestled into the verdant mountains to the south. The design brief called for a space appropriate for funerals, while subtly integrating the building into the surrounding parkland.

The concept was to respond not with a conventional massive crematorium, but with a space formed by a sculptural roof that resembles a cloud which, drifting through the sky, has come to settle upon the site. Here, a gently curved reinforced concrete shell structure forms a wave-like roof. The final shape of the roof structure was determined by an algorithm that generated the optimum structural solution. Below the roof, four structural cores and twelve columns with built-in rainwater collection pipes are placed to achieve structural balance within the main ground level space. Ceremonial spaces, as well as technical areas associated with the furnaces, are placed between the cores and columns. The smooth curvature of the roof surface articulates the ceiling in the interior. Indirect light which enters the building via expanses of frameless, full height clear glazing softly illuminates the curved ceiling. Intermediate spaces between the sombre stone cores and the full height perimeter glazing are used as gathering spaces for family and friends.

1 The building nestles between wooded hills on the south and a small artificial lake on the north side.
2 The 20 centimetre (8 inch) thick roof, made up of concave and convex forms, flows into twelve tapered columns, its weight also borne on the two-storey core.
3 Randomly placed between the columns and the core are marble-clad, introverted cuboid volumes in which all the rituals of parting are performed, including the cremation of the body.
4 Clear, full height glazing, cut to fit the contours of the ceiling reveals uninterrupted views over the pond from the waiting room.
5 View of the main hall. The marble clad cores contain the main functions of the cemetery such as the inurnment rooms and furnaces.

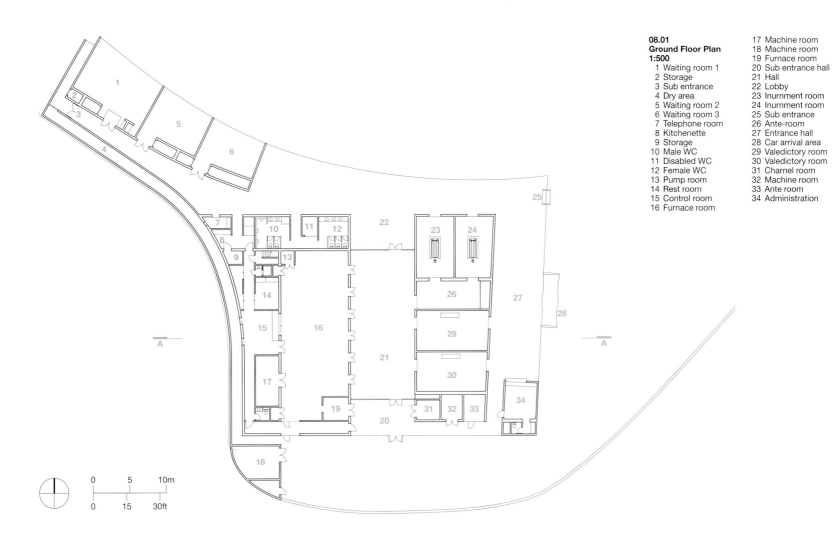

08.01
Ground Floor Plan
1:500

1 Waiting room 1	17 Machine room
2 Storage	18 Machine room
3 Sub entrance	19 Furnace room
4 Dry area	20 Sub entrance hall
5 Waiting room 2	21 Hall
6 Waiting room 3	22 Lobby
7 Telephone room	23 Inurnment room
8 Kitchenette	24 Inurnment room
9 Storage	25 Sub entrance
10 Male WC	26 Ante-room
11 Disabled WC	27 Entrance hall
12 Female WC	28 Car arrival area
13 Pump room	29 Valedictory room
14 Rest room	30 Valedictory room
15 Control room	31 Charnel room
16 Furnace room	32 Machine room
	33 Ante room
	34 Administration

08.02
Section A–A
1:500
1 Furnace
  equipment room
2 Dry area
3 Control room
4 Furnace room
5 Hall
6 Valedictory room
7 Entrance hall
8 Car arrival area
9 Driveway

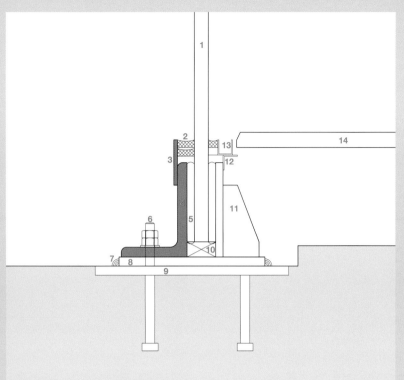

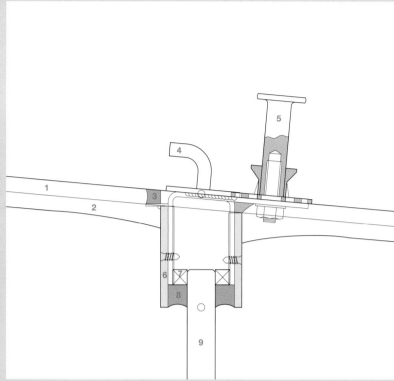

08.03
Exterior Glass Wall Detail at Floor
1:5
 1 Tempered glass exterior glazing
 2 Sealant
 3 Stainless steel flat bar
 4 Steel fixing angle
 5 Foam filler between steel angle and glazing
 6 Anchoring bolt
 7 Welded joint
 8 Steel flat bar

stiffener
 9 Steel wall plate cast into reinforced concrete floor slab
 10 Timber setting block
 11 Ribbed stiffening plate
 12 Setting angle for condensation catchment groove
 13 Stainless steel condensation catchment groove
 14 Marble flooring

08.04
Exterior Glass Wall Detail at Roof
1:2
 1 Roof sheet structure from heat insulating mortar (upper layer)
 2 Roof sheet structure from heat insulating mortar (lower layer)
 3 Waterproof seal
 4 Cast-in U-shaped anchor

 5 Cast-in anchor between roof sheet structure elements
 6 Stainless steel frame plate
 7 Timber backing plate
 8 Sealant
 9 Tempered glass exterior glazing

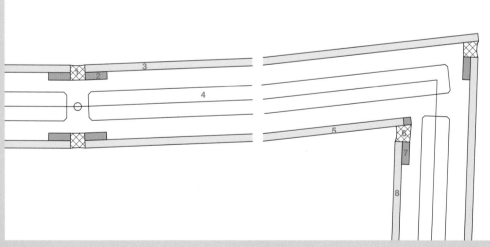

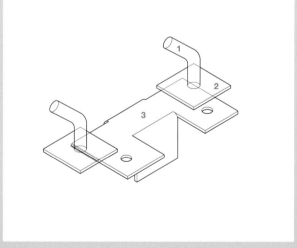

08.05
Exterior Glass Wall Plan Detail
1:2
 1 Sealant
 2 Vulcanized rubber buffer fillet
 3 Stainless steel frame plate
 4 Tempered glass exterior glazing
 5 Stainless steel frame plate
 6 Sealant
 7 Vulcanized rubber

buffer fillet
 8 Stainless steel frame plate

08.06
Steel Roof Junction Assembly Detail
1:5
 1 Cast-in U-shaped anchor
 2 Steel base plate
 3 Steel plate for cast-in U-shaped anchor

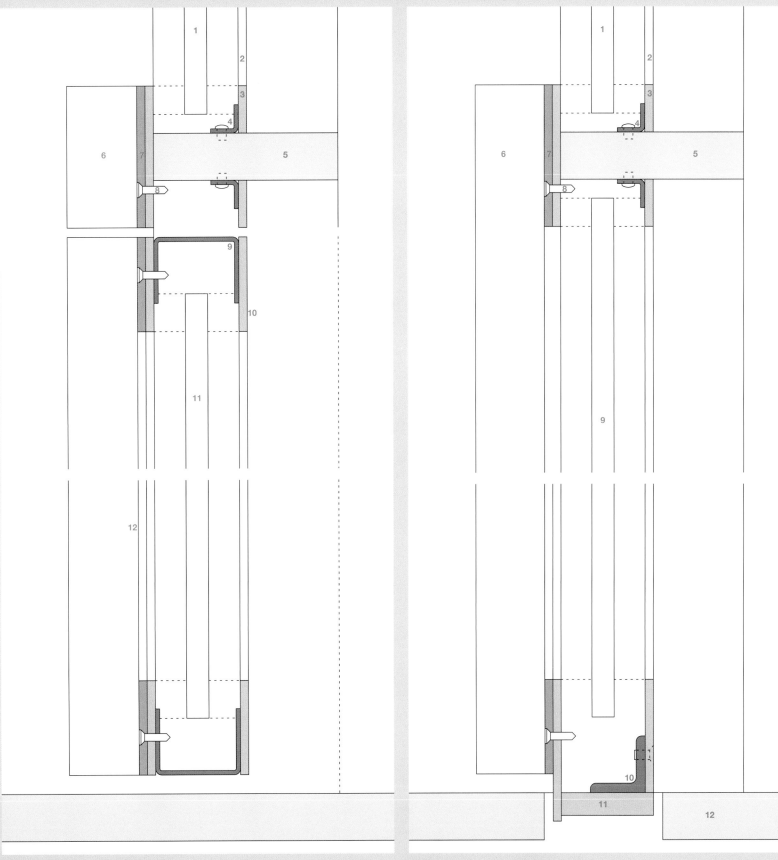

08.07
Glazed Wall and Door
Detail 1
1:5
1 Tempered fixed
glass wall panel
2 Vertical part of steel
frame
3 Horizontal part of
steel frame
4 Setting bed for
glazing frame
5 Transom bar
6 Bent steel flat bar
stiffener

7 Setting bed for flat
bar stiffener
8 Mild steel screw
fixing
9 Steel U-channel
door frame
10 Horizontal part of
steel plate frame to
glazed door
11 Tempered glazed
door
12 Vertical part of steel
plate frame to glazed
door

08.08
Glazed Wall and Door
Detail 2
1:5
1 Tempered fixed
glass wall panel
2 Vertical part of steel
frame
3 Horizontal part of
steel frame
4 Setting bed for
glazing frame
5 Transom bar
6 Bent steel flat bar
stiffener

7 Setting bed for flat
bar stiffener
8 Mild steel screw
fixing
9 Tempered glazed
door
10 Steel angle setting
bed for door frame
11 Bottom plate to
door frame
12 Marble flooring

Nelson-Atkins Museum of Art
Kansas City, Missouri, USA

Client
Nelson-Atkins Museum of Art

Project Team
Steven Holl, Chris McVoy, Martin Cox,
Richard Tobias

Structural Engineer
Guy Nordenson and Associates

Local Architect
BNIM Architects

The expansion of The Nelson-Atkins Museum of Art fuses architecture with landscape to create an experiential architecture that unfolds as it is perceived by each visitor. The new addition, named the Bloch Building, engages the existing sculpture garden, transforming the entire museum site into the precinct of the visitor's experience. The new addition extends along the eastern edge of the campus, and is distinguished by five glass lenses, traversing from the existing building through the sculpture garden to form new spaces and angles of vision. As visitors move through the new addition, they experience the flow of light, art, architecture and landscape, with views from one level to another, and from inside to outside. The threaded movement between the light-gathering lenses of the new addition weaves the new building into its landscape.

The first of the five lenses forms a bright and transparent lobby, with cafe, art library and bookstore, inviting the public into the museum and encouraging movement via ramps toward the galleries. From the lobby, a new cross-axis connects through to the original building's grand spaces. At night the glowing glass volume of the lobby provides an inviting transparency, drawing visitors to events and activities. The lenses' multiple layers of translucent glass gather, diffuse and refract light. During the day the lenses inject varying qualities of light into the galleries, while at night the sculpture garden glows with their internal light. The galleries, organized in sequence to support the progression of the collections, gradually step down into the park, and are punctuated by views into the landscape.

1 The five glass lenses of the new museum extend from the existing classical building, through the sculpture park to create new interstitial spaces for engaging with the art and architecture.
2 The glass lenses are made of a double-layer glass assembly with a pressurized air cavity between the layers. The outer layer consists of double interlocked glass planks with translucent insulation in between. The inner layer consists of translucent laminated low iron glass, with an acid etched finish.
3 The lenses are woven into the landscape of the 9 hectare (22 acre) sculpture garden.
4 Optimum light levels for all types of art and media installations are ensured through the use of computer-controlled screens and special translucent insulating material embedded in the glass cavities.

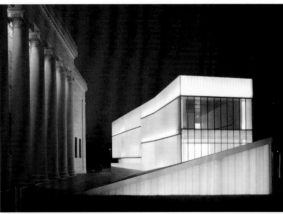

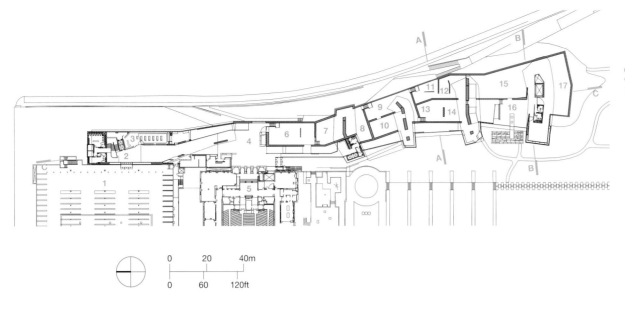

09.01
Ground Floor Plan
1:2000
1 Parking
2 Lower lobby
3 Museum store
4 Lower lobby
5 Lobby of original
 museum building
6 Contemporary art
 gallery
7 Contemporary art
 gallery
8 Contemporary art
 gallery

9 Contemporary art
 gallery
10 Contemporary art
 gallery
11 Photography
 gallery
12 Photography
 gallery
13 African art gallery
14 African art gallery
15 Special exhibitions
16 Noguchi gallery
17 Special exhibitions

09.02
Section A–A
1:1000
1 African art gallery
2 Photography
 gallery
3 Collection storage

09.03
Section B–B
1:1000
1 Noguchi Court
2 Special exhibitions
3 Art receiving bay

09.04
Section C–C
1:1000
1 Upper lobby
2 Multipurpose room
3 Lower lobby
4 Art service level
5 Contemporary art
 gallery
6 Art service level
7 Contemporary art
 gallery

8 Contemporary art
 gallery
9 Art service level
10 Photography
 gallery
11 Featured
 exhibitions gallery
12 Featured
 exhibitions gallery

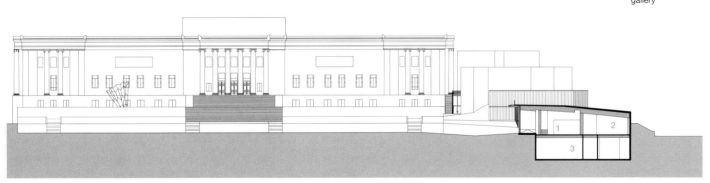

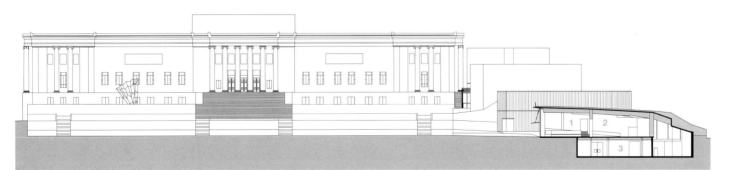

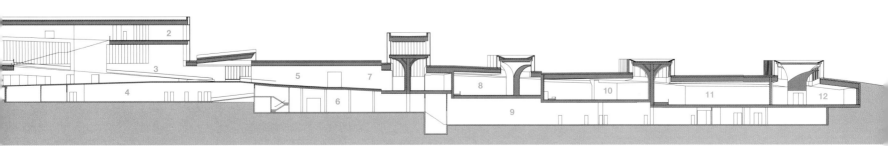

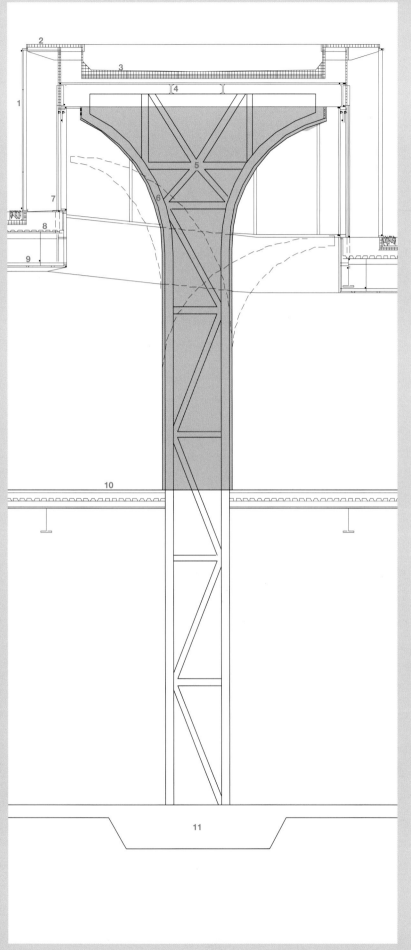

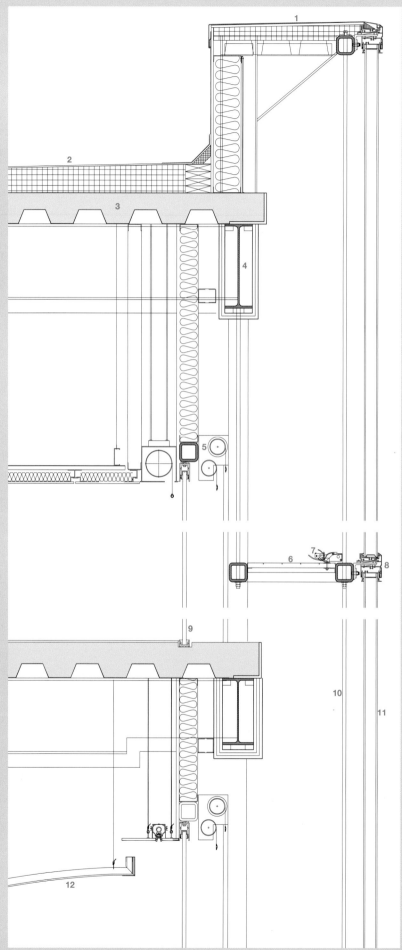

09.05
T-Section Detail at Lens 3
1:50
1 Low-emissivity glass facade with aluminium framed double glazing units with internal translucent Okalux insulation
2 Aluminium flashing painted light grey over 12 mm (1/2 inch) gypsum board panel, sloping layer of 80 mm (3 1/8 inch) corrugated sheeting
3 Waterproofing asphalt membrane sloping insulation layer and composite slab consisting of lightweight concrete fill
4 Steel structure
5 Trussed structure comprised of welded double T-section beams bolted with plates to structural beam
6 Trussed structure comprised of welded double T-section beams bolted with plates to structural beam
7 Sun blind
8 Corrugated sheeting
9 Suspended ceiling
10 Paladiana flooring with recycled glass aggregate composite slab consisting of lightweight concrete fill over corrugated sheeting
11 Reinforced concrete floor slab and footings

09.06
Typical Section Detail Through Glass Lens
1:20
1 Painted aluminium coping
2 EPDM roofing over sloped insulation
3 Composite lightweight concrete and steel deck
4 Steel framing with fireproof treatment
5 Motorized solar control shades
6 Welded catwalk assembly anchored to structural stay for horizontal load resistance
7 Light fixture
8 Intermediate channel slip connection on steel angle with slotted attachment to catwalk assembly
9 Inner facade of single layer of laminated glass
10 White painted suspension rod
11 Outer facade of double layer of low iron U-profile glass units with translucent insulation
12 White gypsum board cladding with light reflective finish fixed to aluminium profile frame suspended by cables from slab

09.07
Catwalk Tube Frame at Soffit Detail
1:10
1 Roller projection screen
2 Facing to projection screen box
3 Aluminium angle
4 Plasterboard ceiling
5 Insulation
6 Extruded aluminium finishing angle with black powdercoat finish
7 Wall in cavity finished up to level of roller shade
8 Structural hanger
9 Structural tube framing to catwalk
10 Metal bar grating
11 Insulation
12 Vapour barrier
13 Catwalk soffit panel
14 Roller shade blackout channel

09.08
Support Detail at Curtain Wall
1:10
1 Metal bar grating
2 Light fixture
3 Catwalk structural tube framing
4 Insulation
5 Vapour barrier
6 Catwalk soffit panel
7 Structural hanger
8 White painted suspension rod
9 Exterior channel glass wall system
10 Exterior face of glass
11 Structural tube framing to catwalk
12 Intermediate channel slip connection on steel angle with slotted attachment to catwalk assembly
13 Steel and glass curtain wall system

09.09
Catwalk Support Detail at Internal Glass Facade
1:10
1 External face of glass
2 Structural steel hanger
3 Support angle to catwalk
4 Steel L-angle
5 Structural tube framing to catwalk
6 Catwalk tube framing
7 Structural tube framing to catwalk
8 Bracket
9 Metal bar grating
10 Steel tube structure

09.10
Intermediate Mullion Detail
1:10
1 Mullion
2 Steel and glass curtain wall system
3 External face of glass

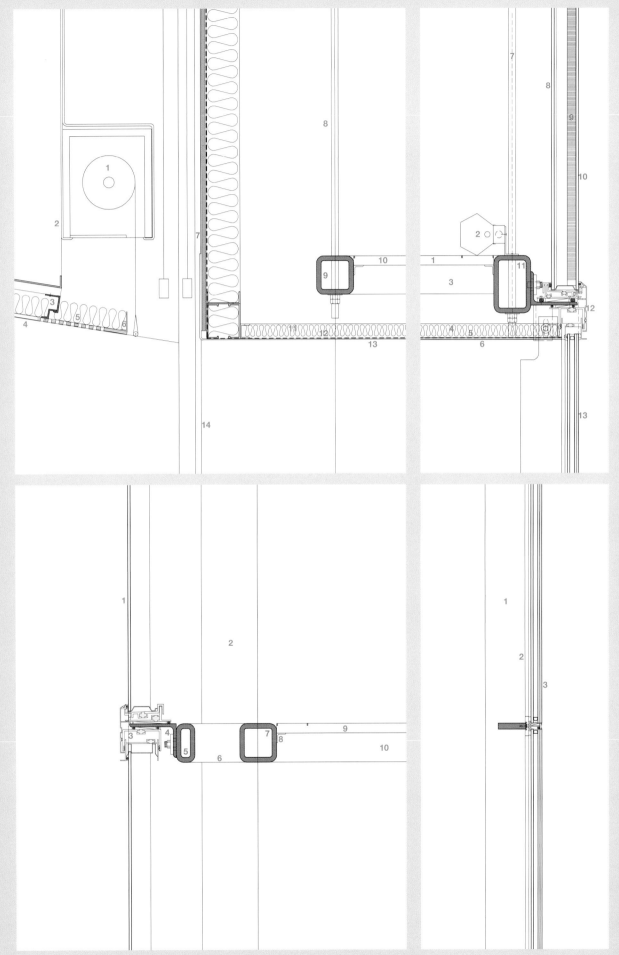

International Chapel, Salvation Army International Headquarters London, England, UK

Client
Salvation Army

Project Team
Luke Lowings, James Carpenter, Valerie Spalding

Structural Engineer
Arup

Main Contractor
Bowmer & Kirklanda

The headquarters of the Salvation Army is on one of the most significant public routes in London, between the Tate Modern gallery, the Millennium footbridge over the Thames and St. Paul's Cathedral. Sheppard Robson, the architects of the main building, have opened up the section of the building with a three storey void from the basement cafe and exhibition area, to the first floor administrative offices which are set back from the facade. The entrance is by means of a bridge across this void, with the chapel overhead, designed by Carpenter Lowings, spanning from the inset floors of the General's suite to the front facade and projecting into the street to form a protective canopy over the entrance doors. The chapel represents the spiritual calling at the heart of the Salvation Army's mission and is also physically in the centre of the facade. It is therefore, despite its small size, extremely significant both architecturally, and for the sense of identity of the institution.

The glowing orange-gold light from within the chapel provides a focus for the facade of the building from the outside and also for the life of the building from inside. Two glass surfaces, one inside the other, one coloured and one of translucent panels, provide a cavity which is lit from within and which also serves to insulate the chapel from the sounds of the entrance area and cafe. At the outer end of the chapel, a series of partially-reflective and translucent blades reflect a view of the sky to the viewer in the chapel while simultaneously obscuring the direct view of the wall outside, and of the chapel from the exterior. The constantly changing London sky is brought into the space to allow the occupant the time and peace of mind to contemplate.

1 View of the entrance to the chapel from the General's suite. At the outer end of the chapel, projecting into the daylight, a series of partially reflective and translucent blades reflect a view of the sky to the viewer in the chapel.
2 The chapel's glowing form at night from the street reflects the history and mission of the Salvation Army as an urban evangelical organization.
3 The glowing orange-gold light from within the chapel provides a focus for the facade of the building from the outside and also for the life of the building from the inside.

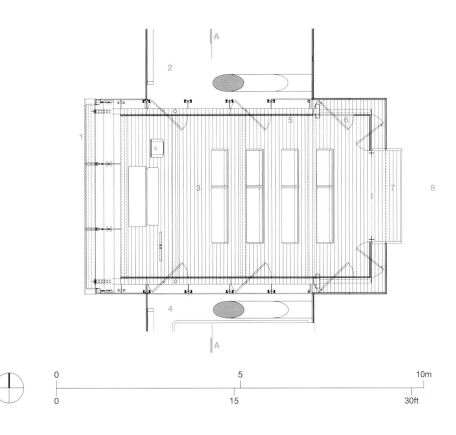

0   5   10m

0   15   30ft

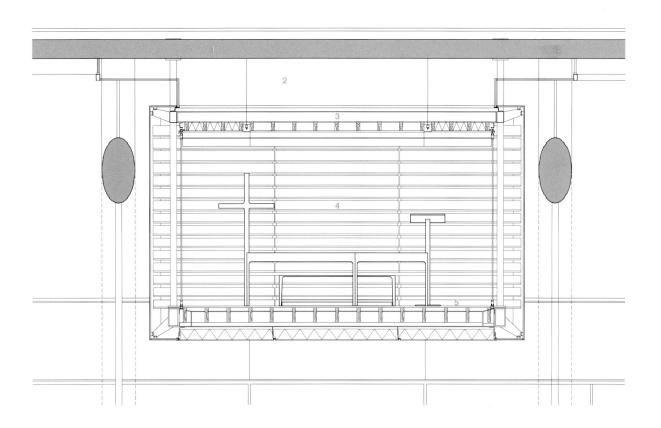

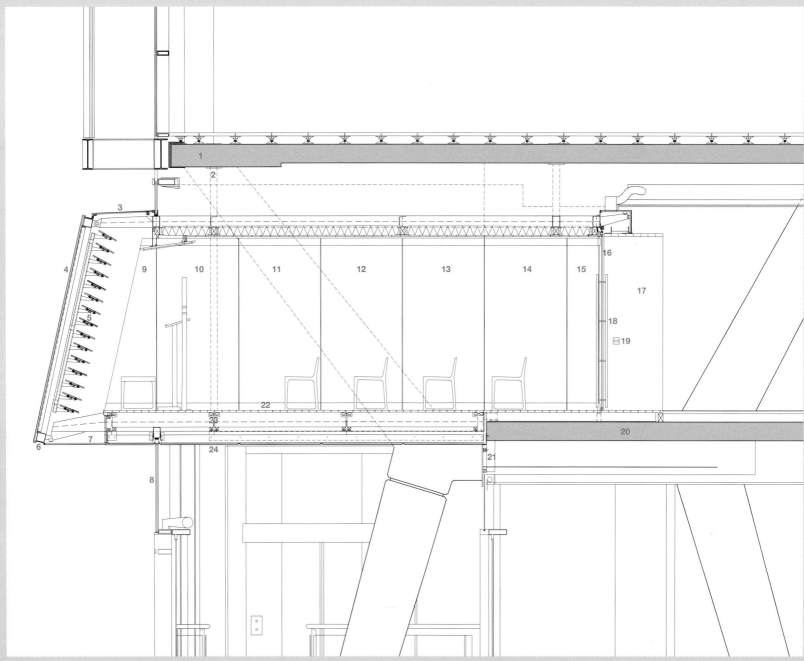

10.03
Long Section Through Chapel 1:50

1 Reinforced concrete floor slab
2 Ceiling frame hangar
3 Translucent exterior glazing
4 West facade of clear solar control glazing
5 Skywall louvres
6 Steel frame to facade structure
7 Translucent exterior glazing
8 External face of building facade
9 Fixed interior glass screen
10 Openable interior glass screen
11 Fixed interior glass screen
12 Openable interior glass screen
13 Fixed interior glass screen
14 Openable interior glass screen
15 Fixed interior glass screen
16 Interior glass screen
17 Timber portal
18 Translucent sliding glass doors
19 Lighting control panel
20 Reinforced concrete floor slab
21 Atrium spandrel panel
22 Timber floorboards
23 Timber floor framing painted with intumescent paint
24 Metal panels to soffit

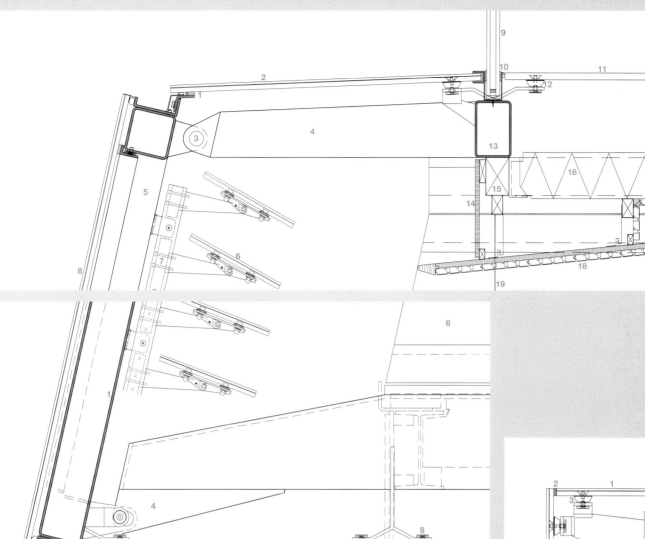

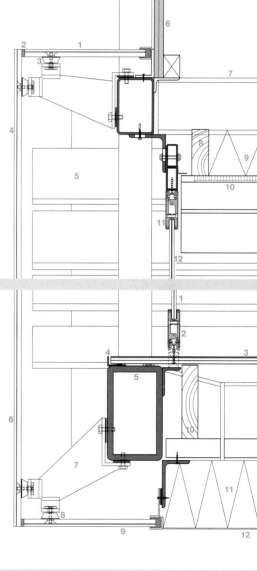

10.04
Top of Front Facade Section Detail
1:10
 1 Structural silicone seal
 2 Exterior translucent glazing
 3 Stainless steel pin connection
 4 West facade steel ceiling cantilever arm
 5 Steel west facade frame
 6 Typical Skywall louvre comprised of clear, semi-reflective coated glass laminated to translucent acid-etched glass
 7 Steel support structure for Skywall louvres
 8 Clear solar control glazing to west facade
 9 Main facade glazing
 10 Structural frame deflection assembly
 11 Translucent glazing to atrium
 12 'Thermospan' laminated bolt to restrain side panels
 13 Rectangular hollow section ceiling frame
 14 Timber closure panel
 15 Timber fixing block
 16 Acoustic insulation
 17 Perforated timber veneered acoustic panel
 18 Perforated timber veneered acoustic panel
 19 Interior glass screen

10.05
Bottom of Front Facade Section Detail
1:10
 1 Steel west facade frame
 2 Site applied structural silicone seal
 3 Glazing fixed to steel supporting angle with structural silicone, with bottom layer of glass recessed to create flush surface with supporting angle
 4 Welded steel lug connecting cantilevered frame element to west facade frame
 5 Exterior translucent glazing
 6 Interior glass screen
 7 Steel floor frame finished with intumescent paint
 8 'Thermospan' laminated bolt to restrain side panels

10.06
Top Section Detail
1:10
 1 Translucent glazing
 2 Silicone joint to accommodate relative movement of floor and ceiling frames and preserve acoustic seal
 3 'Thermospan' laminated bolt to restrain side panels
 4 Translucent glazing
 5 Glass screen supported at floor to accommodate relative movement of floor and ceiling frames at head
 6 Framed drywall interior lining
 7 Ceiling framing
 8 47 x 122 mm (1^7/$_8$ x 4^4/$_5$ inch) timber joists at 295 mm (11^5/$_8$ inch) centres
 9 Acoustic insulation at minimum density of 30 kg per cubic metre
 10 Slots and holes in plank to stop short 30 mm (1^1/$_4$ inch) from edge of plank
 11 Machine anodized top rail of interior glass screen
 12 Interior glass screen

10.07
Bottom Section Detail
1:10
 1 Interior glass screen
 2 Machine anodized bottom rail of interior glass screen
 3 Timber floor
 4 Anodized aluminium floor edge angle
 5 Rectangular hollow section steel floor framing finished with intumescent paint
 6 Translucent glazing
 7 Painted mild steel cantilever bracket
 8 'Thermospan' laminated bolt, site welded to floor frame
 9 Translucent glazing
 10 44 x 195 mm (1^3/$_4$ x 7^2/$_3$ inch) timber floor joist at 300 mm (11^4/$_5$ inch) centres
 11 Mineral wool thermal insulation with minimum density of 30 kg per cubic metre
 12 Metal panels

**11 March Memorial
Madrid, Spain**

Client
Madrid City Council and RENFE

Project Team
Esaú Acosta, Raquel Buj, Pedro Colón
de Carvajal, Mauro Gil-Fournier,
Miguel Jaenicke

Structural Engineer
Schlaich, Bergermann und Partner

Main Contractor
Dragados

The monument for the victims of the
terrorist attacks in Madrid in 2004 is a
unique structure employing massive
glass blocks connected with a
transparent adhesive to form a glass
cylinder. The outer layer of the
monument consists of approximately
15,100 borosilicate glass blocks, each
weighing 8.4 kilograms (18 pounds)
which were specially manufactured to
be convex on the one side and
concave on the other in order to make
it possible to bond the blocks together
in circular rows to create the
cylindrical form. The monument
consists of two parts – the glass
cylinder and an underground
presentation room linked by a circular
rooflight. This arrangement is
designed to create a 'shimmer of
hope', rising up towards the city from
the depths of the station, which in the
context of the memorial is designated
as the 'site of sorrow'.

Inside the glass cylinder,
expressions of sorrow taken from the
thousands of messages left at the
station by mourners in the days after
the bombing, are engraved onto a
transparent plastic film that spirals
upwards towards the circular window
above. After dark, the volume radiates
softly from lights embedded in the
base of the monument. During the
day, sunlight produces an ethereal
glow as it filters through the glass
tower and reflects off the deep blue
surfaces in the underground chamber.
Visitors stream through a double set of
steel and glass security doors into the
lower chamber. The otherwise dark
chamber features blue walls, ceiling
and floor, and has no furniture apart
from a long black steel bench where
visitors can sit in contemplation of life
and death. The names of the victims
of the bombings are engraved on a
frosted glass panel between the first
and second entrance doors.

1 The apparently
fragile structure has
been designed to
withstand extreme
wind forces and
changes in
temperature that are
typical of Madrid's
climate.
2 Inside the glass
cylinder, curving
sheets of pressure
treated Ethylene
tetraflouroethylene
(ETFE) foil is printed
with thousands of
messages of
condolence left by
mourners in the days
after the attacks which
occurred on the 11
March, 2004. The
memorial was
inaugurated on the
third anniversary of the
bombings.
3 The luminous
monument is built from
over 15,000 curved
glass blocks glued
together with a
liquid-acrylic
transparent adhesive
hardened by ultraviolet
lamps.

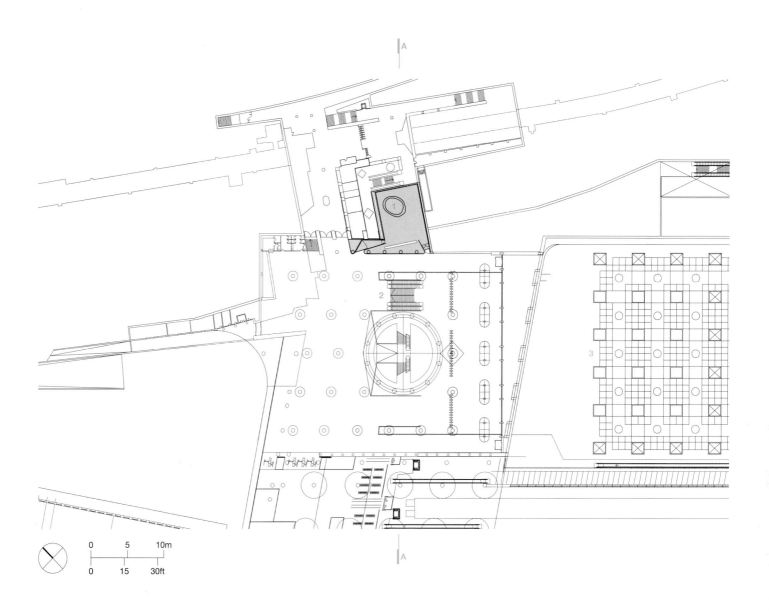

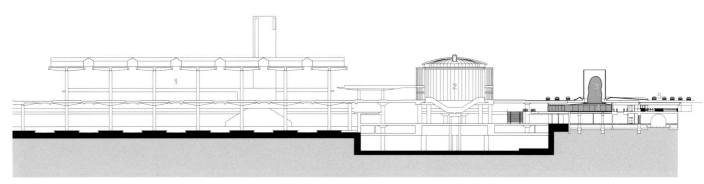

11.01
Site Plan
1:500
1 Madrid Memorial
2 Atocha Station
  entrance
3 Station plaza

11.02
Section A–A
1:500
1 Station platforms
2 Atocha Station
  entrance
3 Madrid Memorial
4 Underground
  memorial chamber
5 Station plaza

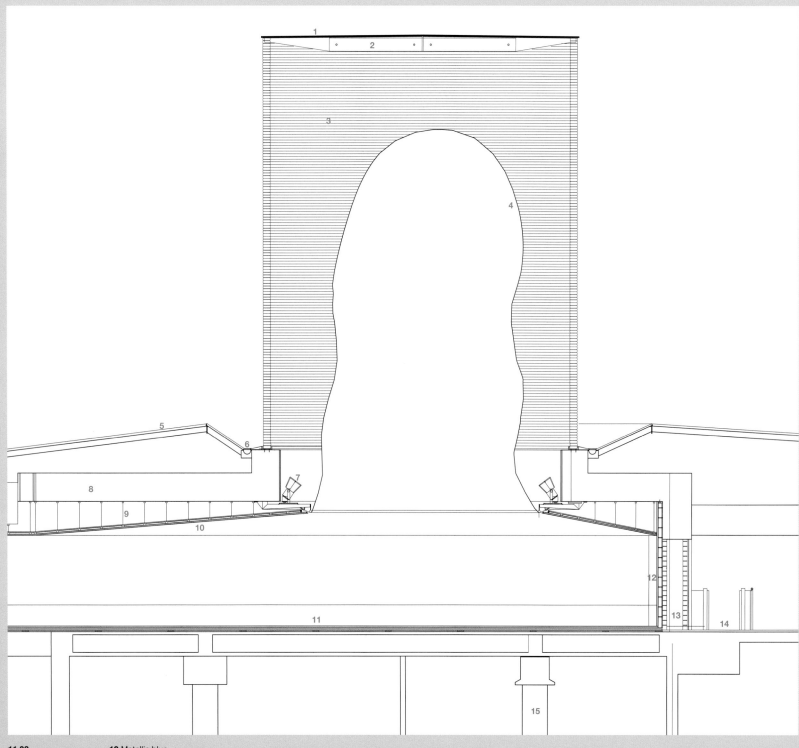

11.03
Section Through
Glass Memorial
Structure and
Underground
Chamber
1:37.5
  1 Laminated glass
  2 Laminated glass
beams
  3 Glass bricks
  4 ETFE (Ethylene
tetrafluoroethylene)
membrane
  5 Volcanic stone
  6 Gutter
  7 Lighting system
  8 Concrete slab
  9 Ceiling structure
10 Ceiling
11 Epoxy resin floor

12 Metallic blue
painted timber panels
13 Acoustic chamber
14 Escalators
15 Existing concrete
structure

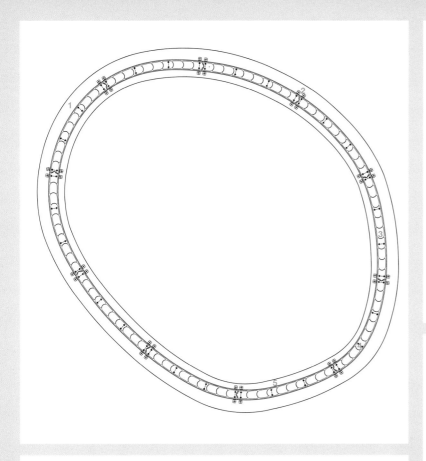

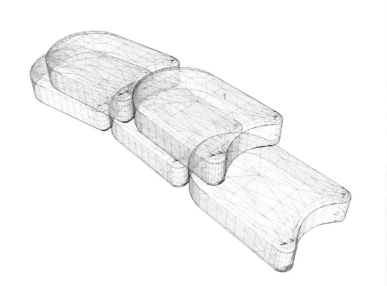

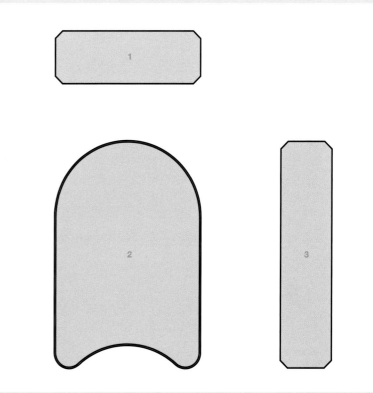

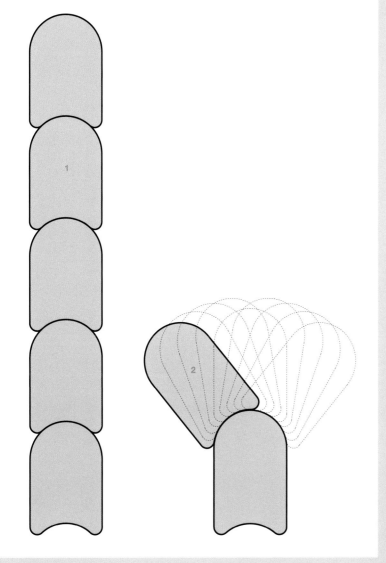

11.04
Plan Detail of Glass Cylinder
1:100
 1 Concrete base
 2 Steel ring
 3 EPDM (ethylene propylene diene Monomer rubber) base
 4 300 x 200 x 80 mm (11⁴/5 x 8 x 3¹/8 inch) borosilicate glass brick
 5 3 mm (¹/16 inch) UV glue

11.05
Typical Glass Block Layering Arrangement Detail
1:10
 1 Three-dimensional view of 300 x 200 x 70 mm (11⁴/5 x 7⁹/10 x 2³/4 inch) glass blocks with 100 mm (4 inch) radius curve to both ends to facilitate end to end connection and variations in angle of connection as dictated by the curve of the exterior wall

11.06
Glass Block Connection System Detail
Not To Scale
 1 300 x 200 x 70 mm (11⁴/5 x 7⁹/10 x 2³/4 inch) glass block with end to end curved connection zone
 2 300 x 200 x 70 mm (11⁴/5 x 7⁹/10 x 2³/4 inch) glass block with 100 mm (4 inch) radius curve to both ends to facilitate end to end connection and variations in angle of connection

11.07
Section and Plan Details of Glass Block
1:5
 1 300 x 200 x 70 mm (11⁴/5 x 7⁹/10 x 2³/4 inch) glass block
 2 300 x 200 x 70 mm (11⁴/5 x 7⁹/10 x 2³/4 inch) glass block with 100 mm (4 inch) radius curve to both ends
 3 300 x 200 x 70 mm (11⁴/5 x 7⁹/10 x 2³/4 inch) glass block with 10 mm (²/5 inch) chamfer to all corners

The Cathedral of Christ the Light
Oakland, California, USA

Client
The Cathedral of Christ the Light

Project Team
Craig Hartman, Gene Schnair, Keith Boswell, Raymond Kuca, Patrick Daly, David Diamond

Structural Engineer
Mark Sarkisian, Peter Lee, Eric Long

Main Contractor
Webcor Builders

Located in downtown Oakland, the 1,350-seat Cathedral of Christ the Light offers a sense of solace, spiritual renewal, and respite from the secular world. The building form is based on a wooden vessel contained within a veil of glass, both of which are anchored on an architectural concrete base. The design conveys an inclusive statement of welcome while recalling the narrative of Noah and his ark. The cathedral employs state-of-the-art technologies to create lightness and space. As its name suggests, the building draws on the tradition of light as a sacred phenomenon. Through its poetic introduction, indirect daylight ennobles modest materials—primarily wood, glass and concrete.

Triangular aluminium panels form the petal-shaped Alpha Window, which diffuses light above the cathedral's entrance, while the Omega Window rises behind the altar, its triangular aluminium panels perforated with 94,000 laser-cut holes. As points of light shine through the holes in varying levels of brightness, a 17.7 metre (58 foot) image of Christ appears and disappears. The lightest ecological footprint was a core design objective. With the exception of evening activities, the cathedral is entirely lit by daylight. The structure's concrete makes use of industrial-waste fly ash, and an advanced version of the ancient Roman technique of thermal inertia maintains the interior climate with radiant heat, while small ducts beneath the pews cool the building from the floor. Douglas fir, obtained through certified harvesting processes, was used throughout the complex and has proven to be aesthetically pleasing, economically sound and structurally forgiving.

1 Located in downtown Oakland on the edge of Lake Merritt, The Cathedral of Christ features a non-linear approach that honours the church's 2,000-year history without forcing a specific point of view. By stripping away received iconography, the design positions symbolic meaning within contemporary culture.
2 Exterior view of the Alpha Window which is formed from triangular aluminium panels, which diffuse light 30 metres (100 feet) above the cathedral's entrance.
3 Once visitors pass through the entrance and under the Alpha Window, they cross the sanctuary's open and ethereal nave. The louvred timber surfaces, constructed from Douglas fir, lend a warmth to the luminous interior.

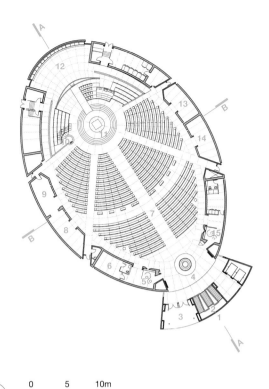

12.01
Ground Floor Plan
1:500
1 Plaza
2 Stairs to
  mausoleum
3 Entrance
4 Baptistry
5 Reconciliation
  chapels
6 Community room
7 Centre aisle
8 Chapel of All
  Saints

9 Chapel of The
  Seasons
10 Ambo (lectern)
11 Altar
12 Blessed
  Sacrament Chapel
13 Chapel of The
  Suffering Christ
14 Chapel of The Holy
  Family
15 Reconciliation
  chapels

12.02
Section A–A
1:500
1 Plaza
2 Stairs to
  mausoleum
3 Entrance
4 Baptistry
5 Mausoleum entry
6 Mausoleum
7 Catafalque
8 Mausoleum
9 Mechanical plant
10 Cathedral seating

11 Choir
12 Altar
13 Cathedra
14 Blessed
  Sacrament Chapel
15 Organ pipes
16 Douglas fir louvred
  interior screen
17 Glass exterior
  curtain wall

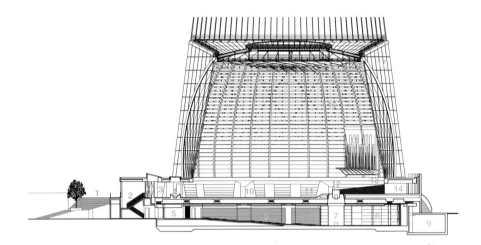

12.03
Section B–B
1:200
1 Loading dock
2 Chapel of All
  Saints
3 Storage
4 Mausoleum
5 Catafalque
6 Mausoleum niches
7 Classroom
8 Parish hall
9 Ambo (lectern)
10 Altar
11 Cathedra
12 Chapel of The Holy
  Family
13 Organ canopy
14 Organ pipes
15 Douglas fir louvred
  interior screen
16 Aluminium panels
  to Omega Window
17 Aluminium panels
  to oculus ceiling
18 Oculus ceiling
  skylight
19 Aluminium vertical
  mullion fin
  extensions
20 Glazed roof
21 Glass exterior
  curtain wall

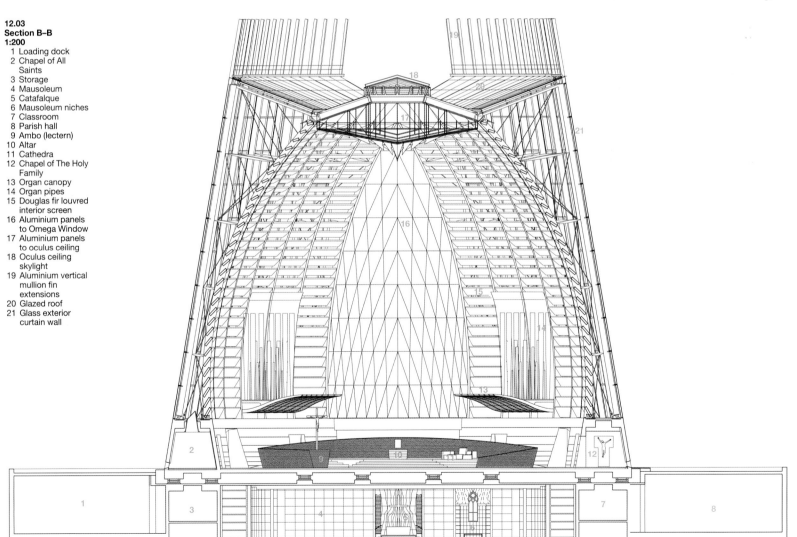

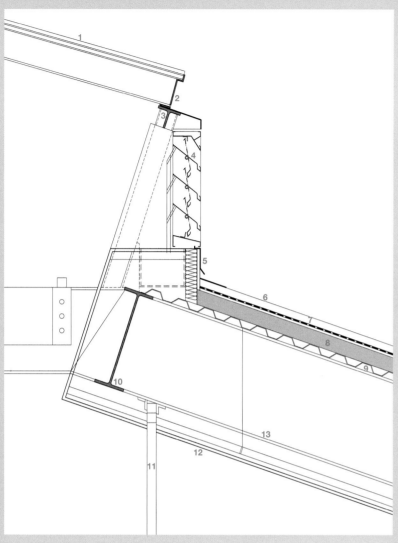

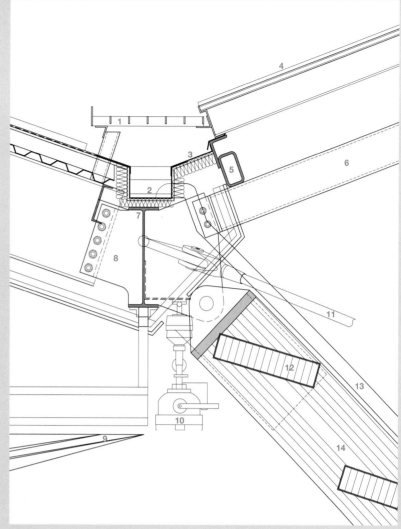

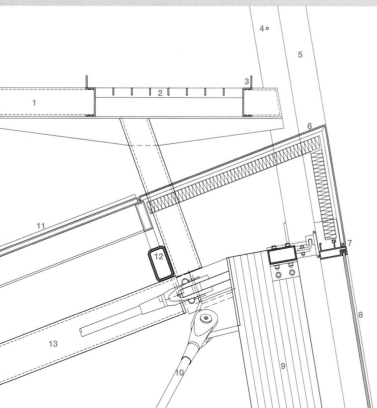

12.04
Oculus Skylight Detail
1:20
1 Aluminium skylight assembly with clear insulated laminated low-E glass
2 Extruded aluminium curb
3 Continuous steel beam
4 Extruded aluminium drainable louvre with electric actuator
5 Stainless steel flashing
6 Standing seam zinc roofing over waterproof membrane
7 Mineral board sheathing
8 76 mm (3 inch) thick semi-rigid insulation
9 38 mm (1¹/2 inch) thick metal roof deck
10 Continuous steel beam
11 Support strut for suspended ceiling
12 Painted gypsum board ceiling on suspended runner
13 Steel framing

12.05
Internal Roof Gutter Detail
1:20
1 Grating formed from aluminium bars
2 Continuous

stainless steel gutter
3 Continuous stainless steel flashing
4 Aluminium skylight assembly with clear insulated laminated low-E glass
5 Rectangular hollow section steel skylight support structure
6 Steel structure
7 Continuous steel beam
8 Formed galvanized steel plate with stiffeners at cable supports
9 Suspended perforated aluminium panels
10 Light fixture
11 Galvanized steel tension rod
12 Glu-laminated timber louvre
13 Copper roof drainpipe
14 Tapered curved Glu-laminated timber rib

12.06
Detail at Junction Between Glazed Roof and Glass Exterior Screen Wall
1:20
1 100 x 150 mm (4 x 6 inch) galvanized steel tube for retractable window washing support
2 Grating formed

from aluminium bars
3 Continuous aluminium toe guard face plate
4 Stainless steel cable guardrail
5 6,096 mm (20 foot) high vertical mullion extensions with stainless steel inserts laminated on south facing side of each vertical mullion beyond top of window wall
6 Aluminium coping with powder-coated finish
7 Sealant with backer rod
8 Unitized aluminium and glass curtain wall with laminated fritted glass
9 Glu-laminated timber rib
10 Galvanized steel tension rod
11 Aluminium skylight assembly with clear insulated laminated low-E glass
12 Steel tube
13 Galvanized steel beam

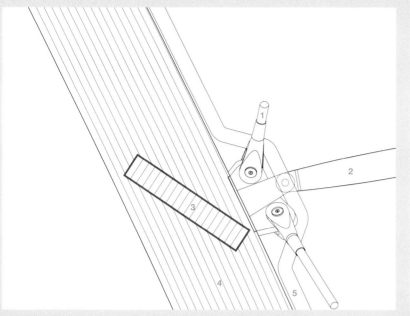

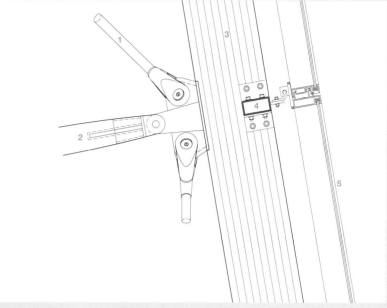

12.07
Timber Louvre Detail
1:20
1 Galvanized steel
tension rod
2 Tapered timber
compression strut
3 Glu-laminated
timber louvre
4 Tapered, curved
Glu-laminated timber
rib
5 Copper roof
drainpipe

12.08
External Glazed
Curtain Wall Detail
1:20
1 Galvanized steel
tension rod
2 Tapered timber
compression strut
3 Glu-laminated
timber rib
4 Galvanized steel
horizontal curtain wall
support tube
5 Unitized aluminium

and glass curtain wall
with laminated fritted
glass

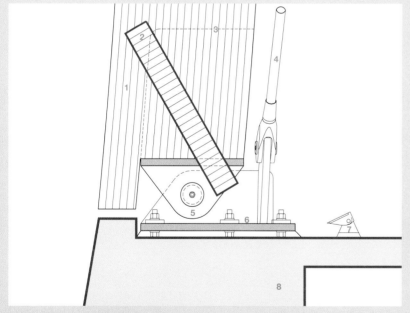

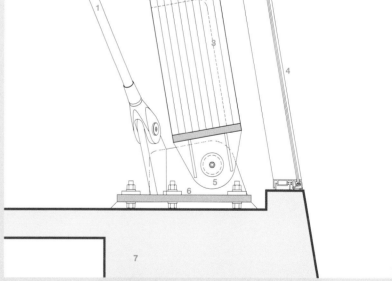

12.09
Detail of Timber
Louvred Wall at Base
1:20
1 Tapered curved
Glu-laminated timber
rib
2 Glu-laminated
timber louvre
3 Galvanized steel
kerf plate
4 Galvanized steel
tension rod
5 Galvanized steel pin
connection
6 Galvanized steel

base plate
7 Light fixture
8 Reinforced
concrete reliquary wall

12.10
Detail of Glazed
Curtain Wall at Base
1:20
1 Galvanized steel
tension rod
2 Glu-laminated
timber rib
3 Galvanized steel
kerf plate
4 Unitized aluminium
and glass curtain wall
with laminated fritted
glass
5 Galvanized steel pin
connection

6 Galvanized steel
base plate
7 Reinforced
concrete reliquary wall

**Norwegian National Opera and
Ballet
Oslo, Norway**

Client
Statsbygg National Governmental
Building Agency

Project Team
Craig Dykers, Tarald Lundevall, Kjetil
Trædal Thorsen

Structural Engineer
Reinertsen Engineering

Structural Contractor
Veidekke Entreprenør

In 1999 the Norwegian National
Assembly voted to build a new Opera
House in Bjørvika, on the seafront of
the Oslo fjord. The building was to be
the foundation for the urban
redevelopment of this area of the
capital. The government wanted the
opera house to be a monumental
building which would mark Norway as
a cultural centre as well as highlighting
the social and cultural importance of
the Norwegian National Opera and
Ballet. The design of the new building
is split in two by a corridor running
north-south, the 'Opera Street'. To the
west of this line are located all the
public areas and stage areas. The
eastern part of the building houses the
production areas which are simpler in
form and finish.

The majority of the building is three
to four storeys above ground with an
additional level below ground. The
sub-stage area is a further three
storeys deep. A marble clad plaza
leads the visitors to the foyer and
other public areas. A secondary
entrance on the north facade gives
direct access to the restaurant and
foyer. To the south, the foyer opens up
to the inner Oslo fjord and views of
Hovedøya island. The high glass
facade over the foyer has a dominant
role in the views of the building from
the south, west, and north. The glass
facade is an important element in the
project – both during the day and
night it acts as a lamp illuminating the
external surfaces. The glass facade,
which in parts is up to 15 metres (50
feet) high, is constructed with an
absolute minimum of columns,
framing, and stiffening steel. The
solution uses glass fins where
minimized steel fixings are
sandwiched inside the laminates.

1 The dividing line
between the ground
and the water is both a
real and a symbolic
threshold which is
made manifest in the
Opera House as an
inclined stone plane
that rises out of the
sea and continues
upwards to form both
the building's roof and
a public plaza.
2 In the foyer, a wave
of timber in the form of
small rectangular
pieces of oak,
envelops an elegant
curve of circulation
that wraps around the
full height of the main
auditorium.
3 The requirements for
the glass's stiffness
increased due to the
need for large panels.
Glass of this size tends
to be tinged with
green. It was therefore
decided that the
facade would use clear
low-iron glass.
4 Oak is used
throughout many of
the public spaces for
the floors, walls and
ceilings.

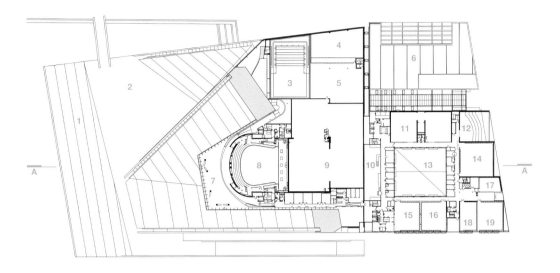

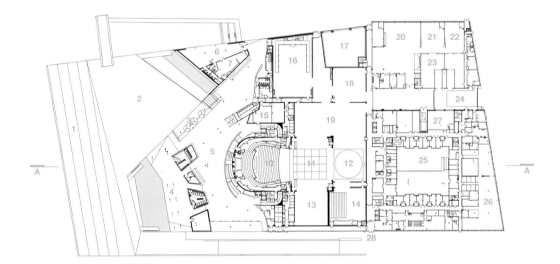

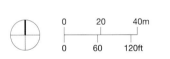

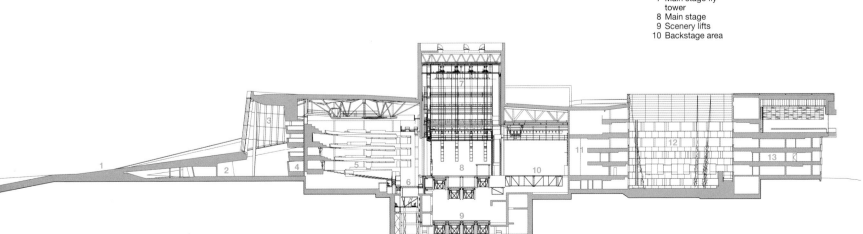

13.01
Third Floor Plan
1:2000
1 Public plaza
   (inclined)
2 Public plaza (flat)
3 Third balcony,
   stage 2
4 Courtyard
5 Technical room
6 Roof to workshop
   areas below
7 Auditorium foyer
8 Main auditorium
9 Void
10 Technical room
11 Void
12 Void
13 Void
14 Ballet rehearsal
   rooms
15 Ballet rehearsal
   rooms
16 Ballet rehearsal
   rooms
17 Opera rehearsal
   room
18 Ballet rehearsal
   rooms
19 Ballet rehearsal
   rooms

13.02
Ground Floor Plan
1:2000
1 Public plaza
   (inclined)
2 Public plaza (flat)
3 Main entrance
4 Public cloakroom
5 Auditorium foyer
6 Restaurant seating
   area
7 Restaurant back
   of house
8 Ticketing and
   information
9 Circulation wall to
   auditorium
10 Main auditorium
   stalls
11 Main stage
12 Backstage area
13 Stage wings
14 Opera rehearsal
   room
15 Lecture room
16 Stage 2
17 Void
18 Assembly hall
19 Stage wings
20 Paint and tapestry
   workshop
21 Wood and metal
   scenery workshop
22 Wood and metal
   scenery workshop
23 Workshop
24 Loading dock
25 Courtyard
26 Costume
   department
27 Storage
28 Backstage
   entrance
29 Ballet dressing
   rooms

13.03
Section A–A
1:1000
1 Public plaza
   (inclined)
2 Public cloakroom
3 Inclined glazed
   wall
4 Circulation wall to
   auditorium
5 Main auditorium
6 Orchestra pit
7 Main stage fly
   tower
8 Main stage
9 Scenery lifts
10 Backstage area

11 Circulation
12 Stone wall to
   courtyard
13 Costume
   department

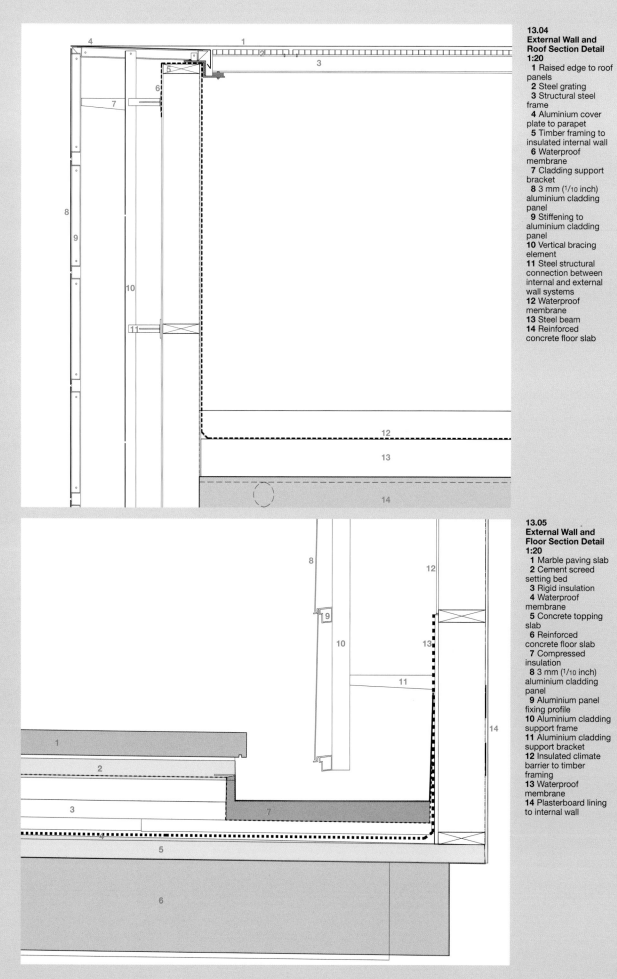

13.04
External Wall and Roof Section Detail
1:20
1 Raised edge to roof panels
2 Steel grating
3 Structural steel frame
4 Aluminium cover plate to parapet
5 Timber framing to insulated internal wall
6 Waterproof membrane
7 Cladding support bracket
8 3 mm (1/10 inch) aluminium cladding panel
9 Stiffening to aluminium cladding panel
10 Vertical bracing element
11 Steel structural connection between internal and external wall systems
12 Waterproof membrane
13 Steel beam
14 Reinforced concrete floor slab

13.05
External Wall and Floor Section Detail
1:20
1 Marble paving slab
2 Cement screed setting bed
3 Rigid insulation
4 Waterproof membrane
5 Concrete topping slab
6 Reinforced concrete floor slab
7 Compressed insulation
8 3 mm (1/10 inch) aluminium cladding panel
9 Aluminium panel fixing profile
10 Aluminium cladding support frame
11 Aluminium cladding support bracket
12 Insulated climate barrier to timber framing
13 Waterproof membrane
14 Plasterboard lining to internal wall

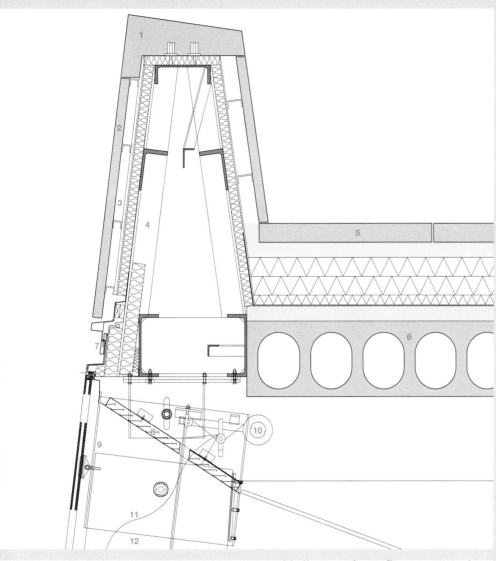

13.06
Parapet to Glazed Wall to Public Foyer Detail
1:20
1 Stone capping with honed top surface and bush hammered side faces
2 50 mm (2 inch) thick bush hammered stone cladding
3 Steel support system for stone cladding
4 Steel structure
5 Roof build up comprised of 80 mm ($3^1/8$ inch) natural stone over 100 mm (4 inch) thick cement-stabilized gravel with 30 mm ($1^1/5$ inch) slurry top layer with embedded lightning conductor grid, over 3 mm ($1/10$ inch) felt layer, over two layers of 100 mm (4 inch) extruded polystyrene, over 50 mm (2 inch) stone wool insulation, over triple layer of 10 mm ($2/5$ inch) asphalt membrane
6 80 mm ($3^1/8$ inch) structural concrete slab
7 Maintenance rail
8 Ventilation grille
9 Fastened guide wire
10 Motorized winding mechanism for interior sun shading system
11 Guide wire for interior sun shading
12 Laminated structural glass fin

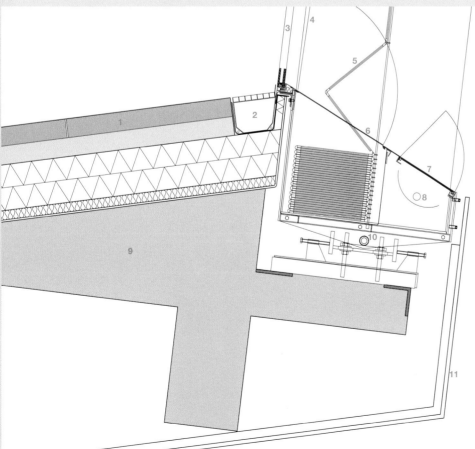

13.07
Glass Wall to Inclined Plaza Detail
1:20
1 Roof build up comprised of 80 mm ($3^1/8$ inch) natural stone over 100 mm (4 inch) thick cement-stabilized gravel with 30 mm ($1^1/5$ inch) slurry top layer with embedded lightning conductor grid, over 3 mm ($1/10$ inch) felt layer, over two layers of 100 mm (4 inch) extruded polystyrene, over 50 mm (2 inch) stone wool insulation, over triple layer of 10 mm ($2/5$ inch) asphalt membrane
2 Stainless steel gutter
3 Double glazed panel
4 Glass pin seen in elevation
5 Sun shading system
6 Wire guide for sun shading system
7 Openable glass cover to light fixture box
8 Light fixture
9 Structural concrete floor slab with articulated edge beams
10 Pin joint for structural glass fin
11 Internal plasterboard lining on timber sections

**Institut Français de la Mode
Paris, France**

Client
Caisse des Dépôts

Project Team
Dominique Jakob, Brendan
MacFarlane

Structural Engineer
C&E ingénierie

Main Contractor
Icade G3A

The Docks of Paris is a long, thin concrete building constructed in 1907 and originally a depot for goods brought up the Seine by barge. The city of Paris launched a competition to create a new cultural building on the site with the option to keep the existing concrete structure. Jakob + MacFarlane opted to retain the structure and use it to influence the new project. The three storey building is comprised of four pavilions. On the level corresponding to the Quai d'Austerlitz, the building is accessible from the street with higher areas above to facilitate the loading of goods for transport. The idea for the new project was to create an external skin, inspired primarily by the flux of the Seine and the walkways along the river bank.

The glass skin both protects the existing structure and forms a new layer containing most of the public circulation systems and added programme, as well as creating a new top floor to the existing building. The structural system supporting the glass skin is the result of a systematic deformation of the existing conceptual grid of the docks building, in which the new building grows out from the old as new branches grow on a tree. This skin is created principally from glass panels, steel structure, timber decking and a grassed, faceted roofscape. The intervention operates not only as a way of exploiting the maximum building envelope but enables a continuous public path to move up through the building from the lowest level alongside the Seine to the roof deck and back down; a kind of continuous loop enabling the building to become part of the urban condition. The programme is a rich mixture, centred on the themes of design and fashion, including exhibition spaces, the French Fashion Institute (IFM), music producers, bookshops, cafes and a restaurant.

1 The concept of the new project is referred to by the architects as a 'Plug-Over' which refers to the way the glass intervention plugs into and climbs over the roof of the existing building to create new circulation zones as well as programmable space.
2 The panels of green tinted glass are fixed to a green painted structural steel skeleton which in turn is fixed to the concrete frame of the existing building.
3 On the street side of the building, the new structure continues over the roof and runs down the side of the building to form a covered circulation zone.
4 Detail view from inside the new glass and steel structure.

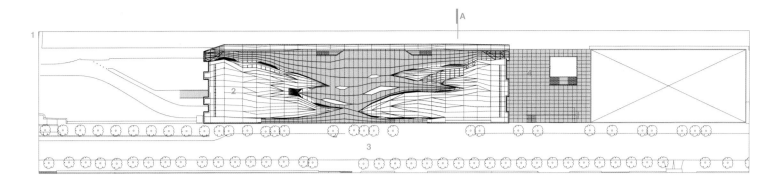

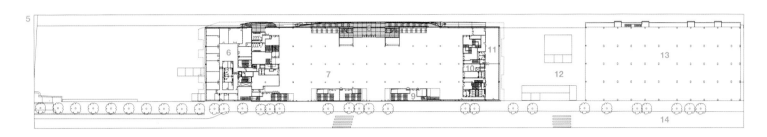

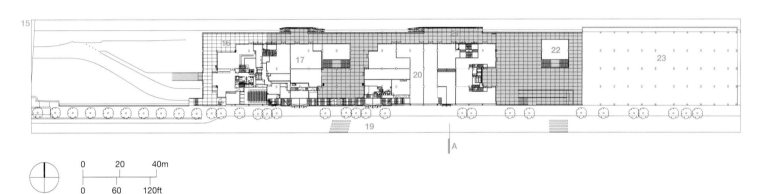

0 20 40m

0 60 120ft

14.01
Floor Plans
1:2000
 1 Roof plan
 2 Landscaped roof
 3 Quai d'Austerlitz
 4 Plaza entrance
 5 First floor plan
 6 French Fashion
    Institute
 7 Exhibition space
 8 Landing
 9 Security exit
    staircases
10 Technical spaces
11 Meeting rooms
12 Plaza
13 Neighbouring
    property
14 Quai d'Austerlitz
15 Ground floor plan
16 Promenade
17 Retail space
18 Public entry
19 Quai d'Austerlitz
20 Retail space
21 Landing
22 Staircase to Quai
    d'Austerlitz
23 Neighbouring
    property

14.02
Section A–A
1:400
 1 Quai d'Austerlitz
 2 Circulation space
 3 Retail space
 4 Landscaped roof
 5 Roof
 6 Exhibition space
 7 Exhibition space
 8 Landing
 9 Technical space
10 Retail space
11 Truck loading dock
12 Retail space
13 Retail space
14 Promenade
15 Quay-side exterior
    exhibition space
16 Public promenade
17 River Seine

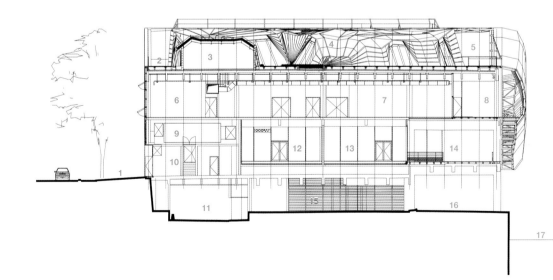

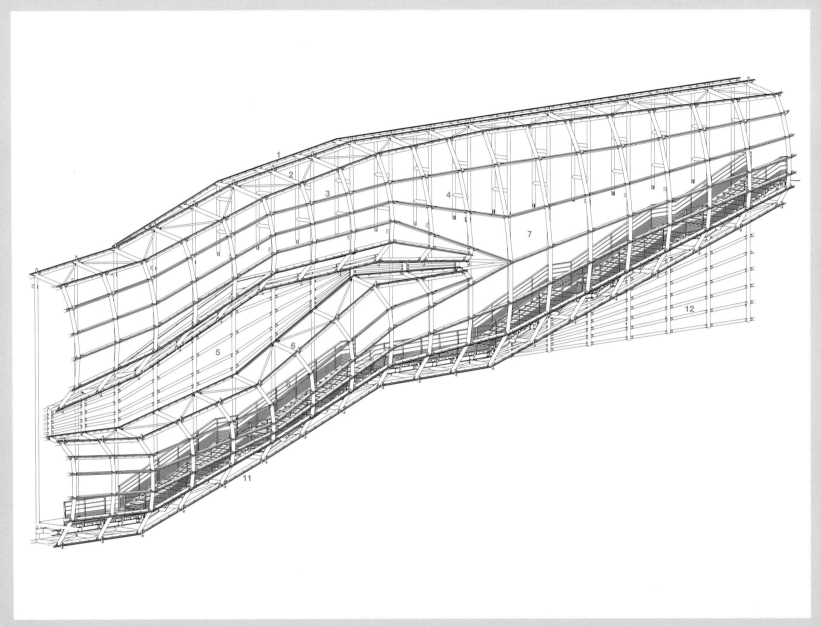

14.03
**Axonometric Stair
and Glass Cladding
Detail**
Not to Scale
1 Intermediate
horizontal span steel
nose capping
2 16.8 mm (2/3 inch)
diameter steel tube
structure
3 Intermediate
horizontal span steel
nose capping
4 Lateral structural
steel support
5 Open section of
facade

6 16.8 mm (2/3 inch)
diameter steel tube
structure
7 Fritted patterned
glass facade panel
8 Fritted patterned
glass facade panel
9 Public walkway
10 Fritted patterned
glass facade panel
11 Intermediate
horizontal span steel
nose capping
12 14 mm (1/2 inch)
diameter structural
steel tube

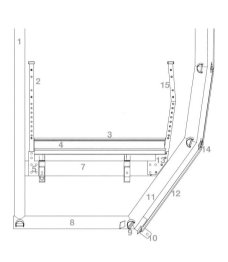

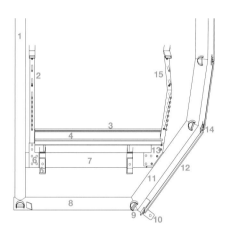

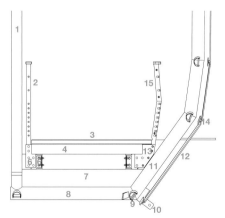

14.04
Section Details
Through External
Circulation and Glass
Cladding
1:50
1 Vertical steel tube
structure
2 Steel flat bar
balustrade upright with
horizontal steel rods
3 Oak board flooring
to bridge floor
4 Steel section
structure
5 Steel handrail fixing
plate with bolted
connections to main
steel structure
6 Steel hollow section
stair support structure
7 Steel horizontal
fixing plate
8 168 mm (6³/₅ inch)
diameter steel tube
structure
9 140 mm (5¹/₂ inch)
diameter structural
steel tube
10 Steel support plate
for glass cleaning
equipment
11 168 mm (6³/₅ inch)
diameter steel tube
structure
12 Fritted patterned
glass facade panel
13 Steel fixing plate
14 Intermediate
horizontal span steel
nose capping
15 Steel balustrade
with drilled holes for
wire rope horizontals

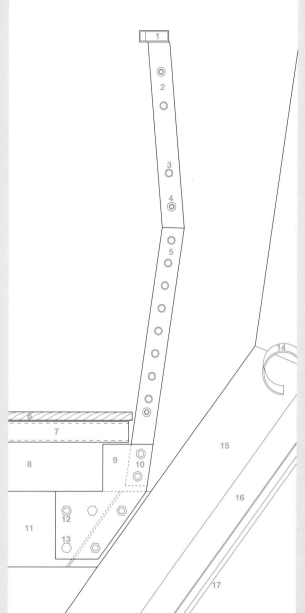

14.05
Walkway Balustrade
and Glass Cladding
Detail
1:10
1 Rectangular hollow
section steel hand rail
2 Steel flat bar
balustrade upright
3 Horizontal steel
rods forming
balustrades
4 Flat screw hat
joining support plates
to steel rod balustrade
horizontals
5 Steel flat bar
balustrade upright
6 Oak board flooring
to bridge and stair
floor
7 Steel section
structure
8 Open tread to stair
9 Steel fixing plate
10 Vertical support
plate between fixing
plates
11 Horizontal support
plate for stair tread
12 Steel handrail fixing
plate with bolted
connections
13 Bolt fixing
14 140 mm (5¹/₂ inch)
diameter structural
steel tube
15 168 mm (6³/₅ inch)
diameter structural
steel tube
16 Void
17 Fritted patterned
glass facade panel

15
João Luís Carrilho da Graça, Architect

Poitiers Theatre and Auditorium
Poitiers, France

Client
Ville de Poitiers

Project Team
Giulia de Appolonia, João Trindade, Nicola Marchi, Giorgio Santagostino, João Manuel Alves, Mónica Margarido, Filipe Homem, Tiago Castela, Anna Lobo Martins, Frederico Santos, Sylvain Grasset, Hervé Beaudouin

Structural Engineer
DL Structures

Acoustic Engineer
Commins Acoustics Workshop

The new performing arts building for Poitiers was designed to be as simple as possible, allowing it to act as a catalyst for artistic activities. The architects wanted the building to have a clear, strong but discreet presence in the city. The limestone platform opens the building to the public and ensures a spatial continuity with the city. Slightly suspended above this monolithic base lie the two main volumes of the building, both clad in white matt glass. Designing a venue exclusively dedicated to the performing arts necessitated the development of optimal acoustics as well as a distinctive architectural expression.

The rectangular glass prism of the hall, with its flat seating area employs a typology inherited from nineteenth-century theatres. The form guarantees the quality of musical performances, as its primary shape suppresses the unwanted reverberations that can be caused by sloped seating areas. Canted walls of timber on the interior that have been arranged to optimize acoustical performance have been detached from the exterior shell to produce a unified space that incorporates both stage and orchestra. Pivoted doors disguised in the walls ensure the continuity of the interior as well as a homogeneous reading of the spatial container. The theatre hall is a versatile space that embraces the technical demands of the 'theatre machine', as well as the requirements for visual and acoustic performance. Here, the audience space is clad in gypsum fibre plates that produce a dark, neutral, monochromatic 'cocoon' punctuated only by the doors and galleries.

1 The plain concrete base and white glass panelled facade act as a neutral reflector in a context of mostly nineteenth century town houses.
2 The veil of the glass facade is attached to a system of galvanized steel supports that are hung from the reinforced concrete primary structure behind.
3 At night, the yellow painted interior lends the building a welcoming golden glow.
4 The primarily white-painted interior public spaces such as the foyer are accented with yellow and black, with floors of natural light timber.

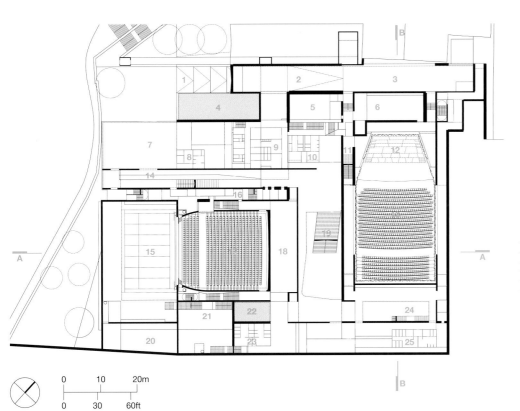

15.01
Ground Floor Plan
1:1000
1 External access
  from surrounding
  public square
2 Cafe and brasserie
  delivery area
3 Auditorium delivery
  area
4 Artist's courtyard
5 Production area
6 Instrument storage
7 Theatre cafe and
  brasserie
8 WCs
9 Staff WCs
10 WCs
11 Auditorium
   backstage area
12 Auditorium stage
13 Auditorium seating
14 Cafe and brasserie
   access
15 Theatre fly tower
16 Lift access
17 Theatre seating
18 Theatre foyer
19 Main foyer
20 Technical area
21 Water storage
22 Courtyard
23 Theatre WCs
24 Auditorium foyer
25 Auditorium WCs

15.02
Section A–A
1:500
1 Theatre fly tower
2 Orchestra pit
3 Theatre seating
4 Light technician
  area
5 Administration
  offices
6 Instrument storage
7 Main foyer
8 Auditorium stage
9 Auditorium seating
10 Surrounding public
   square

15.03
Section B–B
1:500
1 Auditorium WCs
2 Auditorium foyer
3 Auditorium foyer
  mezzanine
4 Light and sound
  technicians area
5 Acoustic ceiling
6 Auditorium
7 Auditorium
  balcony
8 Auditorium seating
9 Auditorium stage
10 Instrument storage
11 Delivery area

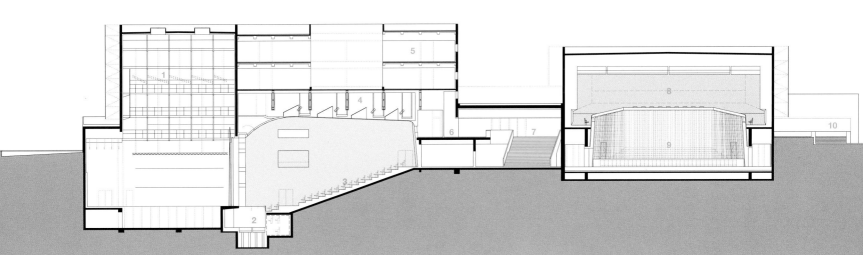

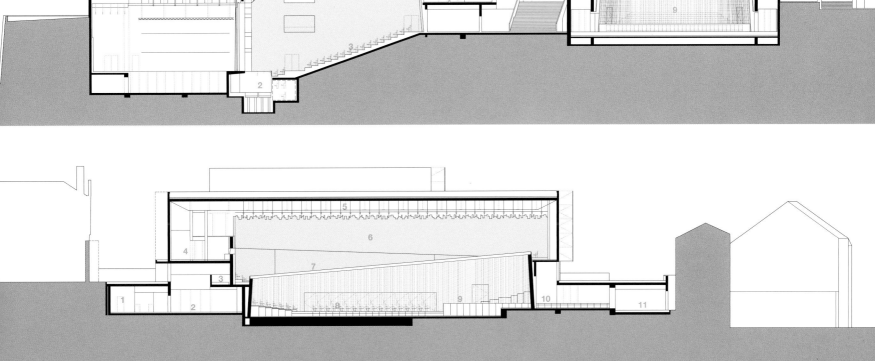

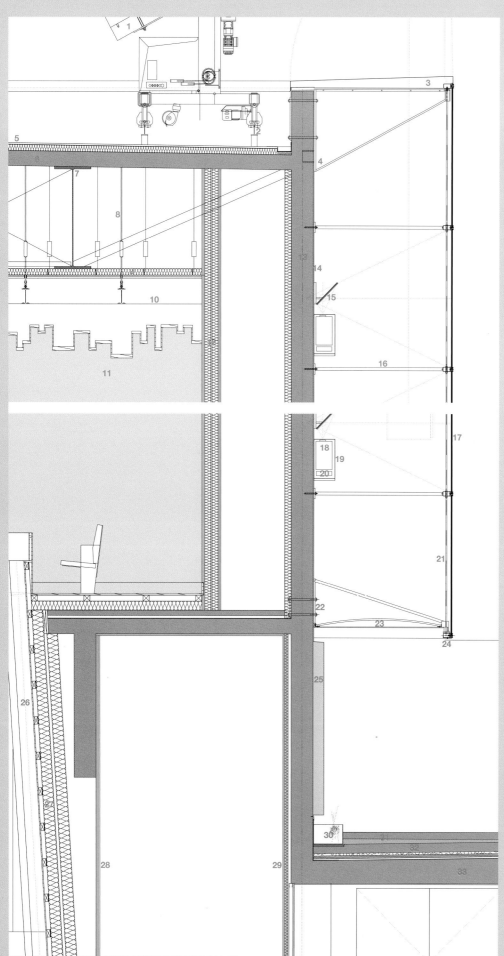

15.04
Detail Section Through Auditorium 1:50
1 Facade maintenance crane
2 Peripheral facade rail system for sliding maintenance crane
3 Removable aluminium parapet cover filled with 5 mm (1/5 inch) polycarbonate
4 Facade fixed back to concrete wall structure with galvanized steel I-sections formed to create angles
5 80 mm (31/8 inch) thermal insulation
6 200 mm (8 inch) prefabricated concrete slab
7 Structural steel section
8 Cable suspension system
9 Ceiling system comprised of one layer of 18 mm (7/10 inch) and two layers of 12.5 mm (1/2 inch) plasterboard and 85 mm (31/3 inch) mineral sound insulation
10 Ceiling comprised of 14 mm (1/2 inch) suspended main plywood frames and Canadian maple plywood
11 Wall comprised of three layers of 12.5 mm (1/2 inch) plasterboard, two layers of 85 mm (31/3 inch) mineral sound insulation and three layers of 12.5 mm (1/2 inch) plasterboard
12 Wall comprised of three layers of 12.5 mm (1/2 inch) plasterboard, two layers of 85 mm (31/3 inch) mineral sound insulation and three layers of 12.5 mm (1/2 inch) plasterboard
13 300 mm (114/5 inch) reinforced concrete wall
14 Render and plaster wall finish
15 Mobile mirror
16 Galvanized steel tension rod
17 Double glazing to facade from 8 mm (1/3 inch) laminated transparent glass with 2 mm (1/16 inch) opal PVB film and 8 mm (1/3 inch) laminated safety glass
18 Video projector
19 Ventilated projection box
20 Computer decoder
21 Vertical pre-stressed cable for facade stabilization
22 Facade fixed back to concrete wall structure with galvanized steel I-sections formed to create angles
23 3 mm (1/8 inch) anodized aluminium expanded metal mesh panels
24 Aluminium glazing section
25 Pre-cast concrete wall panel
26 Canadian maple plywood wall cladding
27 Two layers of 150 mm (6 inch) thick mineral sound insulation
28 Wall system comprised of one layer of 18 mm (7/10 inch) and two layers of 12.5 mm (1/2 inch) plasterboard
29 Two layers of 12.5 mm (1/2 inch) plasterboard over 48 mm (14/5 inch) thermal insulation
30 5 mm (1/5 inch) galvanized steel gutter filled with soil and climbing plants
31 110 mm (41/3 inch) concrete upstand to contain compacted bed of cracked gravel
32 120 mm (43/4 inch) concrete screed separating layer over 30 mm (11/5 inch) gravel bed and 40 mm (13/5 inch) thermal insulation
33 Reinforced concrete slab with 20 mm (3/4 inch) black asphalt and 3 mm (1/10 inch) elastometric bitumen membrane

15.05
Facade Plan Detail 1 1:50
1 50 x 50 mm (2 x 2 inch) steel angles for fixing mesh panels
2 Facade fixed back to concrete wall structure with galvanized steel I-sections formed to create angles
3 Supporting aluminium structure
4 3 mm (1/8 inch) anodized aluminium expanded metal mesh panels
5 Double glazing to facade from 8 mm (1/3 inch) laminated transparent glass with 2 mm (1/16 inch) opal PVB film and 8 mm (1/3 inch) laminated safety glass
6 Facade fixings to primary structure using galvanized steel I-sections
7 10 mm (2/5 inch) void between anodized aluminium expanded metal mesh panels
8 60 x 60 mm (21/3 x 21/3 inch) curved steel angle for hanging anodized aluminium expanded metal mesh panels
9 Facade fixings to primary structure using galvanized steel I-sections
10 10 mm (2/5 inch) void between anodized aluminium expanded metal mesh panels

15.06
Facade Plan Detail 2 1:10
1 5 mm (1/5 inch) vertical black sheet aluminium facing with invisible fixings
2 Vertical steel section structure
3 Black sheet aluminium facing fixed with lateral black screws
4 5 mm (1/5 inch) vertical black sheet aluminium facing with invisible fixings
5 Double glazing to facade from 8 mm (1/3 inch) laminated transparent glass with 2 mm (1/16 inch) opal PVB film and 8 mm (1/3 inch) laminated safety glass
6 Limit of aluminium glass clamps
7 Facade fixing to concrete structural wall using galvanized steel I-sections
8 300 mm (114/5 inch) reinforced concrete wall
9 Steel plate
10 60 x 60 mm (21/3 x 21/3 inch) curved steel angle for hanging anodized aluminium expanded metal mesh panels
11 3 mm (1/8 inch) anodized aluminium expanded metal mesh panels
12 60 x 40 mm (21/3 x 13/5 inch) steel angle bearing surface for expanded metal mesh panels

15.07
Facade Section Detail 1:5
1 Double glazing to facade from 8 mm (1/3 inch) laminated transparent glass with 2 mm (1/16 inch) opal PVB film and 8 mm (1/3 inch) laminated safety glass
2 Galvanized steel head I-section
3 Vertical pre-stressed cable
4 Punctured steel wedge
5 Aluminium Stabalux section
6 120 x 25 mm (43/4 x 1 inch) aluminium section
7 60 x 40 mm (21/3 x 13/5 inch) steel angle bearing surface for expanded metal mesh panels
8 Lower limit of steel section
9 3 mm (1/8 inch) anodized aluminium expanded metal mesh panels supported on steel angles
10 Timber fixing block
11 Threaded bolt fixing for occasional removal of mesh panel for maintenance
12 Steel plate
13 300 mm (114/5 inch) reinforced concrete wall
14 Pre-cast concrete wall panel

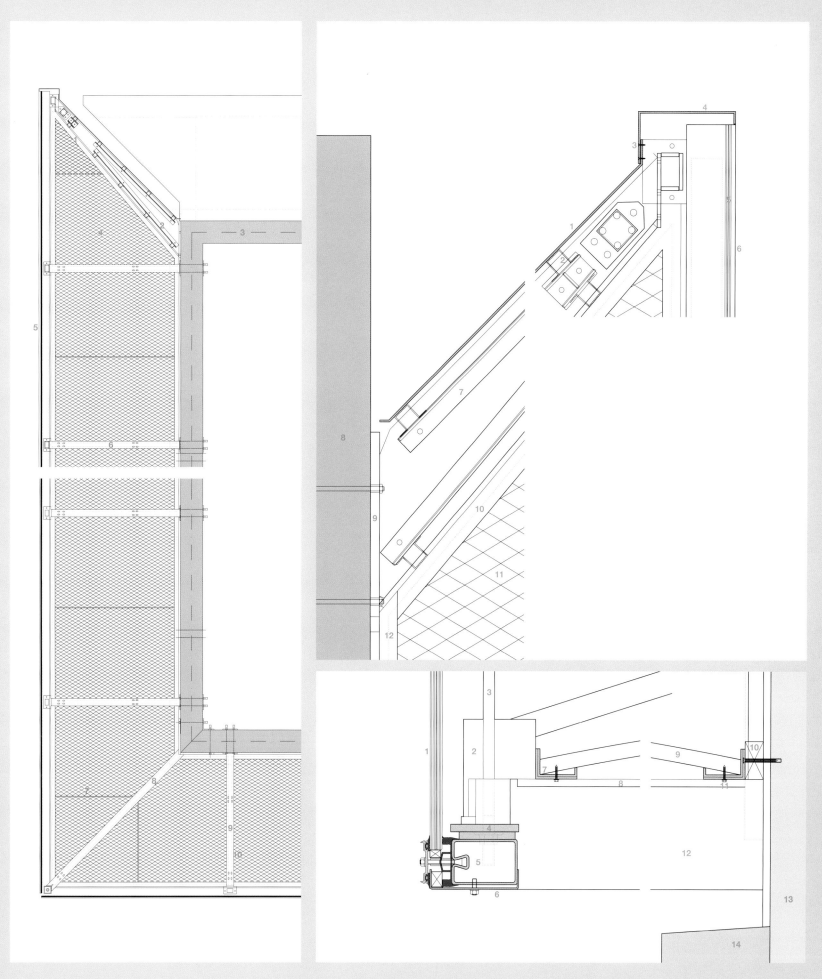

Taubman Museum of Art
Roanoke, Virginia, USA

Client
Taubman Museum of Art

Project Team
Randall Stout, John Murphey, Sandra
Hutchings, Cynthia Bush, Hugo
Ventura, Niel Prunier, Rashmi
Vasavada

Structural Engineer
DeSimone Consulting Engineers

Main Contractor
Balfour Beatty Construction

To accommodate rapid growth in its
collections, the Taubman Museum of
Art commissioned Los Angeles based
architect Randall Stout, to design a
new building commensurate with its
ambition to become a gateway arts
institution in western Virginia. The
building, with forms and materials
chosen to pay homage to the famed
Blue Ridge and Appalachian
Mountains, features flexible exhibition
galleries for the museum's important
permanent collection, contemporary
art, education facilities, a multipurpose auditorium, a theatre, cafe
and outdoor terraces. The finish on
the undulating, stainless steel roof
forms reflects the rich variety of colour
found in the sky and the seasonal
landscape.

Inspired by mountain streams,
translucent glass surfaces emerge
from the building's mass to create
canopies of softly diffused light over
the public spaces and gallery level. As
it rises to support the stainless steel
roof, a layered pattern of angular
exterior walls are surfaced in shingled
patinated zinc to give an earthen and
aged quality to the facade. The
building occupies three levels with a
central atrium, around which all
functions are organized. The glass
atrium allows the lobby to be filled
with natural light during the day, while
at night, the translucent glass roof
surfaces are illuminated. From the
lobby, illuminated glass treads lead
the visitor up the grand staircase to
the gallery level. At the landing, a
ceiling of cascading, backlit,
translucent polycarbonate panels
leads the visitor through the central
gallery hall to the permanent collection
galleries. In the contemporary and
American galleries the luminous
ceiling extends into the space to
diffuse the daylight from clerestory
windows and skylights overhead.

1 The glass atrium
allows the lobby to be
filled with natural light
during the day. At
night, the translucent
glass roof surfaces are
illuminated, allowing
the volume to glow like
a beacon and draw
visitors and the
community to the
museum's activities.
2 Evoking a grand
mountain outcropping,
a faceted glass form
soars skyward at the
centre of the overall
composition, providing
a glowing interior
space for information,
ticketing, temporary art
installations,
scheduled museum
functions and informal
encounters.
3 A dramatic
composition of
flowing, layered forms
in steel, patinated zinc
and high performance
glass, the building
pays sculptural tribute
to the famous Blue
Ridge Mountains that
frame the city and
shape the region's
spirit.
4 Illuminated glass
treads lead the visitor
up the grand staircase
from the ground floor
lobby to the two
gallery levels above.

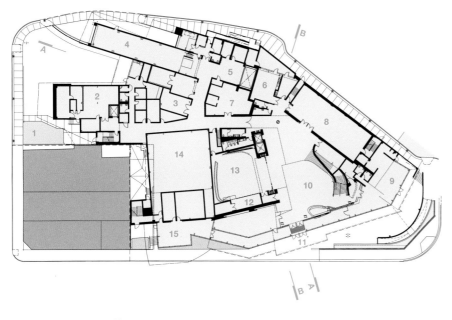

16.01
Ground Floor Plan
1:1000
1 Electrical plant
2 Mechanical plant
3 Museum services
4 Art handling
5 Protective services
6 Education studio
7 Catering kitchen
8 Art Venture Gallery
9 Museum cafe
10 Museum lobby
11 Salem Avenue
entrance
12 Museum store
13 Auditorium
14 Theatre
15 Theatre foyer

0 10 20m
0 30 60ft

16.02
Section A–A
1:500
1 Staff break room
2 Registration work
area and
temporary storage
3 Registrar and
unloading area
4 Corridor
5 Catering kitchen
6 WC
7 Central hall gallery
8 Gallery entry
9 Museum lobby
10 Entry vestibule
11 Office
12 Office
13 Office
14 Copy and fax area
15 Director's
reception area
16 Corridor
17 WC
18 Office reception
area

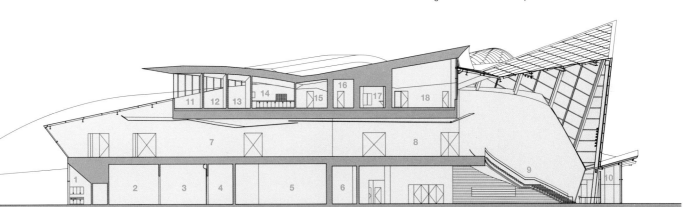

16.03
Section B–B
1:500
1 Entry vestibule
2 Museum lobby
3 Birthday room
4 Gallery lobby
5 Temporary
exhibitions gallery
6 Shared office
reception area
7 Library

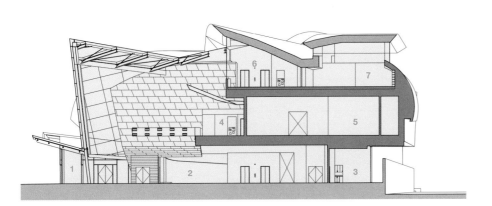

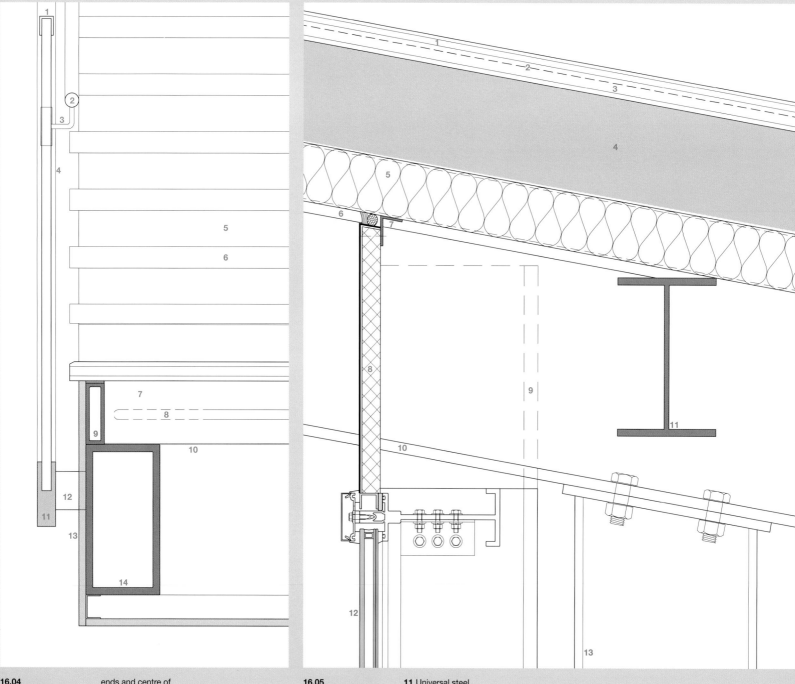

16.04
Grand Stair Tread
Section Detail
1:10
 1 Stainless steel
handrail cap
 2 38 mm (1¹/2 inch)
diameter stainless
steel handrail
 3 12 mm (¹/2 inch)
diameter handrail
support
 4 Butt jointed glass
guardrail panels at
1,524 mm (5 foot)
vertical intervals
 5 Removable
timber-faced stair riser
with access to light
fitting behind
 6 Translucent glass
tread
 7 Steel tube to
support back of tread
and lighting
 8 Light fixture
 9 Custom steel
triangle to support

ends and centre of
tread
10 18 gauge sheet
metal light fixture
support
11 Stainless steel
channel guardrail
support
12 Stainless steel
channel support
anchored to structure
13 Timber underside
to stair
14 Rectangular hollow
section steel structure

16.05
Vestibule Roof and
Wall Section Detail
1:5
 1 Standing seam
metal roofing
 2 Continuous
waterproof membrane
 3 Oriented Strand
Board sheathing
 4 Insulation
 5 Acoustic metal
decking
 6 Steel rafter beyond
 7 Thermal break at
exterior–interior
connections and
penetrations
 8 Insulated metal
panel in glazing
system, formed to fit
around rafter
penetrations and
sealed all round
 9 Vertical mullion
beyond rafter shown
dotted
10 Steel beam

11 Universal steel
beam primary structure
12 Double glazed
window
13 Composite steel
column

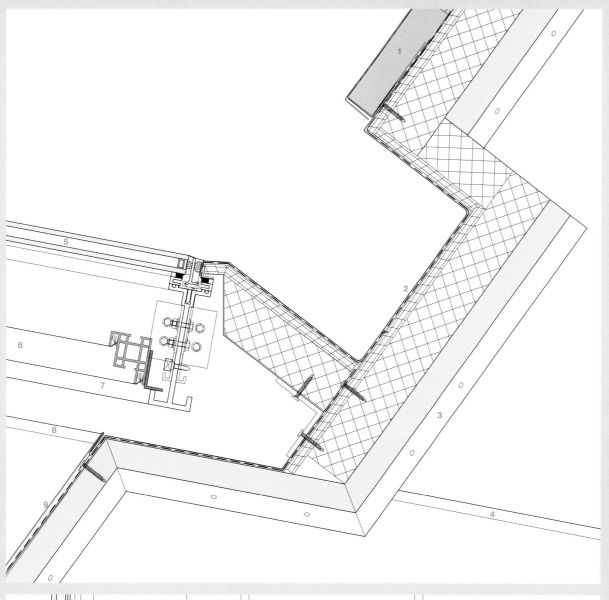

16.06
Metal and Glazed
Roof Closure Section
1:5
1 Metal cladding over air and water barrier
2 Stainless steel gutter assembly
3 Prefabricated panel assembly
4 Steel beam beyond
5 Double glazed roof panel
6 Dual membrane stretched fabric ceiling panel
7 Line of rafter mullion beyond
8 Steel beam beyond
9 Metal cladding

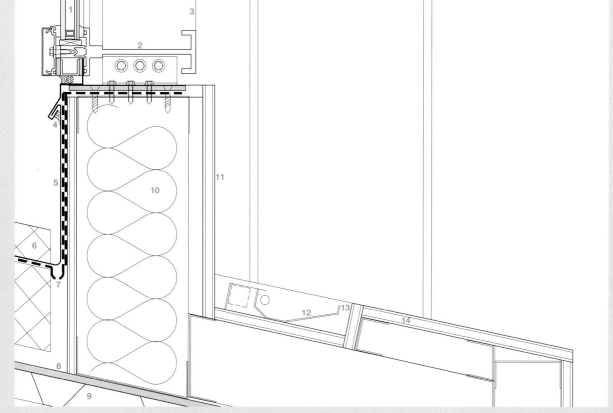

16.07
Light Cove at Clerestory Window Detail
1:5
1 Double glazed clerestory window
2 Horizontal transom
3 Back of vertical mullion
4 Drip profile
5 Counterflashing over membrane tie-in
6 Rigid insulation
7 Water barrier
8 Sheathing board
9 Corrugated steel deck
10 Insulated metal studs
11 Painted gypsum board
12 Light fixture
13 Light cove to full length of window
14 Standing seam roofing covering beyond

Kazuyo Sejima + Ryue Nishizawa / SANAA

**Toledo Museum of Art Glass Pavilion
Toledo, Ohio, USA**

Client
Toledo Museum of Art

Project Team
Kazuyo Sejima, Ryue Nishizawa,
Toshihiro Oki, Florian Idenburg,
Takayuki Hasegawa, Mizuki Imamura,
Junya Ishigami, Hiroshi Kikuchi,
Tetsuo Kondo, Keiko Uchiyama

Structural Engineer
SAPS / Sasaki and Partners

Main Contractor
Rudolph / Libbe

The Glass Pavilion, an annexe of the Toledo Museum of Art, contains an extensive art glass collection, temporary exhibition galleries and glass-making facilities. Due to its location in a park at the southernmost end of a historical housing district, it was necessary to consider the preservation of both the 150 year old trees in the park and the surrounding historical neighbourhood in conceiving the design. SANAA designed the museum as a low, single-storey pavilion with a series of courtyards open to the sky, so that visitors, when inside the building, still feel they are walking under the trees.

The museum's visionary programmatic requirement of combining the two somewhat contradictory uses of the 'rough' glass-making studio and the 'refined' museum galleries was the catalyst for the design. Bringing the surrounding park into the building, not only visually but also as an experience, adds to the complexity of the floor plan. The curved glass walls that separate the spaces within the building give visitors visual contact with the exterior, the glass-making activities, and the art at all times. The shape of the glass walls guide visitors in different directions, creating unique experiences throughout the sequence of spaces. The 2,973 square metre (32,000 square feet) of glass originates from a single batch of float glass in Germany. Prior to being shipped to the site in Toledo, the glass was curved and laminated in southern China. Very slender solid steel columns for vertical loads and solid plate steel wall panels for lateral bracing create a lightness of structure to enhance the sense of transparency and clarity.

1 Opened in 2006, the glass pavilion is home to the Toledo Museum of Art's world-renowned glass collection, featuring more than 5,000 works of art from ancient to contemporary times.
2 The glass pavilion is itself a work of art. All of the exterior and nearly all of the interior walls consist of large panels of curved glass, resulting in a transparent structure that blurs the boundaries between interior and exterior spaces.
3 Each of the more than 360 panels, many of them curved, that make up the glass walls measures approximately 2.4 metres (8 feet) wide by 4 metres (13 feet) high.
4,5 Elegantly simple in appearance but complex in organization, the pavilion's 6,875 square metre (74,000 square feet) contains a main floor and full basement.

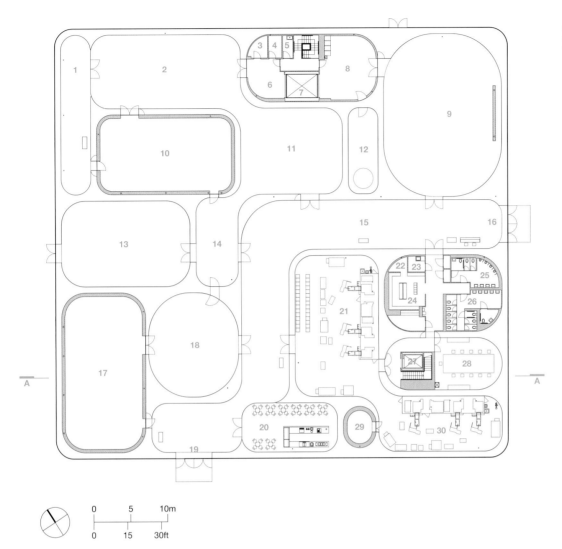

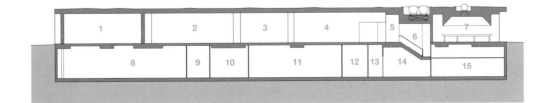

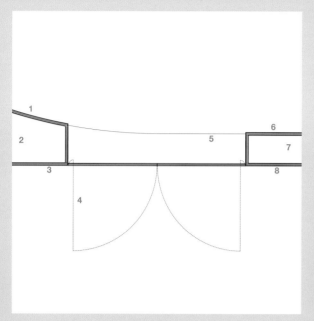

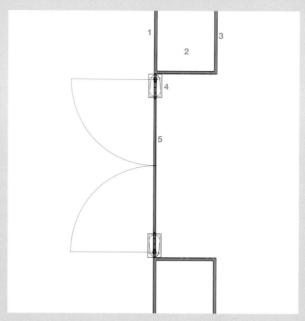

17.03
Door 3 Plan Detail
1:50
 1 Double layer of 10 mm (3/8 inch) thick low-iron laminated glass
 2 Cavity
 3 Double layer of 10 mm (3/8 inch) thick low-iron laminated glass
 4 Tempered low-iron glass door
 5 Line of glass header above
 6 Double layer of 10

mm (3/8 inch) thick low-iron laminated glass
 7 Cavity
 8 Double layer of 10 mm (3/8 inch) thick low-iron laminated glass

17.04
Door 15 Plan Detail
1:50
 1 Double layer of 12 mm (1/2 inch) thick low-iron laminated glass
 2 Cavity
 3 Double layer of 10 mm (3/8 inch) thick low-iron laminated glass
 4 Recessed floor door closer
 5 Tempered low-iron glass door

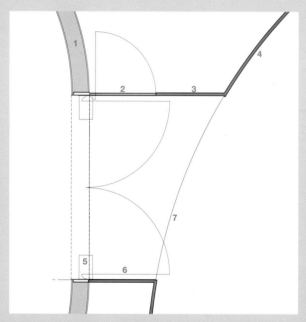

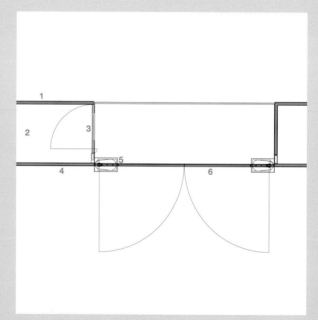

17.05
Door 10 Plan Detail
1:50
 1 Stud wall
 2 Tempered low-iron glass cavity access door
 3 Double layer of 10 mm (3/8 inch) thick low-iron laminated glass
 4 Double layer of 10 mm (3/8 inch) thick low-iron laminated glass
 5 Recessed floor door closer

 6 Opaque hollow metal door
 7 Line of glass header above

17.06
Door 12 Plan Detail
1:50
 1 Double layer of 10 mm (3/8 inch) thick low-iron laminated glass
 2 Cavity
 3 Tempered low-iron glass cavity access door
 4 Double layer of 10 mm (3/8 inch) thick low-iron laminated glass
 5 Recessed floor door closer

 6 Tempered low-iron glass door

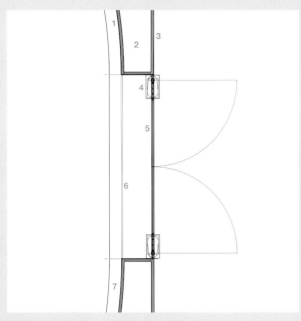

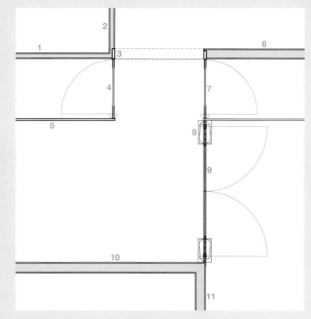

17.07
Door 16 Plan Detail
1:50
1 Double layer of 10 mm (3/8 inch) thick low-iron laminated glass
2 Cavity
3 Double layer of 10 mm (3/8 inch) thick low-iron laminated glass
4 Recessed floor door closer
5 Tempered low-iron glass door
6 Line of glass header

above
7 Perimeter floor grille

17.08
Door 6 Plan Detail
1:50
1 Plasterboard-clad timber stud wall
2 Plasterboard-clad timber stud wall
3 Line of doorway header above
4 Tempered low-iron glass cavity access door
5 12.7 mm (1/2 inch) steel plate wall
6 Plasterboard-clad

timber stud wall
7 Tempered low-iron glass cavity access door
8 Recessed floor closer
9 Tempered low-iron glass door
10 Plasterboard-clad timber stud wall
11 Plasterboard-clad timber stud wall

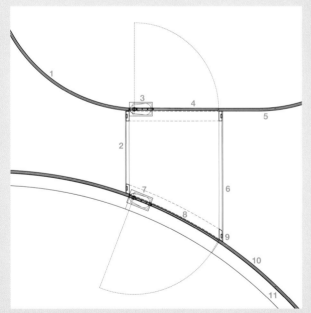

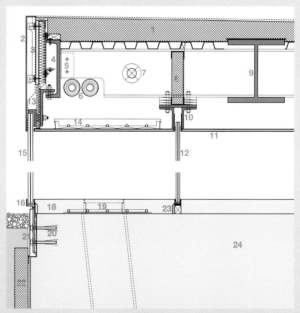

17.09
Door 17 Door Plan
1:50
1 Double layer of 10 mm (3/8 inch) thick low-iron laminated glass
2 Temporary acrylic panel
3 Recessed floor door closer
4 Tempered low-iron glass door
5 Double layer of 10 mm (3/8 inch) thick low-iron laminated glass

6 Temporary acrylic panel
7 Recessed floor door closer
8 Line of door header above
9 Stainless steel door frame
10 Double layer of 10 mm (3/8 inch) thick low-iron laminated glass
11 Perimeter floor grille

17.10
Exterior Glass Wall and Roof Section Detail
1:20
1 Roof system comprised of roofing membrane, insulation, vapour barrier and metal decking
2 6 mm (3/16 inch) thick clear anodized aluminium capping
3 Fascia attachment frame

4 Perimeter roof steel beam
5 Bolted connection
6 Insulated piping
7 Beam penetration for duct and pipe runs
8 Insulated vapour barrier
9 Steel girder
10 Glass header channel
11 Gypsum wall board ceiling
12 Double layer of 10 mm (3/8 inch) thick

low-iron laminated glass
13 Flashing
14 Radiant heating panels in ceiling void
15 Double layer of 12 mm (1/2 inch) thick low-iron laminated glass
16 Bottom channel
17 Gravel fill
18 76 mm (3 inch) thick concrete topping
19 Radiant heating system imbedded in

concrete topping over feed duct
20 Anchor bolts
21 Perimeter flashing
22 Rigid insulation
23 Bottom glass channel
24 Structural concrete floor slab

77

Salburúa Nature Interpretation Centre
Vitoria, Spain

Client
Centre for Environmental Studies

Project Team
José María García Del Monte, Ana María Montiel Jiménez, Fernando García Colorado

Structural Engineer
José Luis Fernández Cabo

Main Contractor
Urazca Construcciones

The starting point for the project was to create a natural wetlands area close to the city, that would act as a threshold between two worlds – the urban and the natural. The wetlands were created by returning previously-drained farmland back to its original condition. Central to the creation of the wetlands area was the inclusion of an interpretation centre as a place to make contact with the wetlands. The centre juts out over the water, placing visitors in a privileged position inside the park looking out over the water, with the city at their backs. The drama is intensified by placing visitors within a steel and glass tube cantilevered 21 metres (69 feet) out over the water.

The two storey timber structure behind the glass viewing platform contains both private and public facilities. On the ground floor are offices, administrative spaces, a conference room, classrooms and a bird treatment room. On the upper level, public facilities include a cafe, permanent and temporary exhibition spaces, outdoor terraces as well as the viewing platform. The entire structure is highly sustainable, using renewable construction materials as well as employing shade and cross ventilation to heat and cool the building, avoiding the need for air conditioning. The structural programme is designed using six identical framed sections that are infinitely repeatable should space requirements change. Concrete is used to bridge the gap between ground and building. Timber is then used in a rigorous vertical rhythm across the main building, which then opens up in the form of steel framing and large glass panels to create the viewing platform.

1 Glass is used in contrast to the rugged concrete and timber in the main part of the building to create a light, cantilevering structure that hovers out over the water.
2 The glazing is held in place and connected to the underlying timber structure using anodized steel angles. The bottom of the glass panes are frameless to accentuate the lightness of the structure.
3 The interior of the viewing platform is characterized by the rhythm of the vertical timber framing, to which the glass is fixed. A large pane of clear glass at the end of the viewing platform reveals uninterrupted views of the wetlands.

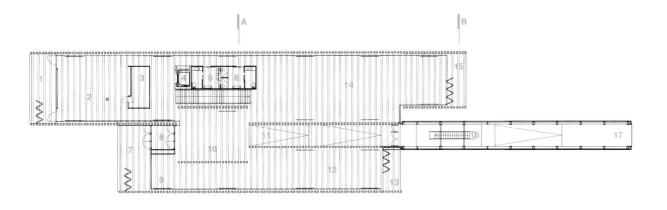

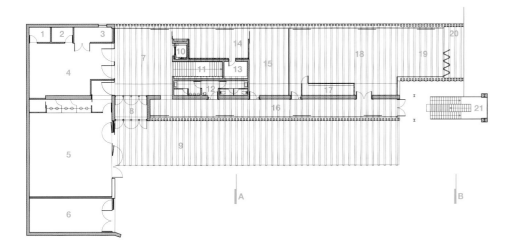

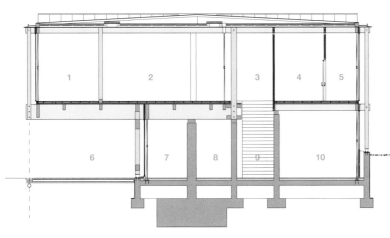

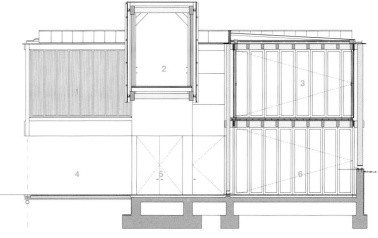

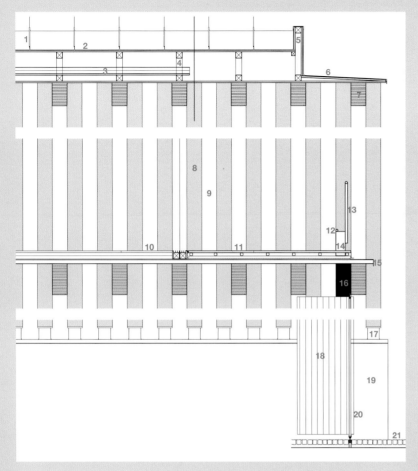

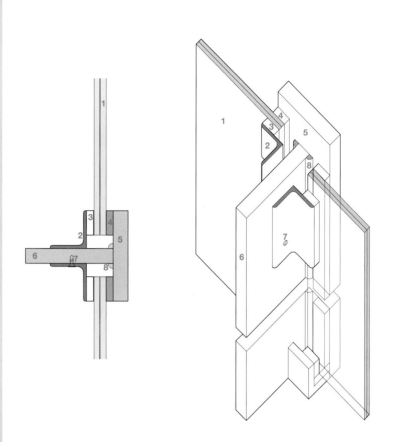

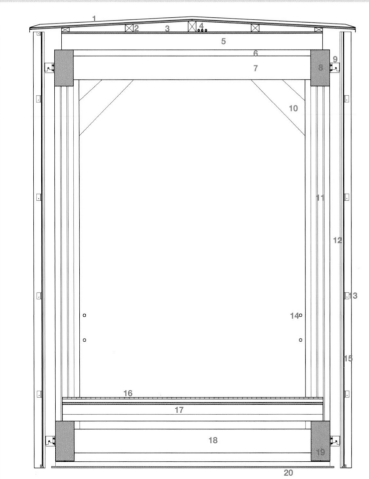

18.05
Main Building Section Detail
1:50
1 Zinc panels
2 13 mm (1/2 inch) agglomerated board
3 80 mm (3 1/8 inch) glass fibreboard
4 Timber structure to facilitate roof falls
5 Vertical gable
6 Zinc on agglomerate board
7 300 x 200 mm (11 3/4 x 8 inch) laminated timber beam
8 200 x 200 mm (8 x 8 inch) laminated timber support
9 Open space between supports
10 Oak flooring
11 Vacuum treated oak boards
12 Steel railing to lower part of balustrade
13 Glass balustrade
14 Vacuum treated oak boards
15 Zinc protection
16 200 x 400 mm (8 x 15 3/4 inch) laminated timber beam
17 Galvanized steel support
18 Steel shutter
19 Concrete wall
20 Steel shutter
21 Portuguese paving stones

18.06
Viewing Platform Glazing Details
1:5
1 Two layers of 8 mm (1/3 inch) laminated safety glass
2 Steel L-angle
3 Expandable joint between steel and glass
4 Continuous elastic bond
5 100 x 20 mm (4 x 3/4 inch) steel plate
6 120 x 20 mm (4 3/4 x 3/4 inch) steel plate
7 Screw fixing
8 Welded joint

18.07
Viewing Platform Section Detail
1:50
1 Zinc panels
2 Timber structure to facilitate roof falls
3 Plywood boarding
4 Electrical conduits
5 20 x 30 mm (3/4 x 1 1/5 inch) laminated timber beam
6 Air gap
7 700 x 200 mm (27 1/2 x 8 inch) laminated timber beam
8 230 x 440 mm (9 x 17 1/3 inch) upper part of micro-laminated beam
9 Galvanized steel support for vertical facade profiles
10 Reinforced beam
11 Diagonal steel bars
12 Two layers of 8 mm (1/3 inch) laminated safety glass
13 100 x 20 mm (4 x 3/4 inch) steel plate
14 Steel railing
15 120 x 20 mm (4 3/4 x 3/4 inch) steel plate
16 Oak flooring
17 100 x 200 mm (4 x 8 inch) laminated timber beam
18 20 x 30 mm (3/4 x 1 1/5 inch) laminated timber beam
19 230 x 440 mm (9 x 17 1/3 inch) upper part of micro-laminated beam
20 Plywood boarding

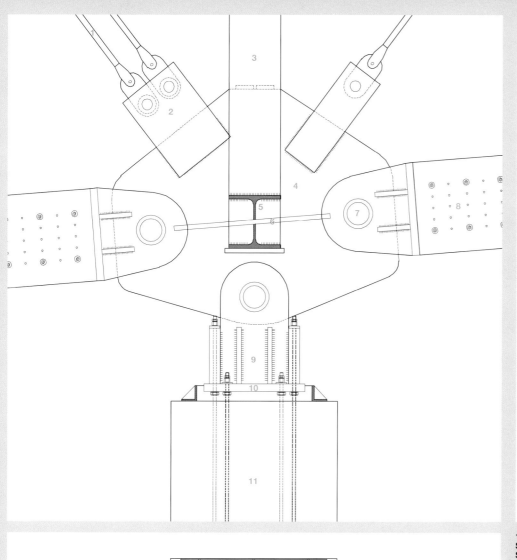

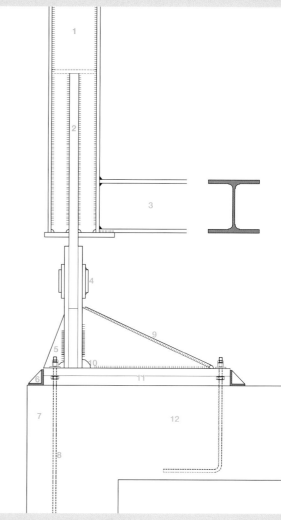

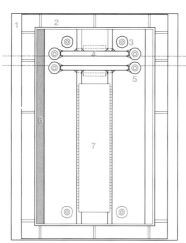

18.08
Steel Structure
Section Detail
1:20
 1 30 mm (1¹/₅ inch) diameter steel rod
 2 500 x 350 x 315 mm (19²/₃ x 13³/₄ x 12²/₅ inch) steel plate
 3 Steel support
 4 50 mm (2 inch) steel plate
 5 Steel beam
 6 200 mm (7⁴/₅ inch) steel plate
 7 120 mm (4³/₄ inch) diameter steel cylinder with greased joint
 8 Lower chord of micro-laminated timber truss
 9 Two layers of 25 mm (1 inch) steel plate
 10 40 mm (1³/₅ inch) steel plate
 11 500 x 900 mm (19²/₃ x 35²/₅ inch) concrete support

18.09
Concrete Pier
Section Detail
1:20
 1 Steel support
 2 50 mm (2 inch) steel plate
 3 Steel beam
 4 120 mm (4³/₄ inch) diameter steel cylinder with greased joint
 5 25 mm (1 inch) rigid steel plate
 6 Steel profile
 7 Concrete support structure
 8 Pre-stressed bar
 9 25 mm (1 inch) rigid steel plate
 10 Welded joint
 11 40 mm (1³/₅ inch) steel plate
 12 Concrete support structure

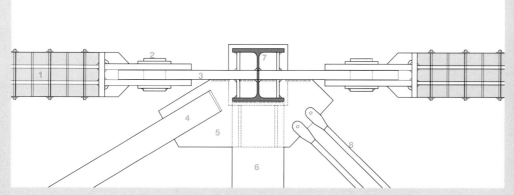

18.10
Concrete Pier
Section Detail
1:20
 1 Outer limit of concrete support
 2 Steel L-profile
 3 20 mm (³/₄ inch) diameter pre-stressed bar
 4 25 mm (1 inch) steel plate
 5 Perforated steel bars
 6 Filling joint
 7 25 mm (1 inch) steel plate

18.11
Steel Structure
Section Detail
1:20
 1 Lower chord of micro-laminated timber truss
 2 Steel joint
 3 Main steel plate
 4 Steel profile
 5 25 mm (1 inch) steel plate
 6 Steel beam
 7 Steel support
 8 30 mm (1¹/₅ inch) diameter steel bar

**New British Embassy
Warsaw, Poland**

Client
Foreign & Commonwealth Office

Project Team
Tony Fretton, Jim McKinney, David
Owen, Donald Matheson, Matthew
Barton, Nina Lundvall, Frank Furrer,
Laszlo Csutoras, Martin Nassen, Max
Lacey, Tom Grieve, Piram Banpabutr,
Chris Snow, Chris Neve

Structural Engineer
Buro Happold Polska

Main Contractor
Porr (Polska)

Set in its own grounds facing onto a
park in an area of the city devoted to
embassies, the building's long form is
centralized by a glazed attic in an
elementally neo-classical manner. The
glass elevations function as the outer
skin of a double facade, which
provides substantial thermal insulation
in winter and relieves heat in the
summer. The outer layer, delineated by
pale bronze aluminium mullions and
mirror glass, reflects the sky and trees
of the surrounding gardens. Behind
this is a more substantial facade of
windows set between solid piers and
spandrels in a modulated composition
of a similar palette.

The embassy is entered through a
gatehouse, after which a carriageway
leads to a porte-cochère at the centre
of the facade. The ground floor is
reserved for public activities and
features a large space for exhibitions
and events, and a cafe that opens
onto the garden. Also on the ground
floor is the Consular Section and UK
Border Agency complete with a public
waiting area accessed via its own
entrance. Administrative offices are
located on the first and second floor
and are amply lit with daylight from
the glass facades and two generous
planted courtyards in the centre of the
plan. In the attic at the second floor is
the Ambassador's suite, which looks
out on either side to extensive roof
terraces. Here, the Ambassador's
offices have the scale and quality of
cabinets, a theme that continues in
the small spaces for sitting that are
cut out from the wide areas of planting
filling the roof terraces on either side.
The roof planting relates to the
terraces in the grounds around the
embassy and the park beyond. With
these simple gestures, the embassy
maintains its important place in the
culture and fabric of Warsaw.

1 The formal
symmetry of the
embassy building is
complemented by the
horizontal elements of
the walls and railings
that define the
boundaries.

2 The external skin of
the double layer
facade is delineated by
pale bronze aluminium
mullions and mirror
glass which reflects
the sky and trees of
the gardens.

3 Behind the external
layer of glazing is a
more substantial
facade of windows set
between solid piers
and spandrel panels.

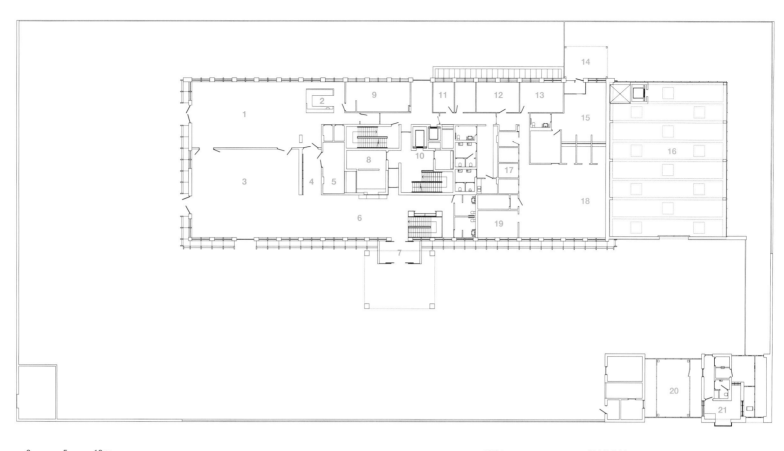

0 5 10m
0 15 30ft

19.01
Ground Floor Plan
1:500
1 Cafe
2 Cafe servery
3 Exhibition and
  conference area
4 Lobby
5 Store
6 Foyer
7 Main entrance
  portico
8 Reception office
  and store
9 Kitchen
10 Lift lobby
11 Office
12 Office
13 Office
14 Consular entrance
   portico
15 Consular and UK
   Border Agency
16 Car park
17 Store
18 Offices
19 Office
20 Vehicular entrance
21 Gate house

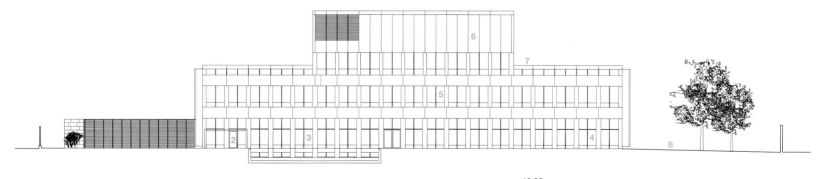

19.02
North Elevation
1:500
1 Car park
2 Consular entrance
3 Office
4 Cafe
5 Consular offices
6 Ambassador's
  suite
7 Roof terraces
8 Embassy grounds

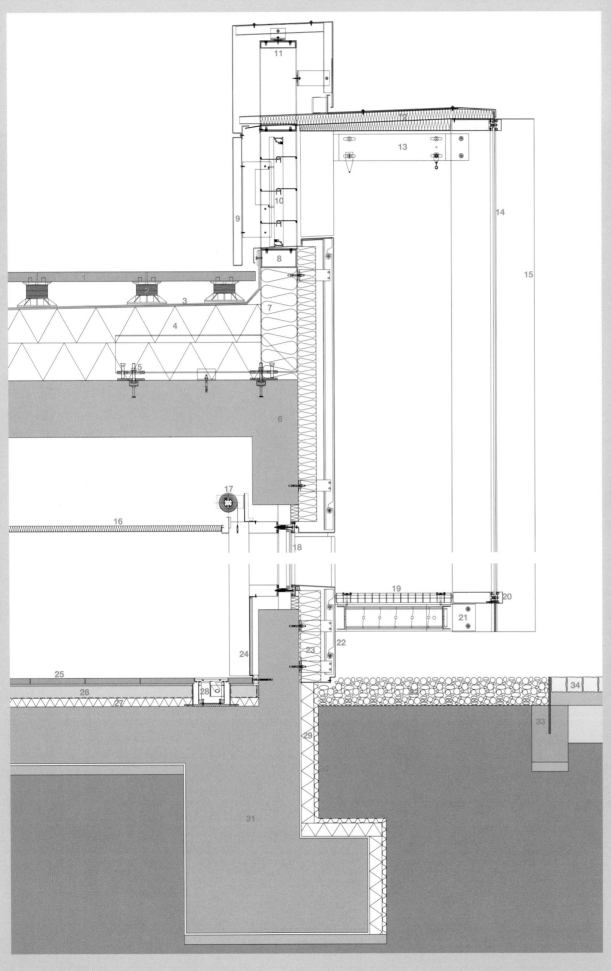

19.03
Section Detail
Through Double
Facade
1:20
1 Polished granite paver
2 Pedestals
3 Waterproof membrane
4 Insulation cut to falls
5 Cast anchors
6 Reinforced, cast in-situ concrete roof slab and downturn
7 Insulation
8 Rectangular hollow section framing
9 Perforated anodized aluminium cladding
10 Anodized aluminium automatic ventilation blades
11 Wind post
12 Insulation
13 Mansafe system
14 Toughened glass with 'Supersilver' coating
15 Anodized aluminium glazing mullion
16 Suspended ceiling
17 Anti-glare blind
18 Laminated, blast resistant double glazing with argon filled cavity
19 Anodized aluminium grid platform for maintenance access
20 Expansion joint to anodized aluminium glazing mullion
21 Stainless steel bracket to support outer layer of glazing
22 Anodized aluminium sheet cladding
23 Semi-rigid insulation
24 Anodized panel
25 Terrazzo tile
26 Screed
27 Insulation
28 Trench heater
29 Insulation
30 Egg crate waterproofing
31 Reinforced, cast in-situ concrete floor slab and footing
32 Gravel
33 Stainless steel path edge
34 Polished granite paving

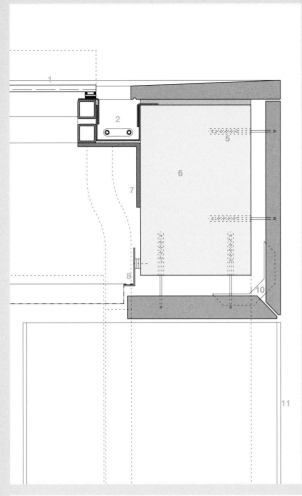

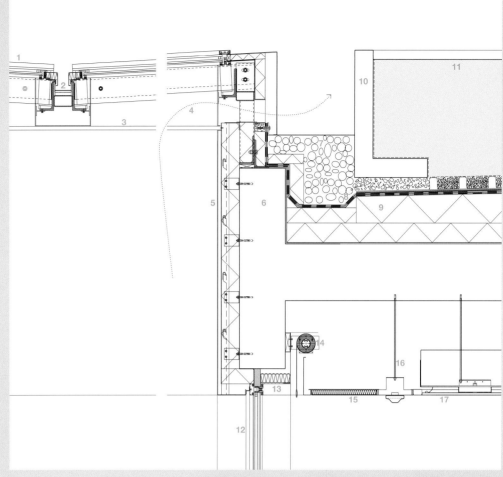

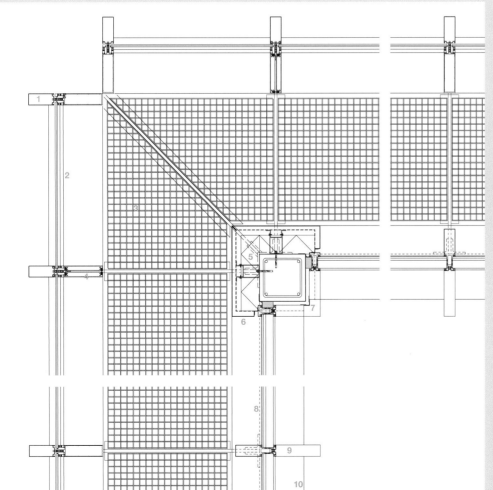

19.04
Entrance Canopy Detail
1:20
1 Glass roof
2 Heated internal gutter
3 Stone coping cut to fall to internal gutter
4 Stone cladding to beam face
5 Bolt fixing between stone cladding and concrete edge beam
6 Reinforced concrete edge beam
7 Glazing bracket
8 Anodized aluminium angle profile fixed straight and level from reinforced concrete beam
9 Stone cladding with polished edges and face to beam soffit
10 Stone fixing
11 Stone column to column beyond

19.05
Section Detail Through First Floor Atrium
1:20
1 Fixed glazing to skylight
2 Stainless steel drainage channel
3 Anodized aluminium panel
4 Line of air path
5 Anodized aluminium cladding
6 Reinforced concrete roof structure
7 Pebble filling to gutter
8 Waterproof membrane
9 Rigid insulation
10 Prefabricated concrete planter
11 Roof comprised of soil to planter box, filtration layer, drainage layer, protection layer, two layers of separating and slip foil, waterproofing root resistant capping sheet, waterproofing underlayer, insulation cut to falls and vapour barrier
12 Double glazed unit
13 Ceiling trim panel
14 Anti-glare blind
15 Suspended ceiling
16 Suspended ceiling system hanger
17 Chilled beam

19.06
Plan Detail Through Facade
1:20
1 Anodized aluminium capping piece
2 Low-iron toughened glass
3 Anodized aluminium grid maintenance walkway
4 Anodized aluminium mullion
5 Styrofoam insulation
6 Anodized aluminium column cladding
7 Extruded anodized aluminium cornerpiece
8 Double glazed unit
9 Anodized aluminium mullion
10 Anodized aluminium sill

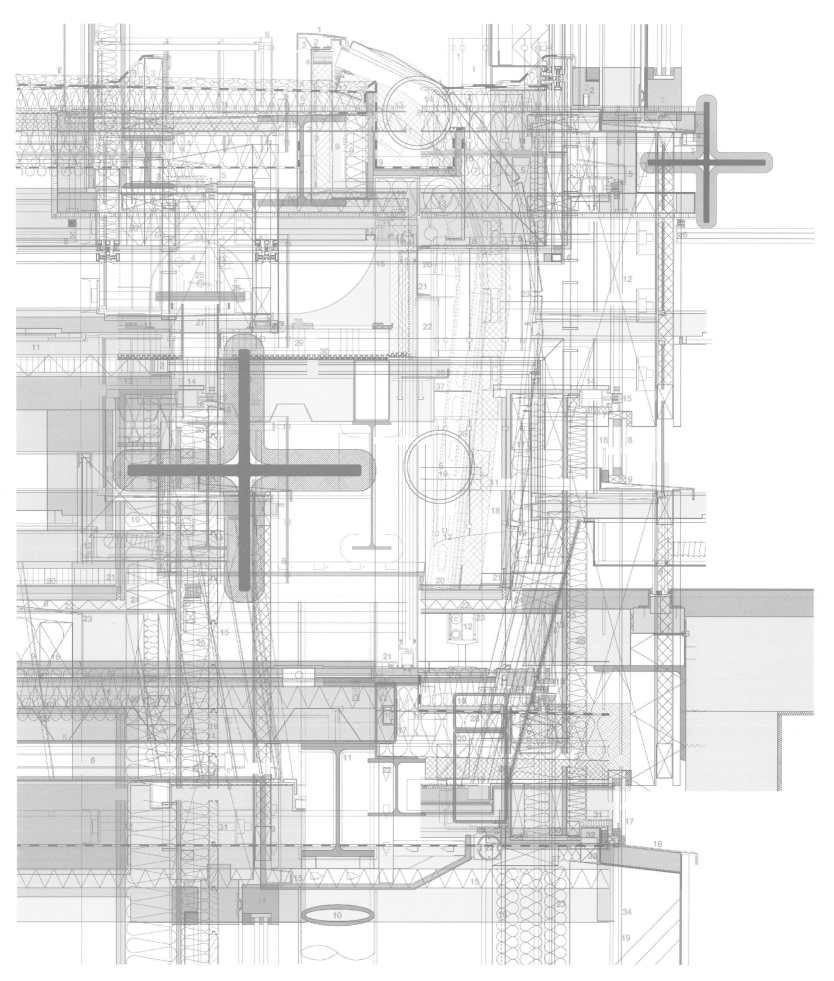

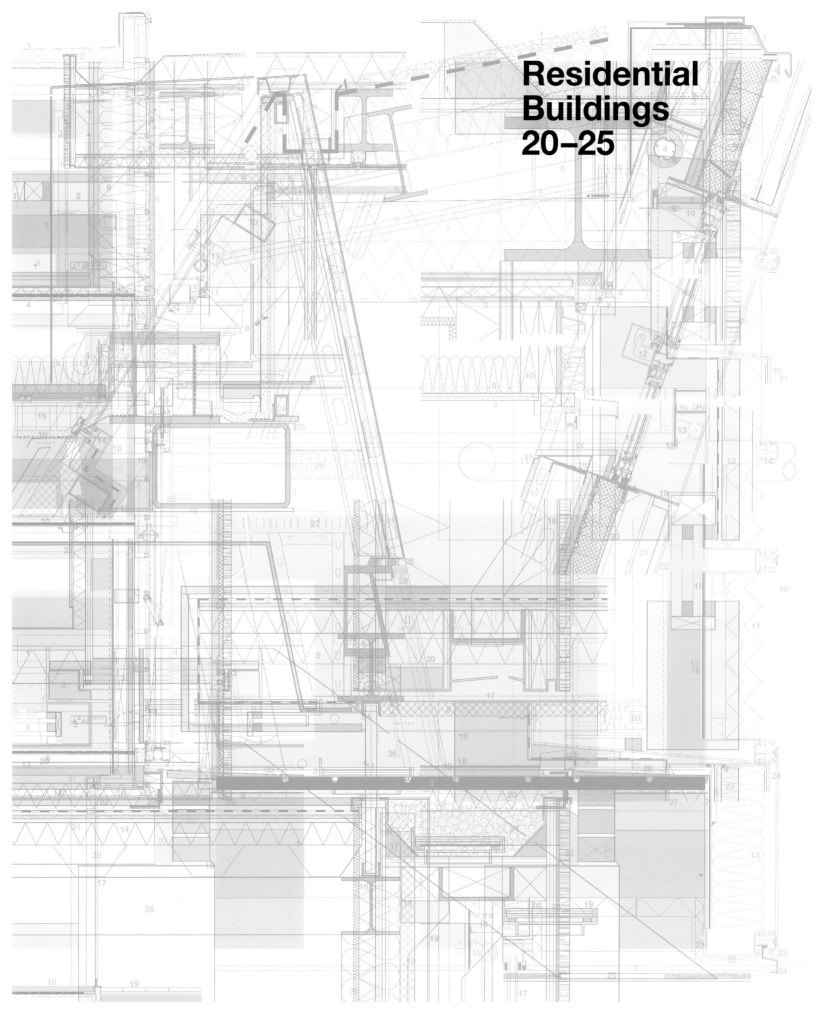

Residential
Buildings
20–25

Villa 1
Veluwe Zoom, The Netherlands

Project Team
Nanne de Ru, Charles Bessard,
Alexander Sverdlov, Nolly Vos, Wouter
Hermanns, Anne Luetkenhues, Bjørn
Andreassen, Joe Matthiessen

Structural Engineer
BREED ID

Main Contractor
Valleibouw BV Veenendaal

Villa 1 enjoys a woodland setting
where it has been sited to take
maximum advantage of views and
sunlight. Half of the programme is
pushed below ground to meet local
zoning regulations. This creates a
bipartite arrangement comprised of a
glass box ground floor where all mass
is concentrated in furniture elements,
and an enclosed basement, where the
spaces are carved out of the mass.

The Y-plan shape is the result of the
optimal configuration of the
programme on the ground floor
towards the sun and views. The study,
music room and library are located in
the northeast wing where the rooms
are shaped by a nut-wood central
furniture piece. The kitchen is shaped
by a slate furniture element in the
small southeast wing which enjoys the
sun all day, while the living room and
studio are defined by concrete walls in
the west wing with full south
exposure. The house opens up to the
views via uninterrupted walls of
custom made full height glass that
curves to define the edges of the
Y-plan shape. Panels of the frameless
glass slide away on concealed tracks
to open the house up in multiple
directions. Covered terraces between
the wings create natural sun shading.
In contrast with the ground floor, the
basement level accommodates the
private spaces. All rooms are massive
except for carefully positioned
windows in the bedrooms. In one
wing, the master bedroom is defined
by a wooden element that contains
the stair, bath, laundry, walk-in-closet
and bed. In the other wing, two guest
rooms are located either side of a
patio. A long vaulted closet-corridor
contains all storage.

1 The house has been
placed gently on its
woodland site, giving
few clues as to the
breadth of the
programme, half of
which is located
underground.

2 The garage is
located underneath the
kitchen where access
to the upper level is via
a ramp that brings
visitors up into the
centrally located
entrance hall.

3 The full height glass
walls make the
landscape an integral
part of the experience
of living in the house. A
solid panel of stone in
the living room wall
slides away to create

uninterrupted access
to the south facing
terrace.
4 Large pieces of
built-in furniture divide
the living spaces on
the ground floor, in this
case a slate-clad box

divides the kitchen
from the dining room.

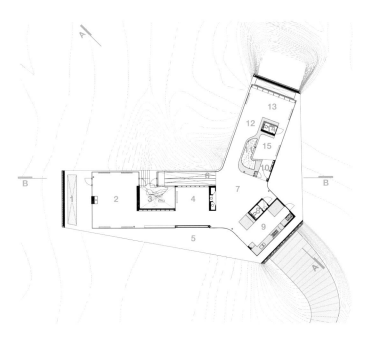

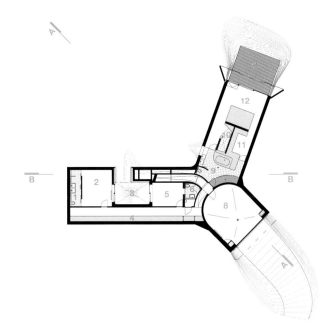

20.01
Ground Floor Plan
1:500
1 Pond
2 Studio
3 Patio
4 Living room
5 Terrace
6 Ramp up from garage
7 Central hall
8 WC
9 Kitchen

10 Entrance
11 Stair down to basement level
12 Music room
13 Library
14 WC
15 Study

20.02
Basement Plan
1:500
1 Bathroom
2 Guest bedroom
3 Patio
4 Storage wall
5 Guest bedroom
6 Bathroom
7 Ramp up to ground floor
8 Garage
9 Bathroom

10 Stair up to ground floor
11 Walk-in closet
12 Master bedroom
13 Terrace

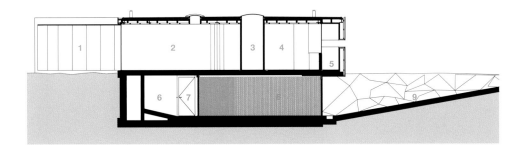

20.03
Section A–A
1:200
1 Glazed wall to music room and library
2 Central hall
3 WC
4 Kitchen
5 Kitchen terrace
6 Ramp up from garage
7 Door to garage
8 Garage
9 Driveway ramp

20.04
Section B–B
1:200
1 Terrace
2 Central hall
3 Bathroom
4 Ramp
5 Patio
6 Studio
7 Guest bedroom
8 Bathroom
9 Terrace

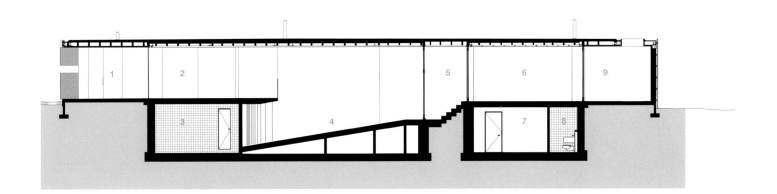

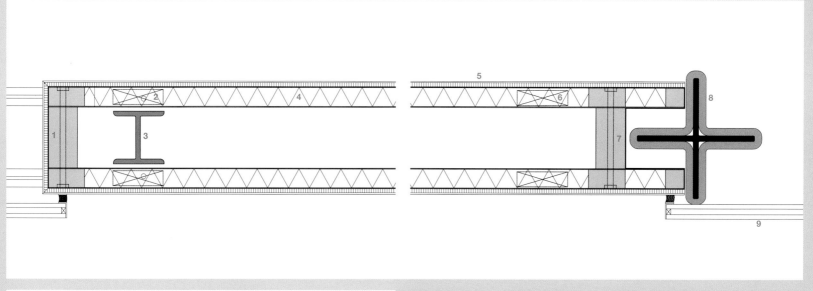

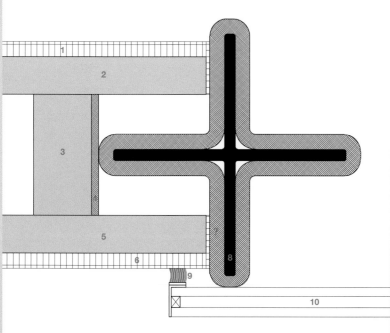

20.05
Marble Sliding Door and Cruciform Column Detail
1:10
1 Aluminium structure to connect both faces of door panel to create 300 mm (11⁴/₅ inch) thick door
2 Wheels
3 Concealed steel H-beam primary structure

4 Door structure comprised of 50 mm (2 inch) thick sandwich panel with aluminium frame, styrofoam filling and boarded with 2 mm (1/16 inch) thick aluminium
5 Stone panelled door cladding comprised of Ultralite green marble panels on 20 mm (3/4 inch) thick aluminium

honeycomb panels glue-fixed to door substructure
6 Wheels
7 Aluminium structure to connect both faces of door panel to create 300 mm (11⁴/₅ inch) thick door
8 320 x 320 mm (12³/₅ x 12³/₅ inch) steel cruciform column clad in 10 mm (3/8 inch) rubber

9 Full height double glazing

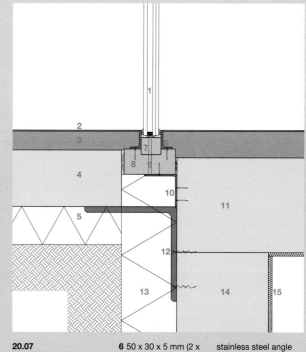

20.06
Cruciform Column Detail
1:5
1 Stone panelled door cladding comprised of Ultralite green marble panels on 20 mm (3/4 inch) thick aluminium honeycomb panels glue-fixed to door substructure

2 Door structure comprised of 50 mm (2 inch) thick sandwich panel with aluminium frame, styrofoam filling and boarded with 2 mm (1/16 inch) thick aluminium
3 Door frame
4 10 mm (2/5 inch) thick rubber
5 Door structure comprised of 50 mm

(2 inch) thick sandwich panel with aluminium frame, styrofoam filling and boarded with 2 mm (1/16 inch) thick aluminium
6 Stone panelled door cladding comprised of Ultralite green marble panels on 20 mm (3/4 inch) thick aluminium honeycomb panels

glue-fixed to door substructure
7 Rubber cladding to cruciform column
8 320 x 320 mm (12³/₅ x 12³/₅ inch) steel cruciform column
9 Draft excluding brush on steel profile
10 Full height double glazing

20.07
Fixed Glazing Detail
1:10
1 Fixed double glazing
2 3 mm (1/8 inch) thick white polyurethane flooring
3 50 mm (2 inch) thick concrete topping screed
4 150 mm (6 inch) thick reinforced structural concrete slab
5 100 mm (4 inch) thick rigid insulation

6 50 x 30 x 5 mm (2 x 1¹/₅ x 1/5 inch) aluminium angle glass holders
7 50 x 51 mm (2 x 2 inch) timber block
8 139 x 67 mm (5¹/₂ x 2²/₃ inch) timber block
9 Condensation channel
10 90 x 90 mm (3¹/₂ x 3¹/₂ inch) steel angle
11 250 mm (9⁷/₈ inch) reinforced structural concrete slab
12 250 x 250 x 25 mm (9⁷/₈ x 9⁷/₈ x 1 inch)

stainless steel angle for terrace floor support
13 150 mm (6 inch) thick rigid insulation
14 250 mm (9⁷/₈ inch) reinforced structural concrete basement wall
15 12 mm (1/2 inch) thick coat of cement render

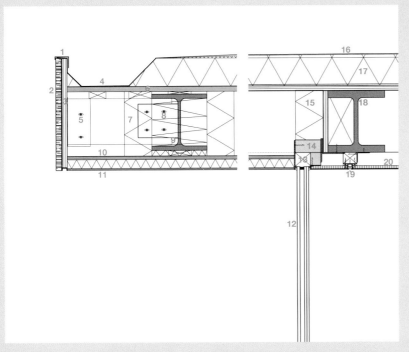

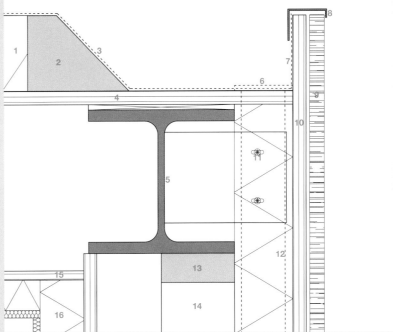

20.08
Roof Overhang Detail
1:12.5
 1 Aluminium parapet cover
 2 400 x 800 x 20 mm (15³/₄ x 31¹/₂ x ³/₄ inch) travertine cladding panels
 3 18 mm (³/₄ inch) Multiplex plywood
 4 Formed gutter
 5 Steel L-profile
 6 18 mm (³/₄ inch)

Multiplex plywood
 7 100 mm (4 inch) thick insulation
 8 Steel panel welded to beam to support roof edge and gutter structure
 9 200 x 200 mm (7⁷/₈ x 7⁷/₈ inch) universal steel beam
 10 12 mm (¹/₂ inch) fibre cement sheet
 11 12 mm (¹/₂ inch) thick insulated panel

ceiling with stucco finish
 12 Fixed structural glass
 13 Void for lifting in glass
 14 90 x 90 mm (3¹/₂ x 3¹/₂ inch) window frame
 15 140 mm (5¹/₂ inch) thick insulation
 16 EPDM rubber roofing membrane
 17 Rigid urethane

insulation panels
 18 Universal steel beam roof structure
 19 Integrated and concealed curtain track
 20 Plasterboard ceiling with stucco finish

20.09
Concealed Gutter Detail
1:5
 1 100 mm (4 inch) thick insulation
 2 Timber filler with mastic coating
 3 EPDM rubber roofing membrane
 4 18 mm (³/₄ inch) Multiplex plywood
 5 200 x 200 mm (7⁷/₈ x 7⁷/₈ inch) universal

steel beam
 6 60 mm (2³/₈ inch) diameter draining pipe
 7 Waterproof mastic coating to timber parapet framing
 8 Aluminium parapet cover
 9 400 x 800 x 20 mm (15³/₄ x 31¹/₂ x ³/₄ inch) travertine cladding panels
 10 18 mm (³/₄ inch) Multiplex plywood

 11 Steel panel welded to beam to support roof edge and gutter structure
 12 Down pipe shown dotted
 13 100 x 56 mm (4 x 2¹/₅ inch) timber support
 14 Timber framing
 15 12 mm (¹/₂ inch) fibre cement sheet
 16 18 mm (³/₄ inch) fibre cement sheet

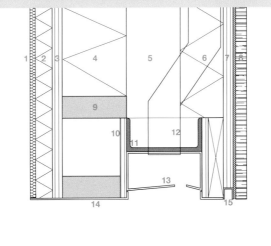

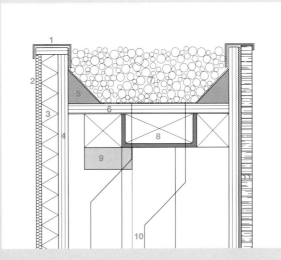

20.10
Ground Floor Overhang Detail
1:10
 1 10 mm (²/₅ inch) Stotherm insulated board with stucco finish to interior wall
 2 30 mm (1¹/₅ inch) insulation
 3 12 mm (¹/₂ inch) fibre cement sheet
 4 60 mm (2¹/₃ inch) timber stud and rails
 5 180 x 67 mm (10¹/₁₆ x 2²/₃ inch) timber stud

 6 18 mm (³/₄ inch) waterproof plywood
 7 400 x 800 x 20 mm (15³/₄ x 31¹/₂ x ³/₄ inch) travertine cladding panels glue-fixed to plywood
 8 Aluminium stucco stop skirting
 9 3 mm (¹/₁₀ inch) thick white Polyurea floor finish
 10 50 mm (2 inch) thick concrete screed floor laid to fall to drain
 11 80 mm (3¹/₁₆ inch) pressure proof

insulation
 12 139 x 54 mm (5¹/₂ x 2¹/₁₀ inch) timber rails
 13 Reinforced concrete floor slab
 14 Concealed rainwater pipe
 15 30 mm (1¹/₅ inch) insulation
 16 10 mm (²/₅ inch) Stotherm insulated board with stucco finish
 17 Aluminium profile

20.11
Waterfall Detail to Kitchen Terrace (Upper Part)
1:7.5
 1 10 mm (³/₈ inch) Stotherm insulated board with stucco finish
 2 30 mm (1¹/₅ inch) insulation
 3 18 mm (³/₄ inch) waterproof plywood
 4 130 mm (5¹/₅ inch) thick insulation
 5 Timber structure
 6 Insulation
 7 18 mm (³/₄ inch) waterproof plywood
 8 400 x 800 x 20 mm (15³/₄ x 31¹/₂ x ³/₄ inch) travertine cladding panels glue-fixed to plywood
 9 130 x 45 mm (5¹/₅ x 1³/₄ inch) timber framing
 10 18 mm (³/₄ inch) waterproof plywood
 11 Steel U-channel to form water outlet
 12 60 mm (2³/₈ inch) diameter water drainage pipe
 13 Powder-coated aluminium formed to create waterfall
 14 Powder-coated aluminium cover plate
 15 Powder-coated aluminium channel

20.12
Waterfall Detail to Kitchen Terrace (Lower Part)
1:7.5
 1 Powder-coated aluminium cover plate
 2 10 mm (³/₈ inch) Stotherm insulated board with stucco finish
 3 30 mm (1¹/₄ inch) insulation
 4 18 mm (³/₄ inch) waterproof plywood
 5 Timber fillet
 6 18 mm (³/₄ inch) waterproof plywood
 7 White stones to drainage gulley on EPDM rubber roofing membrane
 8 Steel U-channel to form water outlet
 9 90 x 56 mm (3¹/₂ x 2¹/₅ inch) timber framing
 10 100 mm (4 inch) drainage pipe
 11 400 x 800 x 20 mm (15³/₄ x 31¹/₂ x ³/₄ inch) travertine cladding panels glue-fixed to plywood

Ring House
Karuizawa, Nagano, Japan

Client
Hill Karuizawa

Project Team
Yuuichirou Katagiri, Hideki Nakamura,
Masaki Watanabe, Seiichi Iwamaru

Structural Engineer
Akira Suzuki

Main Contractor
Niitsu-gumi Co.

Lighting Designer
Masahide Kakudate Lighting

Karuizawa is a mountain resort at the foot of the active volcano Mount Asama in Nagano Prefecture which is located at an altitude of roughly 1,000 metres (3,280 feet). Second home owners, in particular those from Tokyo for whom it is only an hour's journey, enjoy a pleasant escape from the summer heat in Karuizawa. The Ring House is a holiday home located in the forest for clients who spend most of their time in the city. They specifically wanted a house that was a complete departure from their weekday lives. The 1,300 square metre (⅓ acre) property is large by Japanese country-house standards, and is also dotted with pine, cherry and a host of other tree species. On the sloped valley site where code-stipulated setbacks defined the lot's buildable area, the forest guided the placement of the structure.

Rather than having a single directional view, a structure has been created in which the forest can be appreciated and experienced from every direction. The choice of a vertical composition with a minimal footprint was chosen to further integrate the house into the forest landscape. As such the house cannot be determined in terms of the number of levels, rather it is a structure that merges within the forest. The tower is clad in alternating bands of timber and glass – an irregularly striped envelope that evenly balances transparency and opacity. As sunlight floods into the interior by day, or glows from within the volume by night, the wrapper allows views straight through the house. The three levels are connected by a lightweight steel and timber stair whose open treads do nothing to obscure the forest view.

1 The timber rings around the facade have been placed so that private spaces and utilities could be appropriately screened. The height of each ring was decided by the function concealed behind it.
2 The black-stained timber bands on the exterior contrast with the primarily white interior.
3 The kitchen joinery and fireplace are carefully placed behind one of the timber rings.
4 A light weight steel and timber stair, placed in one corner of the square plan, links all three storeys of the house.

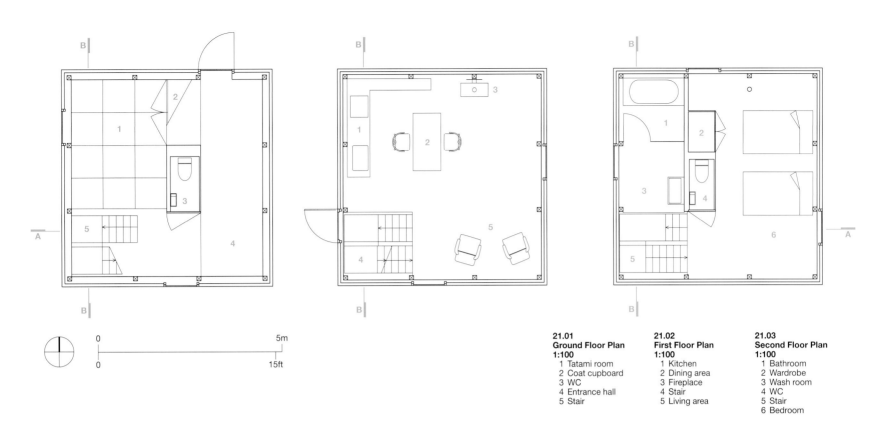

21.01
Ground Floor Plan
1:100
1 Tatami room
2 Coat cupboard
3 WC
4 Entrance hall
5 Stair

21.02
First Floor Plan
1:100
1 Kitchen
2 Dining area
3 Fireplace
4 Stair
5 Living area

21.03
Second Floor Plan
1:100
1 Bathroom
2 Wardrobe
3 Wash room
4 WC
5 Stair
6 Bedroom

21.04
Section A–A
1:100
1 Balustrade to roof
2 Pitched roof
3 Wash room
4 Door to WC
5 Bedroom
6 Stair
7 First floor entrance
8 Living, dining and kitchen
9 Tatami room
10 Door to WC
11 Entrance hall

21.05
Section B–B
1:100
1 Balustrade to roof
2 Pitched roof
3 Bathroom
4 Wash room
5 Stair
6 Living, dining and kitchen
7 Coat cupboard
8 Tatami room

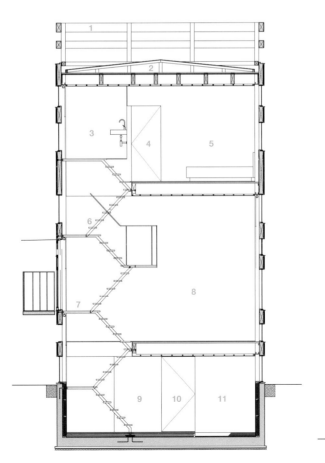

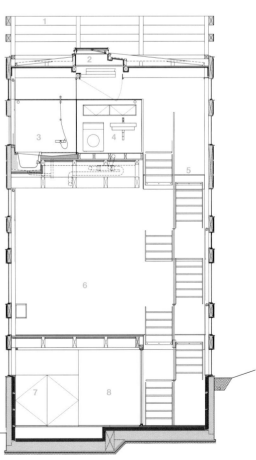

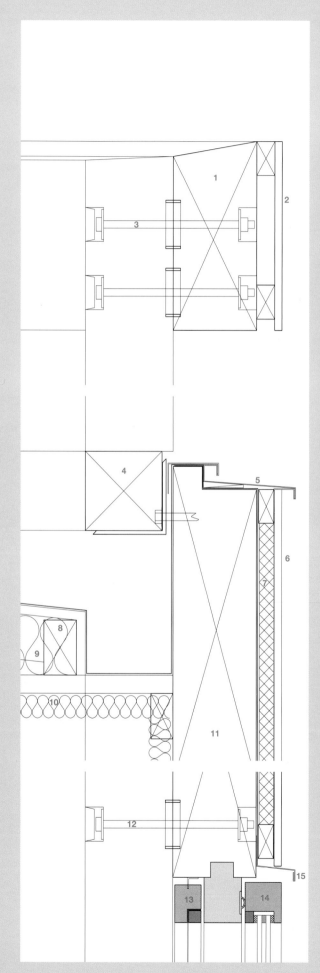

21.05
External Wall Section
Detail 1
1:5
 1 Timber roof
balustrade from 115 x
210 x 240 mm (4^{1}/$_{2}$ x
8^{1}/$_{4}$ x 9^{1}/$_{2}$ inch)
Douglas fir
 2 10 mm (3/8 inch)
burnt cedar cladding
with preservative
treatment
 3 Bolt fixing between
structural framing and
facade
 4 Handrail base from
105 x 105 mm (4^{1}/$_{8}$ x
4^{1}/$_{8}$ inch) timber
section on 100 x 100
mm (4 x 4 inch) steel
angle
 5 Galvanized sheet
metal flashing
 6 10 mm (3/8 inch)
burnt cedar cladding
with preservative
treatment
 7 20 mm (3/4 inch)
thick styrofoam
insulation
 8 Timber framing
 9 Grouted glass wool
insulation on 24 mm
(1 inch) thick structural
plywood
 10 Sprayed urethane
insulation
 11 Timber wall framing
from 115 x 210 x 240
mm (4^{1}/$_{2}$ x 8^{1}/$_{4}$ x 9^{1}/$_{2}$
inch) Douglas fir
 12 Bolt fixing between
structural framing and
facade
 13 Window screen
frame from American
cypress with
preservative
treatment
 14 Window frame from
American cypress with
preservative treatment
 15 Galvanized sheet
metal flashing

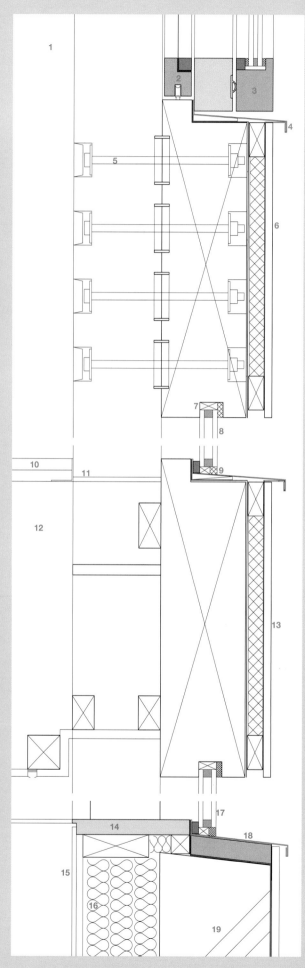

21.06
External Wall Section
Detail 2
1:5
 1 120 x 120 mm (4^{3}/$_{4}$
x 4^{3}/$_{4}$ inch) Douglas fir
laminated lumber
column
 2 Window screen
frame from American
cypress with
preservative treatment
 3 Window frame from
American cypress with
preservative treatment
 4 Galvanized sheet
metal flashing
 5 Stainless steel bolt
with timber cover plate
to interior face
 6 10 mm (3/8 inch)
burnt cedar cladding
with preservative
treatment over
styrofoam insulation
and waterproof
building paper
 7 20 x 10 mm (3/4 x
3/8 inch) timber glazing
frame
 8 Clear double
glazing
 9 Structural silicone
seal
 10 Japanese birch
flooring with integrated
electric underfloor
heating over structural
plywood
 11 Steel plate over 6
mm (1/4 inch) structural
plywood
 12 105 x 300 mm (4^{1}/$_{8}$
x 11^{4}/$_{5}$ inch) Douglas
fir beam
 13 10 mm (3/8 inch)
burnt cedar cladding
with preservative
treatment over
styrofoam insulation
and waterproof
building paper
 14 Timber window
frame
 15 9 mm (1/3 inch)
structural plywood
interior lining
 16 Grouted urethane
insulation
 17 Clear double
glazing
 18 Galvalume plate sill
with watertight seal
 19 Concrete blockwork
with waterproof paint
finish

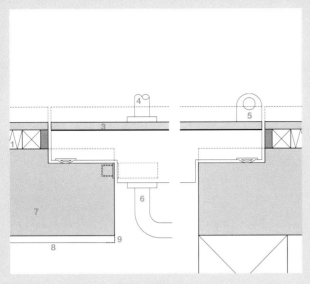

21.07
Steel Entrance Door
Detail
1:5
 1 25 mm (1 inch)
thick rigid foam
insulation
 2 Caulking
 3 10 mm (3/8 inch)
burnt cedar cladding
with preservative
treatment
 4 Stainless steel door
handle
 5 Stainless steel
hinge
 6 Stainless steel door
handle
 7 Douglas fir wall
framing

 8 9 mm (1/3 inch)
insulating fibreboard
 9 Corner profile,
puttied in place

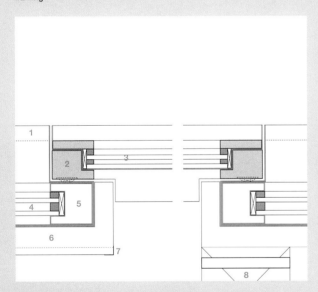

21.08
Glazed Door Detail
1:5
 1 Galvanized steel
plate flashing
 2 Cypress door frame
 3 Double glazed door
comprised of 6 mm
(1/4 inch) glass, 12 mm
(1/2 inch) air gap and 6
mm (1/4 inch) glass
 4 Double glazing
comprised of 6 mm
(1/4 inch) glass, 12 mm
(1/2 inch) air gap and 6
mm (1/4 inch) glass
 5 Timber glazing
frame
 6 Douglas fir cladding
below

 7 Corner profile,
puttied in place
 8 120 x 120 mm (4³/4
x 4³/4 inch) timber
column

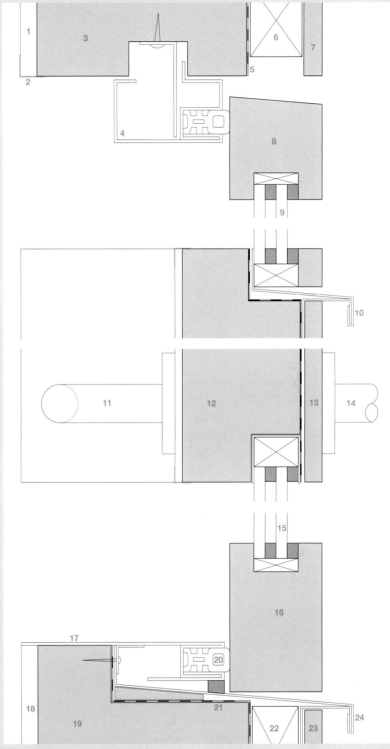

21.09
Steel Door Section
Detail
1:2
 1 9 mm (1/3 inch)
insulating fibreboard
 2 Corner profile,
puttied in place
 3 Douglas fir framing
 4 1.5 mm (1/20 inch)
steel plate door head
profile
 5 Waterproof
membrane
 6 Timber framing
 7 10 mm (2/5 inch)
burnt cedar cladding
with preservative
treatment
 8 Cypress frame

 9 Clear double
glazing
 10 Galvanized sheet
flashing
 11 Stainless steel door
handle
 12 Douglas fir door
panel
 13 10 mm (3/8 inch)
burnt cedar cladding
with preservative
treatment
 14 Stainless steel door
handle
 15 Clear double
glazing
 16 Cypress frame
 17 2 mm (1/16 inch)
stainless steel
 18 9 mm (1/3 inch)

insulating fibreboard
 19 Douglas fir framing
 20 1.5 mm (1/20 inch)
steel plate door sill
profile
 21 Waterproof
membrane
 22 Timber blocking
 23 10 mm (3/8 inch)
burnt cedar cladding
with preservative
treatment
 24 Galvanized sheet
flashing

Peabody Trust Housing
London, England, UK

Client
Peabody Housing

Project Team
Niall McLaughlin, Gus Lewis, Bev
Dockray, Matt Driscoll

Structural Engineer
Whitby Bird Associates

Main Contractor
Sandwood Construction

The project was won in a competition
titled 'Fresh Ideas for Low Cost
Housing' for three sites in the
Silvertown area of East London. Niall
McLaughlin Architects won the
competition to develop the largest
site. The scheme consists of 12
apartments. In each dwelling a high,
bright space has been designed
adjacent to the best prospect of the
outside, towards the street, balcony or
garden. Each living space contains a
large area of full height glazing
opening towards views along and
across the existing streets. The main
south facade is made up of individual
double glazed panels that act as a
rainscreen cladding system. The
windows and the facade use the same
curtain walling system allowing them
to be flush with each other. The 200
mm (8 inch) deep facade units contain
two groups of offset louvres – the first
centred within the depth of the case,
and the second on the back wall.

The louvres are fabricated from
sheet acrylic, each with a covering of
dichroic film. The film, which contains
no actual colour of its own, is
comprised of layers of colourless
metal oxides that generate shifting
spectra. The eighteenth-century
French physicist, Fresnel, discovered
that spectra occur on a surface
because light is reflected from the
different layers within the material,
generating patterns of interference on
its way out. The dichroic film,
manufactured for use in astronomy,
exploits this phenomenon. The result
is a strikingly colourful and truly kinetic
facade which is a result entirely of
reflection and not related to the
transmission of light through the
glazing. The colours change
constantly as one moves past the
building, as the sun moves in the sky
and as the reflection of trees shift in
the wind.

1 The main facade
along Evelyn Road
features a three-storey
high wall of glass
louvres which are
opened from each of
the living rooms in the
12 apartments.

2 The apartments are
located in the East End
of London, within sight
of the regenerated
Docklands.
3 View of the louvred
facade at night.
4 The striking effect of

the dichroic film
bonded to each of the
louvres is illustrated
here with the full
spectrum of colours
on view.

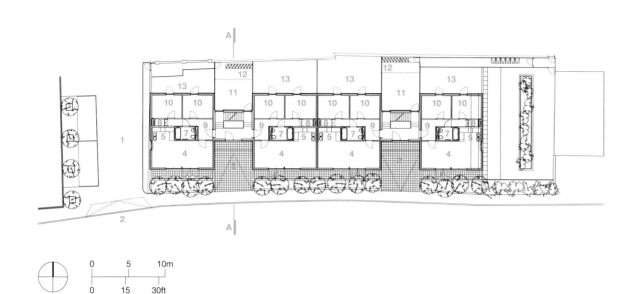

1 Julia Garfield
  Mews
2 Evelyn Road
3 Entrance hall
4 Living room
5 Kitchen
6 Balcony
7 Bathroom
8 Store
9 Apartment
  entrance hall
10 Bedroom
11 Communal garden
12 Bicycle store
13 Garden

1 Bicycle store
2 Communal garden
3 Brick garden wall
4 Main entrance
5 Communal stair
6 Balcony
7 Louvred wall
8 Flat roof
9 Smoke vent
10 Louvred wall

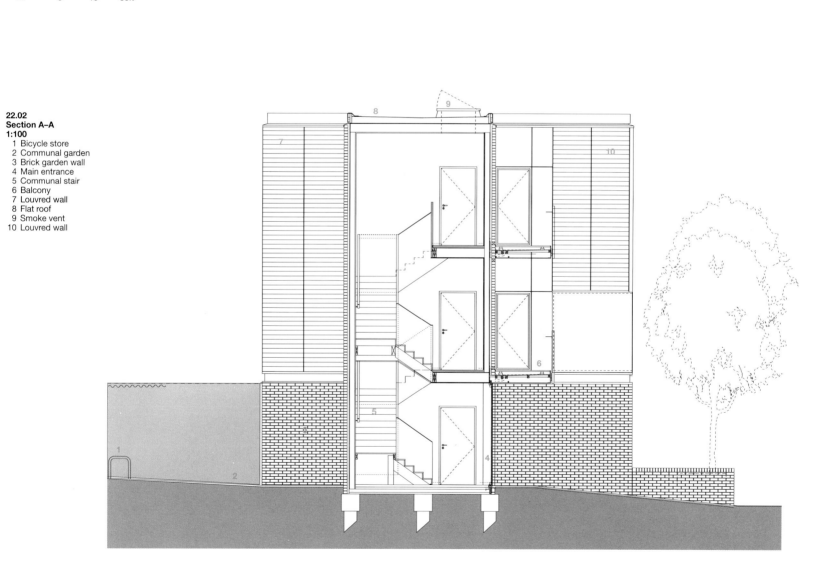

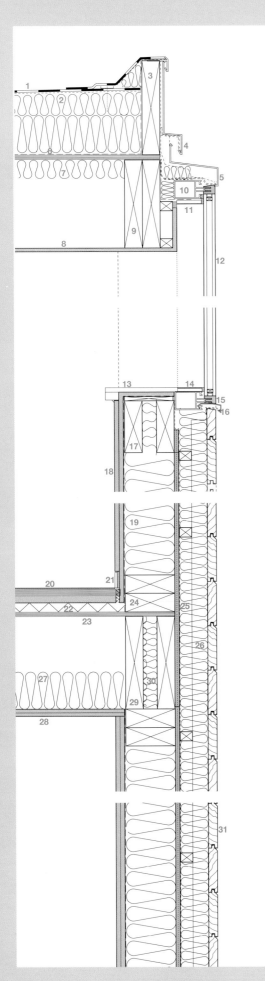

22.03
Window Head and Sill
Detail 1
1:10
1 Polymeric roofing membrane system bonded to insulation
2 Thermal insulation
3 Softwood verge upstand
4 Polyester powder-coated pressed aluminium flashing
5 Polyester powder-coated pressed aluminium flashing
6 Damp proof membrane
7 Thermal insulation between joists
8 12.5 mm ($1/2$ inch) plasterboard
9 Structural timber frame
10 Flush glazed polyester powder-coated aluminium carrier system
11 Brushed stainless steel bonded to 10 mm ($3/8$ inch) Superflex board
12 Double glazed unit structurally bonded to polyester powder-coated aluminium carrier profile
13 Painted MDF window sill
14 Brushed stainless steel bonded to 10 mm ($3/8$ inch) Superflex board
15 Flush glazed polyester powder coated aluminium carrier system
16 Polyester powder coated aluminium flashing
17 Softwood member
18 Two layers of 12.5 mm ($1/2$ inch) plasterboard and vapour barrier
19 Thermal insulation
20 Carpeting on 18 mm ($3/4$ inch) plywood and 19 mm ($3/4$ inch) fire resistant sheeting
21 Painted MDF skirting
22 25 mm (1 inch) rigid foam insulation
23 15 mm ($5/8$ inch) plywood
24 Softwood member
25 Fire resistant sheeting, windproof layer and 10 mm ($3/8$ inch) oriented strand board
26 Thermal insulation
27 Thermal insulation
28 Two layers of 12.5 mm ($1/2$ inch) plasterboard
29 Structural timber frame
30 Thermal insulation
31 24 mm (1 inch) larch boarding

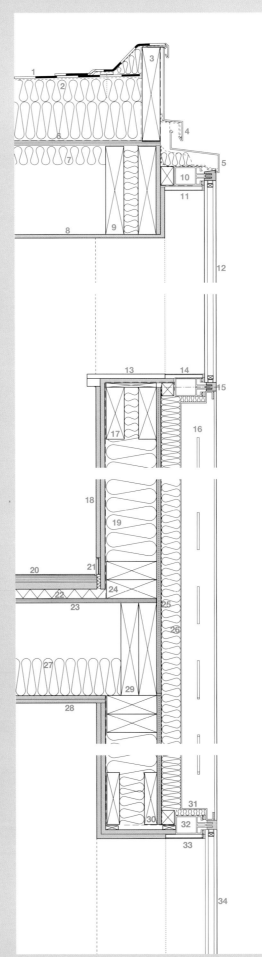

22.04
Window Head and Sill
Detail 2
1:10
1 Polymeric roofing membrane system bonded to insulation
2 Thermal insulation
3 Softwood verge upstand
4 Polyester powder-coated pressed aluminium flashing
5 Polyester powder-coated pressed aluminium flashing
6 Damp proof membrane
7 Thermal insulation between joists
8 12.5 mm ($1/2$ inch) plasterboard
9 Structural timber frame
10 Flush glazed polyester powder-coated aluminium carrier system
11 Brushed stainless steel bonded to 10 mm ($3/8$ inch) Superflex board
12 Double glazed insulated unit structurally bonded to polyester powder-coated aluminium carrier profile
13 Painted MDF window sill
14 Brushed stainless steel bonded to 10 mm ($3/8$ inch) Superflex board
15 Flush glazed polyester powder-coated aluminium carrier system
16 Curtain wall cladding panel
17 Softwood members
18 Two layers of 12.5 mm ($1/2$ inch) plasterboard and vapour barrier
19 140 mm ($51/2$ inch) thermal insulation
20 Carpeting on 18 mm ($3/4$ inch) plywood and 19 mm ($3/4$ inch) fire resistant sheeting
21 Painted MDF skirting
22 25 mm (1 inch) rigid foam insulation
23 15 mm ($5/8$ inch) plywood
24 Softwood members
25 Fire resistant sheeting, windproof layer and 10 mm ($3/8$ inch) oriented strand board
26 Continuous firestop
27 Thermal insulation
28 Two layers of 12.5 mm ($1/2$ inch) plasterboard
29 Structural timber frame
30 Softwood members
31 Aluminium tray with slits at sides for fixing
32 Flush glazed polyester powder-coated aluminium carrier system
33 Brushed stainless steel bonded to 10 mm ($3/8$ inch) Superflex board
34 Double glazed insulated unit

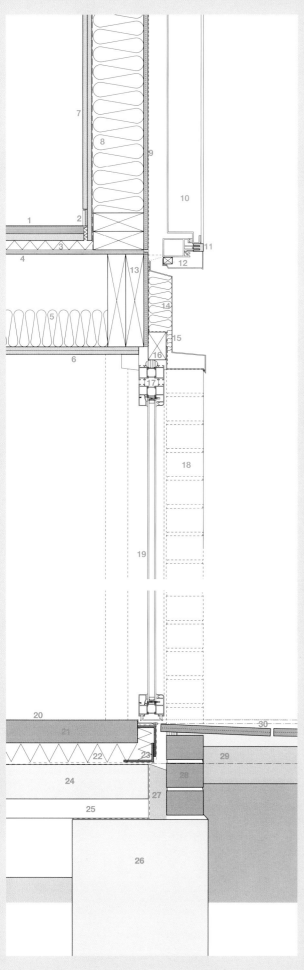

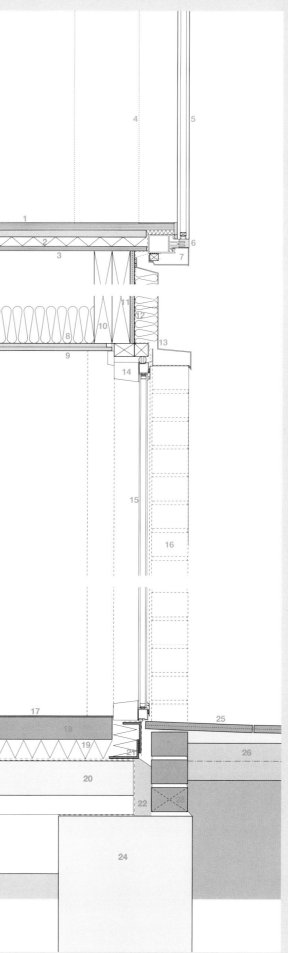

22.05
**Glazed Door Head
and Sill Detail 1**
1:10
  1 Carpeting on 18 mm (3/4 inch) plywood and 19 mm (3/4 inch) fire resistant sheeting
  2 Painted MDF skirting
  3 25 mm (1 inch) rigid foam insulation
  4 15 mm (3/8 inch) plywood
  5 Thermal insulation
  6 Two layers of 12.5 mm (1/2 inch) plasterboard
  7 Two layers of 12.5 mm (1/2 inch) plasterboard and vapour barrier
  8 140 mm (51/2 inch) thermal insulation
  9 50 mm (2 inch) ventilated cavity
  10 Glazing unit structurally bonded to aluminium carrier profile
  11 Flush glazed polyester powder-coated aluminium carrier system
  12 Polyester powder-coated pressed aluminium flashing
  13 Structural timber frame
  14 Thermal insulation
  15 Powder-coated pressed aluminium flashing with integrated slot ventilator
  16 Softwood members
  17 Polyester powder-coated aluminium door frame
  18 Engineering brick facing skin
  19 Double glazed insulated unit to door
  20 Linoleum flooring
  21 Concrete floor screed
  22 Rigid insulation
  23 Structural steel angles
  24 Beam and block floor planks
  25 Cavity
  26 Strip foundation
  27 Mortar infill
  28 Engineering bricks
  29 100 mm (4 inch) consolidated hardcore
  30 25 mm (1 inch) thick paving slabs on 25 mm (1 inch) sand cement bed

22.06
**Glazed Door Head
and Sill Detail 2**
1:10
  1 Carpeting on 18 mm (3/4 inch) plywood and 19 mm (3/4 inch) fire resistant sheeting
  2 25 mm (1 inch) rigid foam insulation
  3 15 mm (5/8 inch) plywood
  4 Structural silicone
  5 Double glazed insulated unit structurally bonded to polyester powder-coated aluminium carrier profile
  6 Flush glazed polyester powder-coated aluminium carrier system
  7 Polyester powder-coated pressed aluminium flashing
  8 Thermal insulation
  9 Two layers of 12.5 mm (1/2 inch) plasterboard
  10 Structural timber frame
  11 Structural timber frame
  12 Thermal insulation
  13 Powder-coated pressed aluminium flashing with integrated slot ventilator
  14 Polyester powder coated aluminium window frame system
  15 Double glazed insulated unit
  16 Engineering brick facing skin beyond
  17 Linoleum flooring
  18 Concrete floor screed
  19 Structural insulation
  20 Beam and block floor planks
  21 Structural steel angles
  22 Mortar infill
  23 Weepholes (this course and above)
  24 Strip foundation
  25 25 mm (1 inch) thick paving slabs on 25 mm (1 inch) sand cement bed
  26 100 mm (4 inch) consolidated hardcore

YVE Apartments
Melbourne, Victoria, Australia

Client
Sunland Group

Project Team
Randal Marsh, Roger Wood, Domenic
Chirico

Structural Engineer
Waley Consulting Group

Services Engineer
Lincolne Scott

The YVE Apartment building has been
designed as a three dimensional
iconographic structure with
predominately glass facings of various
textures and layers. The intention was
to create a subtle building that would
sit harmoniously in its location and at
the same time present a positive
contribution to the streetscape. The
building is symmetrical in plan and
elevation. Floors above 45 metres
(148 feet) step inward from the
corners, and to a lesser extent, from
the centre. This movement forces the
perspective and creates a crown to
the building without altering the overall
building language.

The facade has many levels which,
when combined with the form,
emphasizes the three dimensional
quality of the building. The inner layer
is a slightly reflective charcoal glass
extending from floor to ceiling. The
charcoal glazing mullions establish a
vertical pattern. The glazing follows
the outer curves and steps back in
places to form balconies and create
shadowed recesses. This layer
contrasts with the horizontal glazed
ribbons of the outer layer. All-concrete
floor plates are screened by a
continuous band of concertina glass
which acts as both a balustrade and
shading device, and provides the
building with its outer layer. Partially
transparent, the concertina glass
forms a shimmering ribbon when
viewed from a distance. These panels
are held off the face of the building,
allowing filtered light to penetrate
through the facade. At street level
the building skirt lifts up centrally
and the ground floor glazing is
recessed so that the building above
appears to float.

1 The outer layer of
glazing, which lends
the geometry of the
building its fluid
movement, acts as a
balustrade to the
wrap-around balconies
and shading device.
2 Detail view
illustrating the two
layers of glazing that
clad the building – a
full height inner layer
that provides security
and protection from
the weather, and the
outer horizontal layer
of balustrading.
3 The raked glazing to
the ground floor is in
various shades of soft
colour to contrast with
the grey shades used
in levels above.

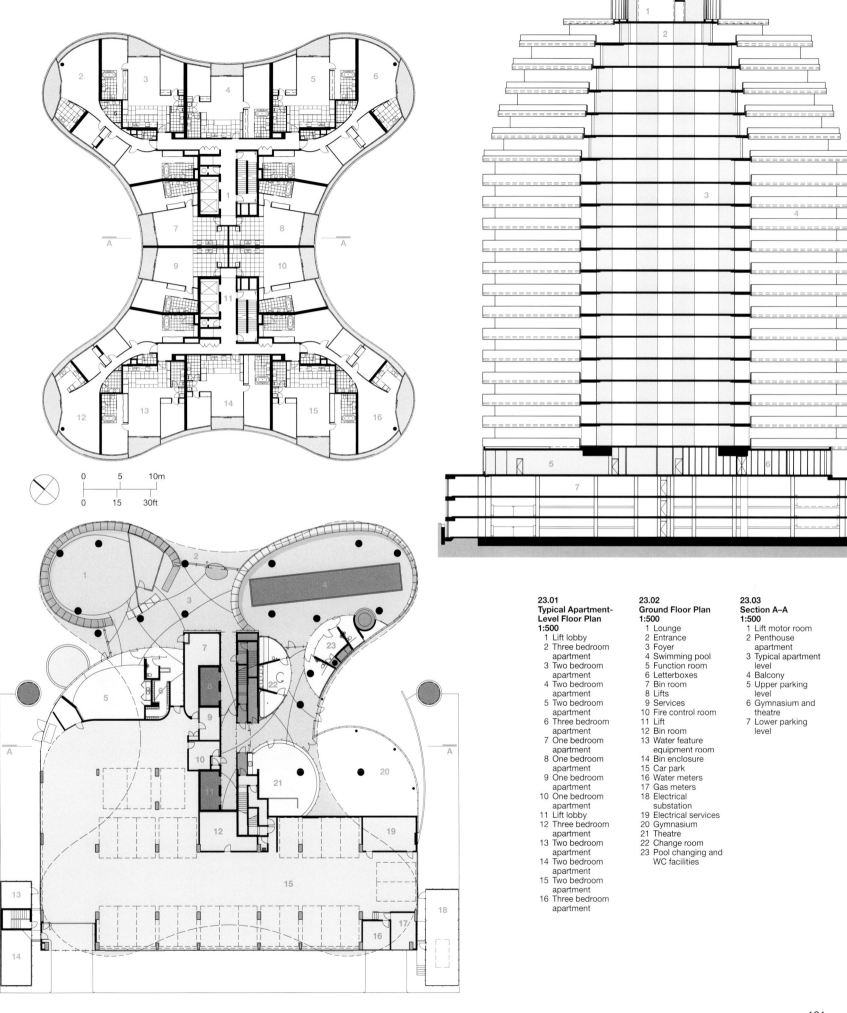

0	5	10m
0	15	30ft

23.01
Typical Apartment-Level Floor Plan
1:500
1 Lift lobby
2 Three bedroom apartment
3 Two bedroom apartment
4 Two bedroom apartment
5 Two bedroom apartment
6 Three bedroom apartment
7 One bedroom apartment
8 One bedroom apartment
9 One bedroom apartment
10 One bedroom apartment
11 Lift lobby
12 Three bedroom apartment
13 Two bedroom apartment
14 Two bedroom apartment
15 Two bedroom apartment
16 Three bedroom apartment

23.02
Ground Floor Plan
1:500
1 Lounge
2 Entrance
3 Foyer
4 Swimming pool
5 Function room
6 Letterboxes
7 Bin room
8 Lifts
9 Services
10 Fire control room
11 Lift
12 Bin room
13 Water feature equipment room
14 Bin enclosure
15 Car park
16 Water meters
17 Gas meters
18 Electrical substation
19 Electrical services
20 Gymnasium
21 Theatre
22 Change room
23 Pool changing and WC facilities

23.03
Section A–A
1:500
1 Lift motor room
2 Penthouse apartment
3 Typical apartment level
4 Balcony
5 Upper parking level
6 Gymnasium and theatre
7 Lower parking level

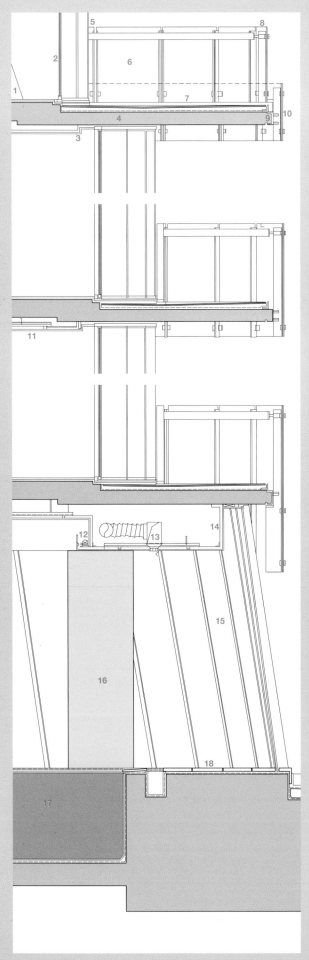

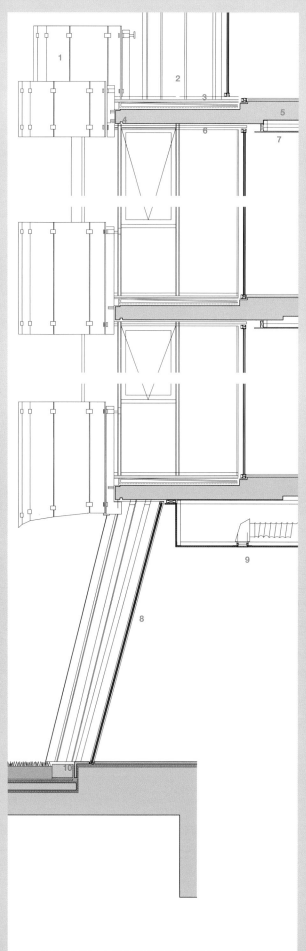

23.04
Facade Section
Detail 1
1:50
1 Sloping concrete column
2 Aluminium framed glazed sliding door in window system with powdercoat finish
3 MDF closing panel to pelmet, painted to match ceiling
4 Reinforced concrete floor slab
5 Cantilevered glass division screen between balcony and ledge
6 Balustrade beyond
7 Tiled finish to balcony floor over screed bed laid to fall and waterproof membrane
8 60 x 40 x 5 mm (2³/8 x 1⁵/8 x ¹/5 inch) angle to back of perimeter frame
9 Rolled, galvanized and painted 90 x 90 mm (3¹/2 x 3¹/2 inch) mild steel angle border to balcony edge
10 Textured glazing faceted to follow slab edge
11 Flush plasterboard suspended ceiling with paint finish
12 Pelmet lighting
13 Mechanical supply air grille with linear slot diffuser and associated ductwork
14 Bulkhead return
15 Glazed facade to ground floor beyond
16 Reinforced concrete structural column with tiled finish
17 Swimming pool
18 Tiled floor finish over screed and waterproof membrane

23.05
Facade Section
Detail 2
1:50
1 Glass balustrade faceted to follow curves of slab edges
2 Faceted glass facade
3 Tiled finish to balcony over screed laid to falls over impact-absorbent mat and waterproof membrane
4 Rolled, galvanized and painted 90 x 90 mm (3¹/2 x 3¹/2 inch) mild steel angle border to balcony edge
5 Reinforced concrete floor slab
6 Paint finish to concrete soffit
7 MDF closing panel to pelmet, painted to match ceiling
8 Line of angled glazed facade to ground floor
9 Mechanical supply air grille with linear slot diffuser and associated ductwork
10 Polished pre-cast edge to lawn perimeter

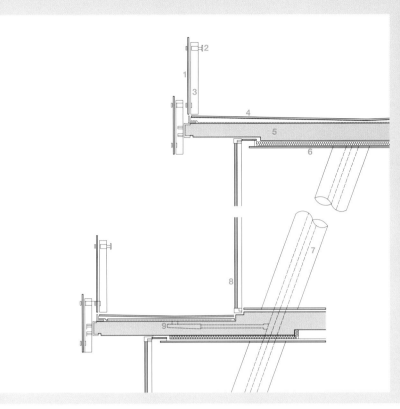

23.06
Glazed Balustrade
Section Detail
1:50
 1 Textured glazing faceted to follow slab edge
 2 Handrail
 3 Stainless steel stanchion
 4 Tile finish to balcony over screed laid to falls and waterproof membrane and incorporating outlets to suit downpipe connection
 5 Reinforced concrete floor slab
 6 Flush plasterboard suspended ceiling over foilboard insulation to achieve thermal rating
 7 Circular reinforced concrete column with applied 6 mm (1/4 inch) skim coat plaster and paint finish with 150 mm (6 inch) downpipe cast in column, shown dotted
 8 Aluminium framed window assembly with powdercoat finish
 9 Terrace rainwater outlet connected to cast-in PVC box catchment with 50 mm (2 inch) pipe connection to downpipe

23.07
Stair detail
1:10
 1 Stringer fixed to wall with countersunk screw fixings with 250 mm (6 inch) stainless steel spacers between wall and stringer
 2 250 mm (6 inch) deep painted mild steel stringer
 3 60 x 40 x 5 mm (2³/8 x 1⁵/8 x 1/5 inch) angle to back of tread perimeter frame
 4 12 mm (1/2 inch) thick laminated glass treads and landing fixed with double sided glazing tape
 5 Painted 40 x 40 x 5 mm (1⁵/8 x 1⁵/8 x 1/5 inch) mild steel perimeter support frame to glass tread
 6 Polished steel 25 mm (1 inch) countersunk pin fixing connection between glass and mild steel stringer
 7 300 x 75 x 12 mm (11⁴/5 x 3 x 1/2 inch) base plate welded to string to enable anchoring to concrete slab with countersunk fixings

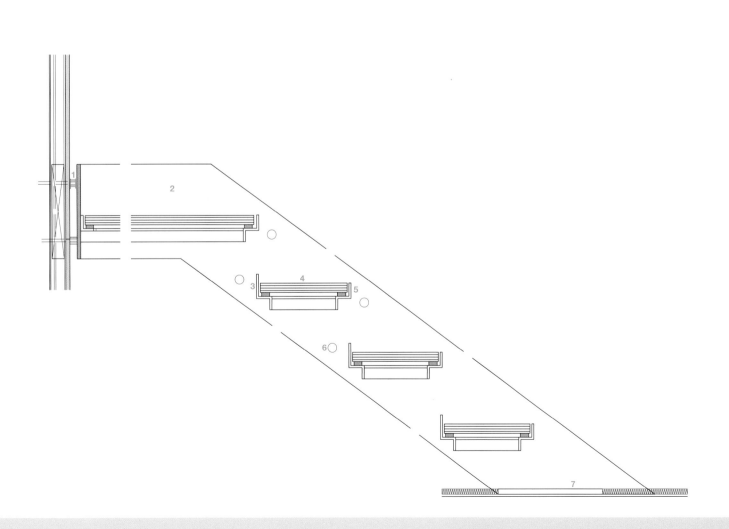

HL23
New York, New York, USA

Client
Highline LLC, Alf Naman Real Estate,
Garrett Heher

Project Team
Neil Denari, Stefano Paiocchi, Duks
Koschitz, David Aguilo, Carmen
Cham, Antonio Torres, Alex Janowski,
Philip Traexler, Yoichiro Mizuno, Rick
Michod, Christian Kotzemanis

Structural Engineer
Desimone Consulting Engineers

Main Contractor
T. G. Nickel and Associates

HL23 is a 14-storey high condominium
tower that responds to a unique and
challenging site directly adjacent to
the High Line at 23rd Street in New
York's West Chelsea art district. The
High Line is a new linear park,
elevated above the street on existing
rail lines, and offers people the
opportunity to interact with the city's
rich architectural heritage. Likewise,
HL23 is a structure precisely shaped
by a confluence of local forces. The
site (and the developer) demanded a
specific response, yielding a project
that is a combination of found and
given parameters and architectural
ambition.

For the client, the question was how
to expand the floor area of a restricted
zoning envelope which included a
setback from the High Line and a
height limit. As a result, a supple
geometry was developed to allow a
larger building to stand in very close
proximity to the elevated park of the
High Line. Together, the demands
produced a reverse tapering building
(a small base, with a larger top) with
one apartment per floor and three
distinct yet coherent facades – a rarity
in Manhattan's block structure. The
main living areas and views are
oriented toward the south, while the
east facade facing the High Line is
formed as a sculptural surface with
smaller windows allowing privacy and
framed views across Manhattan. A
custom-designed, spandrel-free
curtain wall of glass and stainless
steel mega panels hangs on a
complex, cantilevered steel frame,
generating expression within
systematic economy. Since the
building sits in the middle of the art
District, it attempts to deliver a
commercially viable, highly crafted
object that can take its place among
the art shown in the nearby galleries.

1 View of the north facade, behind which most of the bedrooms are located. A custom-designed glass and stainless steel curtain wall creates a dynamic geometric that complements the changing landscape of the High Line park.
2 The glazed south facade brings soft diffused light into the living areas.
3 View of the expansive terrace of the penthouse apartment.
4 A double height apartment on level two features a large terrace protected by overscaled planting.

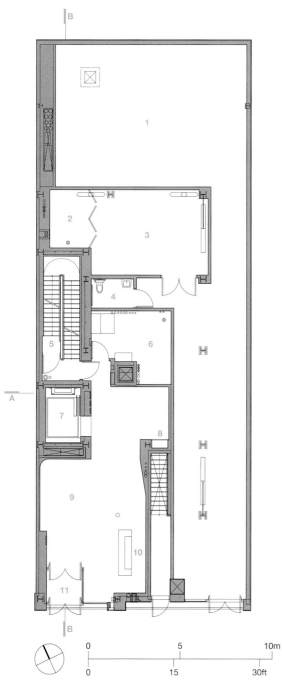

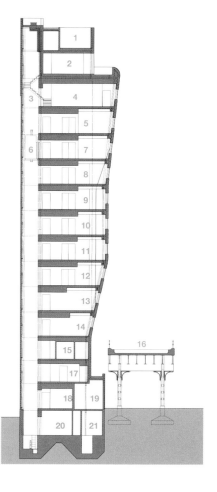

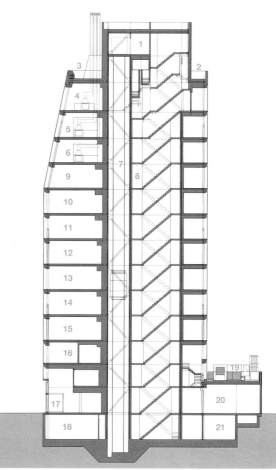

0   5   10m

0   15   30ft

24.01
Ground Floor Plan
1:200
1 Retail space
2 Mechanical closet
3 Office
4 Bathroom
5 Stair
6 Mechanical room
7 Lift
8 Mailboxes
9 Lobby
10 Reception
11 Entrance

24.02
Seventh Floor Plan
1:200
1 Bathroom
2 Bedroom
3 Stair
4 Bathroom
5 Bedroom
6 Rubbish chute
7 Lift
8 Apartment
   entrance
9 Powder room
10 Study
11 Kitchen

12 Living and dining
   area

24.03
Section A–A
1:500
1 Mechanical plant
   on roof
2 Penthouse
   apartment upper
   level
3 Internal stair to
   penthouse
   apartment
4 Penthouse
   apartment lower
   level
5 Single level
   apartment
6 Lift
7 Single level
   apartment
8 Single level
   apartment
9 Single level
   apartment
10 Single level
   apartment
11 Single level
   apartment

12 Single level
   apartment
13 Single level
   apartment
14 Single level
   apartment
15 Single level
   apartment
16 High line
17 Single level
   apartment
18 Entrance lobby
19 Retail space
20 Electrical service
   room
21 Mechanical room

24.04
Section B–B
1:500
1 Electrical room
2 Terrace to
   penthouse
3 Terrace to
   penthouse
4 Penthouse
   apartment lower
   level
5 Single level
   apartment

6 Single level
   apartment
7 Lift
8 Stair
9 Single level
   apartment
10 Single level
   apartment
11 Single level
   apartment
12 Single level
   apartment
13 Single level
   apartment
14 Single level
   apartment
15 Single level
   apartment
16 Single level
   apartment
17 Entrance lobby
18 Electrical service
   room
19 Terrace
20 Retail space
21 Mechanical room

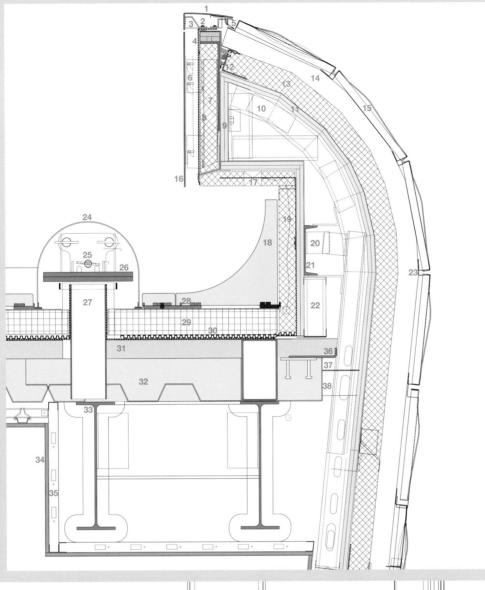

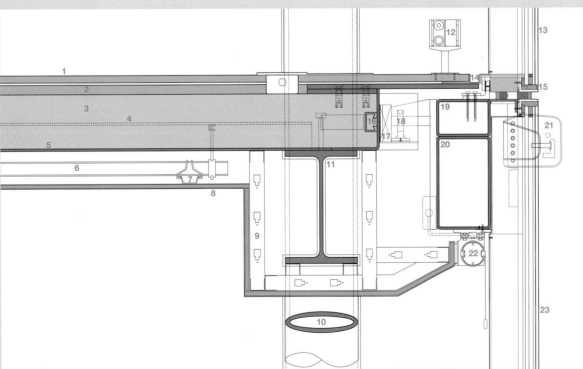

24.05
Section Detail at Roof Parapet
1:20
1 Aluminium cover plate
2 Aluminium cover plate support
3 Cover support bracket
4 Aluminium coping
5 Aluminium flashing
6 75 mm (3 inch) steel support system
7 Insulation
8 Vapour shield membrane
9 Densglass sheathing panel engineered with water-resistant treated core and surfaced with glass mat facings
10 100 mm (4 inch) panel frame
11 50 x 16 mm (2 x 5/8 inch) Glasroc glass reinforced gypsum board
12 Trimmed corner to roof purlin
13 89 mm (3 1/2 inch) unfaced Thermafiber insulation
14 Extruded aluminium purlin
15 Stainless steel panel cladding system
16 Aluminium panel
17 Recessed light fitting
18 Prefabricated concrete paver corner piece
19 Electrical conduit
20 100 mm (4 inch) panel frame
21 89 mm (3 1/2 inch) unfaced membrane installed with primer
22 Site framing
23 Purlin
24 Davit cover
25 Davit base
26 Steel plate
27 Davit pedestal
28 Stackable pedestal
29 Rigid insulation
30 Waterproofing
31 Sloped topping slab
32 75 mm (3 inch) composite metal deck used as formwork for reinforced concrete roof slab
33 Steel beam
34 Gypsum wall board
35 Steel stud framing
36 152 x 25 mm (6 x 1 inch) continuous erection angle
37 Smoke sealant
38 100 mm (4 inch) Firestop mineral wool

24.06
Typical Floor Detail
1:10
1 19 mm (3/4 inch) rift cut oak flooring
2 Subfloor
3 Reinforced concrete floor slab
4 Reinforcing bar
5 Composite steel decking
6 Ceiling channel
7 Hat channel
8 Waterproof suspended ceiling system
9 Steel stud framing
10 200 mm (8 inch) diameter circular hollow section steel column
11 Steel beam with intumescent fireproof coating
12 Runtal perimeter heating
13 Glass curtain wall
14 Timber floor expansion joint
15 Aluminium cassette
16 Halfen anchor channel
17 Steel shims
18 Anchor
19 Curtain wall spreader beam
20 Curtain wall spreader beam
21 Intermittent stabilization anchor for facade access
22 Solar blind housing
23 Glass curtain wall

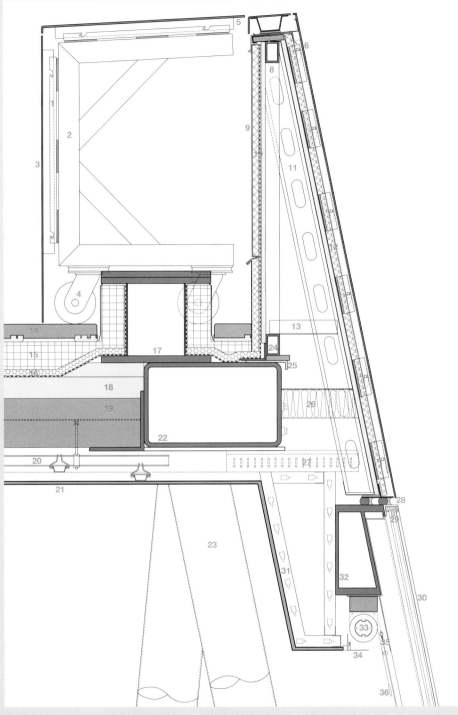

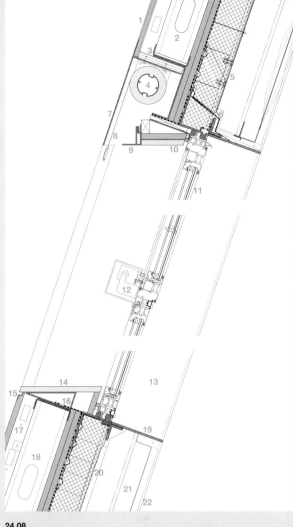

24.07
Sloped Parapet Detail
1:12.5
 1 Mild steel plate
support system
 2 Rollaway parapet
cart
 3 Aluminium panel
 4 Pneumatic wheel
 5 Vapour shield
 6 Stainless steel
metal cladding system
 7 Spacer
 8 Steel tube frame
 9 Rigid insulation
 10 Densglass
sheathing panel
engineered with
water-resistant treated
core and surfaced with
glass mat facings
 11 100 mm (4 inch) 16
gauge shop welded
steel studs at 406 mm

(16 inch) centres as
parapet framing
 12 16 gauge metal flat
stock cladding support
 13 Angle kicker
 14 Pre-cast concrete
paver
 15 Rigid insulation
 16 Waterproofing
 17 Steel plate
 18 Topping slab
 19 75 mm (3 inch)
composite metal deck
as formwork for
concrete roof slab
 20 Support plate to
suspended ceiling
system
 21 Waterproof
suspended
plasterboard ceiling
system
 22 Rectangular hollow
section steel framing

 23 Diagonal braces
 24 Dead load clip
angle
 25 Dead load support
angle
 26 100 mm (4 inch)
minimum fire stop and
smoke seal
 27 Lateral support
angle brace
 28 Backer rod and
caulking
 29 Milled aluminium
panel perimeter
extrusion
 30 Glass curtain wall
 31 Support bracket
 32 Curtain wall
spreader beam
 33 Roller blind tube
with assembly motor
inside tube
 34 Standard 75 mm
(3 inch) closure plate in

standard white
 35 Spring loaded
tension cable
 36 Hem bar sealed
inside shade cloth

24.08
Detail at Sloped
Glazed Wall
1:10
 1 Gypsum wall board
interior lining
 2 100 mm (4 inch)
steel framing
 3 19 mm ($^3/_4$ inch)
continuous framing
 4 Roller blind
 5 Protective
membrane
 6 Continuous
aluminium flashing
 7 Stainless steel
shade fascia
 8 Guide cable to
roller blind
 9 Closure angle
 10 Painted timber
 11 Operable window
 12 Window motor
 13 Aluminium trim
 14 Timber sill
 15 Z reveal
 16 Levelling track
 17 Slip joint
connection
 18 100 mm (4 inch)
steel framing
 19 6 mm ($^1/_4$ inch)
aluminium trim
 20 Protective
membrane
 21 Hanger profile
 22 Line of fascia
beyond

**House Ray 1
Vienna, Austria**

Client
Delugan Meissl

Project Team
Anke Goll, Christine Hax, Martin Josst

Structural Engineer
Werkraum ZT

Main Contractor
Baumeister Tupy

Situated on the flat roof of a 1960s office building in the middle of the rooftop landscape of Vienna's fourth district, Ray 1 evolved out of the direct stimuli and spatial quality of the location. The juxtaposition of the static mass of the existing building and the dynamic form of architecture in motion serves to charge the structure. The new building evolved out of the connection between the two buildings on either side, continuing the line of projection of the gables to bridge the gap. The house that is the result is seen as a permeable border zone between earth and sky that becomes a space for living.

Recesses and folds create transparent zones and sheltered terraced landscapes on both sides of the building, providing opportunities for experiencing the structure's open layout, from the entrance all the way up to the accessible roof area. The interior space is designed as a loft whose various functional areas are defined by different floor levels. Stairs and ramps throughout the mainly open space, connect zones for eating, living and relaxing in the centre and southern end of the structure, with more private quarters for sleeping and bathing at the northern end. Various covered outdoor spaces provide far reaching views in both directions across the city. The outer skin, which is coated with Alucobond, defines the contours of the apartment's interior, suggesting varying subtleties for different zones and niches. The intention was to create a shell that would function as a changeable backdrop for the furniture, much of which is custom-designed and built.

1 The nondescript office building is transformed by the addition of the folded, layered architecture of Ray 1.
2 Great swathes of clear glazing connect the interior to various terraces. Timber floorboards, used both inside and out, create a seamless transition between indoors and out.
3 At night, the strips of glazing provide glimpses into the living spaces.
4 A ramped timber floor and an elevated white ramp and walkway structure lend an unexpected dynamism to the main living level. The kitchen consists of a long recess tucked into the wall behind the floating ramp.

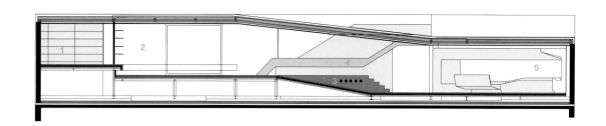

25.01
Section A–A
1:200
1 Study
2 Dining area
3 Ramped timber
  floor
4 Kitchen
5 Bedroom 2

25.02
Floor Plan
1:200
1 Bedroom 1
2 Bath
3 WC and shower
4 Bedroom 2
5 Bathroom
6 Utility room
7 Entrance
8 Terrace
9 Ramped timber
  floor
10 Entrance
11 WC

12 Kitchen
13 Pool
14 Pool terrace
15 Living room
16 Dining area
17 Study
18 Terrace

25.03
Section B–B
1:100
1 Bedroom 1
2 Timber floor
3 Ramp
4 Entrance stair

25.04
Section C–C
1:100
1 Study
2 Living area
3 Dining area

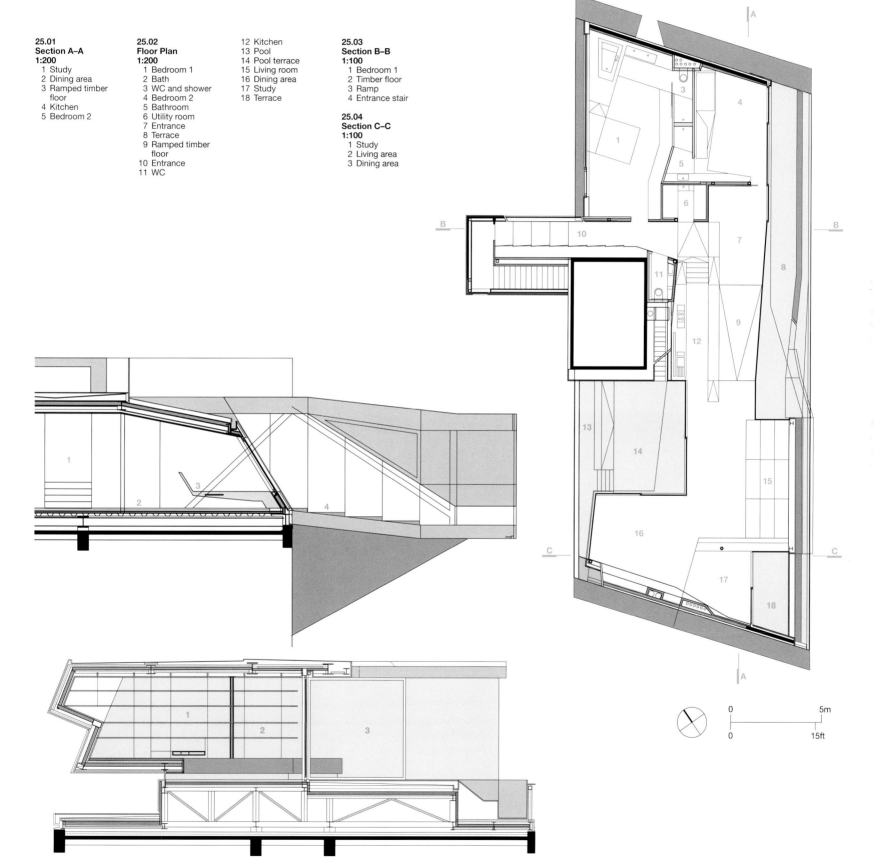

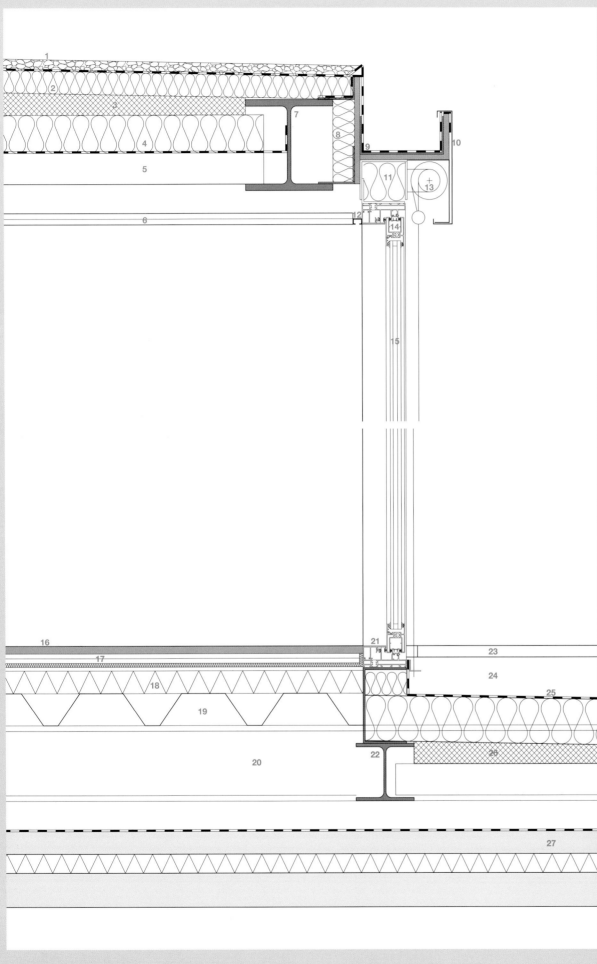

25.05
Roof, Gutter, Sliding Glass Door and Floor Detail
1:10
1 10 mm (3/8 inch) quartz sand-surfaced membrane over 20 mm (3/4 inch) Sarnafil oriented strand board panel laid to fall
2 60 mm (23/8 inch) thermal insulation
3 85 mm (33/8 inch) thermal insulation with corrugated metal sheet in between
4 15 mm (5/8 inch) Thermax board over edge bonded vapour barrier
5 50 mm (2 inch) electrical wiring zone
6 125 mm (5 inch) plasterboard finished with joint compound and painted
7 240 mm (91/2 inch) steel I-beam
8 Thermal insulation
9 Waterproof membrane to structural plywood formed gutter
10 Folded aluminium gutter capping
11 Insulation
12 Aluminium shadow line rebate profile
13 External roller blind
14 Sliding mechanism to glazed door
15 Double glazed door
16 20 mm (3/4 inch) thick timber parquet to interior floor
17 25 mm (1 inch) cement bed over 10 mm (3/8 inch) thick noise dampening layer
18 10 mm (3/8 inch) gypsum fibreboard
19 60 mm (23/8 inch) rigid thermal insulation
20 85 mm (33/8 inch) corrugated metal sheet
21 Aluminium profile door sill
22 Steel I-beam
23 Timber boards to terrace
24 Air space and substructure
25 Sarnafil sealant over 15 mm (3/5 inch) oriented strand board laid to fall
26 120 mm (43/4 inch) thermal insulation
27 85 mm (33/8 inch) thermal insulation with corrugated metal sheet in between

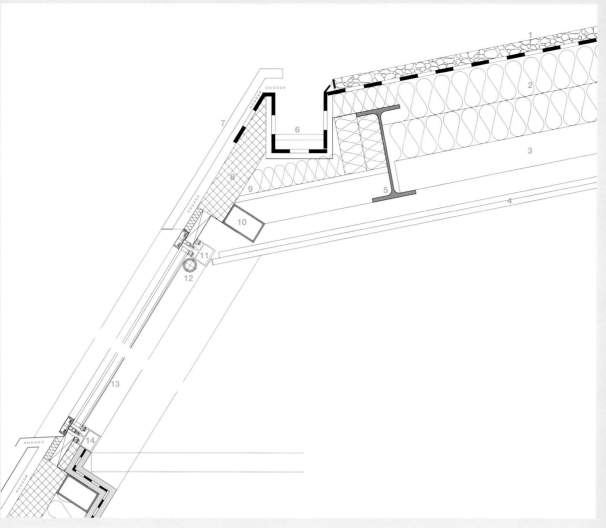

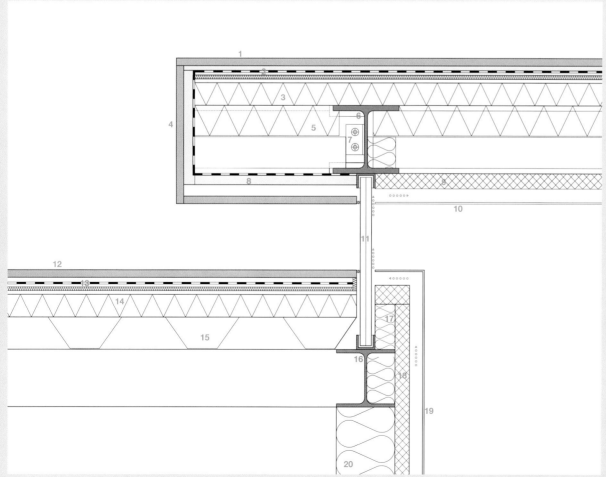

111

112

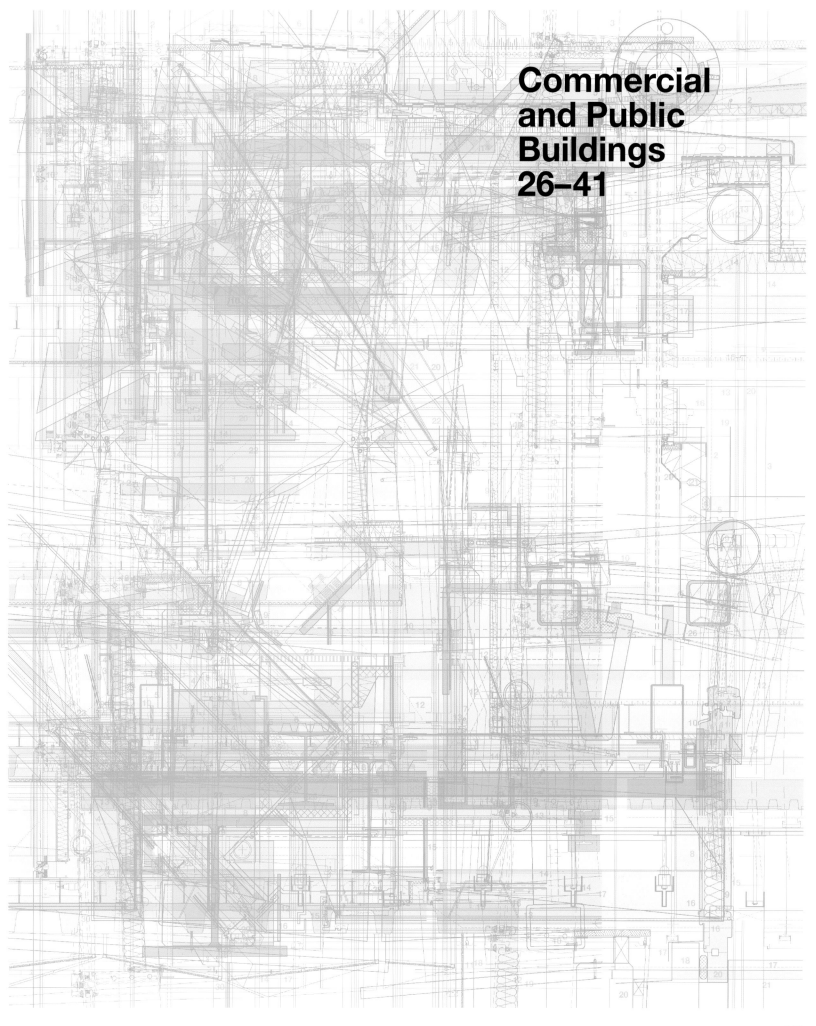

Commercial
and Public
Buildings
26–41

**John Lewis Department Store,
Cineplex and Footbridges
Leicester, England, UK**

Client
GP Limited : Hammerson / Hermes

Project Team
Farshid Moussavi, Alejandro Zaera-Polo

Structural Engineer
Adams Kara Taylor

Main Contractor
Sir Robert McAlpine

The new John Lewis Department Store was commissioned within a larger city centre regeneration scheme for Leicester. The department store and cineplex challenge the conventional blank envelopes which typify these buildings and explore new ways for them to connect to an urban context. In order to produce a unique experience and a unique building, a number of cultural and historical references have been used to animate the structure and enrich the retail and leisure experience. Department stores are conventionally designed as blank enclosures to allow retailers the flexibility to rearrange their interior layouts. However, the concept for the John Lewis store is a net curtain that provides privacy to the interior without blocking natural light.

The design provides the flexible layout required without dissociating the interior from the urban experience. The cladding is designed as a double glazed facade with a net-curtain like function. This allows for a controlled transparency that brings in views of the exterior and natural light to penetrate the retail floors. The glazing pattern references Leicester's 200 year history of textile design and weaving, the vibrancy of saris worn by the large Indian community in Leicester, as well as John Lewis' own tradition of producing quality fabrics. The pattern itself is formed from four panels of differing density which allow for a variable degree of transparency. These meet seamlessly across the perimeter, producing a textile-like cladding. Viewed from the retail floors, the double facade layers align to allow views out, whilst an oblique view from street level displaces the two patterns and creates a moiré effect, reducing visibility and increasing visual complexity.

1 A fritted mirror pattern has been applied to both layers of the glass curtain wall. The mirrored pattern reflects its surroundings and in doing so becomes further integrated into its context.
2 In order to establish a consistent identity between the department store (left) and the cinema (right) the curtain concept is extended. The curtain wall to the cinema is designed as an opaque stainless steel rainscreen.
3 Two new footbridges form part of a pedestrian route connecting the Shires shopping centre to the new John Lewis.
4 The walkway is set within the volume of the store, connecting through a covered and naturally ventilated pedestrian bridge over Vaughan Way to the multi-storey car park.

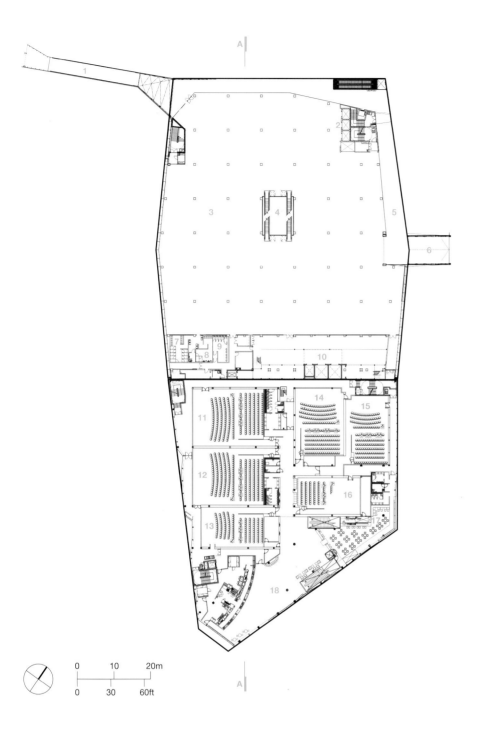

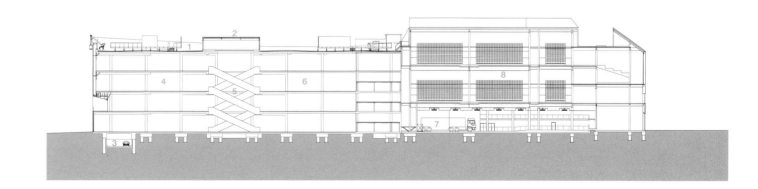

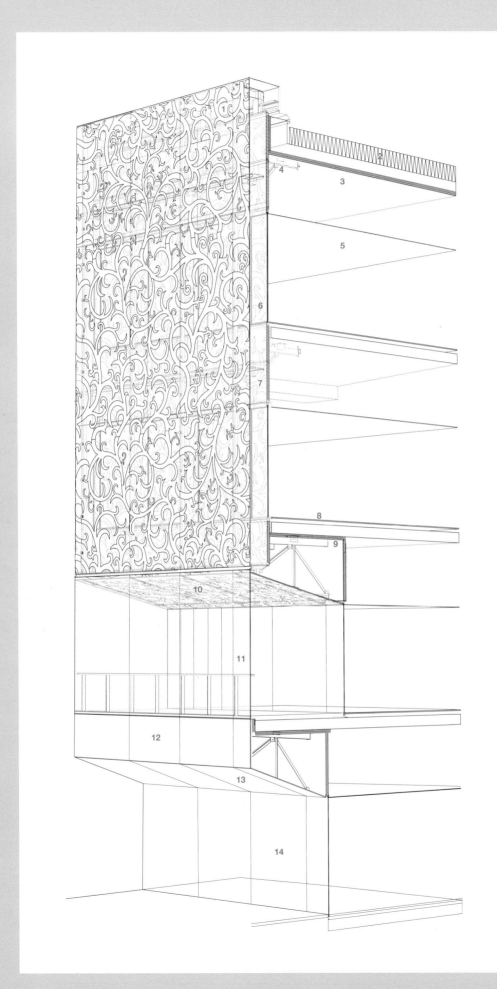

26.03
Sectional
Axonometric Through
Department Store
Exterior Glazed
Cladding
Not to Scale
1 Single glazed
cladding with mirror frit
pattern
2 Asphalt roof over
reinforced concrete
floor slab
3 Under-slab
insulation
4 Spandrel panel
support system
5 Suspended ceiling
system to retail area
6 Double glazed
cladding with ceramic
frit pattern
7 Insulated spandrel
glazing with ceramic
frit pattern
8 Laminated glass
walkway with anti-slip
frit pattern
9 Under-slab
insulation
10 Inclined glazing
with mirror frit pattern
11 Single glazed
cladding
12 Opaque spandrel
glazing
13 Stainless steel soffit
14 Single glazed
cladding

26.04
Facade Layering
System Detail 1
1:100
1 Cleaning cradle
2 Glazed parapet
capping
3 Single glazing with
mirror frit pattern
4 Color Blast 12 light
fitting at 2400 mm
(94½ inch) centres
5 Asphalt roof
6 Insulated glass
spandrel panel with
pattern
7 27 mm (1 inch)
thick laminated glass
walkway with anti-slip
fritted pattern
8 Suspended ceiling
system to retail area
9 Single glazed outer
layer of facade
cladding with fritted
mirror pattern
10 Double glazed inner
layer of facade
cladding with fritted
pattern
11 Insulated glass
spandrel panel with
pattern
12 27 mm (1 inch)
thick laminated glass
walkway with anti-slip
fritted pattern
13 Suspended ceiling
system to retail area
14 Metal channel
shadow gap
15 Double glazed inner
layer of facade
cladding with fritted
pattern
16 Single glazed outer
layer of facade
cladding with fritted
mirror pattern
17 Insulated glass
spandrel panel with
pattern
18 27 mm (1 inch)
thick laminated glass
walkway with anti-slip
fritted pattern
19 Color Blast light
fitting
20 Eye bolts to resist
horizontal and vertical
loads fixed to hanger
21 Color Blast light
fitting
22 Inclined glazing
with fritted pattern
23 Clear single glazed
cladding
24 Single glazed
cladding
25 Stone floor finish
26 Metal guard rail
with integral lighting
27 Lower portion of
glazing to slab and
ceiling zones to have
opaque spandrel panel
bonded to rear
28 Stainless steel
panels
29 Continuous lighting
strip
30 Single glazed
cladding

26.05
Facade Layering
System Detail 2
1:100
1 Single ply
membrane roof with
semi rigid insulation
cut to falls and vapour
barrier
2 Stainless steel
gutter
3 Polished stainless
steel cladding
4 Dry lining installed
to interior of cinema
facade
5 Cinema auditorium
6 Dry lining to
partition wall
7 Dry lining to
corridor face of
partition
8 Polished stainless
steel cladding
9 Eye bolt fixings at
2400 mm (94½ inch)
centres for fixing of
Christmas decorations
10 Dry lining to
corridor face of
partition
11 Polished stainless
steel shingle cladding
12 Stainless steel soffit
with vent holes
13 Continuous lighting
14 Mirror polished
stainless steel cladding
15 Retail unit
16 Floor finish over
concrete slab installed
by tenant

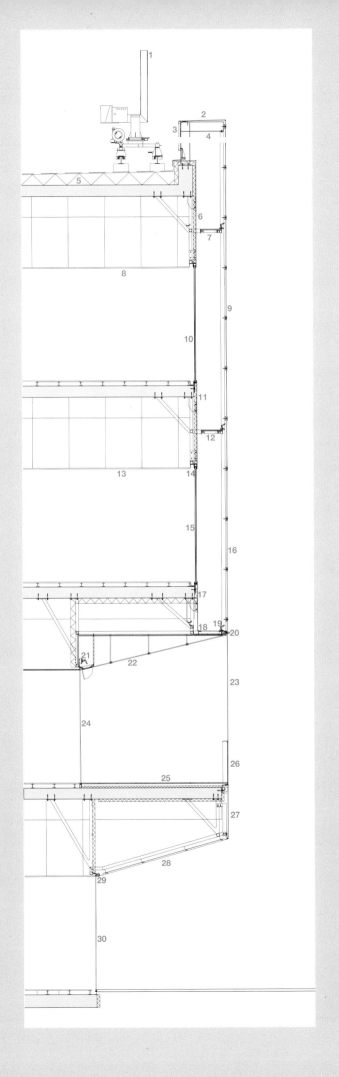

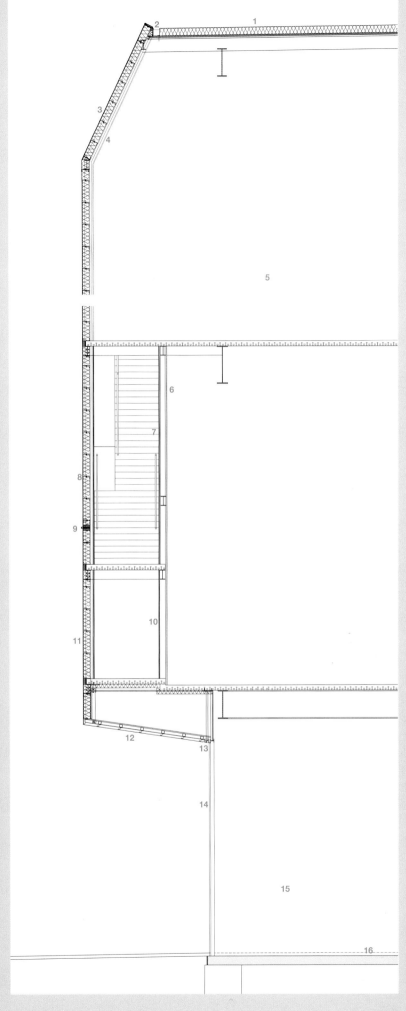

BMW Welt
Munich, Germany

Client
BMW AG

Project Team
Wolf D. Prix, Paul Kath, Tom
Wiscombe, Waltraut Hohenender,
Mona Marbach

Structural Engineer
B+G Ingenieure, Bollinger und
Grohmann

Main Contractor
Ingenieurbüro Schoenenberg

The realization of BMW Welt, a
multi-functional customer experience
and exhibition facility, led to a design
comprised of three thematic blocks
named Premiere, Forum and Double
Cone, all of which are connected by a
lightweight, sweeping bridge
structure. At the heart of BMW Welt is
vehicle delivery, which forms both the
spatial hub and the functional
backbone of the building. New
vehicles are delivered to their own
loading yard on the lower floors and
from there are transported in
transparent glass elevators to the
delivery stage, dubbed Premiere. The
vehicles are handed over to
customers on rotating platforms.
Another key function of BMW Welt is
represented by the Forum, at the heart
of which is an auditorium for 800
people. Equipped with a variable
topography of hydraulic platforms, it
can be used for a variety of events,
from conferences to theatre
productions. On the lower floors, the
Forum includes a truck loading dock,
catering kitchens, artists' dressing
rooms and interpreter booths as well
as storage and service spaces.
   The Tower, like the Forum, offers
both interior rooms with sight lines out
into the Hall and toward the
Olympiapark as well as indoor and
outdoor terraces. The four-storey
underground base of BMW Welt
contains two parking levels for 600
cars. Overall the underground service
areas cover 48,000 square metres
(516,670 square feet), double the floor
area of the above-ground levels. The
Double Cone is a full-service event
realm extending over several levels,
including infrastructure for events
such as concerts and exhibitions. All
of these structures take the form of
walk-through sculptures in an urban
landscape that is overarched by the
virtually free-floating roof that
originates out of the Double Cone.

1 View of BMW Welt
illustrating the Double
Cone (foreground),
Premiere with its
glazed facade and the
Tower in the
background. The
connecting bridge

extends out over
Lerchenauerstrasse to
the BMW areas on the
opposite side of the
street including the
administration
headquarters and
museum.

2 The facade was
conceived as a
modified post-and-
beam system leaning
ten degrees out of the
vertical. The glazing is
clamped directly to the
beams and glued in

the butt joints. It is
slogged as closely to
the edge as possible in
order to minimize
bending loads from the
beams.
3 The Double Cone
takes the form of two

leaning truncated
cones with a rounded
transition between
them. It is conceived
as a framework shell
made of horizontal
rings and two
ascending diagonal

bands.
4 View of the Premiere
new vehicle handover
space.

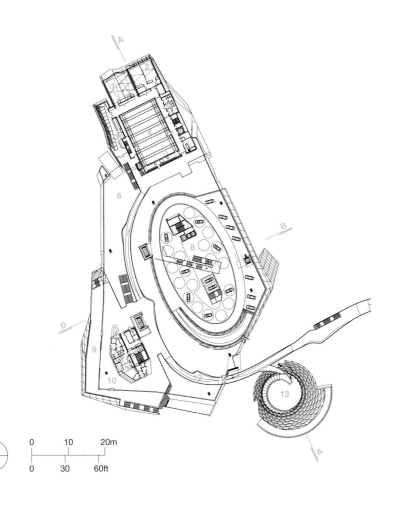

27.01
Second Floor Plan
1:1000
1 Forum Foyer business centre
2 Forum business centre
3 Forum Foyer business centre
4 Auditorium
5 WCs
6 Ground floor car showroom below
7 Connecting bridge
8 Premiere new car handover area
9 Restaurant terrace
10 Restaurant
11 Restaurant back of house facilities
12 Connecting bridge
13 Double Cone void

27.02
Section A–A
1:500
1 Double Cone
2 Connecting bridge
3 Underground car park
4 Premier car delivery service
5 VIP lounge
6 Glass lift for Premier car delivery service
7 Loading yard
8 Lift
9 Ceiling to curved roof
10 Forum motorbike showroom
11 Exterior terrace to Forum
12 Forum business centre
13 Auditorium
14 Technical space for hydraulics platforms
15 Technical rooms
16 Access ramp for car loading trucks

27.03
Section B–B
1:500
1 Connecting bridge to BMW Museum
2 Double Cone roof structure
3 Double Cone main entrance
4 Loading yard car storage
5 Main entrance to BMW Welt
6 Connecting bridge
7 Top light to restaurant
8 Premier car preparation area
9 Premier car delivery
10 Restaurant
11 Offices
12 Loading yard

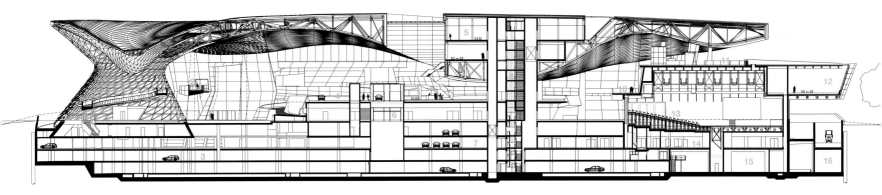

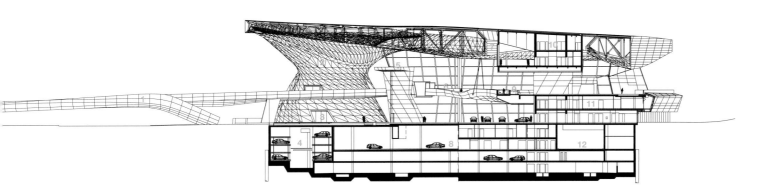

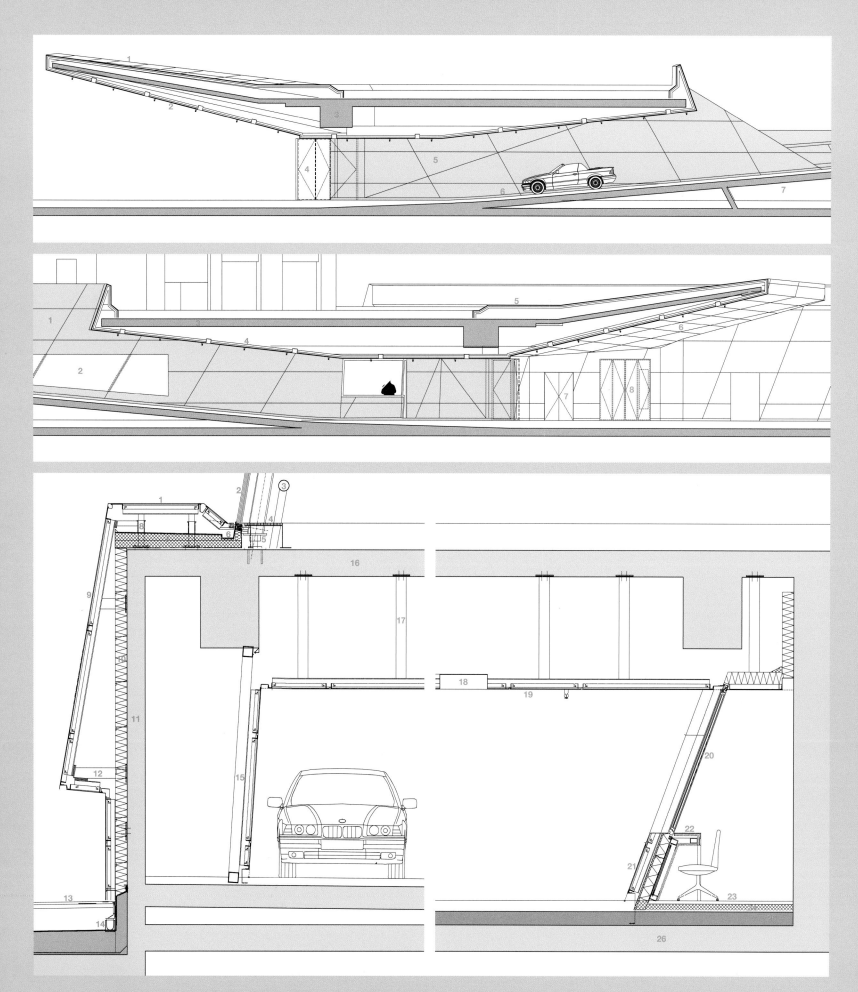

27.04
Premiere Area Exit Ramp Section Detail 1:200
1 Stainless steel cladding and waterproofing to cantilevered canopy
2 Stainless steel cladding with integrated sprinklers and lighting
3 Transom beam
4 Rapid action door
5 Stainless steel cladding to ramp walls
6 Cement screed floor to ramp
7 Technical spaces

27.05
Premiere Area Ramp Section Detail 1:200
1 Stainless steel cladding to ramp walls
2 Window to porter's room
3 Cement screed floor to Premier area above
4 Stainless steel cladding to ramp ceiling
5 Stainless steel cladding and waterproofing of cantilevered canopy
6 Stainless steel cladding with integrated sprinklers and lighting to cantilevered canopy
7 Staff entrance
8 VIP car delivery exit

27.06
Premiere Glazed Wall Section Detail 1:50
1 Stainless steel cladding
2 Double glazing comprised of 10 mm (3/8 inch) glass, 16 mm (5/8 inch) air gap and two layers of 8 mm (1/3 inch) heat strengthened glass
3 Protective bumper with integrated lighting
4 Steel grid covering convector heater
5 Convection heater
6 Water drainage
7 Waterproofing and thermal insulation
8 Substructure
9 Stainless steel cladding
10 Thermal insulation
11 Cast in-situ cast concrete
12 Substructure
13 Exterior concrete paving slabs
14 Slot channel for facade water drainage
15 Stainless steel cladding to interior
16 Concrete roof slab
17 Suspended ceiling system
18 Lighting fixtures
19 Stainless steel suspended ceiling
20 Window to porter's room
21 Interior facade comprised of stainless steel cladding, substructure, thermal insulation and gypsum board cladding on substructure
22 Porter's desk
23 Timber floor
24 Thermal insulation
25 Cement floor screed
26 Reinforced

concrete floor slab

27.07
Lounge Wall Section Detail 1:20
1 Stainless steel cladding to roof
2 Waterproofing foil
3 Rockwool thermal insulation
4 Moisture barrier
5 Stainless steel to roof
6 Waterproofing foil
7 Substructure to attic
8 3 mm (1/10 inch) stainless steel L-profile
9 Liner tray wall system with Rockwool insulation
10 Facade substructure
11 Stainless steel cladding
12 Concrete slab
13 Metal deck to roof structure
14 Fire protection
15 Primary structure I-beam
16 Stainless steel capping to corner
17 Bent edge stainless steel U-profile as shadow gap to glass facade
18 Sun screen roller blind
19 Black anodized aluminium pressure cap
20 Exterior glazing
21 Timber floor
22 Stainless steel linear grille
23 Convector heater
24 Concrete slab on metal deck
25 Fire protection
26 Primary structure I-beam

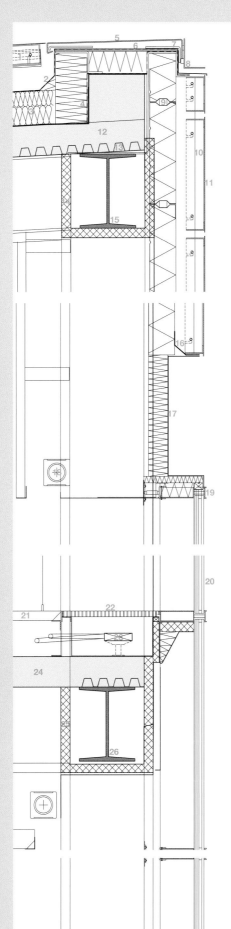

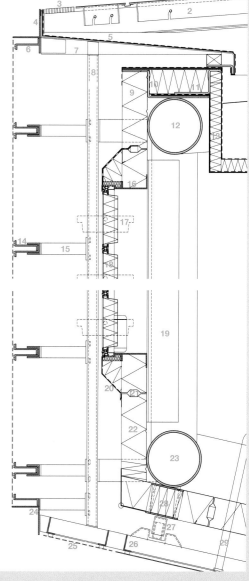

27.08
Roof Structure Detail 1:20
1 Stainless steel roof cladding
2 Stiffener for roof cladding
3 Drainage grid
4 3 mm (1/10 inch) stainless steel L-profile
5 Waterproofing foil
6 Aluminium bearings for perforated steel facade cladding
7 Substructure to roof construction
8 200 x 80 mm (73/4 x 31/8 inch) rectangular hollow section cladding substructure
9 Linear tray wall system with rock wool insulation
10 Substructure for roof construction and emergency overflow of roof drainage
11 Substructure for roof construction and emergency overflow of roof drainage
12 300 mm (114/5 inch) circular hollow section steel truss upper chord
13 Drainage gutter
14 Aluminium bearings for perforated steel facade cladding
15 90 x 90 mm (31/2 x 31/2 inch) rectangular hollow section as substructure to facade
16 Steel U-profile as bottom coverage of liner tray wall system
17 Aluminium ventilation lamella in open position
18 Aluminium ventilation lamella in closed position
19 300 mm (114/5 inch) circular hollow section steel truss
20 Connection to lamella system
21 Wind barrier in liner tray system wall
22 Liner tray wall system with Rockwool insulation
23 300 mm (114/5 inch) circular hollow section steel truss bottom chord
24 3 mm (1/10 inch) stainless steel L-profile
25 3 mm (1/10 inch) perforated stainless steel ceiling cladding
26 Substructure to perforated stainless
steel ceiling panels
27 Suspended ceiling system
28 Insulation
29 Sprinkler system

**Citroën Flagship Showroom
Paris, France**

Client
Citroën

Project Team
Manuelle Gautrand, Anne Feldman

Structural Engineer
Khephren

Mechanical Engineer
ALTO

The new Citroën showroom on the Champs Elysées in Paris features a dramatic glass facade that incorporates the iconic Citroën chevron motif built into the design. The higher up the building one looks, the more three-dimensional the facade becomes with the introduction of prisms that bring new depths to the design. Finally, the top section of the building resembles a great glass sculpture, recalling origami in its complexity. The brand's signature colour red was originally proposed for the entire facade but this was considered to be too bold given the historic context of the Champs Elysées. Instead, a filter that on first sight masks the red colour from the exterior, is cleverly constructed inside the finished glass. The filter also minimizes heat gain and creates a diaphanous pearly white atmosphere inside the building.

The main function of the building is as a car showroom and the shape of the building itself is inspired by the shape of a car. As such, the building does not appear as an object with a front, a roof and a rear, but something that has been sculpted with curves and fluidity, creating unity between the place and the product. The interior features eight circular platforms each of which is a car display area. The six metre (19.5 feet) diameter platforms revolve to display the cars in the round and have mirrored bases to reflect the car below. Visitors are led by a series of staircases and walkways that spiral past the cars, more in the manner of a museum or a cultural building, a space which encourages people to spend time enjoying both the cars and exceptional views of Paris.

1 By day, the specially filtered glass lends the sculptural facade a dignity that respects its neighbours on the Champs Elysées.
2 At night, the iconic red Citroën chevron logo is apparent as the interior lighting overrides the effects of the filters.
3 Bridges and ramps that travel the height of the building afford breathtaking views across the city.
4 Eight revolving platforms with mirrored bases display the cars to great dramatic effect.

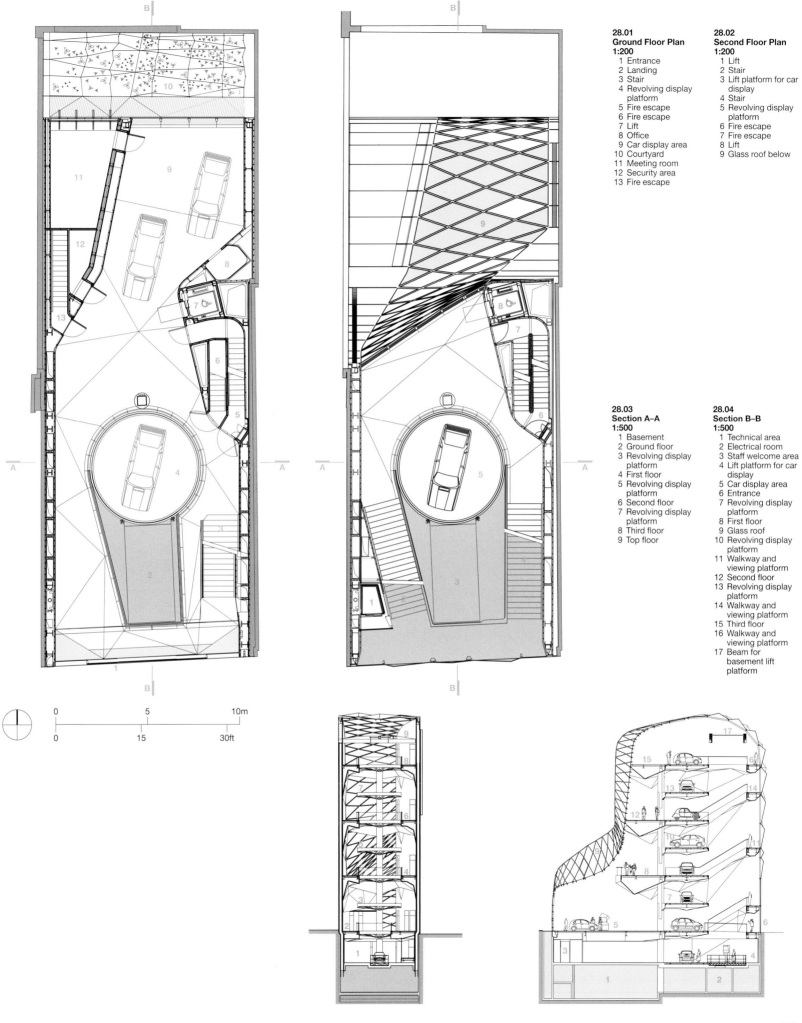

28.01
Ground Floor Plan
1:200
1 Entrance
2 Landing
3 Stair
4 Revolving display
platform
5 Fire escape
6 Fire escape
7 Lift
8 Office
9 Car display area
10 Courtyard
11 Meeting room
12 Security area
13 Fire escape

28.02
Second Floor Plan
1:200
1 Lift
2 Stair
3 Lift platform for car
display
4 Stair
5 Revolving display
platform
6 Fire escape
7 Fire escape
8 Lift
9 Glass roof below

28.03
Section A–A
1:500
1 Basement
2 Ground floor
3 Revolving display
platform
4 First floor
5 Revolving display
platform
6 Second floor
7 Revolving display
platform
8 Third floor
9 Top floor

28.04
Section B–B
1:500
1 Technical area
2 Electrical room
3 Staff welcome area
4 Lift platform for car
display
5 Car display area
6 Entrance
7 Revolving display
platform
8 First floor
9 Glass roof
10 Revolving display
platform
11 Walkway and
viewing platform
12 Second floor
13 Revolving display
platform
14 Walkway and
viewing platform
15 Third floor
16 Walkway and
viewing platform
17 Beam for
basement lift
platform

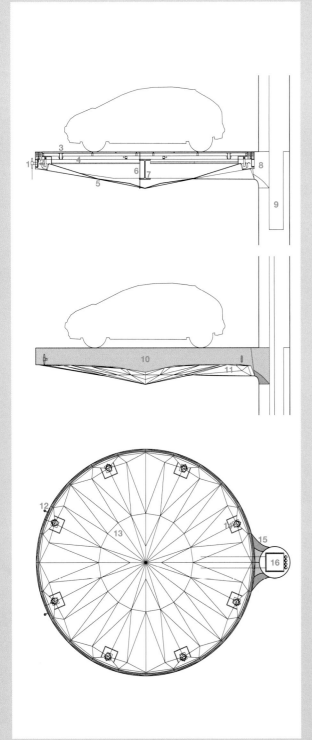

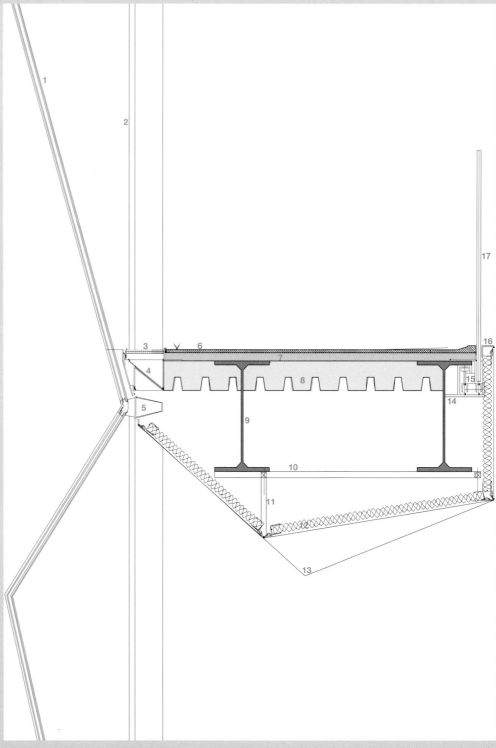

28.05
Revolving Display Platform Section, Elevation and Plan Detail
1:100
1 Guide for lift platform
2 Fixing rail
3 Resin mortar flooring
4 Aluminium structure flooring
5 Inox mirror base
6 Aluminium structure
7 Steel beam
8 Resin beam
9 Steel pole
10 Resin floor
11 Inox mirror base
12 Guide for basement

lift platform
13 Inox mirror base
14 Spotlight
15 Steel support frame
16 Beam pole junction

28.06
Detail Section Through Facade and Mezzanine Walkway
1:20
1 Continuous glazed facade
2 Mortar structure
3 Stainless steel grille to floor edge
4 Ceiling edge panel
5 Steel frame supporting glazed facade
6 Resin floor
7 Upper part of aluminium and plastic floor profile system
8 Lower part of aluminium and plastic floor profile system

9 Steel beam structure
10 Aluminium structure
11 Aluminium structure
12 Acoustic insulation board
13 Aluminium structure
14 Steel beam structure
15 System of bearing and guides for maintenance
16 Aluminium and plastic floor profile system
17 Laminated glass balustrade

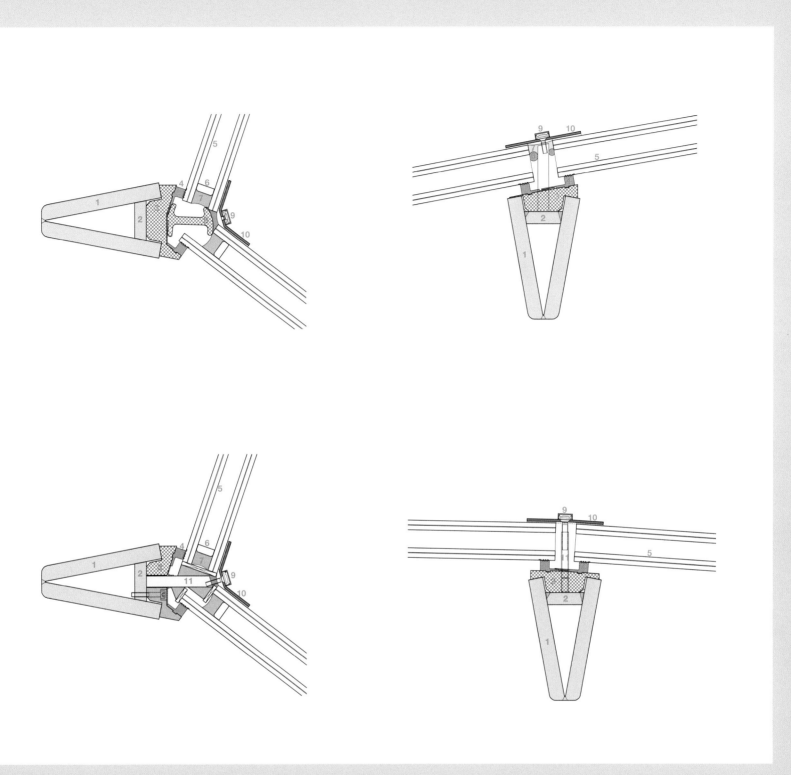

28.07
Typical Glazing
Junction Details
1:5
  1 Door sill profile
  2 Sill profile element
  3 Grooved aluminium
section
  4 Silicone joint
  5 Double glazing
  6 Glazing profile
  7 Silicone joint
  8 Cover strip
  9 Glazing profile
10 Glazing profile
cover panel
11 Rubber seal

185 Post Street
San Francisco, California, USA

Client
185 Post Street

Project Team
Koonshing Wong, Maryam A. Belli

Structural Engineer
Murphy Burr Curry

Main Contractor
Plant Construction

185 Post Street is located at the southeast corner of Post Street and Grant Avenue within the Kearny-Market-Mason-Sutter Conservation District. The client had purchased the building with the intention of creating a modern and distinctive commercial facility. The project is comprised of a shell and core modernization of an existing six-storey retail and office building. The original structure is an unreinforced masonry building from 1908 which had been completely re-clad during numerous alterations beginning in 1951. This current modernization by Brand + Allen preserves the original masonry shell from 1908 while stripping away the later additions, as well as replacing the metal panel facades, the cast iron columns and wood joist flooring systems. Also included in the renovation are new centralized mechanical systems, vertical circulation systems and a complete seismic retrofit of the building to meet current standards.

The metal panel facade from 1951 has been replaced with a translucent glass curtain wall enclosure. The new glass curtain wall is constructed with a 228 millimetre (9 inch) void between it and the original masonry structure to allow for an intermediate air space to mitigate the temperature differential between the interior and exterior. This glass facade and intermediate air space is internally illuminated. The existing masonry walls and window openings are visible through the transparent and silk-screened glass panels. The new double wall shell and new core enable the building to meet the most current design criteria in energy efficiency requirements for building systems, and in building environments in terms of natural light, and thermal and acoustic insulation.

1 The existing historic building is shrouded in a diaphanous glass screen which allows the texture and history of the existing structure to be an integral part of the new aesthetic.
2 The glass curtain wall serves as a foil between the new and historic and is enriched by the existing structure beneath.
3 The unique and dynamic quality of the facade allows the glass skin to reflect the richly detailed historic buildings nearby without completely obscuring the existing building beneath. A robust lighting scheme brings the building to life at night.

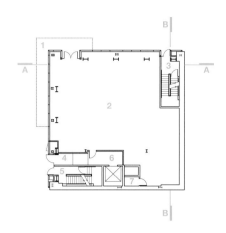

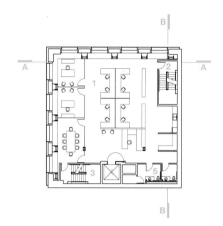

29.01
Ground Floor Plan
1:500
1 Line of roof
2 Retail space
3 Escape stair
4 Mechanical
  plenum
5 Escape stair
6 Lift lobby
7 Store

29.02
First Floor Plan
1:500
1 Office space
2 Escape stair
3 Escape stair
4 Lift
5 Bathrooms

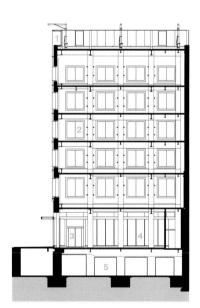

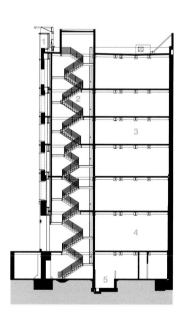

29.03
Section A–A
1:500
1 Roof parapet
2 Office space
3 Entrance
4 Retail space
5 Basement

29.04
Section B–B
1:500
1 Roof parapet
2 Escape stair
3 Office space
4 Retail space
5 Basement delivery
  dock

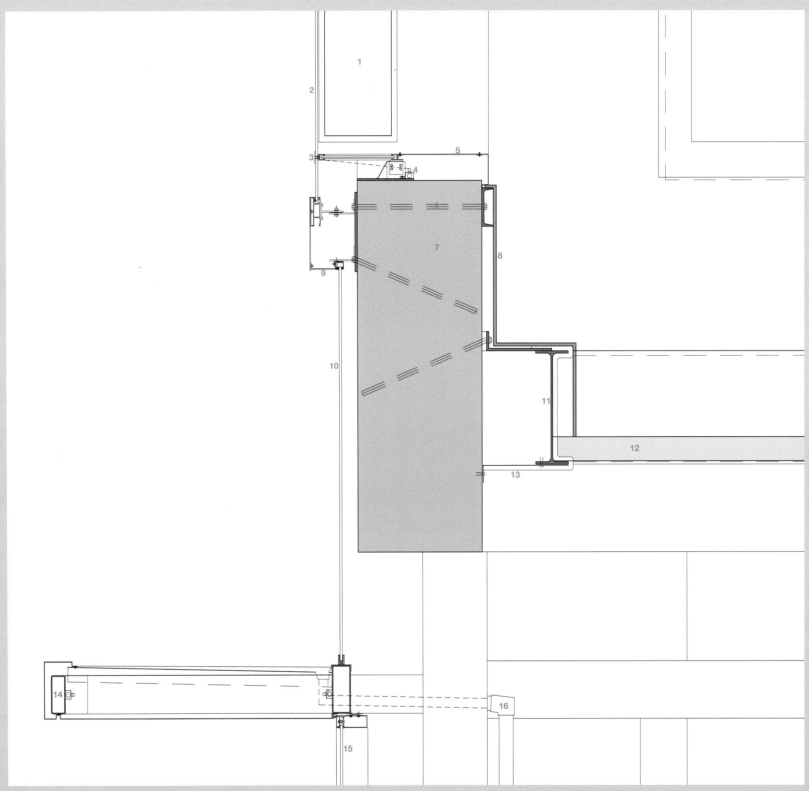

29.05
Facade Section
Detail 1
1:20
1 25 mm (1/2 inch)
frosted glass window
liner, backlit top and
bottom
2 25 mm (1/2 inch)
clear glass curtain wall
facade
3 Painted curtain wall
intermediate support
4 Continuous
horizontal mullion
fluorescent light

5 Diffuser panel
enclosure
6 Drilled and epoxied
anchor bolt
7 Original painted
brick facade
8 5 mm (3/16 inch)
aluminium floor closure
plate
9 Continuous air vent
10 25 mm (1/2 inch)
clear glass curtain wall
facade
11 Structural I-beam
support
12 Concrete floor

decking
13 Aluminium ceiling
fascia plate
14 Perforated stainless
steel canopy with
continuous lighting to
front and back edge
15 Aluminium store
front system
16 Canopy drainage
pipe

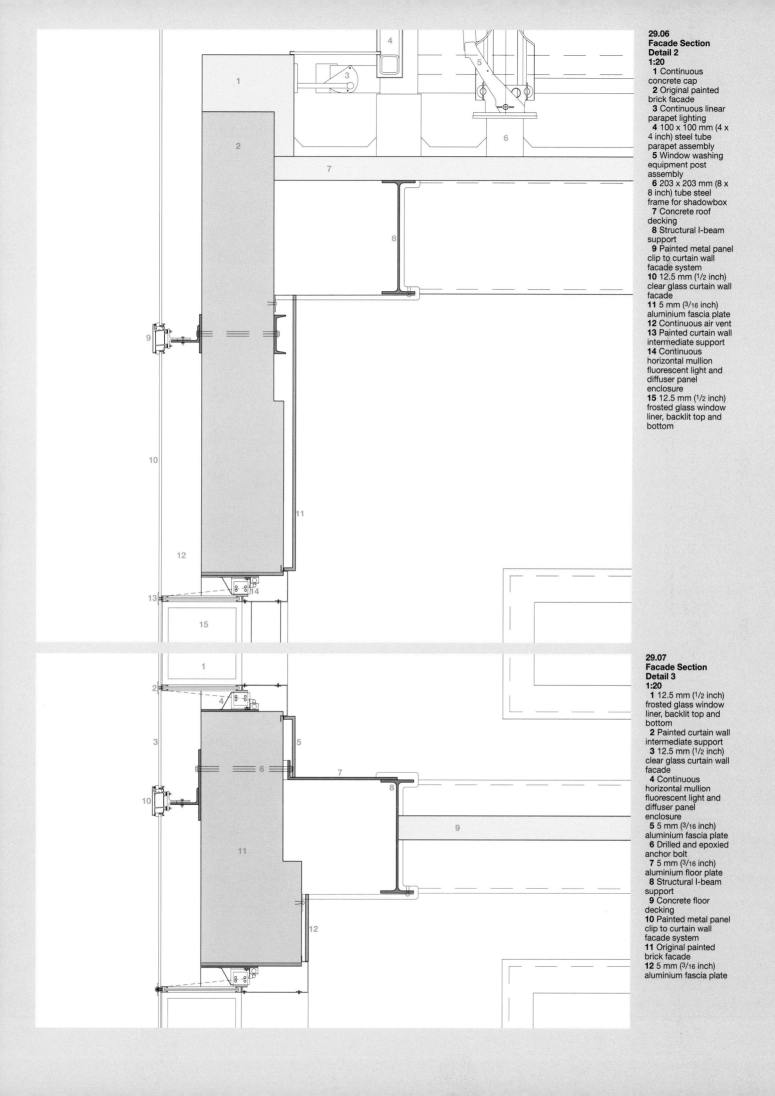

29.06
Facade Section
Detail 2
1:20
  1 Continuous
concrete cap
  2 Original painted
brick facade
  3 Continuous linear
parapet lighting
  4 100 x 100 mm (4 x
4 inch) steel tube
parapet assembly
  5 Window washing
equipment post
assembly
  6 203 x 203 mm (8 x
8 inch) tube steel
frame for shadowbox
  7 Concrete roof
decking
  8 Structural I-beam
support
  9 Painted metal panel
clip to curtain wall
facade system
  10 12.5 mm (^{1}/2 inch)
clear glass curtain wall
facade
  11 5 mm (^{3}/16 inch)
aluminium fascia plate
  12 Continuous air vent
  13 Painted curtain wall
intermediate support
  14 Continuous
horizontal mullion
fluorescent light and
diffuser panel
enclosure
  15 12.5 mm (^{1}/2 inch)
frosted glass window
liner, backlit top and
bottom

29.07
Facade Section
Detail 3
1:20
  1 12.5 mm (^{1}/2 inch)
frosted glass window
liner, backlit top and
bottom
  2 Painted curtain wall
intermediate support
  3 12.5 mm (^{1}/2 inch)
clear glass curtain wall
facade
  4 Continuous
horizontal mullion
fluorescent light and
diffuser panel
enclosure
  5 5 mm (^{3}/16 inch)
aluminium fascia plate
  6 Drilled and epoxied
anchor bolt
  7 5 mm (^{3}/16 inch)
aluminium floor plate
  8 Structural I-beam
support
  9 Concrete floor
decking
  10 Painted metal panel
clip to curtain wall
facade system
  11 Original painted
brick facade
  12 5 mm (^{3}/16 inch)
aluminium fascia plate

Galleria Department Store
Seoul, South Korea

Client
Hanwha Stores

Project Team
Ben van Berkel and Caroline Bos with
Astrid Piber, Ger Gijzen, Cristina Bolis,
Markus Hudert, Colette Parras, Arjan
van der Bliek, Christian Veddeler,
Albert Gnodde, Richard Crofts, Barry
Munster, Mafalda Bothelo, Elke Uitz,
Harm Wassink

Structural Engineer
Arup

Main Contractor
Dongshin Glass

The Galleria Department Store,
together with the Galleria Masterpiece
Hall nearby, carries a large number of
highly prestigious fashion brands and
is located prominently in the
Apgujeong-dong district in one of the
most popular commercial districts in
Seoul. However, from the outside the
store originally appeared
unremarkable. The Galleria hired
UNStudio to design a new facade
which involved the application of
4,330 glass discs on a metal
substructure attached directly to the
existing facade. The glass discs
generate a lively surface that looks
different from every viewpoint and at
different times of the day and year.

The glass discs are made of
sandblasted laminated glass treated
with a special iridescent foil which
causes constant changes in the
perception of the facade. A special
lighting scheme, designed
cooperatively by UN Studio and Arup
Lighting, has an LED-light source
behind each of the glass discs which
are controlled individually to
manipulate colour and light, and are
programmable to create a multitude of
effects. The interior renovation
focused on the general areas in
between the individual branded
shops. The circulation spaces were
streamlined, providing 'catwalks' of
light-coloured, glossy coordinated
walkways and ceilings, which improve
orientation and give the store a
super-bright, fresh image.

1 The glass facade
has the potential to be
adapted for special
occasions and can be
changed according to
the seasons, fashion
events or artistic
expression.
2 During the day the
atmospheric and
weather changes
influence the degree of
reflection and
absorption of light and
colour on the glass
discs, so that from
different viewpoints
the appearance of
each disc and the total
surface changes
constantly.
3 The main circulation
corridors feature a
continuous lighting
element integrated
within the dropped
ceiling.
4 The walls enclosing
the vertical circulation
space are comprised
of a series of vertical
beams that are clad
from both sides with
glass. The inside glass
face of the escalators
is finished with a
partially transparent,
reflective foil.

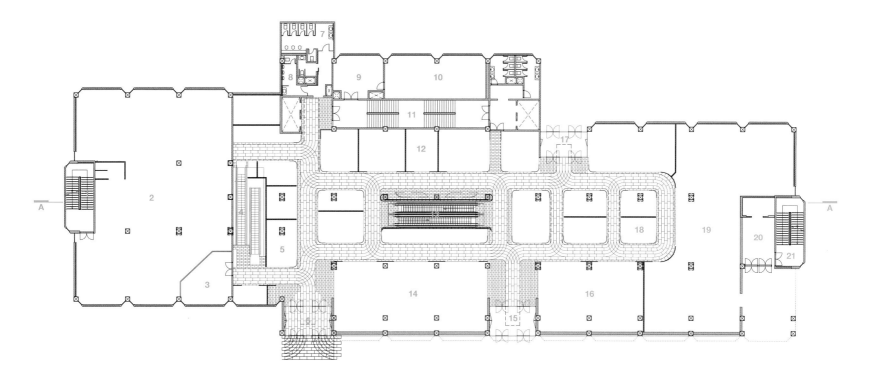

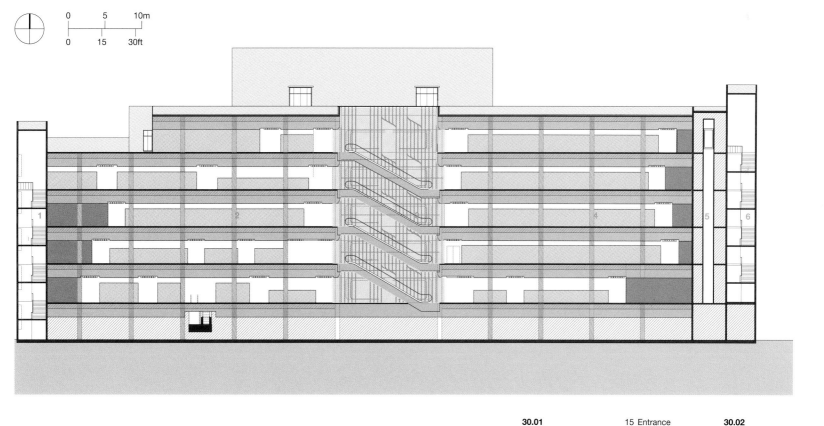

30.01
Ground Floor Plan
1:500
1 Fire stair
2 Retail unit
3 Concierge
4 Escalators
5 Retail unit
6 Entrance
7 Female WCs
8 Male WCs
9 Retail unit
10 Retail unit
11 Circulation stair
12 Retail unit
13 Escalators
14 Retail unit

15 Entrance
16 Retail unit
17 Entrance
18 Retail unit
19 Retail unit
20 Entrance
21 Fire stair

30.02
Section A–A
1:500
1 Fire stair
2 Retail units
3 Escalators
4 Retail units
5 Lift
6 Fire stair

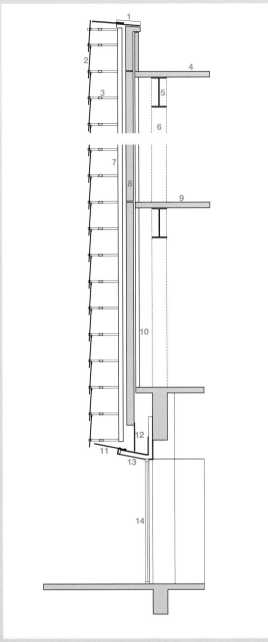

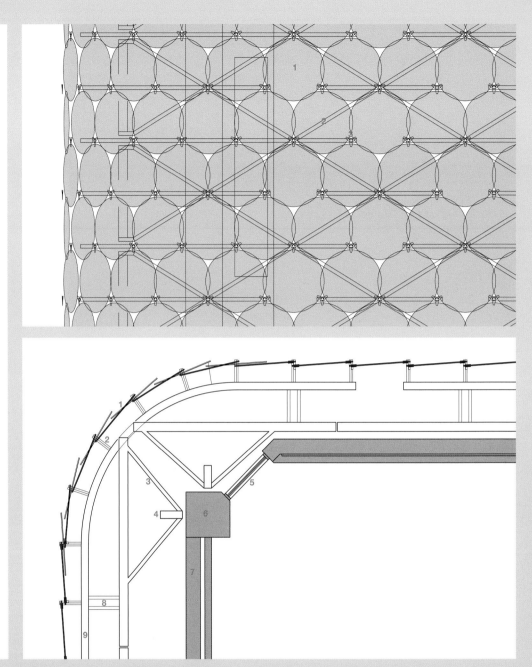

30.03
Typical Glass Disc
Facade Section
1:100
1 Toughened glass
clamped onto
galvanized steel strips
2 830 mm (32²/₃ inch)
diameter, 10 mm (³/₈
inch) thick toughened
glass disc cladding
with two layers of foil
3 Galvanized steel
spacer between glass
disc cladding and
surface of building
4 Existing reinforced
concrete roof slab
5 Existing
prefabricated steel
beam
6 Existing
prefabricated steel
column
7 Galvanized
diagonal steel
structure
8 Existing
prefabricated facade
structure
9 Existing reinforced
concrete floor slab

10 Existing
prefabricated facade
structure
11 Cantilevered double
layer toughened glass
12 Cladding with
coloured folded
aluminium plate
13 Galvanized steel
tube structure with
coloured folded
aluminium plate
14 Glazed entrance
doors

30.04
Glass Disc Facade
Corner Detail 1
1:50
1 830 mm (32²/₃ inch)
diameter, 10 mm (³/₈
inch) thick toughened
glass disc cladding
with two layers of foil
2 Galvanized
diagonal steel
structure
3 Stainless steel
clamp

30.05
Glass Disc Facade
Corner Detail 2
1:50
1 830 mm (32²/₃ inch)
diameter, 10 mm (³/₈
inch) thick toughened
glass disc cladding
with two layers of foil
2 Galvanized
diagonal steel
structure
3 Galvanized steel
spacer between glass
disc cladding and
surface of building
4 Vertical spine
structure connected to
existing structural
columns
5 Existing glazing
6 Existing column
7 Existing
prefabricated facade
elements
8 50 x 50 mm (2 x 2
inch) galvanized steel
spacer
9 Cladding structure

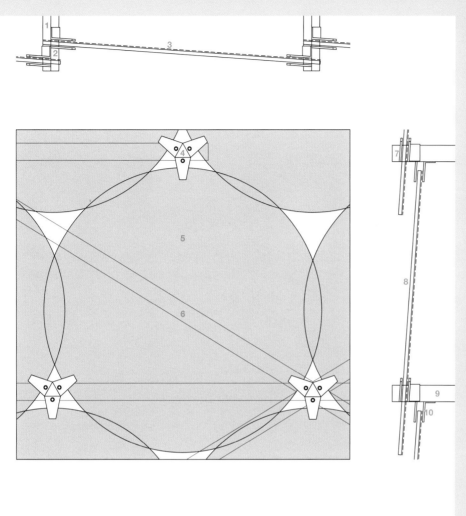

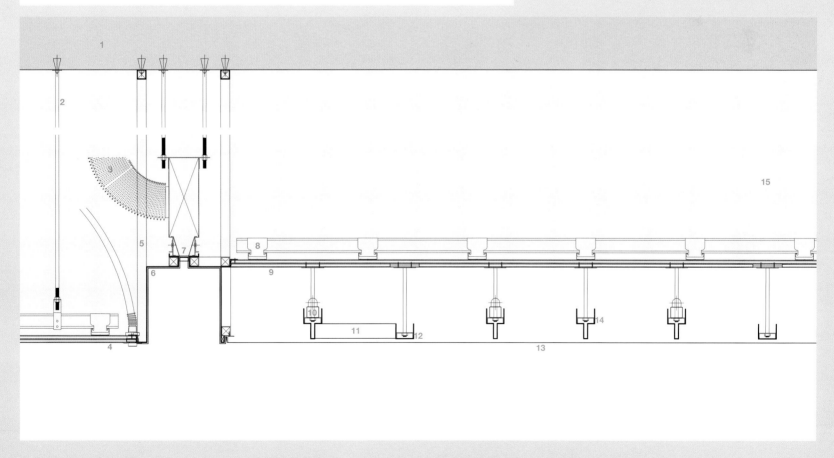

CUBE Biberwier-Lermoos Hotel
Biberwier, Austria

Client
T1 Hotelerrichtungsgesellschaft

Project Team
Christian Reischauer, Stephan
Marending, Christian Bregulla,
Matthias Dörer, Gregor Fasching,
Gerhard Müller, Michaela Rajcekova,
Kari Silloway, Veronika Hamsikova,
Martin Palzenberger, Corina Bender,
Tim P. Brendel

Structural Engineer
DI Heinz Nemec

Main Contractor
Team GMI

CUBE is an innovative hotel concept
that serves as a base for young and
young-at-heart sports enthusiasts,
combining sport, entertainment,
design and community. Of the several
CUBE destinations in Switzerland and
Austria, CUBE Biberwier is the latest
incarnation. Here, a compact,
cube-shaped structure is surrounded
by a delicate glass shell. The concept
of a club-like atmosphere and
associated facilities is reflected in the
architecture. Spacious public areas on
all levels encourage communication.
In the lobby, the centre of life at
CUBE, leather sofas and a large open
fireplace suggest a comfortable home
away from home. The interior is simple
with a functional approach that
pervades the building from top to
bottom, and is particularly manifest in
the ramp-and-walkway concept. The
ramps – also called gateways –
connect the atrium with the various
levels. The ramps enable guests to
easily transport all manner of sports
equipment, such as skis and bikes, to
their rooms. The rooms are divided
into a sleeping area and a glass-
fronted anteroom. The latter serves as
a store for sports equipment, and
comes complete with special fixtures
to hang all types of equipment as well
as shoe dryers. Special attention was
paid to the effects of light throughout
CUBE. Static elements with colourful
glass shells on the ground floor, large
coloured glass surfaces on all levels,
and translucent glass panel on the
facade help to define the mood at
CUBE. In addition to the interior
lighting, coloured beams of light are
projected onto the exterior, turning it
into an optical centre of attraction.

1 The CUBE concept
stands for
unconventional
architecture and urban
design embedded in a
dramatic alpine
landscape. All of the
CUBE hotels offer
innovative sports
programmes
encompassing new
and classic summer
and winter activities.
2 The Wellness area
on the top floor of
CUBE has access to a
wrap around terrace
with spectacular
mountain views.
3 A system of
concrete ramps
traverse the central
atrium allowing guests
to transport sports
equipment to their
rooms. Coloured glass
balustrades lend a
festive atmosphere to
the public spaces.
4 Detail view of the
glass facade which is
fixed to a system of
galvanized steel
sections, which in turn
is attached to the
concrete structural
frame.

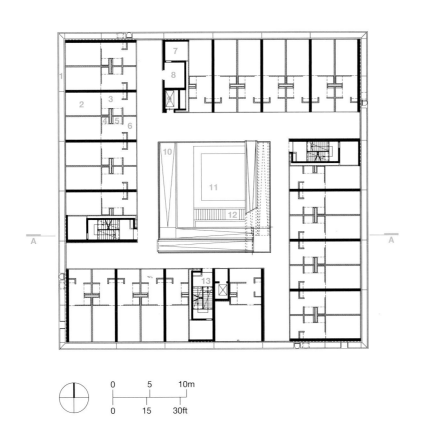

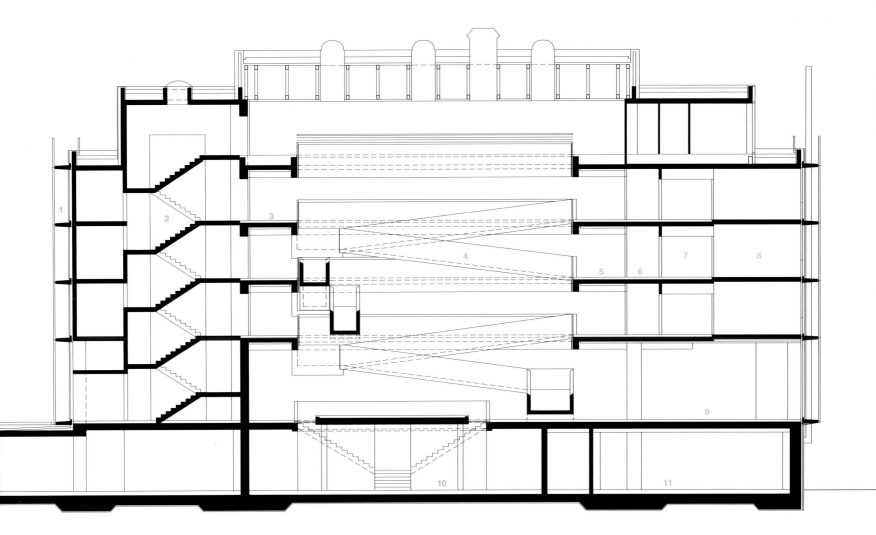

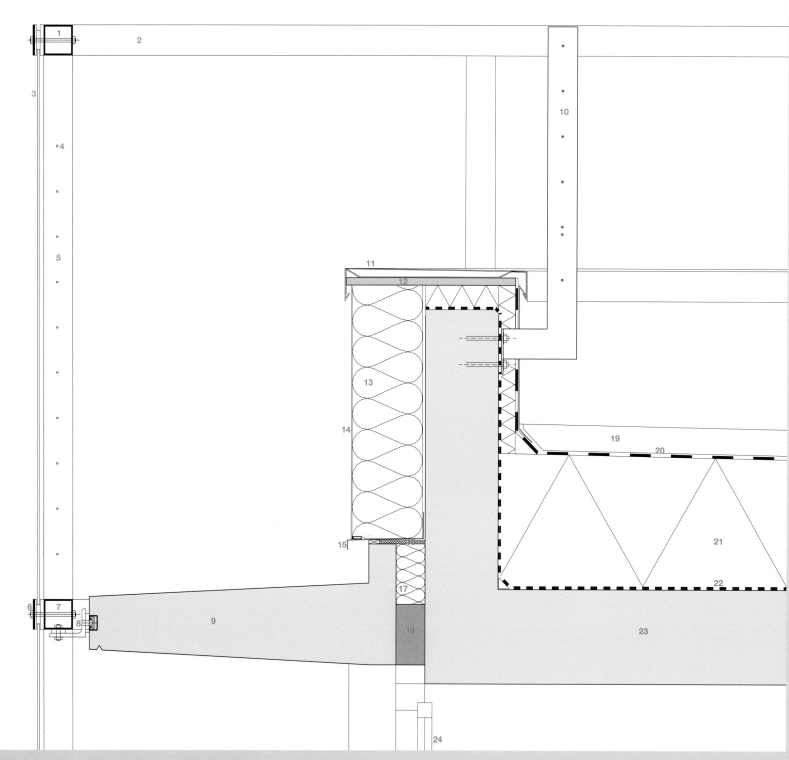

31.03
External Terrace Detail at Roof Levels 1:10

1 Galvanized steel 80 x 80 mm (3¹/₈ x 3¹/₈ inch) square hollow section handrail framing
2 Galvanized steel 80 x 80 mm (3¹/₈ x 3¹/₈ inch) square hollow section handrail framing
3 Facade glazing from translucent laminated safety glass with acid-etched satin finish

4 Steel cable balustrade between steel uprights
5 Galvanized steel 80 x 80 mm (3¹/₈ x 3¹/₈ inch) square hollow section handrail and glazing framing
6 Plastic glass stop profile with 80 x 100 x 5 mm (3¹/₈ x 4 x ¹/₅ inch) galvanized steel covering
7 Galvanized steel 80 x 80 mm (3¹/₈ x 3¹/₈ inch) square hollow section glazing framing
8 100 x 75 x 10 mm (4 x 3 x ³/₈ inch) steel

L-angle for flexible connection between steel facade framing and concrete structure
9 Precast concrete cantilevered balcony with Isokorb insulation
10 Galvanized steel 80 x 80 mm (3¹/₈ x 3¹/₈ inch) square hollow section handrail with steel cable balustrade between steel uprights
11 Formed profile capping
12 Structural plywood parapet substructure
13 External wall insulation system

14 Rendered wall finish
15 Aluminium drip profile
16 Waterproof joint tape
17 Heat insulation
18 Isokorb anchored isolation element
19 Gravel layer
20 Damp proof layer
21 Insulation
22 Vapour barrier
23 Reinforced concrete roof slab and upstand
24 Double glazed window unit

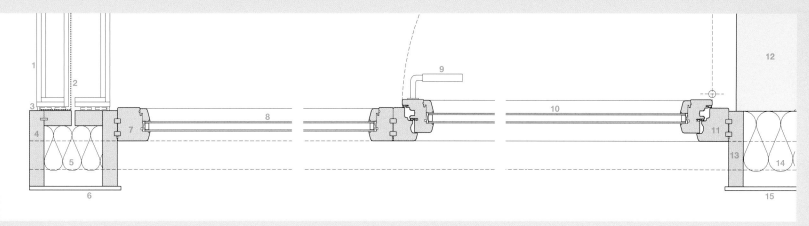

31.04
Plan Detail of Fixed and Openable Windows
1:10
1 Gypsum plasterboard wall
2 Bitumen layer
3 Acrylic joint
4 Timber counter frame
5 Insulation
6 Fibre cement panel
7 Timber window frame
8 Fixed glazed window
9 Metal handle to openable window
10 Openable glazed window
11 Timber window frame
12 Reinforced concrete wall
13 Timber counter

frame
14 Insulation
15 Fibre cement panel

31.05
Atrium Balustrade and Walkway Detail 1
1:20
1 60 x 30 mm ($2^3/_8$ x $1^1/_5$ inch) steel section
2 60 x 50 mm ($2^3/_8$ x 2 inch) steel section
3 Laminated safety

glass balustrade with screen print pattern
4 Steel section
5 Steel L-angle
6 Natural rubber flooring
7 Floor substructure
8 Reinforced concrete cantilevered floor slab to walkway
9 Bolted connection between glass balustrade and

reinforced concrete downstand
10 Reinforced concrete downstand beam
11 Concealed light fixture
12 Wood fibre insulating board
13 Steel section

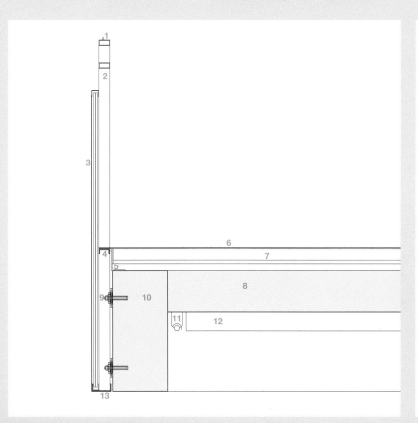

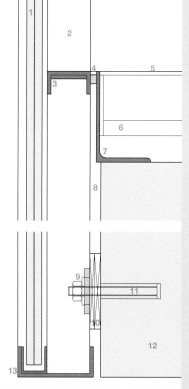

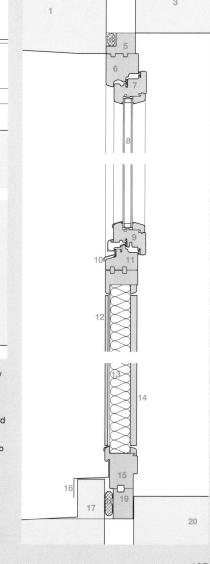

31.06
Atrium Balustrade and Walkway Detail 2
1:5
1 Laminated safety glass balustrade with screen print pattern
2 60 x 50 mm ($2^3/_8$ x 2 inch) steel section
3 Welded steel composite sections
4 Silicone joint
5 Natural rubber flooring
6 Floor substructure
7 75 x 150 mm (3 x 6 inch) steel section
8 Air gap
9 Secure nut

assembly
10 Washer
11 Resin bolt
12 Reinforced concrete downstand beam
13 Steel U-section

31.07
Openable Window and Fixed Facade Panel Detail
1:10
1 Prefabricated reinforced concrete element
2 Isokorb anchored isolation element
3 Reinforced concrete floor slab
4 Sealing cord
5 Counter frame
6 Timber window frame
7 Window casement
8 Laminated safety glass

9 Casement window
10 Weather seal to window sill
11 Timber window frame
12 Fibre cement board to exterior face
13 Insulation
14 Timber panelling to interior face
15 Window frame
16 Drip profile
17 Prefabricated concrete upstand
18 Sealing strip
19 Counter frame
20 Reinforced concrete floor slab

SOHO Shangdu
Beijing, China

Client
SOHO China

Project Team
Peter Davidson, Donald Bates, Mike Buttery, Melissa Bright, Wayne Sanderson, Matt Foley

Structural Engineer
Arup

Main Contractor
CSCEC

The SOHO Shangdu project is a mixed-use retail and office building located in Beijing's new eastern business district. The organization of the retail component was designed on the principle of reinterpreting a traditional Chinese hutong with a series of internal streets and passages which vary in their position, width and height from floor to floor, thus generating different circulation patterns which in turn create localized and specialist retail zones. Two large internal courtyards, which spiral vertically and link all floors, provide a navigational and activity focus to the retail's 'east-' and 'west-ends', facilitating a range of events from fashion parades to commercial launches and concerts.

The facetted facades of the two 32-level towers and one 8-level tower are clad in a random pattern of grey glass and aluminium panels. The dynamic qualities of the pattern readily allows the proportion of glass orientated to the south and west to be reduced, thus lowering the heat gain to units facing those directions. Inscribed within the facade is a large-scale parametric network of lines which at night lend the project its distinctive nocturnal image. The pattern chased over the facade was generated using the same principles as the traditional Chinese ice-ray pattern that provides a cultural bridge to unite various aspects of the project. Unlike the majority of adjacent mixed-use projects, which are internalized, SOHO Shangdu relates directly to the established street pattern by increasing the site coverage and creating activated street frontages to all the major and minor adjacent streets. This was achieved by limiting the main retail areas to four storeys, rather than building up to the 12 storeys the site development criteria allowed.

1 The facetted facades of SOHO Shangdu are clad in grey glass and aluminium panels.
2 Inscribed within the facets of glass that make up the facade is a super-scale geometric network of lines which at night create continuous light-lines across the length and breadth of the building.
3 The floor levels in the tower elements increase in size further up the building to increase the amount of lettable area, while maintaining the scale of the development in keeping with the existing urban patterns.
4 Two large internal courtyards spiral vertically through the building to link all floors and provide space for a range of events from fashion parades, commercial launches to concerts and talks.

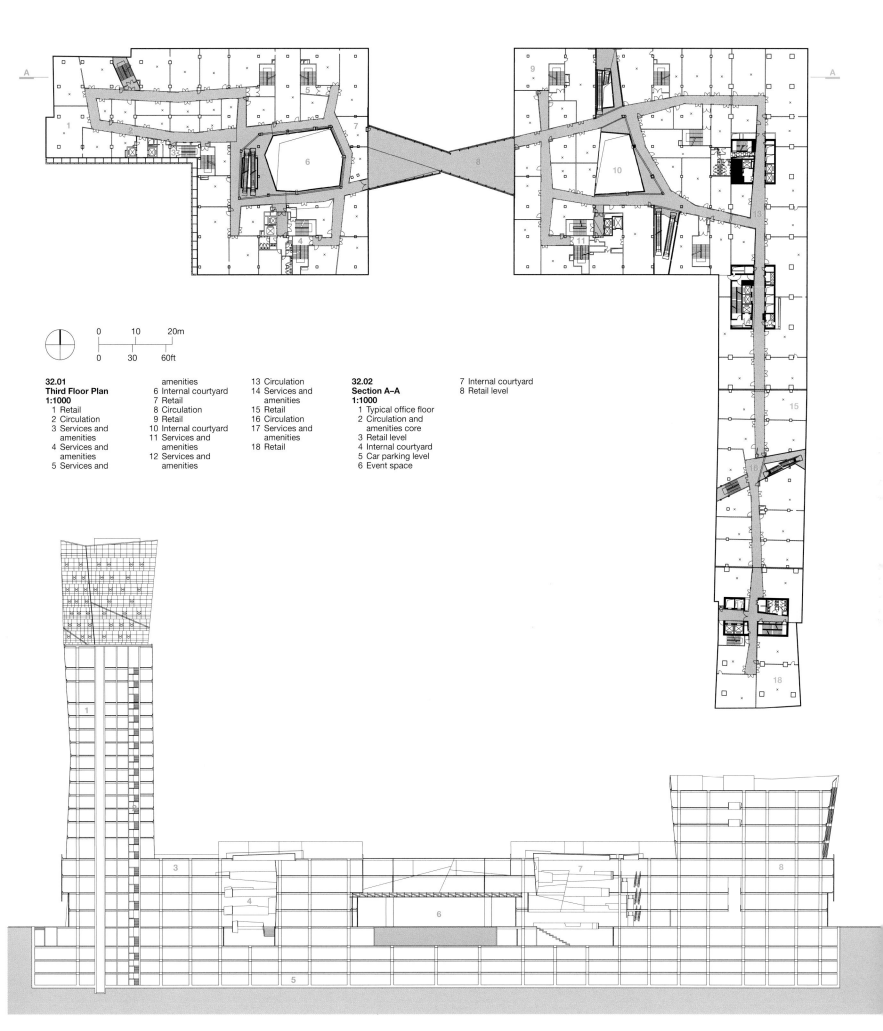

32.01
Third Floor Plan
1:1000
1 Retail
2 Circulation
3 Services and
  amenities
4 Services and
  amenities
5 Services and
  amenities
6 Internal courtyard
7 Retail
8 Circulation
9 Retail
10 Internal courtyard
11 Services and
   amenities
12 Services and
   amenities
13 Circulation
14 Services and
   amenities
15 Retail
16 Circulation
17 Services and
   amenities
18 Retail

32.02
Section A–A
1:1000
1 Typical office floor
2 Circulation and
  amenities core
3 Retail level
4 Internal courtyard
5 Car parking level
6 Event space
7 Internal courtyard
8 Retail level

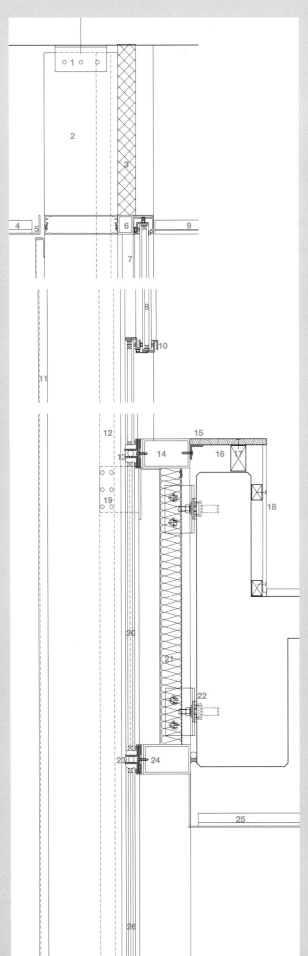

32.03
**Operable Header and
Sill to Glass Facade
Detail**
1:10
 1 Deflection of head
fixed to underside of
concrete structure
 2 Extruded aluminium
mullion
 3 Rigid thermal
insulation
 4 Soffit lining
suspended grid
system
 5 Prefinished
aluminium soffit
cladding
 6 Extruded aluminium
transom
 7 Interlocking double
glazed window system
 8 Insulated double
glazed unit
 9 Internal ceiling
lining on suspended
ceiling grid
10 Extruded aluminium
frame with weather
seals
11 External signage
panel
12 Signage panel
support mullion
13 Extruded aluminium
frame with weather
seals
14 Extruded aluminium
transom and internal
lining support
15 Internal sill lining
16 Air gap
17 Internal sill lining
support block
18 Internal wall lining
19 External signage
panel with concealed
connection bracket
20 Insulated double
glazed unit with
opaque back panel
21 Aluminium
prefinished back panel
with bonded rigid
insulation
22 Facade connection
bracket with discrete
fixings
23 Structural silicone
weather seal
24 Extruded aluminium
transom
25 Internal ceiling
lining on suspended
ceiling grid
26 Insulated double
glazed unit

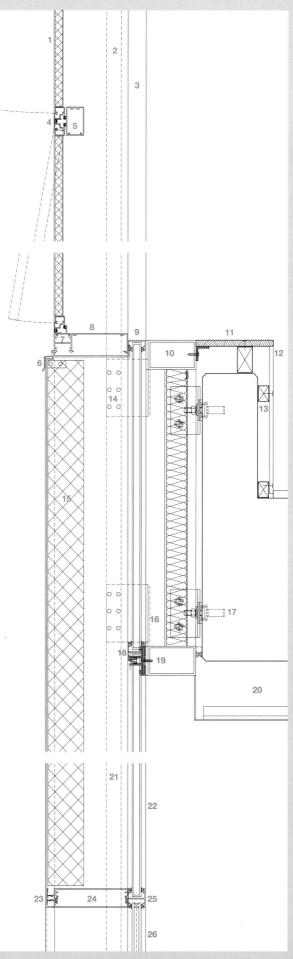

32.04
**Operable Mullion and
Sill to Aluminium
Panel Facade Detail**
1:10
 1 Aluminium cladding
panel with rigid
insulation
 2 Signage panel
support mullion
 3 Extruded aluminium
mullion beyond
 4 Extruded aluminium
transom
 5 Horizontal
aluminium transom
support channel
 6 Aluminium sill
flashing
 7 Openable panel
seal extrusion
 8 Extruded aluminium
sill
 9 Folded aluminium
sill lining support
10 Internal transom
11 Internal sill lining
12 Internal wall lining
13 Air gap
14 External signage
panel with concealed
connection
15 Rigid thermal
insulation fixed to
cladding panel
16 Facade connection
bracket with discrete
fixings
17 External signage
panel with concealed
connections
18 Glazing panel
support recesses
19 Spandrel panel
aluminium intermediate
support
20 Internal ceiling
lining on suspended
ceiling system
21 Signage panel
support mullion
22 Insulated double
glazed spandrel vision
panel
23 Signage panel
cladding sill member
24 Extruded aluminium
signage panel transom
25 Glazing panel
support recesses
26 Insulated double
glazed spandrel vision
panel

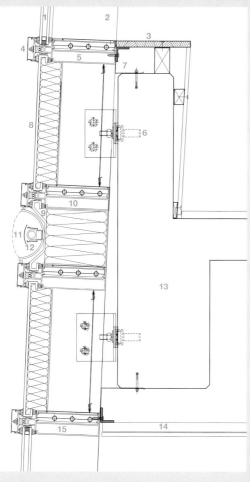

32.05
Typical Facade Section
1:10
1 Insulated double glazed unit
2 Extruded aluminium mullion beyond
3 Internal lining
4 Extruded aluminium transom cap
5 Extruded aluminium transom
6 Uni-strut facade bracket connection
7 Folded stainless steel air seal flashing
8 Aluminium composite spandrel panel
9 Folded support angle
10 Extruded aluminium transom
11 LED light
12 Light support bracket
13 Concrete structure
14 Internal ceiling lining on suspended ceiling grid
15 Extruded aluminium head member

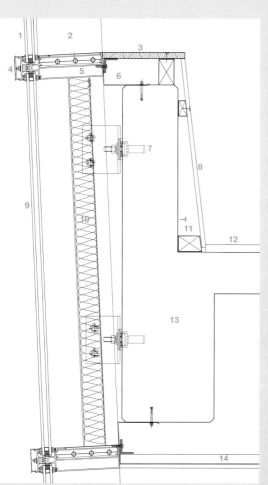

32.06
Typical Wall Section at Spandrel Panel
1:10
1 Insulated double glazed unit
2 Extruded aluminium mullion beyond
3 Internal sill lining
4 Extruded aluminium transom cap
5 Extruded aluminium transom
6 Folded stainless steel air seal flashing
7 Uni-strut facade bracket connection
8 Internal wall lining
9 Aluminium composite spandrel panel
10 Thermal insulation fixed to cladding panel
11 Internal wall lining support block
12 Internal floor finish
13 Concrete structure
14 Internal ceiling lining on suspended ceiling grid

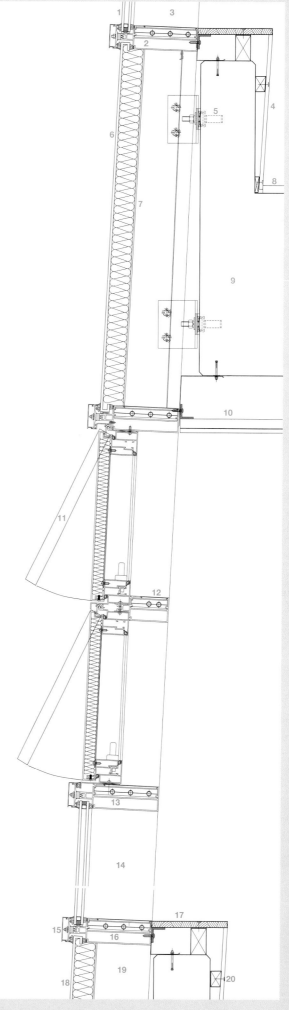

32.07
Section Detail Through Typical Glazing and Operable Shutters
1:10
1 Insulated double glazed unit
2 Extruded aluminium transom
3 Extruded aluminium mullion beyond
4 Internal wall lining
5 Uni-strut facade bracket connection
6 Aluminium composite spandrel panel
7 Thermal insulation fixed to cladding
8 Internal floor finish
9 Concrete structure
10 Internal ceiling lining on suspended support system
11 Openable opaque panel
12 Extruded aluminium transom
13 Extruded aluminium transom
14 Extruded aluminium mullion beyond
15 Extruded aluminium transom capping
16 Extruded aluminium transom
17 Internal sill lining
18 Aluminium composite spandrel panel
19 Concrete structure
20 Internal wall lining

**Natural Gas Headquarters
Barcelona, Spain**

Client
Torremarenostrum and Gas Natural

Project Team
Josep Ustrell, Elena Rocchi, Andrea
Salies Landell de Moura, Lluis
Corbella, Roberto Sforza, Montse
Galindo, Marco Dario Chirdel, Eugenio
Cirulli, Adriana Ciocoletto, Liliana
Sousa

Structural Engineer
MC2 Estudio de Ingenieria

Quantity Surveyor
M.Roig i Assoc

Services Group
PGI Grup

The Natural Gas Group's new
headquarters on the Barcelona
waterfront in the La Barceloneta
district brought the company back to
its origins. The site was the location of
Spain's first natural gas production
plant, built 160 years ago. The
building and its relationship with the
outskirts of the city make the structure
an important architectural icon in a
group of contemporary buildings that
is changing the city's skyline. The
volume is fragmented into a series of
constructions which together form a
single body that in turn responds to
the different scales of Barceloneta.
The complex includes not only the
central tower block but three
additional architectural structures – a
four-storey building shaped like a
waterfall flowing into the sea, a
building cantilevered 35 metres (115
feet) out of the centre of the tower
and, finally, a jagged shard over the
main entrance. The lower part of the
latter volume features 100 trapezoidal
panels of stratified glass of different
sizes, with high breakage resistance
and rigidity. The highly reflective mirror
glass used to clad the entire structure
allows the building to reflect the
complex urban surroundings as well
as the sky.

1 The Natural Gas
Headquarters is
situated in a traditional
neighbourhood that
features a great
diversity of existing
building stock. In such
disparate

surroundings, the
powerful architectural
image created by
EMBT succeeds in
creating a new
coherence for
Barceloneta.
2 The incorporation of

an open landscaped
space at the base of
the building provides a
much needed public
gathering space for the
area as well as defining
the entrance.
3 Each panel of glass

used in the facade
consists of an inner
layer of 8 millimetre (1/3
inch) thick tempered
glass plus a 1.52
millimetre (1/20 inch)
layer and an outer
layer of 8 millimetre

(1/3 inch) thick
tempered glass.

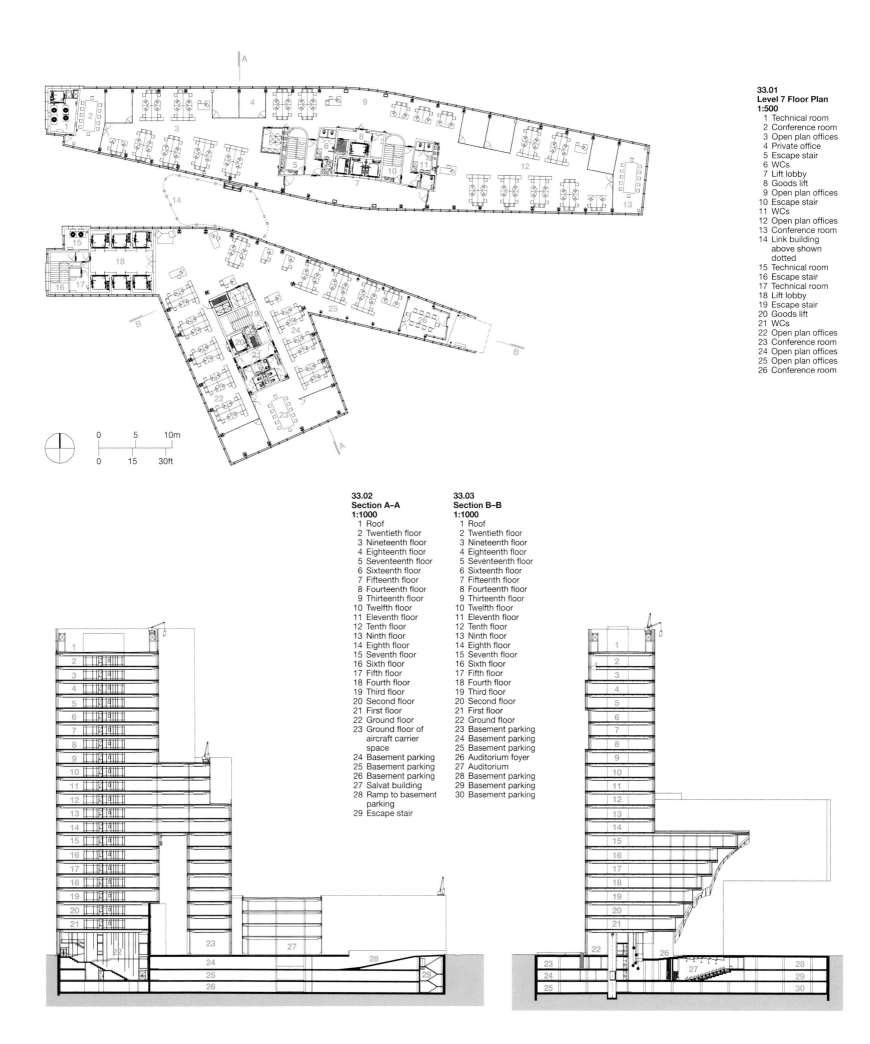

33.01
Level 7 Floor Plan
1:500
1 Technical room
2 Conference room
3 Open plan offices
4 Private office
5 Escape stair
6 WCs
7 Lift lobby
8 Goods lift
9 Open plan offices
10 Escape stair
11 WCs
12 Open plan offices
13 Conference room
14 Link building
above shown
dotted
15 Technical room
16 Escape stair
17 Technical room
18 Lift lobby
19 Escape stair
20 Goods lift
21 WCs
22 Open plan offices
23 Conference room
24 Open plan offices
25 Open plan offices
26 Conference room

33.02
Section A–A
1:1000
1 Roof
2 Twentieth floor
3 Nineteenth floor
4 Eighteenth floor
5 Seventeenth floor
6 Sixteenth floor
7 Fifteenth floor
8 Fourteenth floor
9 Thirteenth floor
10 Twelfth floor
11 Eleventh floor
12 Tenth floor
13 Ninth floor
14 Eighth floor
15 Seventh floor
16 Sixth floor
17 Fifth floor
18 Fourth floor
19 Third floor
20 Second floor
21 First floor
22 Ground floor
23 Ground floor of
aircraft carrier
space
24 Basement parking
25 Basement parking
26 Basement parking
27 Salvat building
28 Ramp to basement
parking
29 Escape stair

33.03
Section B–B
1:1000
1 Roof
2 Twentieth floor
3 Nineteenth floor
4 Eighteenth floor
5 Seventeenth floor
6 Sixteenth floor
7 Fifteenth floor
8 Fourteenth floor
9 Thirteenth floor
10 Twelfth floor
11 Eleventh floor
12 Tenth floor
13 Ninth floor
14 Eighth floor
15 Seventh floor
16 Sixth floor
17 Fifth floor
18 Fourth floor
19 Third floor
20 Second floor
21 First floor
22 Ground floor
23 Basement parking
24 Basement parking
25 Basement parking
26 Auditorium foyer
27 Auditorium
28 Basement parking
29 Basement parking
30 Basement parking

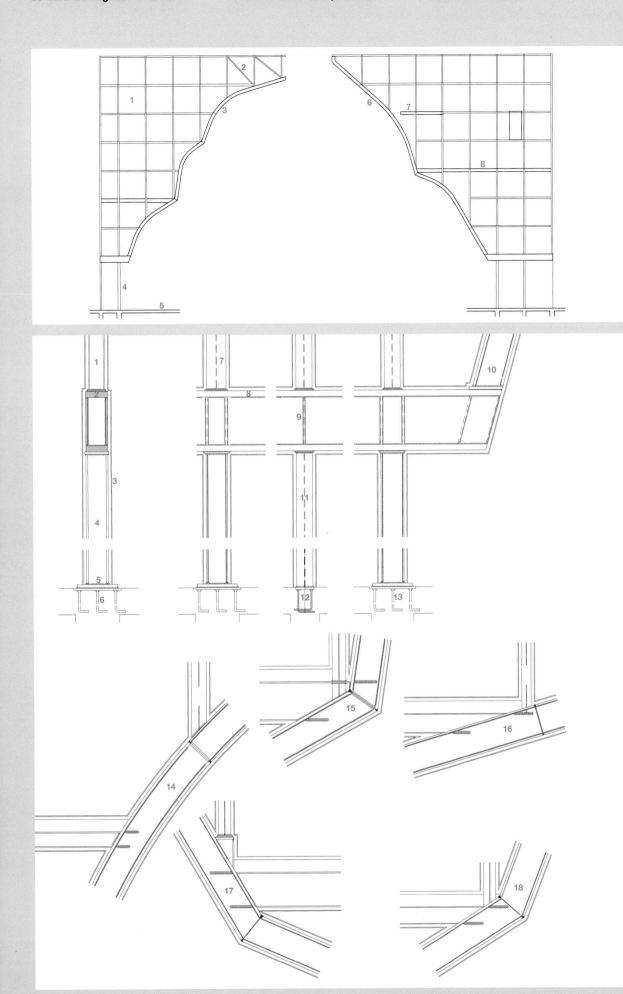

33.04
Glass Facade at Cantilever Detail
1:500
1 Vierendeel steel cantilever facade system
2 Diagonal steel tie bracing
3 Steel edge box beam
4 Reinforced column to ground floor
5 Beam to ground floor
6 Steel edge box beam
7 Cantilevered floor beam
8 Floor beam

33.05
Structural Steel to Cantilever Detail
1:50
1 Structural steel column
2 Formed steel box beam
3 Sprayed fire protection layer
4 Reinforced steel column
5 Steel base plate with bolt fixings
6 Base plate anchor system into reinforced concrete floor beam
7 Structural steel column
8 Steel floor beam
9 Steel floor beam
10 Steel box beam
11 Reinforced steel column
12 Base plate anchor system into reinforced concrete floor beam
13 Base plate anchor system into reinforced concrete floor beam
14 Curved edge box beam intersection between floor beams and column
15 Curved edge box beam intersection between floor beams and column
16 Curved edge box beam intersection between floor beams and column
17 Curved edge box beam intersection between floor beams and column
18 Curved edge box beam intersection between floor beams and column

33.06
Typical Exterior Glazed Wall Section Detail
1:20
1 Aluminium profile facade system
2 Raised floor system
3 Adjustable feet for levelling raised floor
4 Compression layer to concrete floor slab
5 Permanent metal deck formwork
6 Glass spandrel panel
7 Rigid insulation
8 Water supply pipe to sprinkler system
9 Universal steel beam with sprayed fire protection
10 Clamp fixing to glass curtain wall
11 Recessed head of roller blind
12 Suspended fixed ceiling panel
13 Aluminium rod for ceiling suspension
14 Perimeter fluorescent light fixing
15 300 x 1200 mm (11⁴/₅ x 47¹/₄ inch) metal suspended ceiling panels
16 Aluminium rod for ceiling suspension
17 Light fixtures in formed aluminium box support
18 Core wall
19 Suspended perimeter ceiling panel
20 760 x 130 x 2800 mm (30 x 5¹/₁₀ x 110¹/₄ inch) vertical steel girder
21 Metal plate over steel box beam

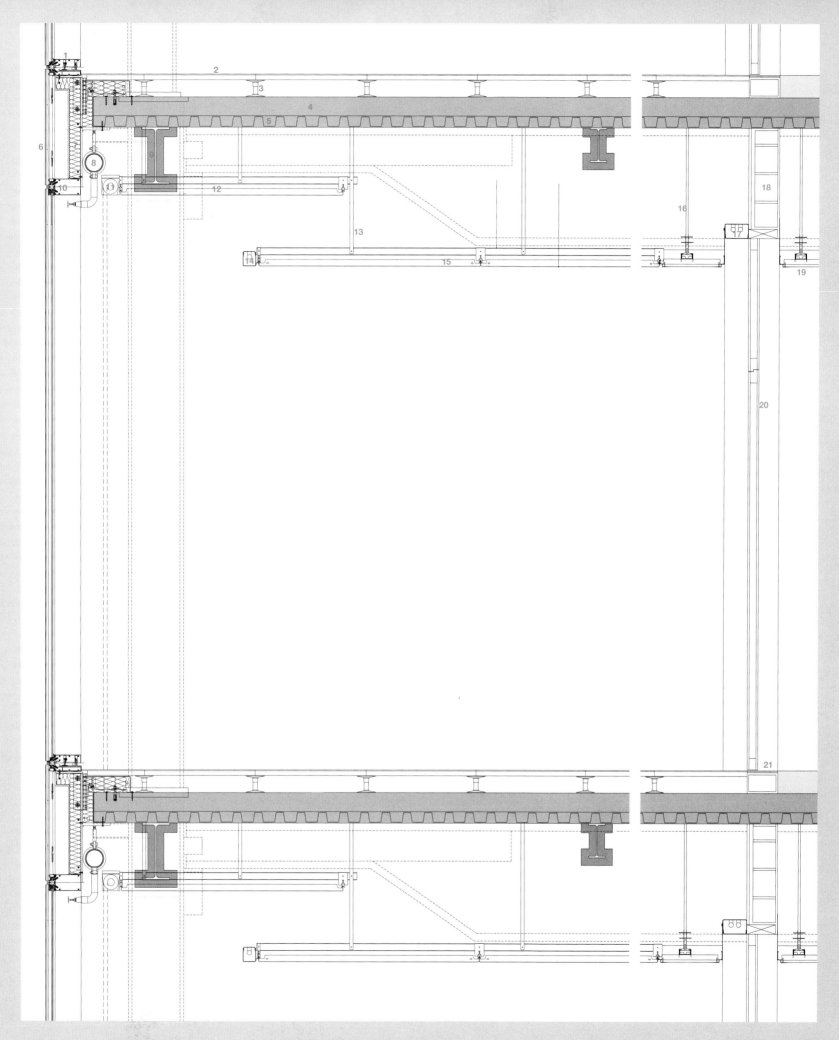

**Merck-Serono Headquarters
Geneva, Switzerland**

Client
Merck–Serono

Project Team
Helmut Jahn, Sam Scaccia, Gordon
Beckman, Scott Pratt, Stephen Kern,
Oliver Henninger, Ingo Jannek, Tobias
Dold, Robert Muller, Susan Pratt, John
DeSalvo, Joachim Schüssler, Joan Hu,
Michaela Fuchs, Bärbel Rudloff, Scott
Becker, Christian Goebel, Christian
Meyer, Anke Wolbrink, Michael
Geroulis

Structural Engineer
Thomas Jundt Ingénieurs

Main Contractor
Steiner Total Services Contractor

The site is in an old industrial district
near Lake Geneva, scattered with
large industrial buildings, some of
which had to be retained. The irregular
site and varied building uses,
including offices, laboratories,
restaurants, shops and meeting
facilities, allowed the architects to
create a lively campus, utilizing a
common and continuous architectural
language. A network of open and
covered spaces lead to the central
Merck-Serono Headquarters with its
operable glass roof and large pivoting
glass doors which blur the boundaries
between inside and outside. The
connectivity at ground level is
continued with bridges at the upper
levels, connected by open stairs and
glazed elevators.

Daylight, natural ventilation, solar
energy, the use of natural resources,
the minimization of mechanical
equipment and the idea that a building
should be able to modulate its own
climate are the concepts that inform
the design. This is evident through the
shingled glass facade which efficiently
handles natural ventilation and
exterior shading. Glass with a high
insulating value, high solar absorption
and reflectivity and maximum daylight
transmission assures an envelope of
optimum physical properties and
control. Structurally integrated heating
and cooling in the floor slabs provides
basic air conditioning, while outside
air is used for additional heating and
cooling if necessary. These systems,
components and materials also
determine the aesthetic so that the
necessary building systems are
elevated to the level of art.

1 View of the entrance
plaza to the
Merck-Serono
Headquarters. The
landscaping, which
transitions seamlessly
from the exterior to the
interior, reinforces the
goal of connectivity
and a sense of place.
2 The glazed facade
features an integrated
louvre system to
promote air circulation
without the need for air
conditioning, while
large pivoting glass
doors lead to the
dramatic entrance
space. Here, trees are
planted in the atrium to
further enhance the
connection to the
landscape.
3 A network of open,
covered or convertible
spaces is threaded
through the campus,
like a public diagram of
streets and places.
4 Open stairs and
glazed elevators on the
upper levels continue
the theme of
connectivity.

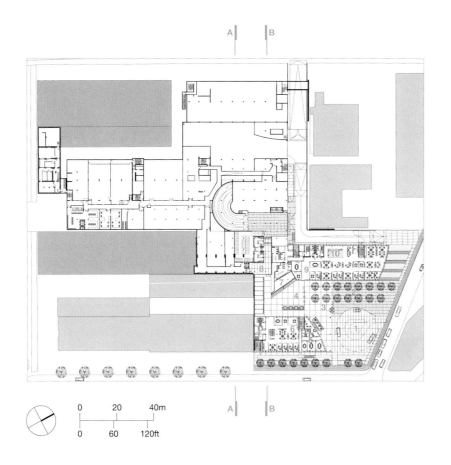

0   20   40m
0   60   120ft

A   B

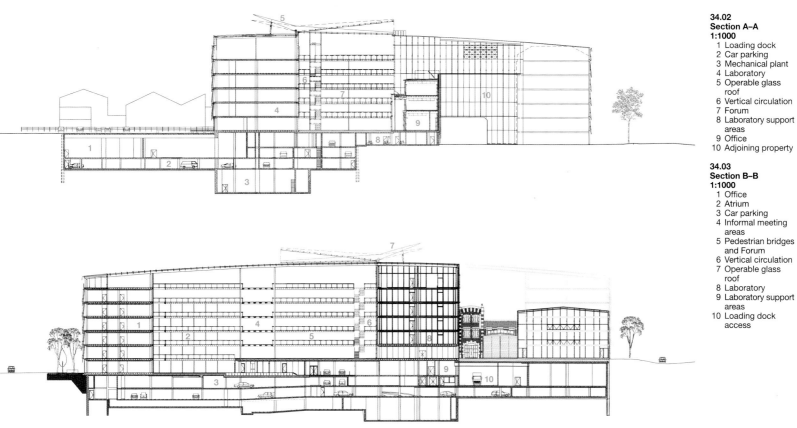

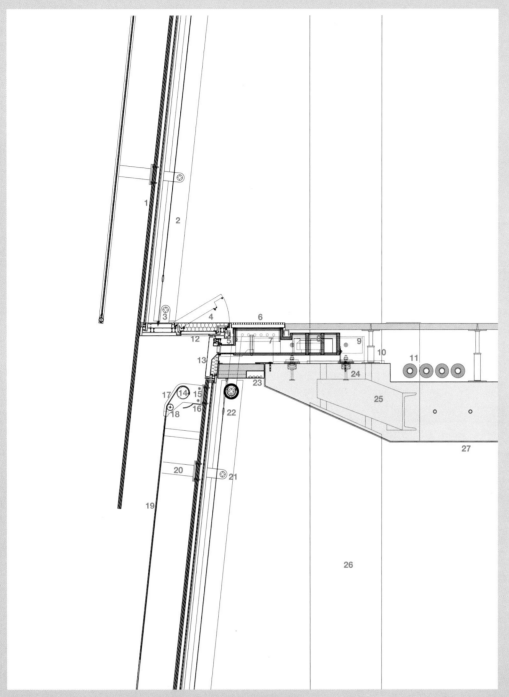

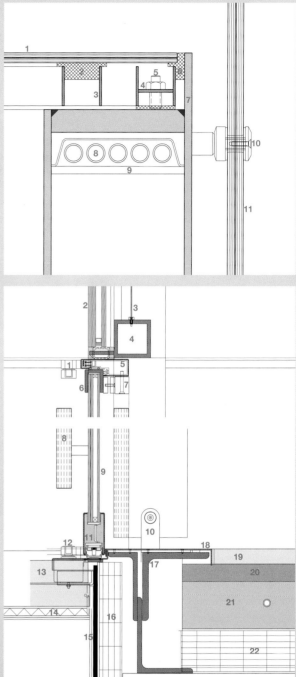

34.04
Vertical Facade
System Detail
1:20
1 Insulated glass unit
2 Stainless steel
mullion
3 Thermally broken
extruded aluminium sill
profile with anodized
finish
4 Insulated stainless
steel operable panel
assembly with
anodized aluminium
sheet to exterior face,
and brushed satin
dimpled stainless steel
to interior face
5 Concealed chain
drive motor operator
6 Stainless steel floor
grille with brushed
satin finish
7 Raised floor frame
member
8 Recessed perimeter

ventilation unit with
integral acoustic baffle
and air intake control
damper
9 Adjustable curtain
wall anchor
10 Raised floor frame
member
11 Perimeter
ventilation unit supply
and return pipework
12 Aluminium bird
screen
13 Formed, perforated
aluminium spandrel
panel with anodized
finish applied after
fabrication
14 Extruded aluminium
roller with concealed
electric motor
15 Cast stainless steel
load glass restraint and
shade bracket
assembly
16 Formed, perforated
stainless steel baffle

17 Formed stainless
steel profile and band
shoe fixture
18 Guide roller with
finish to match
stainless steel shade
fabric
19 Stainless steel track
with brushed satin
finish
20 Cast stainless steel
glass restraint
21 Cast stainless steel
glass fixing assembly
22 Extruded aluminium
roller shade hem bar
23 Stainless steel clad
closure profile with
integral cable tray and
fire protection
24 Cast-in steel insert
25 Reinforced
concrete floor slab
26 Reinforced
concrete column
27 Skim coat plaster

34.05
Entry Hall Glazed
Floor and Facade
Detail
1:5
1 Laminated low-iron
clear tempered glass
floor panel
2 Clear silicone
rubber bearing pad
3 Pressure locked
stainless steel grating
glass floor support
with brushed satin
finish applied prior to
assembly
4 Stainless steel plate
restraint welded to
grating panel
5 Stud bolt
6 Extruded black
EPDM perimeter joint
profile
7 Built up rectangular
hollow section steel
primary girder to
bridge

8 Galvanized steel
conduit secured to
internal stiffeners
9 Steel plate internal
stiffener
10 Reinforced
stainless steel point
fixing assembly in
brushed satin finish
11 Tempered,
laminated low-iron
clear cantilevered,
point supported glass
panel

34.06
Glazed Door Detail
1:10
1 Offset pivot
2 Insulated glass unit
3 Cable
4 Glass support
profile
5 Door frame
6 Stainless steel
top rail
7 Magnetic lock

8 Door pull
9 Insulated glass
door panel
10 Bracket
11 Stainless steel
bottom rail
12 Offset pivot
13 Concealed floor
closer
14 Pavement
15 Waterproofing
16 Thermal insulation
17 Threshold
substructure
18 Stainless steel
threshold
19 Natural stone floor
20 Mortar setting bed
21 Concrete topping
with radiant heating
22 Thermal insulation

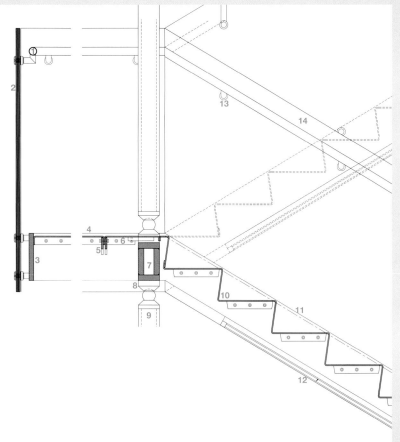

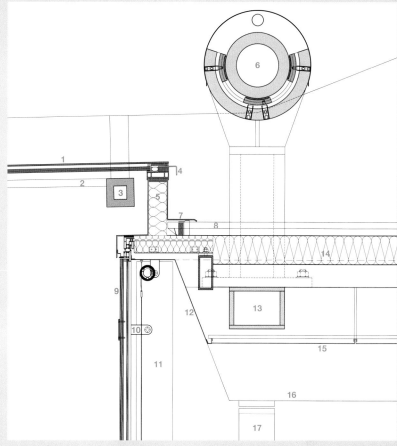

34.07
Entry Hall Stair Detail
1:20
1 Stainless steel point fixed rail bracket assembly with brushed satin finish
2 Tempered, laminated low-iron, point supported clear cantilevered glass panel
3 Steel plate stringer
4 Steel plate stringer
5 Tapered stainless steel plate reinforcement with brushed satin finish
6 Formed, perforated stainless steel stair landing plank with brushed satin finish
7 Built up steel plate stair cross member
8 Steel node assembly
9 Seamless steel circular hollow section stair column with cast spherical bearing assembly
10 Formed, perforated stainless steel stair treads and risers with alternating perforation pattern
11 Steel plate stringer
12 Tempered, laminated low-iron,
point supported clear cantilevered glass panel
13 Stainless steel point fixed rail bracket assembly with brushed satin finish
14 Tempered, laminated low-iron, point supported clear cantilevered glass panel

34.08
Upper Forum Roof Edge Detail
1:10
1 Insulated glass unit to roof
2 Secondary glazing profile
3 Primary glazing profile
4 Flashing
5 Insulated curb
6 Operable roof
bearing block and pivot assembly
7 Roof flashing
8 Standing seam metal roof
9 Insulated glass assembly
10 Cast stainless steel glass fixing assembly
11 Stainless steel mullion
12 Formed stainless steel continuous
closure channel with mounting assembly
13 Steel duct
14 Thermal insulation
15 Anodized suspended aluminium panel ceiling system with concealed suspension system
16 Built up steel plate roof girder
17 Seamless steel circular hollow section
column with articulated bearing connections to top and bottom

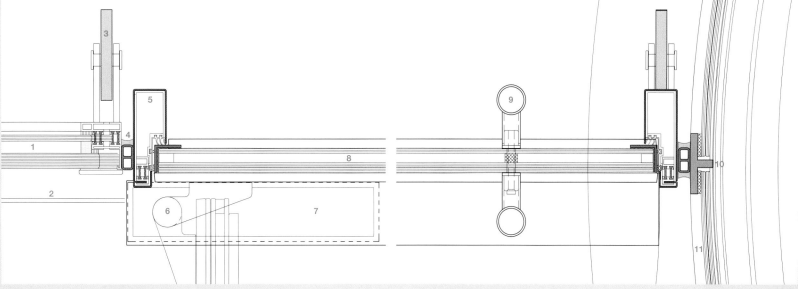

34.09
Revolving Door Plan Detail
1:5
1 Insulated glazing unit
2 Drainage opening in pavement
3 Stainless steel mullion
4 Weather seal
5 Power assisted frameless glass
revolving door
6 Offset pivot hinge in stainless steel clad aluminium
7 Recessed door closer with integral hold open device
8 Double glazing to door leaf
9 Stainless steel door pull with brushed satin finish
10 Stainless steel
profile
11 Laminated glass revolving door enclosure

TRUTEC Building
Seoul, South Korea

Client
TKR Sang-Am

Project Team
Martina Bauer, Matthias Graf von
Ballestrem, Markus Bonauer, Michael
Schmidt, Elke Sparmann, Jan-Oliver
Kunze

Structural Engineer
Schlaich Bergermann and Partner,
Jeon and Lee Partners

Main Contractor
Dongbu Corporation

The Digital Media City is situated in
Seoul between the international
airport and city centre. Given the
uncertainty of adjacent neighbouring
buildings in this new urban quarter,
the design of the TRUTEC building is
intentionally self-referential. An
11-storey high mid-rise building is
clad in a skin of faceted reflective
glass panels articulated into a series
of crystalline projecting bays. This
pattern refracts light and images,
rendering the facade an abstract
surface, where contextual images
such as buildings, traffic, pedestrians
and the weather are fragmented upon
the glass. The building core has been
placed at the eastern extremity of the
building and is clad in dark zinc
shingles. This location facilitates the
placement of large rentable spaces
fronting either the street or to the side
near the parking entrance. The ground
floor features a double height, column
free showroom and a lobby with a
partial first floor mezzanine, which
serves as a coffee shop for the
building. The second and third levels
offer additional showroom space while
the upper seven levels accommodate
office space. The facade continues up
to a roof garden on the twelfth floor
which acts as an open-air courtyard
between the core and facade. A large
triangular indentation, exaggerating
the folding system, marks the formal
entrance to the building.

1 The building is
located within a new
industrial park in
Seoul, and with the
neighbouring buildings
still undecided, it is
unabashedly
self-referential.
2 The exterior
cladding is a mirrored
fractal glass system
articulated into a series
of crystalline-formed
bays that project 200
millimetres (8 inches)
from the surface of the
building.
3 Detail view of the
faceted glass facade.

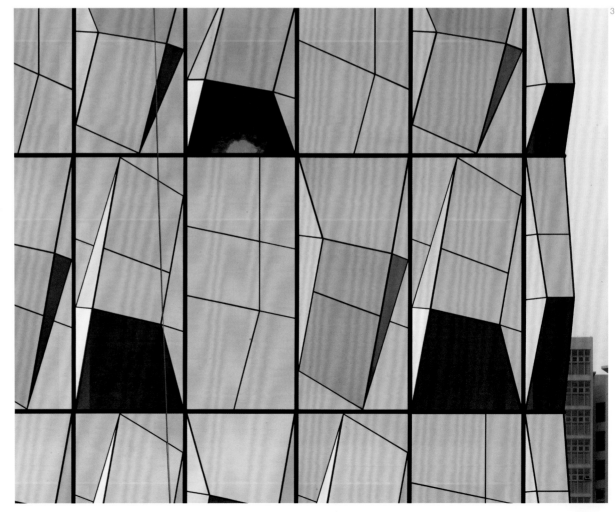

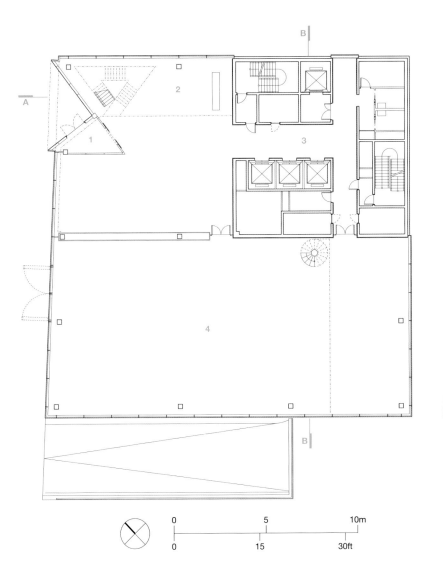

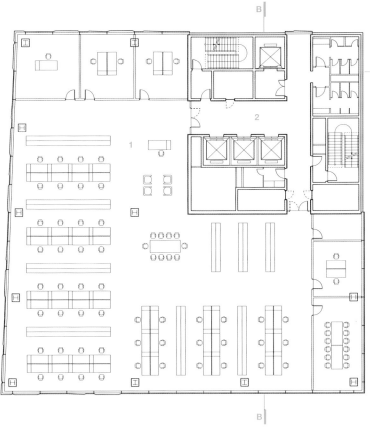

35.01
Ground Floor Plan
1:200
1 Entrance vestibule
2 Entrance lobby
3 Circulation and
 services core
4 Application centre

35.02
Fifth Floor Plan
1:200
1 Office space
2 Circulation and
 services core

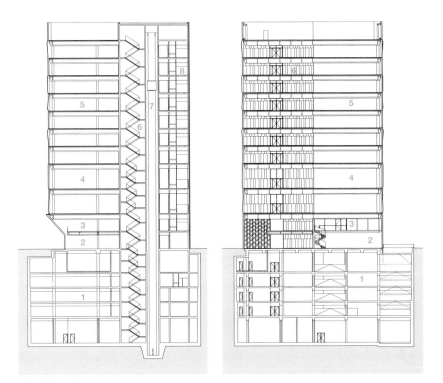

35.03
Section A–A
1:500
1 Basement level
2 Ground floor
 showroom
3 Mezzanine coffee
 shop
4 Showroom levels
5 Office levels
6 Fire stair core
7 Lift core
8 Services core

35.04
Section B–B
1:500
1 Basement level
2 Ground floor
 showroom
3 Mezzanine coffee
 shop
4 Showroom levels
5 Office levels
6 Circulation core

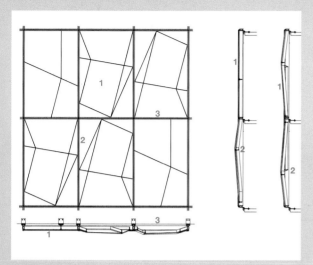

35.05
Partial Facade
Elevation, Sections
and Plan Details
1:100
 1 2D glazing panel
 2 3D glazing panel
 3 3D glazing panel,
rotated 180 degrees

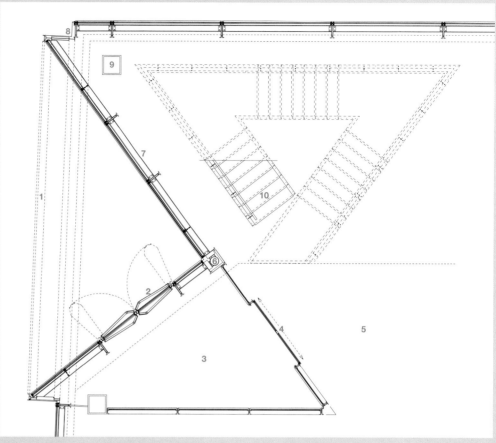

35.06
Ground Floor
Entrance Doors
Partial Plan Detail
1:50
 1 Line of glass facade
over shown dotted
 2 Glass entrance
doors
 3 Entrance vestibule
 4 Sliding glass doors

 5 Entrance lobby
 6 Steel column
 7 Glass facade
 8 Corner jamb detail
 9 Steel column
 10 Suspended stair to
mezzanine

35.07
Entrance Doors Plan
Detail
1:10
 1 Steel column
 2 Typical facade
panel
 3 Motor to drive
openable facade panel
 4 Motor-driven
telescopic arm
 5 Frame stiffener
 6 Floor guides
 7 Insulated low-E
glass

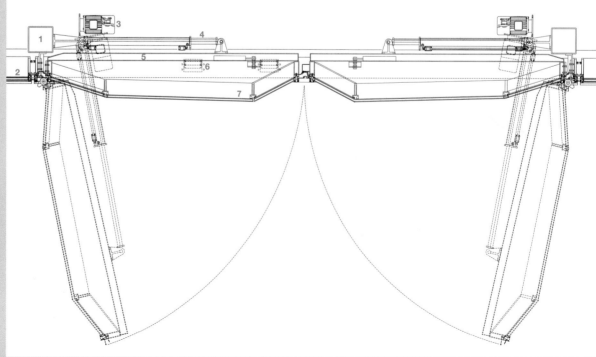

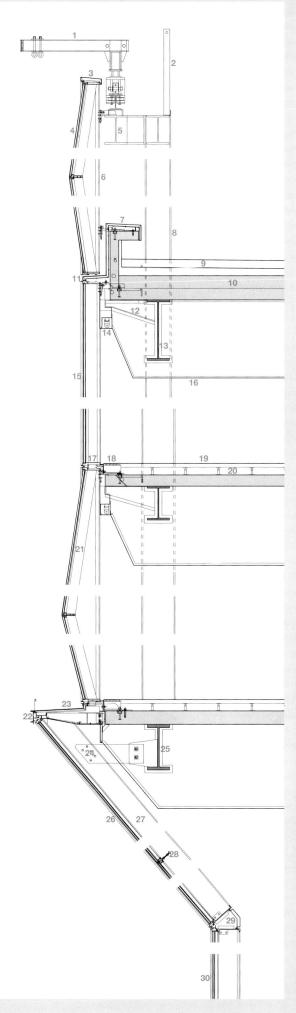

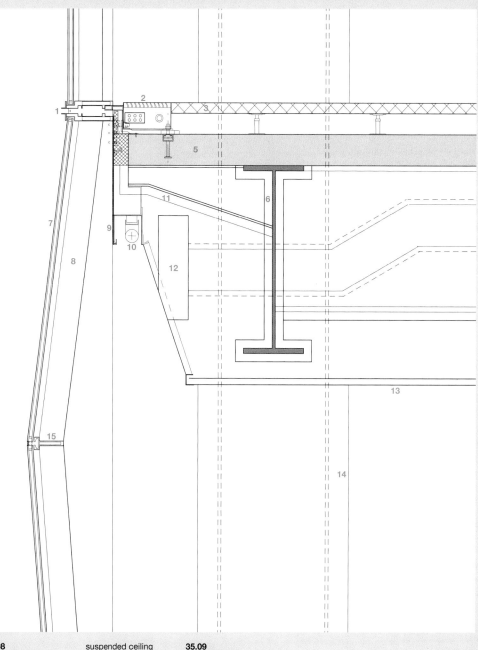

35.08
Detail Section
Through Facade 1
1:50
1 Window washing
apparatus
2 Steel balustrade to
building maintenance
access walkway
3 Folded sheet metal
parapet capping
4 Glass screen wall at
roof level
5 Steel support beam
to window washing
equipment
6 Facade framing
7 Folded sheet metal
parapet capping
8 Steel column clad
in galvanized metal
panels
9 Poured concrete
deck
10 Concrete floor on
corrugated metal
permanent formwork
11 Sill
12 Tapered steel beam
13 Universal steel
beam
14 Anti-glare roller
blind
15 Typical two
dimensional facade
glazing element with
low-E insulating glass
16 Galvanized
perforated panel

suspended ceiling
17 Horizontal transom
18 Floor level grille
with convector heater
and integrated uplight
19 Raised access floor
20 Void under raised
access floor
21 CNC (computer
numerical control) cut
out aluminium
extrusion glazing bar
22 Steel framing to
entrance canopy
23 Flashing
24 Bolted steel
connector plate
between steel beam
and entrance canopy
structure
25 Universal steel
beam
26 Low-E insulating
glass to entrance
canopy
27 CNC (computer
numerical control) cut
out aluminium
extrusion glazing bar
28 Facade module
frame connector
29 Mullion
30 Low-E insulating
glass to entrance

35.09
Detail Section
Through Facade 2
1:20
1 Aluminium
horizontal mullion
2 Floor level grille
with convector heater
and integrated uplight
3 Raised access floor
4 Insulation
5 Concrete floor on
corrugated metal
permanent formwork
6 Universal steel
beam
7 Low-E insulating
glass
8 CNC (computer
numerical control) cut
out aluminium
extrusion glazing bar
9 Perforated metal
tile
10 Anti-glare roller
blind
11 Tapered steel beam
12 Ceiling edge void
13 Galvanized
perforated panel
suspended ceiling
14 Steel column clad
in galvanized metal
panels
15 Facade module
frame connector

**Shanghai World Financial Center
Shanghai, China**

Client
Shanghai World Financial Center
Corporation

Project Team
Eugene Kohn, William Pedersen, Paul
Katz, Joshua Chaiken, Ko Makabe,
David Malott, Roger Robison, John
Koga AIA

Structural Engineer
Leslie Robertson Associates

Main Contractor
China State Construction Engineering
Corporation, Shanghai Construction
Group

Soaring 101 storeys above the city
skyline, the Shanghai World Financial
Center (SWFC) stands as a symbol of
commerce and culture that speaks of
the city's emergence as a global
capital. It features the highest
occupied floor and highest public
observatory in the world. A virtual city
within a city, SWFC houses a mix of
office and retail uses, as well as a Park
Hyatt Hotel on the 79th to 93rd floors.
Occupying the tower's uppermost
floors, the SWFC Sky Arena offers
visitors aerial views of the historic
Lujiazui district and the winding river
below as well as the chance to walk
almost 500 metres (1,640 feet) above
the city via the Sky Walk on the 100th
floor. A large retail volume wraps
around the base of the tower and
faces a planned public park on the
site's eastern side, further activating
the sphere of activity at street level.

Originally conceived in 1993, the
project was put on hold during the
Asian financial crisis in the late 1990s
and was later redesigned to its current
height—32 metres (105 feet) higher
than before. The new, taller structure
not only had to be made lighter, but
also needed to resist higher wind
loads and utilize the existing
foundations which had been
constructed prior to the project delay.
The innovative structural solution
involved abandoning the original
concrete frame structure in favour of a
diagonal-braced frame with outrigger
trusses coupled to the columns of the
mega-structure. This enabled the
weight of the building to be reduced
by more than ten per cent,
consequently reducing the use of
materials and resulting in a more
transparent structure in visual and
conceptual harmony with the tower's
elegant form.

1 A square prism—the
symbol used by the
ancient Chinese to
represent the earth—is
intersected by two
cosmic arcs,
representing the
heavens, here in the
form of the tower. The
interaction between
these two realms gives
rise to the building's
form, with a square sky
portal at the top of the
tower that lends
balance to the
structure and links the
two opposing
elements of heaven
and earth.
2 The symbolic
representation of
heaven and earth
appear again in the
podium where an
angled wall
representing the
horizon cuts through
an overlapping circle
and square. The
angled wall organizes
the ground level to
provide separate
entrances for office
workers, hotel guests
and public access to
elevator service for
Sky Walk visitors.
3 In the public foyer,
one stone wall is
constructed in Jura
yellow limestone, while
the base of the tower
is clad in Maritaca
green Brazilian granite
with a split-face finish,
both of which contrast
beautifully with the
metal of the circular
diaphanous glass skin
enveloping the retail
volume.

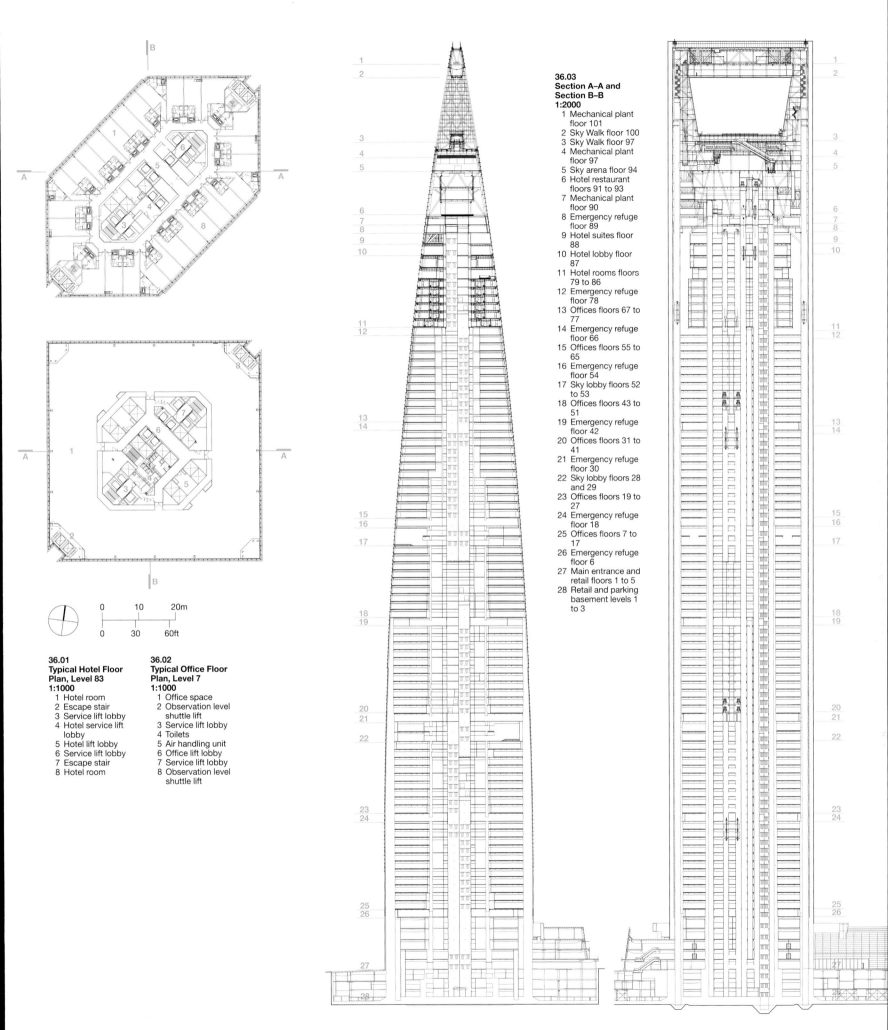

36.01
Typical Hotel Floor
Plan, Level 83
1:1000
1 Hotel room
2 Escape stair
3 Service lift lobby
4 Hotel service lift lobby
5 Hotel lift lobby
6 Service lift lobby
7 Escape stair
8 Hotel room

36.02
Typical Office Floor
Plan, Level 7
1:1000
1 Office space
2 Observation level shuttle lift
3 Service lift lobby
4 Toilets
5 Air handling unit
6 Office lift lobby
7 Service lift lobby
8 Observation level shuttle lift

36.03
Section A–A and
Section B–B
1:2000
1 Mechanical plant floor 101
2 Sky Walk floor 100
3 Sky Walk floor 97
4 Mechanical plant floor 97
5 Sky arena floor 94
6 Hotel restaurant floors 91 to 93
7 Mechanical plant floor 90
8 Emergency refuge floor 89
9 Hotel suites floor 88
10 Hotel lobby floor 87
11 Hotel rooms floors 79 to 86
12 Emergency refuge floor 78
13 Offices floors 67 to 77
14 Emergency refuge floor 66
15 Offices floors 55 to 65
16 Emergency refuge floor 54
17 Sky lobby floors 52 to 53
18 Offices floors 43 to 51
19 Emergency refuge floor 42
20 Offices floors 31 to 41
21 Emergency refuge floor 30
22 Sky lobby floors 28 and 29
23 Offices floors 19 to 27
24 Emergency refuge floor 18
25 Offices floors 7 to 17
26 Emergency refuge floor 6
27 Main entrance and retail floors 1 to 5
28 Retail and parking basement levels 1 to 3

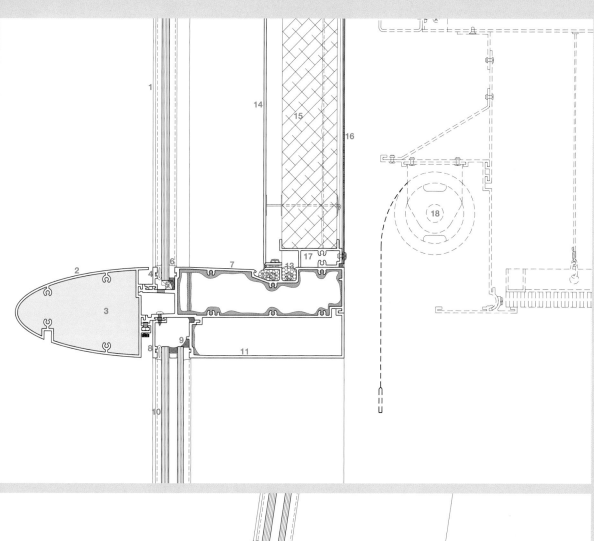

36.04
Typical Horizontal Transom Detail at Flat Wall
1:5
1 Fixed glass spandrel panel
2 Anodized aluminium extruded horizontal primary bullnose mullion
3 Aluminium end cap
4 Painted extruded aluminium upper glazing transom
5 Setting block at quarter point span
6 Sealant compatible rubber set in gasket
7 Painted extruded aluminium intermediate horizontal transom
8 Painted extruded aluminium lower transom glazing capture
9 Perimeter weather sealant
10 Double glazed window
11 Painted extruded aluminium horizontal transom removable glazing adaptor
12 Condensation weep hole with baffle foam
13 Condensation weep hole with baffle foam
14 3 mm (1/10 inch) thick painted aluminium sheet
15 75 mm (3 inch) thick semi-rigid thermal insulation
16 1.5 mm (1/16 inch) thick galvanized sheet
17 Painted extruded aluminium insulation chair
18 Roller blind

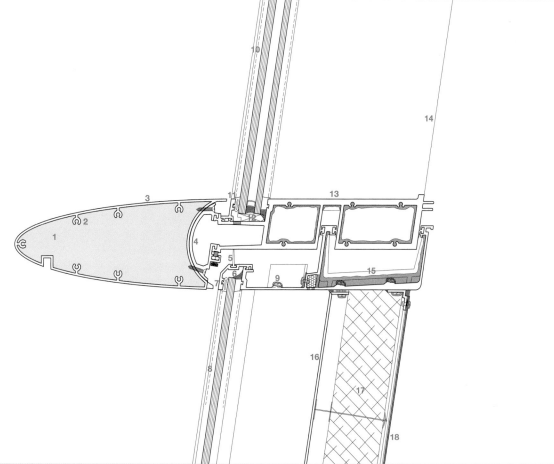

36.05
Typical Stack Joint Detail at Curved Wall
1:5
1 Fixing rivets at ends
2 End cap
3 75 mm (3 inch) thick semi-rigid thermal insulation
4 End cap to bullnose mullion
5 Baffle gasket
6 Perimeter weather sealant
7 Painted extruded aluminium lower transom glazing capture
8 Glass spandrel panel
9 Painted extruded aluminium horizontal male stack joint
10 Double glazed window
11 Wedge gasket
12 Setting block at quarter point span
13 Painted extruded aluminium horizontal female stack joint
14 Painted extruded aluminium vertical dummy mullion
15 Extruded aluminium stack joint sleeve
16 3 mm (1/10 inch) thick painted aluminium sheet
17 75 mm (3 inch) thick semi-rigid thermal insulation
18 1.5 mm (1/16 inch) thick galvanized sheet

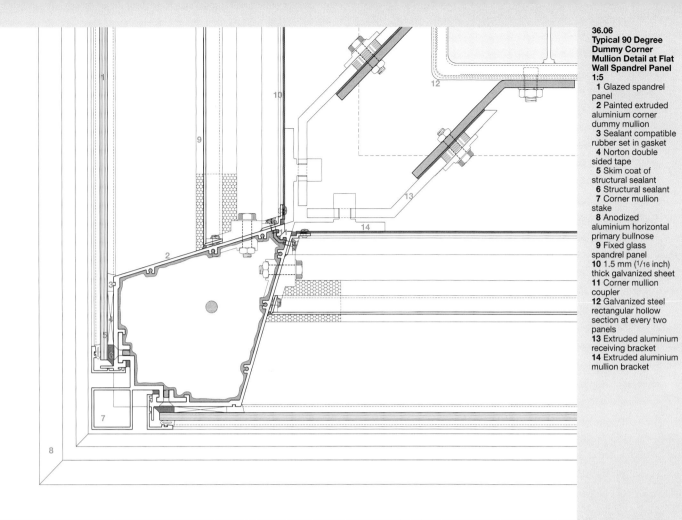

36.06
Typical 90 Degree Dummy Corner Mullion Detail at Flat Wall Spandrel Panel
1:5
1 Glazed spandrel panel
2 Painted extruded aluminium corner dummy mullion
3 Sealant compatible rubber set in gasket
4 Norton double sided tape
5 Skim coat of structural sealant
6 Structural sealant
7 Corner mullion stake
8 Anodized aluminium horizontal primary bullnose
9 Fixed glass spandrel panel
10 1.5 mm (1/16 inch) thick galvanized sheet
11 Corner mullion coupler
12 Galvanized steel rectangular hollow section at every two panels
13 Extruded aluminium receiving bracket
14 Extruded aluminium mullion bracket

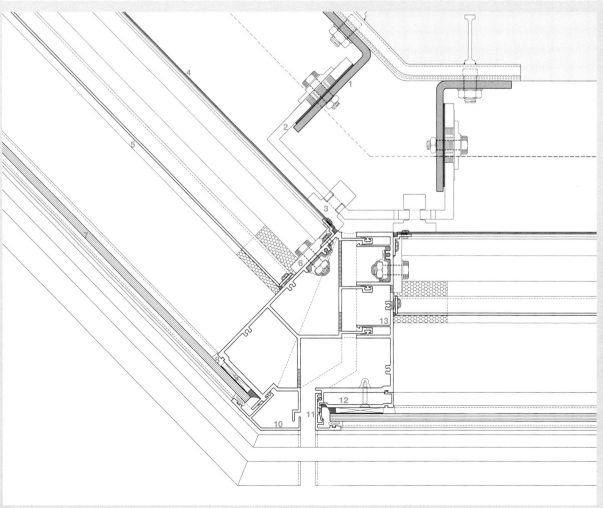

36.07
Typical 135 Degree Split Mullion Detail Above 25th Floor at Flat and Curved Wall Spandrel Panels
1:5
1 Galvanized steel angle at every two panels
2 Extruded aluminium receiving bracket
3 Extruded aluminium mullion bracket
4 1.5 mm (1/16 inch) thick galvanized sheet
5 Fixed glass spandrel panel
6 Painted aluminium vertical male mullion
7 Fixed glazed spandrel panel
8 Sealant compatible rubber set in gasket
9 Norton double sided tape
10 Painted extruded aluminium vertical glazing capture
11 Painted extruded aluminium vertical glazing capture
12 Painted extruded aluminium vertical glazing bead
13 Painted extruded aluminium vertical female mullion

157

Cocoon
Zurich, Switzerland

Client
Swiss Life

Project Team
Marco Noch, Stefan Camenzind,
Susanne Zenker

Structural Engineer
Gruner

Project Management
S+B Baumanagement

Cocoon is located in Zurich's Seefeld district on a hillside which enjoys views over the lake and mountains. Located in a park-like setting, the elliptical structure reads as a freestanding sculptural volume that gracefully spirals up from the landscape. The stainless steel mesh enveloping the building combines visual privacy with restrained elegance. Cocoon can be thought of as a 'communication landscape' that creates a unique spatial configuration and working environment in a matchless setting. The stepped, upward-winding sequence of segments are arranged along a gently rising ramp, which wraps around a central, light-filled atrium.

The space planning concept dispenses with the traditional division into horizontal storeys, in favour of a seemingly endless sequence of elliptical floor segments. By eliminating the usual barriers to communication, this generates a unique spatial experience and working environment that unlocks a host of intriguing possibilities for interaction and cooperation. Internally, the widening atrium forms the centrepiece of Cocoon. Around this, the circulation and communication ramp winds its way upwards in gently curving contours. Externally, the building adopts the guise of a dynamic, upward-reaching sculpture wrapped in a fine veil of stainless steel wire mesh. This curtain curls elegantly upwards in soft lines around the expanding spiral, its junction with the roof terrace accentuated by an open facade frame. The shrouded, sculptural structure, introverted during the daytime as it looks inwards towards the atrium, is recast in the evening as a transparent shining beacon.

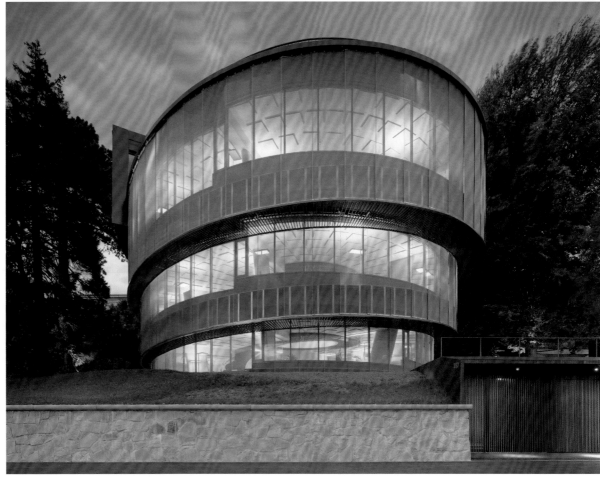

1 The distinctive park-like setting features great stands of mature trees that surround the building.
2 During the day, the stainless steel wire mesh lends privacy and protection from the sun to the interior working environment.
3 The light-filled atrium forms the centrepiece of the design and floods the interior with natural light.
4 The floorspace design is occupancy-neutral and provides for fully flexible partitioning together with the adaptability necessary to meet the shifting needs of future users. Together, the various elements – lift, spiral ramp, floor segments and stairwell – constitute a clearly structured, versatile circulation system.

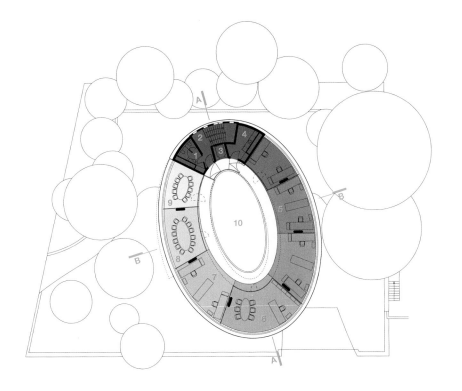

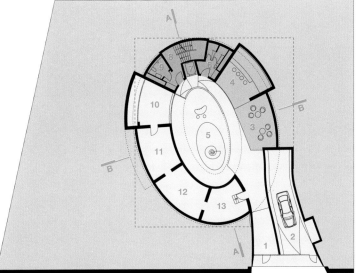

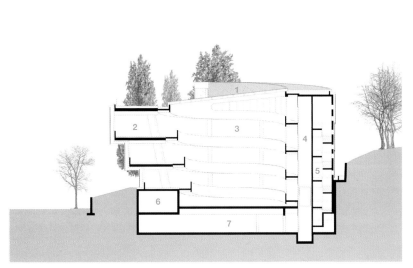

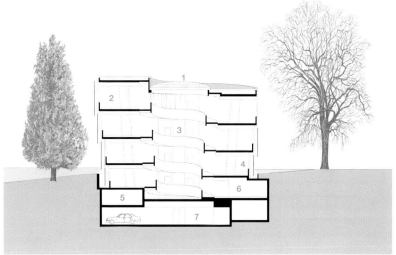

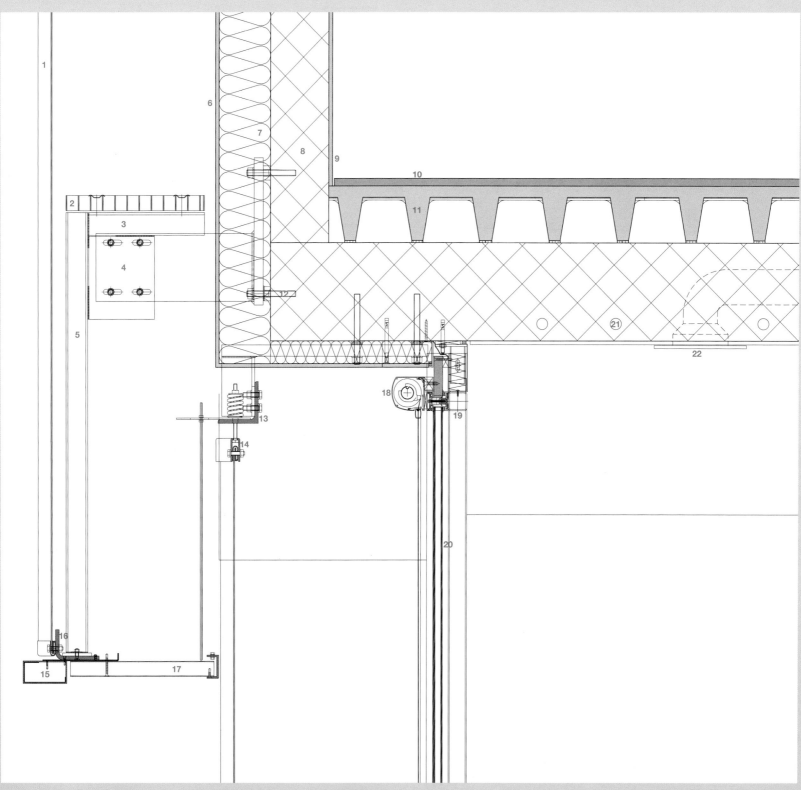

37.05
Facade Detail
1:10

1 Stainless steel metal mesh screen
2 Metal grid maintenance and access catwalk
3 50 x 50 mm (2 x 2 inch) post and mullion construction
4 Steel flange
5 60 x 80 mm (2^3/$_8$ x 3^1/$_8$ inch) steel profile
6 Insulation with skimmed plaster finish
7 Insulation

8 Reinforced concrete wall
9 Skim plaster finish
10 Smoked oak parquet floor
11 Egg crate raised floor
12 Bolt fixing
13 110 x 110 mm (4^1/$_3$ x 4^1/$_3$ inch) steel L-profile
14 Stainless steel woven mesh screen with spring tensioned fixing
15 120 x 60 mm (4^3/$_4$ x 2^3/$_8$ inch) continuous

aluminium box section
16 60 x 120 mm (2^3/$_8$ x 4^3/$_4$ inch) steel L-profile
17 40 x 20 mm (1^5/$_8$ x ^{3}/$_4$ inch) aluminium section ceiling rib elements, centrally aligned
18 Roller-blind sunshade
19 50 x 50 mm (2 x 2 inch) steel profile post and beam facade structure
20 26 mm (1 inch) insulated double

glazing comprised of 6 mm (^{1}/$_4$ inch) glass, 16 mm (^{2}/$_3$ inch) air gap and 4 mm (^{1}/$_6$ inch) glass
21 Thermo-active heating and cooling system
22 Air supply duct

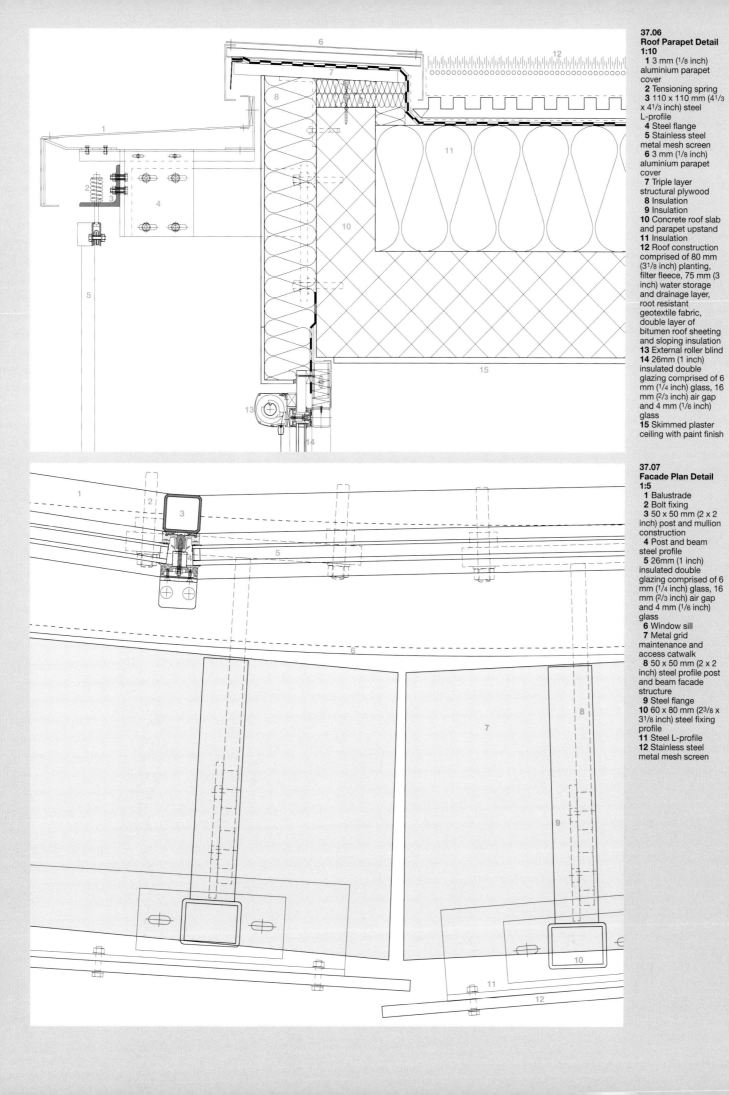

37.06
Roof Parapet Detail
1:10
1 3 mm (1/8 inch) aluminium parapet cover
2 Tensioning spring
3 110 x 110 mm (4 1/3 x 4 1/3 inch) steel L-profile
4 Steel flange
5 Stainless steel metal mesh screen
6 3 mm (1/8 inch) aluminium parapet cover
7 Triple layer structural plywood
8 Insulation
9 Insulation
10 Concrete roof slab and parapet upstand
11 Insulation
12 Roof construction comprised of 80 mm (3 1/8 inch) planting, filter fleece, 75 mm (3 inch) water storage and drainage layer, root resistant geotextile fabric, double layer of bitumen roof sheeting and sloping insulation
13 External roller blind
14 26mm (1 inch) insulated double glazing comprised of 6 mm (1/4 inch) glass, 16 mm (2/3 inch) air gap and 4 mm (1/6 inch) glass
15 Skimmed plaster ceiling with paint finish

37.07
Facade Plan Detail
1:5
1 Balustrade
2 Bolt fixing
3 50 x 50 mm (2 x 2 inch) post and mullion construction
4 Post and beam steel profile
5 26mm (1 inch) insulated double glazing comprised of 6 mm (1/4 inch) glass, 16 mm (2/3 inch) air gap and 4 mm (1/6 inch) glass
6 Window sill
7 Metal grid maintenance and access catwalk
8 50 x 50 mm (2 x 2 inch) steel profile post and beam facade structure
9 Steel flange
10 60 x 80 mm (2 3/8 x 3 1/8 inch) steel fixing profile
11 Steel L-profile
12 Stainless steel metal mesh screen

Erick van Egeraat

INHolland University of Applied Sciences
Rotterdam, The Netherlands

Client
INHolland University of Applied Sciences

Project Team
Erick van Egeraat, Alberte van Santen, Daniel Rodrigues

Structural Engineer
ABT-C Delft

Services Engineer
Deerns Raadgevende Ingenieurs

In order to accommodate the rapid growth of INHolland University in Rotterdam, a new 15,000 square metre (161,500 square foot) building housing study areas, classrooms, commercial functions and offices were added to the original building. Both the new and the old buildings were designed by Erick van Egeraat who also designed the masterplan and the landscaped courtyard. The extension consists of three interconnected parts. A lower, three-level building is situated parallel to and connecting with the original building. This supports one end of a nine-level bridge building that spans 35 metres (115 feet) over the courtyard and underlying Metro line, and rests on a student apartment building at the other end. Finally a higher volume, partially cantilevered from the bridge building, offers panoramic views towards Rotterdam harbour.

The facades of each of the three elements differ, while their architectural language relates to the original INHolland University building to form a coherent ensemble. Screen-printed patterns in gold tones are used on the glass facades of the low and high volumes, while the horizontal glazing of the bridge building recalls the louvres of the original building. Extensive use of glass underlines the open character of the university while the significant height intensifies its corporate image. Thanks to the flexible layout, individual parts of the complex can be used autonomously, if desired. This flexibility and the high building density on the plot, combined with the clever use of sustainable solutions, considerably prolong the lifespan of the project.

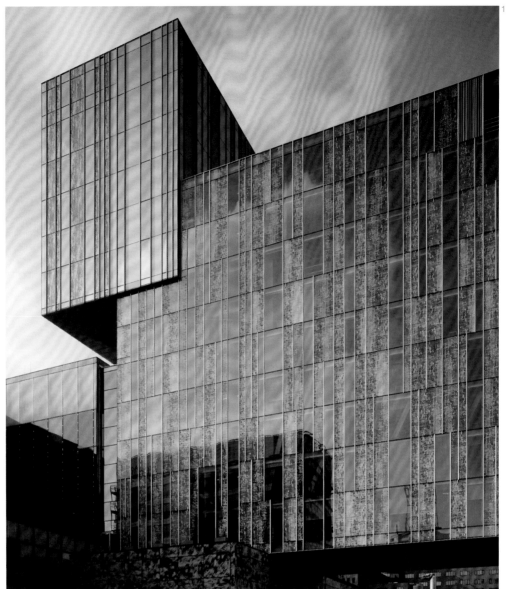

1 The scheme consists of elemental rectangular prisms that are stacked and interlocked to create a lively composition which is further enhanced by the detail and colour in the screen-printed glass facades.
2 The composition of the building consists of a lower and upper volume, both of which are distinguished by their screen printed glazing in tones of gold, and a bridge building with a facade of horizontal blue glazing which echoes the geometry of the existing building.
3 Panes of both clear and screen-printed glazing reveal panoramic views of Rotterdam Harbour from the highest volume of the new building.

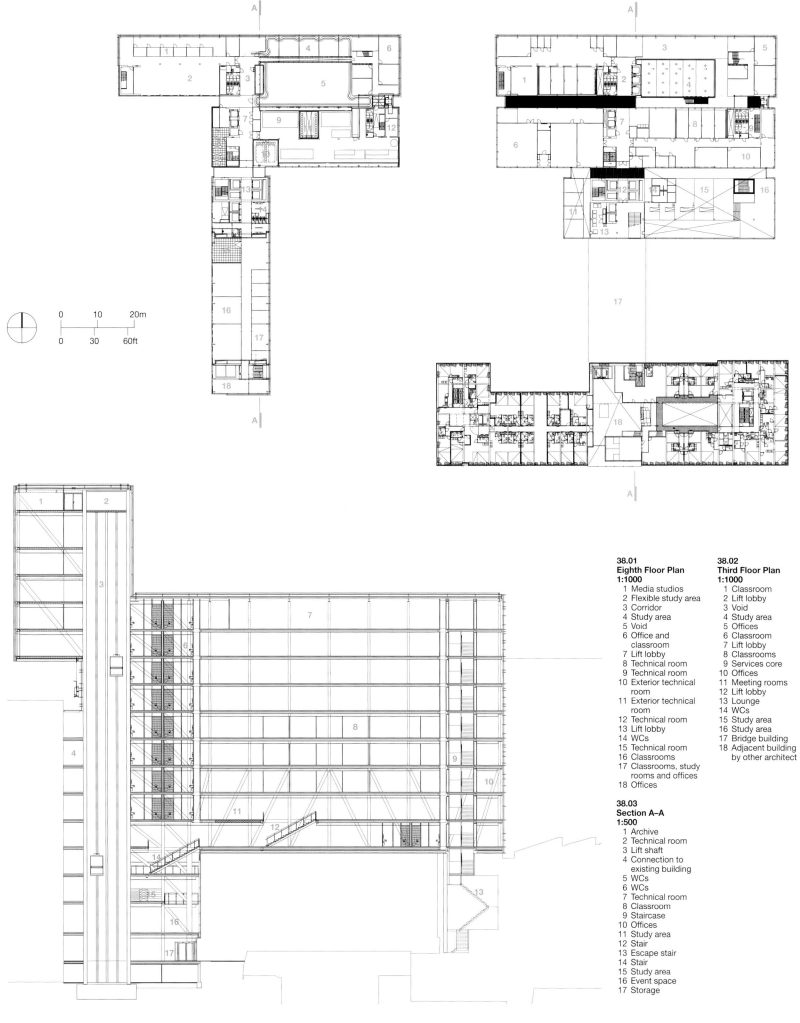

38.01
Eighth Floor Plan
1:1000
1 Media studios
2 Flexible study area
3 Corridor
4 Study area
5 Void
6 Office and
  classroom
7 Lift lobby
8 Technical room
9 Technical room
10 Exterior technical
   room
11 Exterior technical
   room
12 Technical room
13 Lift lobby
14 WCs
15 Technical room
16 Classrooms
17 Classrooms, study
   rooms and offices
18 Offices

38.02
Third Floor Plan
1:1000
1 Classroom
2 Lift lobby
3 Void
4 Study area
5 Offices
6 Classroom
7 Lift lobby
8 Classrooms
9 Services core
10 Offices
11 Meeting rooms
12 Lift lobby
13 Lounge
14 WCs
15 Study area
16 Study area
17 Bridge building
18 Adjacent building
   by other architect

38.03
Section A–A
1:500
1 Archive
2 Technical room
3 Lift shaft
4 Connection to
  existing building
5 WCs
6 WCs
7 Technical room
8 Classroom
9 Staircase
10 Offices
11 Study area
12 Stair
13 Escape stair
14 Stair
15 Study area
16 Event space
17 Storage

163

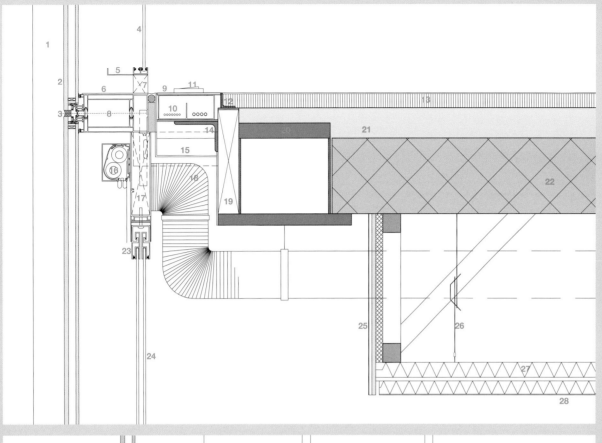

38.04
Glazed Facade at
Floor Junction Detail
Type 1
1:10
 1 Vertical facade
structure
 2 Double glazed
curtain wall facade
 3 Joint between glass
panels
 4 Glass sliding panels
 5 Aluminium profile
 6 Horizontal panel for
sound insulation break
 7 Ventilation opening
 8 Horizontal glazing
frame profile
 9 Plate decking for
cable trough
 10 Cable trough
 11 Floor mounted
electrical outlet
 12 L-angle to floor
finish edge
 13 Cement screed
floor finish
 14 L-angle support to
cable trough
 15 Coated steel plate
 16 Sun shade roller
blind

 17 Mounting section
for sliding glass panel
assembly below
 18 Climate control
ventilation duct
 19 Coated steel plate
 20 Steel beam
 21 Pressure treated
concrete subfloor
 22 Channel plate floor
 23 Frame to sliding
glass panels
 24 Double glazed
sliding panel
 25 Painted plywood
panel
 26 Suspended ceiling
system hanger
 27 Sound insulation
 28 Aluminium ceiling

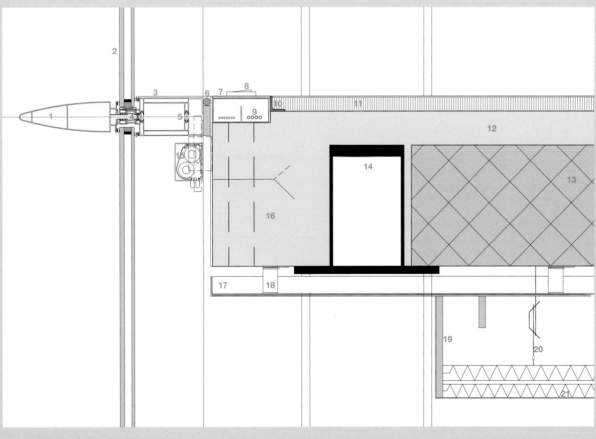

38.05
Glazed Facade at
Floor Junction Detail
Type 2
1:10
 1 Aluminium
horizontal profile
 2 Double glazed
curtain wall facade
 3 4 mm (1/8 inch)
steel plate for sound
insulation
 4 Glazing system
framing profile
 5 Glazing subframe
 6 Sealant
 7 Plate decking for
cable trough
 8 Floor mounted
electrical outlet
 9 Cable trough
 10 L-angle to floor
finish edge
 11 Cement screed
floor finish
 12 Pressure treated
concrete subfloor
 13 Channel plate floor
 14 Steel beam
 15 Sun shade roller
blind
 16 Reinforced

concrete downstand
floor beam
 17 Coated steel plate
 18 Ceiling system
hanger
 19 Painted plywood
ceiling edge panel
 20 Suspended ceiling
system hanger
 21 Insulated aluminium
ceiling

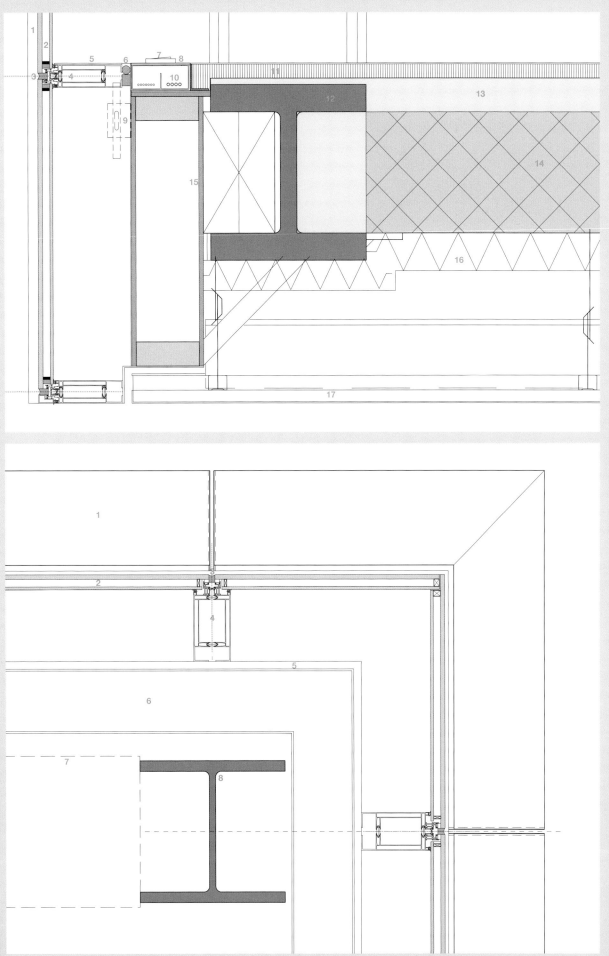

38.06
**Glazed Facade at
Floor Junction Detail
Type 3**
1:10
1 Vertical profile
glazing framing
2 Double glazed
curtain wall facade
3 Sealant
4 Horizontal glazing
frame profile
5 Steel plate sound
insulation
6 Sealant
7 Floor mounted
electrical outlet
8 Plate decking for
cable trough
9 Coated plate
shadow box
10 Cable trough
11 Cement screed
floor finish
12 Steel beam
13 Pressure treated
concrete subfloor
14 Channel plate floor
15 Welded structural
steel plate box section
16 Insulation
17 Coated steel plate

38.07
**Glazed Facade Plan
Detail**
1:10
1 Horizontal profile
glazing framing
2 Double glazed
curtain wall facade
3 Sealant
4 Vertical glazing
frame profile
5 Horizontal sealant
6 Cable trough
7 Line of perimeter
ceiling panel overhead
8 Steel column

**Basque Health Department
Headquarters
Bilbao, Spain**

Client
Gobierno Vasco

Project Team
Juan Coll-Barreu, Daniel Gutiérrez
Zarza, Fernando de la Maza, Jorge
Bilbao, Pablo Castro, Gorka García

Structural Engineer
Mintegia y Bilbao

Electrical and Mechanical Engineer
Indotec

The new Basque Health Department
headquarters is located on the last
empty site at the new administrative
and business centre for Bilbao.
Previously, the institution had to
accommodate staff in several
buildings, and as a consequence had
no public presence or recognizable
identity. The new building brings
together staff and technical services in
one location. The site is located at the
crossroads of two important historic
streets in Ensanche. Restrictive city
rules compel new structures to repeat
the form of existing buildings which
feature chamfered corner towers.

Coll-Barreu have reinterpreted the
restrictions to create an innovative
answer that, while complying with the
regulations, is contemporary and
functional. The faceted glass building
concentrates services and
communications, which serve seven
open-plan office floors, in a vertical
spine along the longest boundary.
Above this are two floors for local
representatives and institutional use.
The board of directors are
accommodated in the double height
space in the tower. The assembly hall,
its lobby and associated service
spaces are situated in the first
basement level, while below this are
two parking levels and a level for
archives. The double glass facade
solves not only urban requirements
but also those concerning energy
efficiency, fire resistance and acoustic
insulation. The folded facade has been
designed to generate multiple vistas
from the work spaces out onto the
streets below and also, from the
highest floors, to the wider urban
landscape.

1 A bold architectural
intervention of faceted
glass brings a new
dynamic to this historic
city neighbourhood.
2 Panels of vertical
glazing create a
seamless interface
between the new
building and its more
traditional neighbour,
which start to change
direction and shape as
the building reaches
and turns the corner.
3 During the day, the
panels of angled glass
reflect intriguing
fragmentary images of
the surrounding urban
landscape.

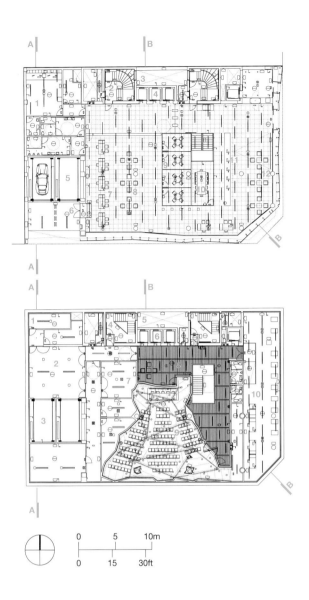

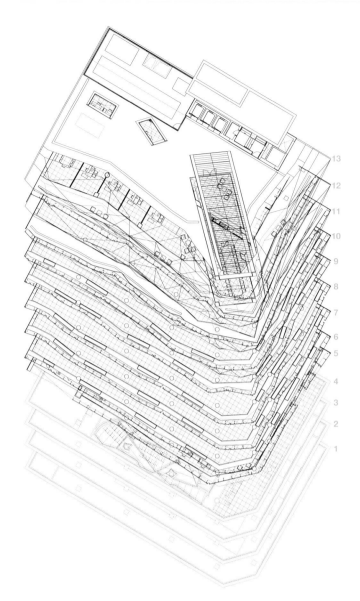

39.01
Ground Floor Plan
1:500
1 Mechanical room
2 Escape stair
3 Service riser
4 Lifts
5 Car park lift system
6 Entrance
7 Administrative area
8 Open meeting area
9 Private meeting room
10 Conference room
11 Computer stations
12 Open meeting area

39.02
First Basement Level Plan
1:500
1 Mechanical room
2 Technical area
3 Car park lift system
4 Escape stair
5 Service riser
6 Lifts
7 Technical area
8 Assembly gathering space
9 Assembly hall
10 Lounge

39.03
Axonometric Plan Diagram
1:500
1 Fourth basement level (archives)
2 Third basement level (car park)
3 Second basement level (car park)
4 First basement level (assembly hall)
5 Ground floor
6 First floor
7 Second floor
8 Third floor
9 Fourth floor
10 Fifth floor
11 Sixth floor
12 Seventh floor
13 Eighth floor

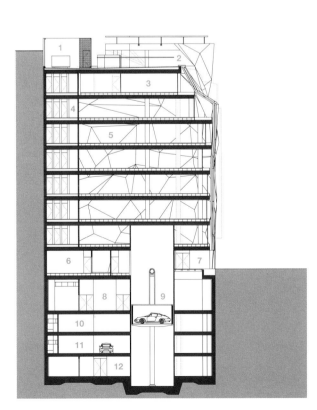

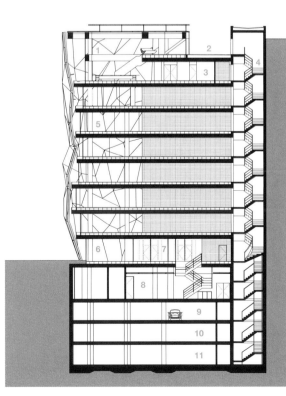

39.04
Section A–A
1:500
1 Rooftop plant
2 Rooftop terrace
3 Board of directors level
4 Circulation core
5 Offices
6 Open meeting areas
7 Circulation
8 Technical area
9 Car park lift system
10 Car park
11 Car park
12 Archives

39.05
Section B–B
1:500
1 Glazed roof space
2 Rooftop terrace
3 Board of directors level
4 Escape stair
5 Offices
6 Open meeting areas
7 Ground floor public area
8 Assembly room lobby
9 Car park
10 Car park
11 Archives

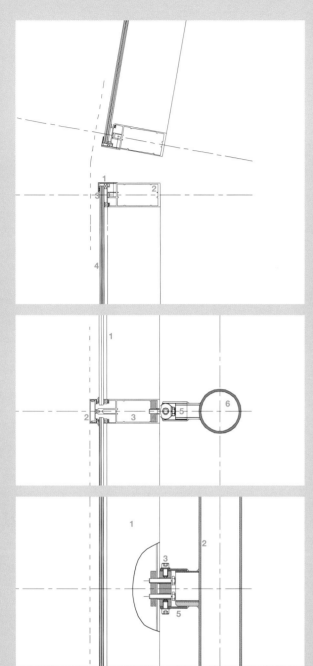

39.06
Glass Facade Plan Detail 1 with 170 Degree Angle
1:10
 1 2 mm ($^1/_{16}$ inch) thick anodized aluminium angle
 2 310 x 135 mm ($12^1/_5$ x $5^1/_3$ inch) extruded aluminium profile glazing frame
 3 Silicone seal
 4 Glazing comprised of polyvinyl butyral (PVB), bonded between two panels of 6 mm ($^1/_4$ inch) laminated glass

39.07
Glass Facade Plan Detail 2
1:10
 1 Glazing comprised of polyvinyl butyral (PVB), bonded between two panels of 6 mm ($^1/_4$ inch) laminated glass
 2 135 mm ($5^1/_3$ inch) anodized aluminium clip
 3 Extruded aluminium profile glazing frame
 4 15 mm ($^3/_5$ inch) stainless steel sheet
 5 Stainless steel profile joint
 6 114 mm ($4^1/_2$ inch) stainless steel circular hollow section

39.08
Glass Facade Section Detail 3
1:10
 1 310 x 135 mm ($12^1/_5$ x $5^1/_3$ inch) extruded aluminium profile glazing frame
 2 114 mm ($4^1/_2$ inch) stainless steel circular hollow section
 3 Stainless steel screw fixing
 4 15 mm ($^3/_5$ inch) stainless steel sheet
 5 Welded stainless steel profile

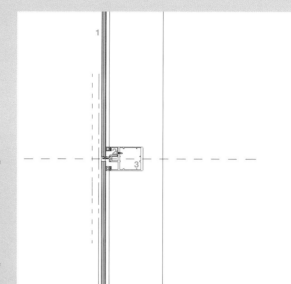

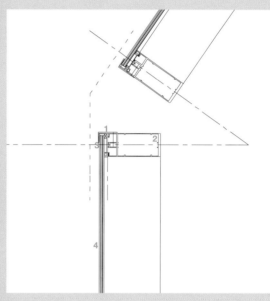

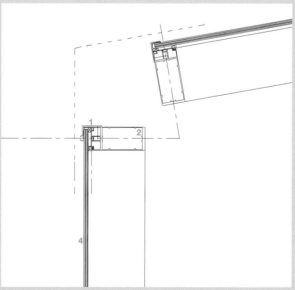

39.09
Glass Facade Plan Detail 4
1:10
 1 Glazing comprised of polyvinyl butyral (PVB), bonded between two panels of 6 mm ($^1/_4$ inch) laminated glass
 2 2 mm ($^1/_{16}$ inch) thick anodized aluminium folded sheet
 3 195 x 135 mm ($7^2/_3$ x $5^1/_3$ inch) extruded aluminium profile glazing frame

39.10
Glass Facade Plan Detail 5 with 145 Degree Angle
1:10
 1 2 mm ($^1/_{16}$ inch) thick anodized aluminium angle
 2 310 x 135 mm ($12^1/_5$ x $5^1/_3$ inch) extruded aluminium profile glazing frame
 3 Silicone seal
 4 Glazing comprised of polyvinyl butyral (PVB), bonded between two panels of 6 mm ($^1/_4$ inch) laminated glass

39.11
Glass Facade Plan Detail 6 with 100 Degree Angle
1:10
 1 2 mm ($^1/_{16}$ inch) thick anodized aluminium angle
 2 310 x 135 mm ($12^1/_5$ x $5^1/_3$ inch) extruded aluminium profile glazing frame
 3 Silicone seal
 4 Glazing comprised of polyvinyl butyral (PVB), bonded between two panels of 6 mm ($^1/_4$ inch) laminated glass

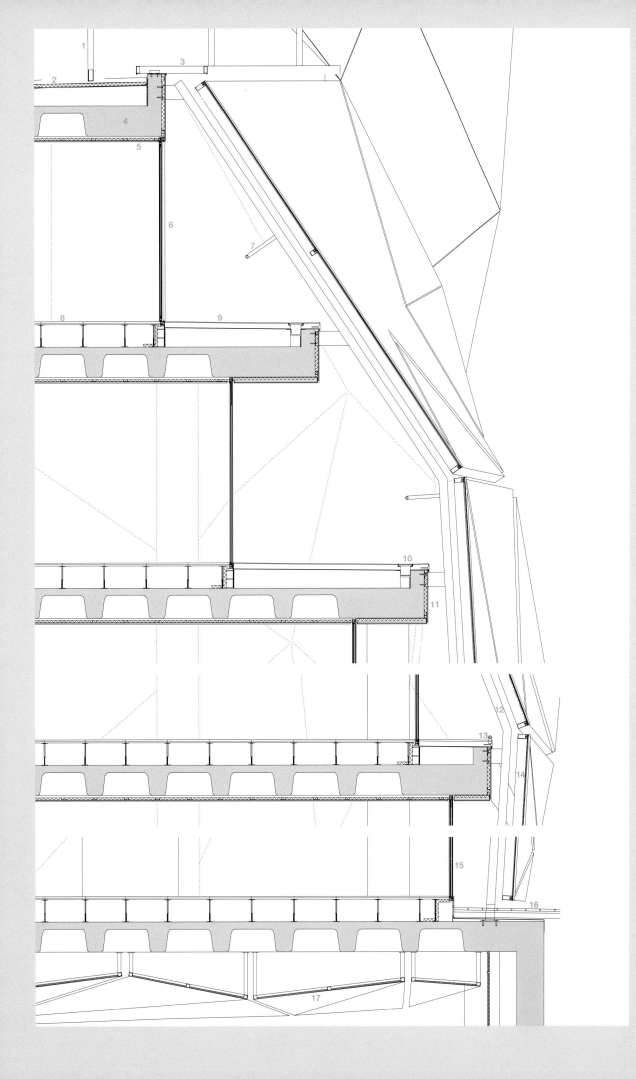

39.12
**Detail Section
Through Facade at
Upper Level**
1:50

1 Balustrade from
stainless steel circular
hollow section verticals
and timber handrail
2 Reinforced
concrete slab with
polished finish to roof
3 Folded aluminium
sheet capping
4 Reinforced
concrete waffle slab
5 Suspended ceiling
from plasterboard
sheets fixed to
galvanized steel
profiles over radiant
ceiling conditioning
system and thermal
insulation
6 Extruded
aluminium-framed
laminated glass doors
with low-E double
glazing
7 Stainless steel
circular hollow section
handrail
8 Raised service floor
over reinforced
concrete waffle slab
9 Mortar bedding
over reinforced
concrete slab with
waterproof membrane
10 Drain cover panel
11 Structural floor
finish from timber
panel over waterproof
cement and thermal
insulation
12 Stainless steel
circular hollow section
stanchion
13 Kick plate to floor
edge from stainless
steel tube profile
14 Exterior glazing
from laminated glass
with sunlight control in
extruded anodized
aluminium framing
15 Double low-E
glazing with interior
security laminated
glass in extruded
anodized aluminium
profile to break thermal
bridge
16 Cement floor tiles
on reinforced concrete
slab with waterproof
membrane
17 Suspended ceiling
to Assembly room
from expanded
stainless steel mesh
over galvanized steel
profiles over acoustic
absorber

**Coimbra Foot and Cycle Bridge
Coimbra, Portugal**

Client
Coimbra Polis / AFA Consulting

Project Team
Cecil Balmond, Daniel Bosia, Charles
Walker, Lip Chiong

Structural Engineer
AFA Consulting

Associate Architect
António Adão da Fonseca

The Rio Mondego, which winds
through the city of Coimbra in central
Portugal, is now traversed by an
innovative new bridge. Designed by
Cecil Balmond, founder of Arup's
Advanced Geometry Unit, and
engineered by António Adão da
Fonseca, a Portuguese bridge
designer, the bridge pushes the limits
of structural dynamics, creating a
seemingly impossible – as well as
unprecedented – structure. The
structure consists of two cantilevered
walkways that appear to be
perpetually caught in the process of
toppling over. In fact, the two halves of
the bridge hold each other up,
restoring equilibrium. The positioning
of the vertical supports and the offset
in plan creates a stiffened structure for
lateral stability. The contradictory
nature of the curving design breaks
the expected, traditional, continuous
sight lines of other bridges.

The displaced supporting structures
of the two bridge halves are pushed to
the outer extremes of each element so
that in sunlight the bridge has
contrasting elevations, one half in
shadow, the other in full sun. As the
joining island section has no deep
beam supports, the visual effect is of
a bridge that does not meet. The
structural dynamic is, however, only
part of a richly conceived design
concept for the architecture of the
bridge. For example, bespoke glass
balustrade panels trapped between a
seemingly random carbon steel
framework catch the dappled light
bouncing off the river. This, and the
landscaping to either side of the
bridge, creates a journey of discovery
in an otherwise open environment.
The design of this unique bridge
provokes the questioning of accepted
practices and methods, using pure
structural techniques to introduce a
new aesthetic to architecture.

1 The surface of the
bridge's walkway
consists of 1,150
square metres (12,378
square feet) of
Guayacan timber
boarding, while the
steel and glass
guard rail stretches
782 metres (2,565 feet)
in total.
2 The faceted panes
of glass in pastel tones
of blue, green, yellow
and pink, cast
coloured shadows
onto the surface of the
walkway.
3 The elemental
structure of white
concrete is juxtaposed
by the crystalline
geometry of the glass
safety rail.
4 Detail view of the
glass balustrade – a
delicate web of carbon
steel with bespoke
circular fixing points
anchor the panels of
coloured glass.

40.01
Bridge Elevation
1:2000
1 Concrete abutment
2 Column support
3 Arch structure
4 Foundations
5 Glass balustrade
6 Staircase

40.02
Bridge Plan
1:2000
1 Earth ramp
2 Bridge approach
  with earth retaining
  wall
3 Staircase
4 Stair
5 Bridge walkway
6 Bridge mid-point

7 Bridge walkway
8 Staircase
9 Bridge approach
  with earth retaining
  wall
10 Earth ramp

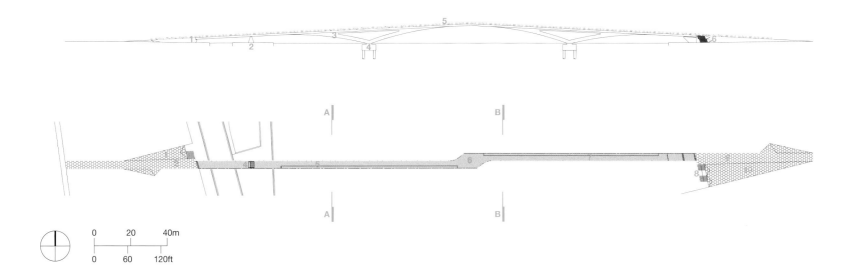

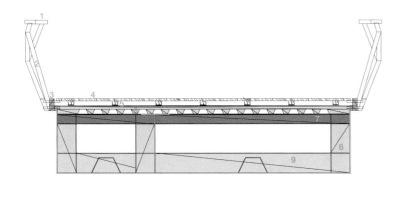

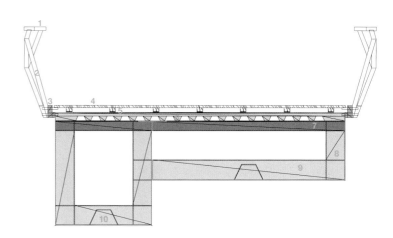

40.03
Section A–A
1:50
1 Handrail
2 Steel balustrade
3 Light embedded in
  timber deck
4 Timber deck
5 Support to deck
6 Structural steel
  deck
7 Structural steel
  member
8 Structural steel
  member
9 Structural steel
  member

40.04
Section B–B
1:50
1 Handrail
2 Steel balustrade
3 Light embedded in
  timber deck
4 Timber deck
5 Support to deck
6 Structural steel
  deck
7 Structural steel
  member
8 Structural steel
  member
9 Structural steel
  member
10 Structural steel
  member
11 Structural steel
  member

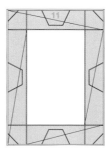

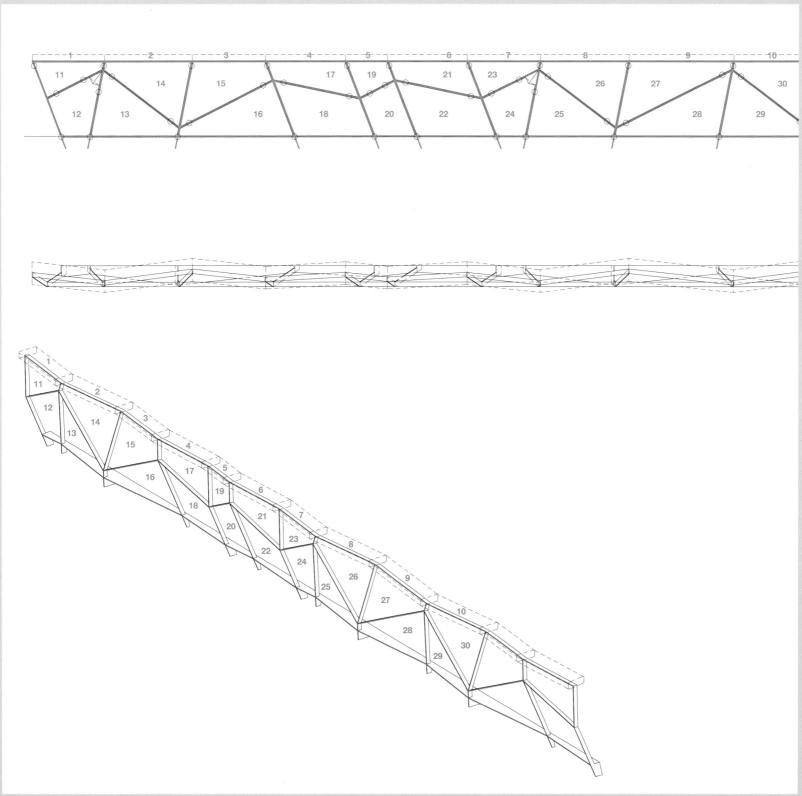

40.05
Balustrade Panels
Detail
1:50
1 997 mm (39¹/₄ inch)
long, 60 x 277 mm
(2³/₈ x 10⁹/₁₀ inch)
timber hand rail
2 1200 mm (47¹/₄
inch) long, 60 x 277
mm (2³/₈ x 10⁹/₁₀ inch)
timber hand rail
3 1003 mm (39¹/₂
inch) long, 60 x 277
mm (2³/₈ x 10⁹/₁₀ inch)

timber hand rail
4 1096 mm (43¹/₈
inch) long, 60 x 277
mm (2³/₈ x 10⁹/₁₀ inch)
timber hand rail
5 581 mm (22⁹/₁₀
inch) long, 60 x 277
mm (2³/₈ x 10⁹/₁₀ inch)
timber hand rail
6 1096 mm (43¹/₈
inch) long, 60 x 277
mm (2³/₈ x 10⁹/₁₀ inch)
timber hand rail
7 997 mm (39¹/₄ inch)
long, 60 x 277 mm

(2³/₈ x 10⁹/₁₀ inch)
timber hand rail
8 1199 mm (47¹/₅
inch) long, 60 x 277
mm (2³/₈ x 10⁹/₁₀ inch)
timber hand rail
9 1419 mm (55⁴/₅
inch) long, 60 x 277
mm (2³/₈ x 10⁹/₁₀ inch)
timber hand rail
10 1200 mm (47¹/₄
inch) long, 60 x 277
mm (2³/₈ x 10⁹/₁₀ inch)
timber hand rail
11 Glass balustrade

panel type 1
12 Glass balustrade
panel type 2
13 Glass balustrade
panel type 4
14 Glass balustrade
panel type 3
15 Glass balustrade
panel type 5
16 Glass balustrade
panel type 6
17 Glass balustrade
panel type 7
18 Glass balustrade
panel type 8

19 Glass balustrade
panel type 9
20 Glass balustrade
panel type 10
21 Glass balustrade
panel type 7
22 Glass balustrade
panel type 8
23 Glass balustrade
panel type 1
24 Glass balustrade
panel type 2
25 Glass balustrade
panel type 4
26 Glass balustrade

panel type 3
27 Glass balustrade
panel type 11
28 Glass balustrade
panel type 12
29 Glass balustrade
panel type 4
30 Glass balustrade
panel type 3

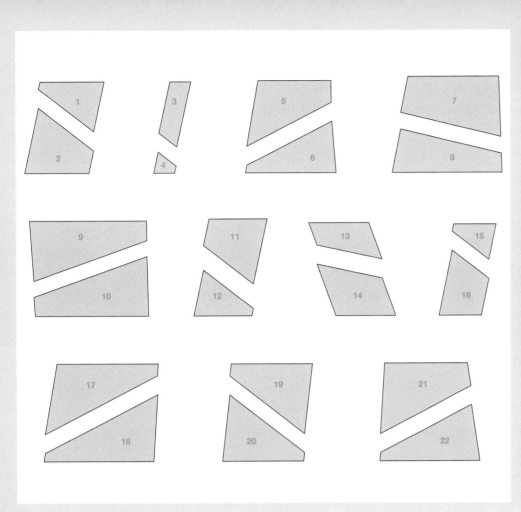

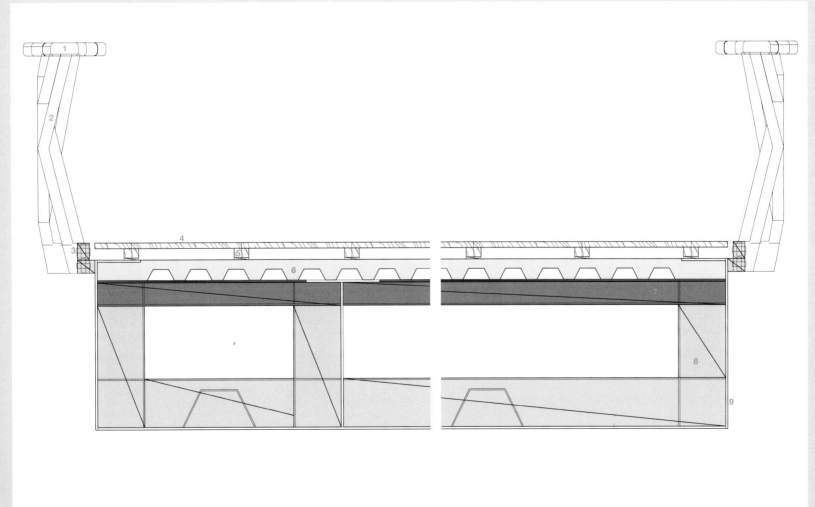

Heneghan Peng Architects in association with Arthur Gibney & Partners

Áras Chill Dara
Naas, County Kildare, Ireland

Client
Kildare County Council

Project Team
Shih-Fu Peng, Roisin Heneghan, Kin Tong, Ulf Klusmann, Paul Giblin, Carmel Murray, Edel Tobin, Martin Rohrmoser, David Harris, Leon Shakeshaft, Susan Early, Claudine Keogh, Padhraic Moneley, Karen Hammond

Structural Engineer
Michael Punch & Partners

Main Contractor
Pierse Contracting

This new building for Kildare County Council is formed around a civic garden where an inclined ground plane gradually ascends from the street to create an amphitheatre. The sloped amphitheatre acts as an 'event surface', opening up the entire site to the town. The two arms that form the building enclose, and are a continuation of, the amphitheatre. The inclined facades form a seamless continuity with the grass surface so that building and park no longer read as two distinct elements but rather combine to create an outdoor room. The link ramps that connect the arms have transparent facades that allow the park to visually flow through the building, while internally, the ramps serve as a place of social interaction. The facade acts as a rainscreen composed of single sheets of glass, with sunshades and louvers helping to provide a moderate internal temperature. The offices are laid out so that all of the departmental elements are grouped together yet none of the departments are given a separate architectural expression. As departments change size over time they can expand and contract without necessitating changes in the building fabric. The east arm houses the main entrance, which is reached from the civic amphitheatre through a natural foyer of retained existing trees. The main entrance – a double height foyer and exhibition space has a strong visual connection to the garden and all of the public spaces. The new civic offices create an environment in which the public is invited to share in the process of government, as well as serving as a resource for the people of Naas and of Kildare.

1 The fully glazed facades and rainscreens incorporate a lighting strategy that maximizes the use of daylighting through the use of a lamella facade which includes louvres within the double glazing that redirect natural light to ceiling mounted reflectors. The artificial lighting system is automatically linked to daylight availability.
2 The ramp structure that links the two glazed wings creates two attractive outdoor spaces either side of the ramp structure.
3 The intersection of the Civic Garden with the existing Central Pavilion creates a small outdoor amphitheatre for public performances.

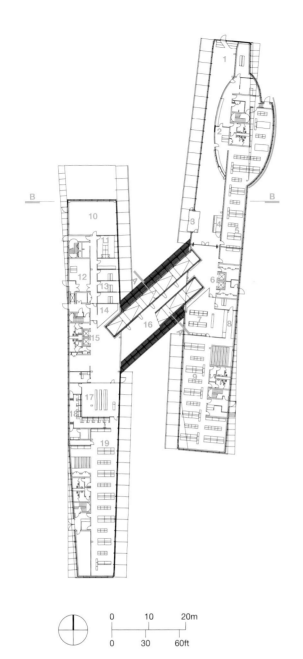

41.01
Ground Floor Plan
1:1000
1 Meeting room
2 Public service counters
3 Main entrance
4 Reception
5 Offices
6 Lift lobby
7 Waiting area
8 Service counters
9 Offices
10 Training suite
11 Meeting room
12 Post and delivery room
13 Interview room
14 Waiting area
15 Lift lobby
16 Ramp link
17 Waiting area
18 Service counters
19 Offices

41.02
Section A–A
1:500
1 Link space roof
2 Glazed facade
3 Ramp
4 Section through sloping external ground
5 Services duct
6 Link cafe

41.03
Section B–B
1:500
1 Aluminium frame curtain walling
2 Office area
3 Main reception
4 Aluminium frame curtain walling
5 Link space glazed facade
6 Glazed garden screen
7 Canteen
8 Plant enclosure
9 Council chamber
10 Aluminium frame curtain walling
11 Approach ramp

0   10   20m

0   30   60ft

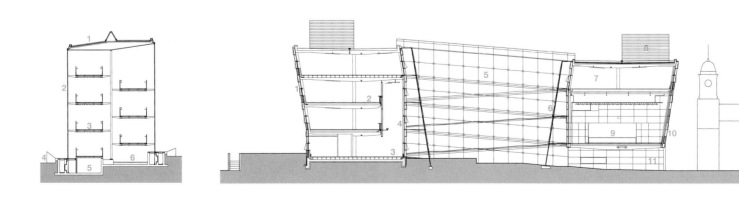

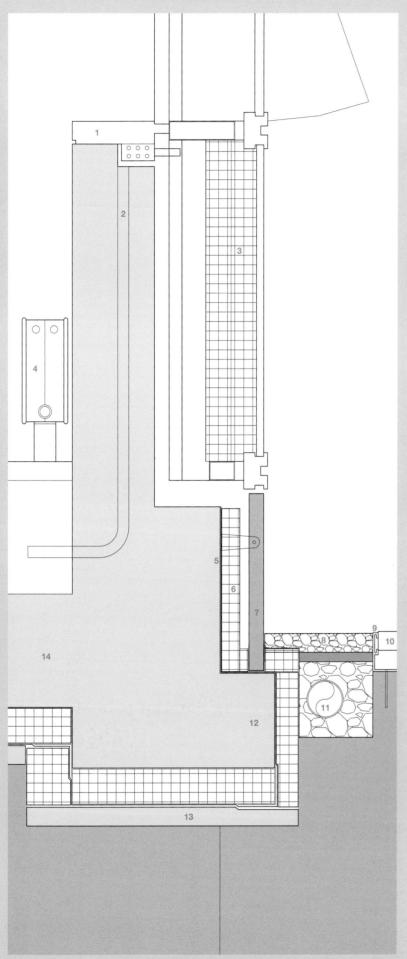

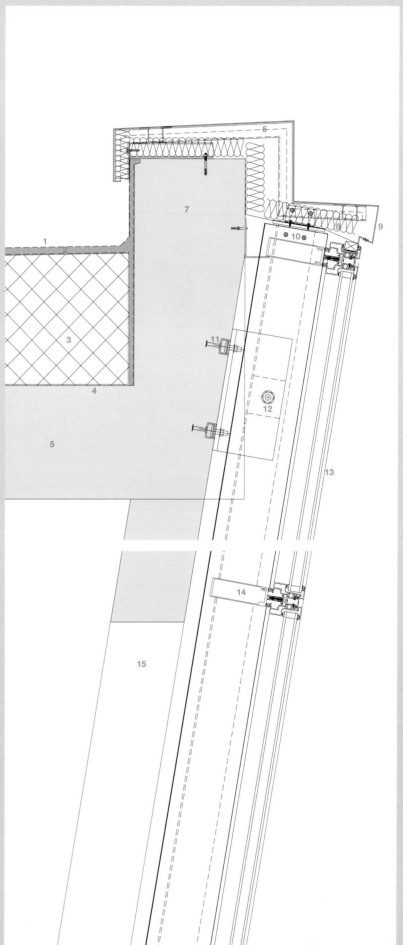

41.04
**Cross Section
Through East Wing
Base Detail**
1:10
  1 Veneer ply with
veneer running over
solid edge to both
ends of window sill
  2 Cast-in conduits at
3 metre (100 foot)
centres
  3 Curtain wall system
  4 Radiator
  5 Radon barrier
  6 Rigid insulation
  7 Stone cladding
  8 Loose gravel
  9 Aluminium restraint
angle
  10 Reinforced grass
  11 Concealed
agricultural drain
  12 Concrete support
footing
  13 Concrete blinding
  14 Reinforced
concrete floor slab

41.05
**Cross Section
Through East Wing
Parapet Detail**
1:10
  1 Asphalt roof
  2 Flax reinforced
black sheathing felt
impregnated with
bitumen
  3 Roof insulation laid
to 1:60 to fall to
rainwater outlets
  4 Vapour control layer
  5 Concrete roof slab
  6 Pressed aluminium
parapet
  7 Concrete upstand
  8 Insulation
  9 Pressed aluminium
capping
  10 Steel closing plate
  11 Cast-in fixing rail
  12 Mullion to bracket
bolt connection
  13 Glazing
  14 Extruded aluminium
transom
  15 Exposed reinforced
concrete wall

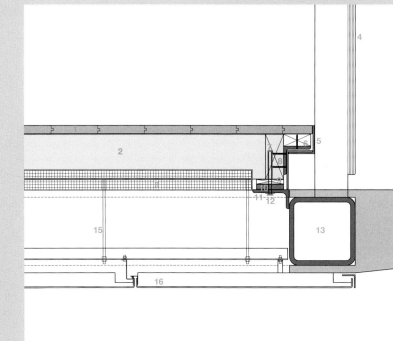

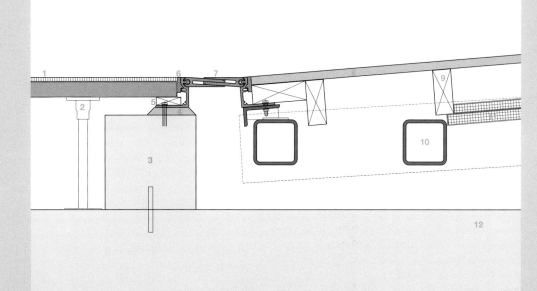

41.06
**Cross Section Detail
Through Ramp Link
Space**
1:10
  1 Longitudinally laid,
fire treated strip-wood
flooring with exposed
expansion joints at
perimeter
  2 Fire treated timber
joists at 350 mm (13³/₄
inch) centres running
across ramp between
steel supports
  3 Rockwool acoustic
insulation in black
surface finish to be 30
mm (1¹/₅ inch) to
underside of joists and
25 mm (1 inch)
between joists
  4 Glass balustrade
  5 4 mm (¹/₈ inch)
anodized continuous

aluminium angles with
concealed fixings
  6 Fire treated
continuous timber
batten, screw fixed to
mild steel angle
  7 Acoustic sleeve for
screw fixing
  8 Continuous
galvanized mild steel
angle support to floor
edge, screw fixed to
timber joists
  9 Fire treated
continuous timber
batten
  10 Continuous resilient
vibration strip
  11 Steel angle
  12 Screw and washer
fixings to joist
  13 Structural steel
tube ramp structure
  14 Trimmed steel
outrigger

  15 Aluminium hangers
for suspended ceiling
system
  16 Suspended ceiling
panel

41.07
**Longitudinal Section
Detail Through Ramp
Link Space**
1:10
  1 Raised access floor
  2 Raised floor props
  3 Continuous
concrete upstand
  4 20 mm (³/₄ inch)
epoxy mortar bed
  5 Fire treated timber
blocking
  6 Compressible
gasket
  7 Expansion joint
cover
  8 Ramp floor
comprised of
longitudinally laid fire
treated timber
floorboards on timber
joists on steel angles
  9 Fire treated timber
joist

  10 Structural steel
tube
  11 Rockwool acoustic
insulation in black,
surface finish to be 30
mm (1¹/₅ inch) to
underside of joists and
25 mm (1 inch)
between joists
  12 Primary structural
slab

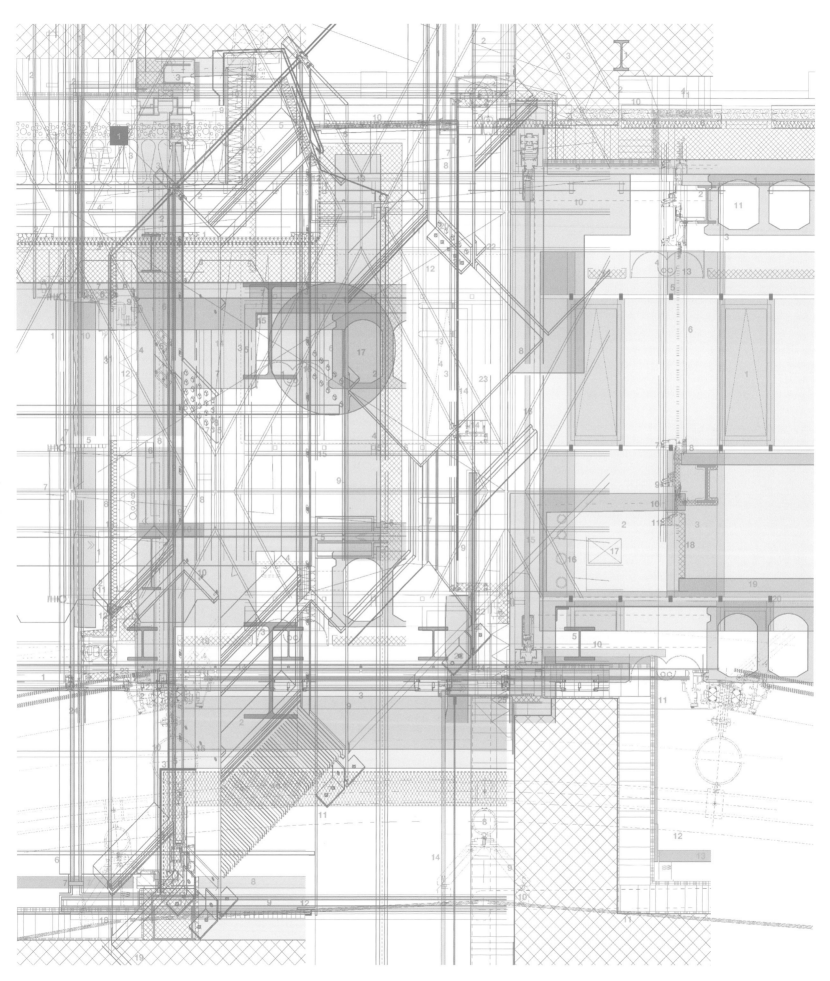

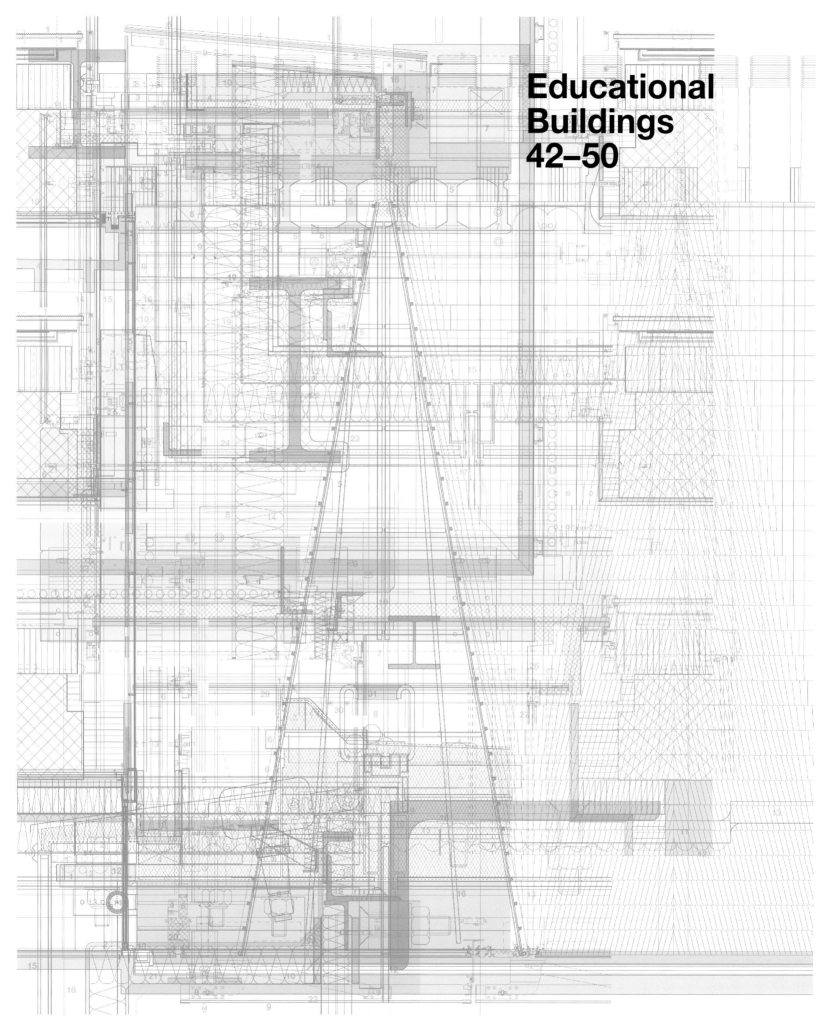

Educational
Buildings
42–50

**Westkaai Apartment Towers
Antwerp, Belgium**

Client
NV Kattendijkdok

Project Team
Diener & Diener, Berlin/Basel with ELD
Partnership, Antwerp

Structural Engineer
Stedec

Facade Planner
AMP Albrecht Memmert & Partner

In the harbour of Antwerp, to the north of the city centre, the Westkaai apartment towers mark a newly conceived cultural axis. The three phase project involves three architectural practices, each of whom will design two towers, each 16 storeys high, that will form a grouping on the public waterfront. The first duo of towers, designed by Diener & Diener, is located close to Amsterdamstraat and is directly on the quay edge. The transparency of the glass-clad towers is in sharp contrast to the phalanx of old narrow, multi-storey row houses elsewhere on the dock. However specific architectural elements in the existing row houses, including the size of openings and textural qualities, inspired the design of the towers.

On the other hand, the homogeneity and horizontality of the existing buildings oppose the dynamic verticality of the towers. The elevations of the two apartment buildings differ as a result of varying the floor plan configurations, which is then reflected in the fenestration. The floor types are repeated in stacks of two, three or four types and then alternated over the height of the tower. Each of these floor types is made up of seven different apartment plans, ranging from two room apartments to five room apartments. The positions of the windows follow the logicality of the floor plans, thus the facades demonstrate varying rhythms across the elevations. Five different window types of either fixed glazing or pivot-hung windows allow light and ventilation to the apartments. The remainder of the facade surface is clad in rippled glass which is fixed by aluminium frames or by individual clips over insulated gold and silver anodized coloured sheet-metal panels.

1 The two apartment towers by Diener & Diener, are the first of six towers to be built as part of the same harbourside development.
2 The entirely glazed facade is made up of either clear fixed or openable glazing to bring light into the apartments, or by rippled glass panels fixed over gold and silver coloured sheet-metal panels.
3 The rhythm of the fenestration is a result of the floor plans which vary over the height of the building and include apartments ranging from two to five bedrooms.
4 Detail view of the corner of one of the towers where it meets the paved surface of the quay.
5 Deep covered terraces feature pivoting glass blades to allow them to be used in a variety of climatic conditions throughout the year.

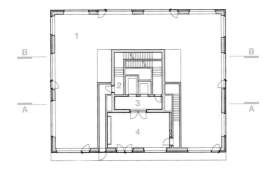

42.01
Tower 1 Ground Floor Plan
1:500
1 Retail or commercial space
2 Escape stair
3 Lift lobby
4 Entrance hall

42.02
Tower 2 Ground Floor Plan
1:500
1 Parking exit
2 Parking entrance

3 Retail or commercial space
4 Escape stair
5 Lift lobby
6 Entrance lobby
7 Retail or commercial space

42.03
Apartment Level Floor Plan Type A
1:500
1 Terrace
2 Living room and Kitchen
3 Bedroom

4 Terrace
5 Living room and Kitchen
6 Living room and Kitchen
7 Terrace
8 Bedroom
9 Living room and Kitchen
10 Terrace
11 Bedroom
12 Bedroom
13 Bedroom
14 Bedroom
15 Bathroom
16 Entrance hall

17 Bathroom
18 Lift lobby
19 Bathroom
20 Entrance hall
21 Bathroom

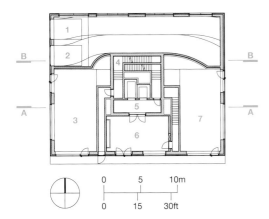

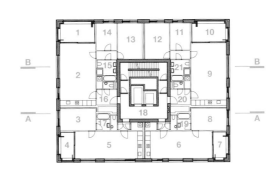

42.04
Section A–A
1:500
1 Service floor and roof
2 Fifteenth floor
3 Fourteenth floor
4 Thirteenth floor
5 Twelfth floor
6 Eleventh floor
7 Tenth floor
8 Ninth floor
9 Eighth floor
10 Seventh floor
11 Sixth floor
12 Fifth floor
13 Fourth floor
14 Third floor
15 Second floor
16 First floor
17 Ground floor
18 First basement level
19 Second basement level

42.05
Section B–B
1:500
1 Service floor and roof
2 Fifteenth floor
3 Fourteenth floor
4 Thirteenth floor
5 Twelfth floor
6 Eleventh floor
7 Tenth floor
8 Ninth floor
9 Eighth floor
10 Seventh floor
11 Sixth floor
12 Fifth floor
13 Fourth floor
14 Third floor
15 Second floor
16 First floor
17 Ground floor
18 First basement level
19 Second basement level

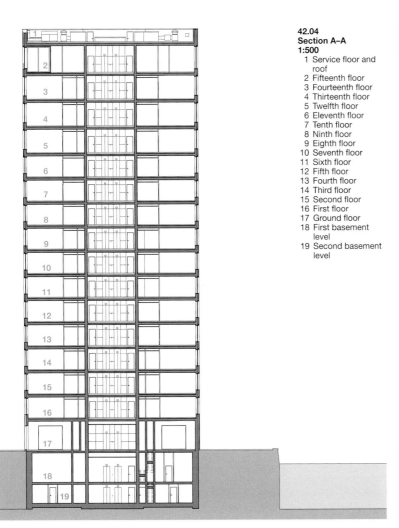

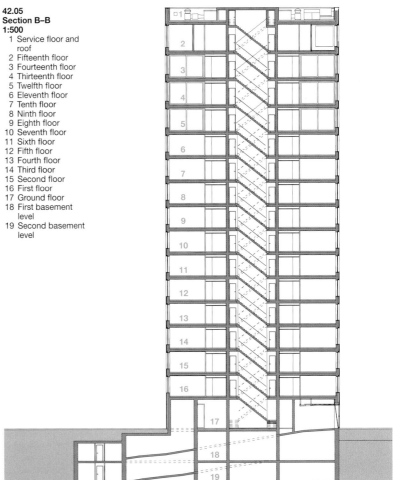

0 5 10m
0 15 30ft

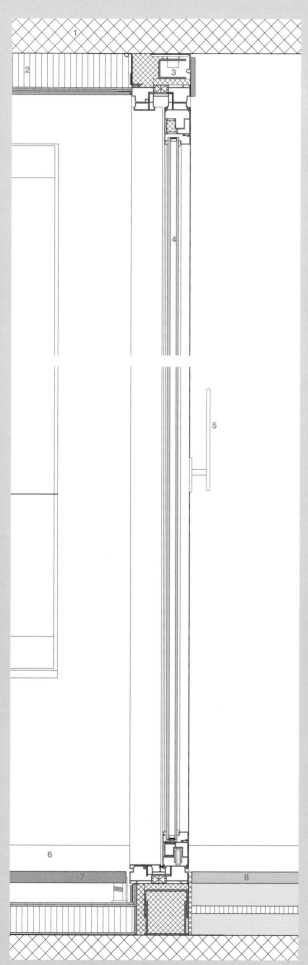

42.06
Sliding Glass Door To Terrace Detail
1:10
1 280 mm (11 inch) reinforced concrete floor slab
2 10 mm (3/8 inch) render ceiling finish over 100 mm (4 inch) insulation
3 Anodized aluminium sliding door frame
4 Sliding glass door with double glazing comprised of 6 mm (1/4 inch) glass, 20 mm (3/4 inch) air gap and 8 mm (1/3 inch) glass
5 Door handle for lifting and sliding door
6 Exterior skirting from 10 mm (3/8 inch) thick granite, set flush with leading edge of plaster finished walls, and bottom edge set flush with bottom edge of granite flooring
7 Exterior flooring from 30 mm (11/5 inch) thick granite with 3 mm (1/8 inch) joints built on height adjustable feet
8 Interior floor from timber parquet laid on cement screed over polythene foil, acoustic layer, layer of concrete with polystyrene grains and concrete floor slab

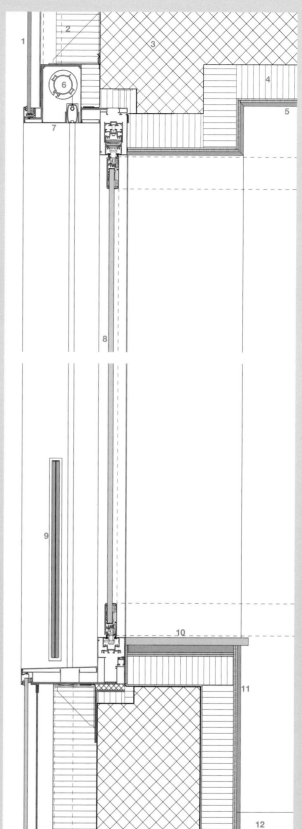

42.07
Glazed Windshield To Terrace Detail
1:10
1 External wall comprised of 12 mm (1/2 inch) cast glass with vertical grooves, aluminium-clip fixing, 30 mm (11/5 inch) ventilated cavity, 3 mm (1/8 inch) aluminium sheet supporting structure, anodized gold or silver coloured sound-deadening coating and 40 mm (15/8 inch) air space
2 120 mm (43/4 inch) Rockwool insulation
3 280 mm (11 inch) reinforced concrete
4 Terrace upstand wall from 100 mm (4 inch) thermal insulation composite panels with painted plaster finish
5 10 mm (3/8 inch) thick skim coat to plaster ceiling
6 External sunscreen with sliding rails for zip system, laterally integrated into opening embrasure
7 42 mm (15/8 inch) anodized aluminium frame to all sides of opening
8 Windbreak blades from sliding and pivoting 12 mm (1/2 inch) thick safety glass with 3 mm (1/8 inch) gaps between blades in anodized aluminium frame with duplex ball-bearing horizontal travelling gear
9 Terrace guardrail from 25 mm (1 inch) thick laminated safety glass with upper edge protected in 25 x 3 mm (1 x 1/8 inch) stainless steel profile
10 Window sill from 20 mm (3/4 inch) thick granite with 2 mm (1/16 inch) joints with minimal bevel to all edges
11 Terrace upstand wall from 100 mm (4 inch) thermal insulation composite panels with painted plaster finish
12 Skirting from 10 mm (3/8 inch) thick granite set flush with leading edge of plaster finished walls, and bottom edge set flush with bottom edge of granite flooring
13 Flooring from 30 mm (11/4 inch) thick granite with 3 mm (1/8 inch) joints built on height adjustable feet
14 External wall comprised of 12 mm (1/2 inch) cast glass with vertical grooves, aluminium-clip fixing, 30 mm (11/4 inch) ventilated cavity, 3 mm (1/8 inch) aluminium sheet supporting structure, anodized gold or silver coloured sound-deadening coating and 40 mm (15/8 inch) air space

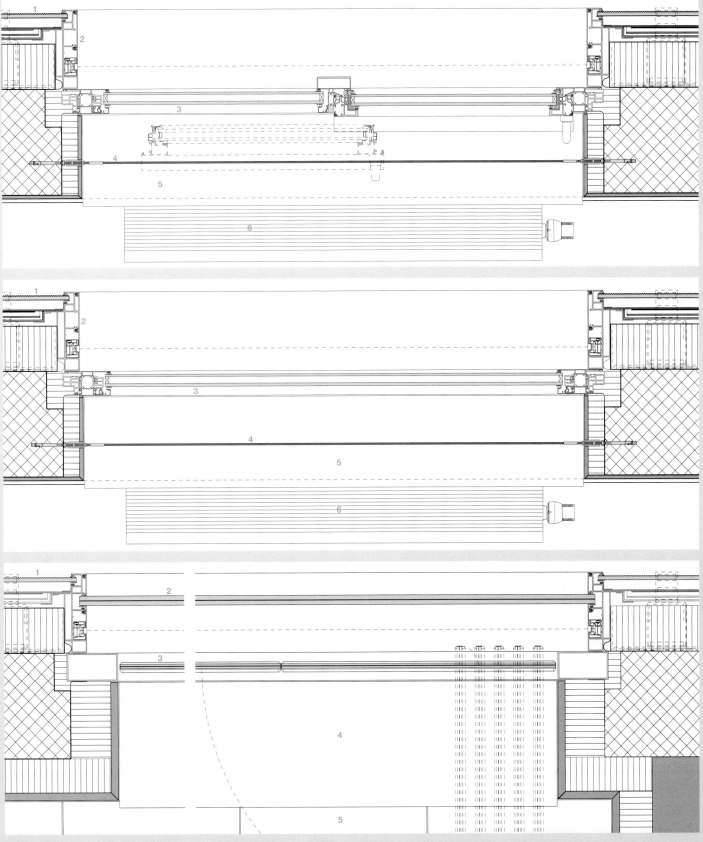

sound-deadening coating and 40 mm (1⁵/₈ inch) air space

2 Terrace guardrail from 25 mm (1 inch) thick laminated safety glass with upper edge protected in 25 x 3 mm (1 x ¹/₈ inch) stainless steel profile

3 Windbreak blades from sliding and pivoting 12 mm (¹/₂ inch) thick safety glass with 3 mm (¹/₈ inch) gaps between blades in anodized aluminium frame with duplex ball-bearing horizontal travelling gear

4 Window sill from 20 mm (³/₄ inch) thick granite with 2 mm (¹/₁₆ inch) joints with minimal bevel to all edges

5 Exterior flooring from 30 mm (1¹/₄ inch) thick granite with 3 mm (¹/₈ inch) joints built on height adjustable feet

**42.08
Typical Sliding
Window Plan Detail
1:10**

1 External wall comprised of 12 mm (¹/₂ inch) cast glass with vertical grooves, aluminium-clip fixing, 30 mm (1¹/₄ inch) ventilated cavity, 3 mm (¹/₈ inch) aluminium sheet supporting structure, anodized gold or silver coloured sound-deadening coating and 40 mm (1⁵/₈ inch) air space

2 42 mm (1²/₃ inch) anodized aluminium frame to all sides of opening

3 Sliding glass window in anodized aluminium frame with double glazing comprised of 6 mm (¹/₄ inch) glass, 20 mm (³/₄ inch) air gap and 8 mm (¹/₃ inch) glass

4 5 mm (¹/₅ inch) diameter horizontal stainless steel rope handrail embedded in embrasure to either side of window with 150 mm (6 inch) gap between ropes

5 Window sill from 20 mm (³/₄ inch) thick granite with 2 mm (¹/₁₆ inch) joints with minimal bevel to all edges

6 200 x 120 mm (7⁷/₈ x 4³/₄ inch) radiator

**42.09
Typical Fixed Window
Plan Detail
1:10**

1 External wall comprised of 12 mm (¹/₂ inch) cast glass with vertical grooves, aluminium-clip fixing, 30 mm (1¹/₄ inch) ventilated cavity, 3 mm (¹/₈ inch) aluminium sheet supporting structure, anodized gold or silver coloured sound-deadening coating and 40 mm (1⁵/₈ inch) air space

2 42 mm (1²/₃ inch) anodized aluminium frame to all sides of opening

3 Fixed glass window in anodized aluminium frame with double glazing comprised of 6 mm (¹/₄ inch) glass, 20 mm (³/₄ inch) air gap and 8 mm (¹/₃ inch) glass

4 5 mm (¹/₅ inch) diameter horizontal stainless steel rope handrail embedded in embrasure to either side of window with 150 mm (6 inch) gap between ropes

5 Window sill from 20 mm (³/₄ inch) thick granite with 2 mm (¹/₁₆ inch) joints with minimal bevel to all edges

6 200 x 120 mm (7⁷/₈ x 4³/₄ inch) radiator

**42.10
Typical Glass
Windshield to Terrace
Plan Detail
1:10**

1 External wall comprised of 12 mm (¹/₂ inch) cast glass with vertical grooves, aluminium-clip fixing, 30 mm (1¹/₄ inch) ventilated cavity, 3 mm (¹/₈ inch) aluminium sheet supporting structure, anodized gold or silver coloured

Information, Communications and Media Center, Brandenburg Technical University Cottbus, Germany

Client
Liegenschafts- und Bauamt Cottbus

Project Team
Jacques Herzog, Pierre de Meuron, Christine Binswanger, Jürgen Johner, Florian Marti

Structural Engineer
Pahn Ingenieure

Main Contractor
Höhler + Partner Architekten und Ingenieure

The new library for the Brandenburg Technical University was designed to stand as a solitary landmark within the surrounding urban architecture that would communicate the new spirit of the university. The amoeba-like ground plan seems to spread and flow into the surrounding landscape. Although it appears, at first sight, to be a purely accidental shape, it is actually a purposeful configuration of many different circulation paths. The glazed building stands opposite the main entrance to the campus, from where it appears to be anchored in its park-like setting.

The organic form allows the creation of reading rooms in many different sizes and oriented in all directions, while maintaining the larger whole of the library as a single, connected interior space. Within the exterior envelope, and following an orthogonal layout, the interior floors are cut back so that each has a different shape, generating a tension between the interior and the continuous shell of the building. As a result, some of the reading rooms are two or three storeys high while others are more intimate with intentionally low ceilings. An expansive spiral staircase, six metres (20 feet) in diameter, cuts through the entire structure and links all nine levels. The delicate facade features a white veil of glass printed on both sides with text in different languages and alphabets. These have been superimposed in a multitude of layers so that they are deliberately illegible. The printed pattern breaks the reflection, eliminates the brittle appearance of the glass and transforms the building into a fragile sculptural presence in the landscape.

1 The layering of white text over the surface of the glass facade results in a design whose origin in the world of written signs is unmistakable.
2 By night, the library appears as an impassive monument anchored in the park.
3 The colour scheme in the reading rooms, with their atmosphere of quiet concentration, is grey and white, allowing the architectural expression of space, light and views to take precedence.
4 Areas in the interior of the building are bathed in colour, including stripes on the floors, supports and walls following the rational, orthogonal building system.

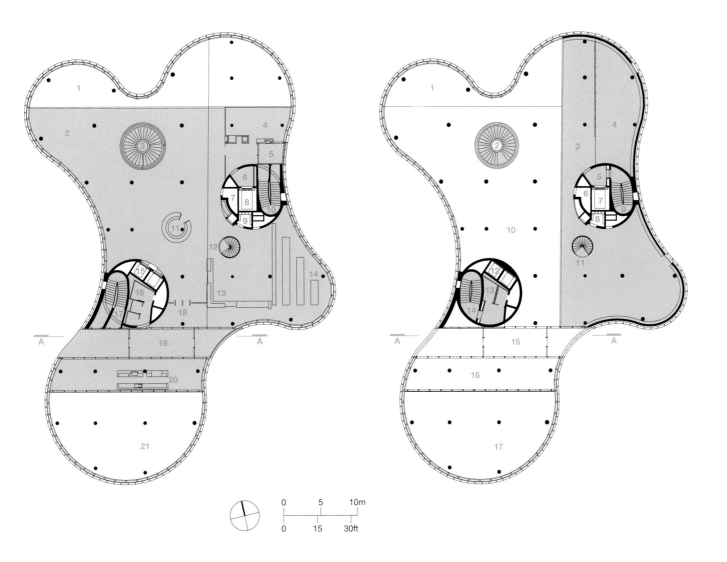

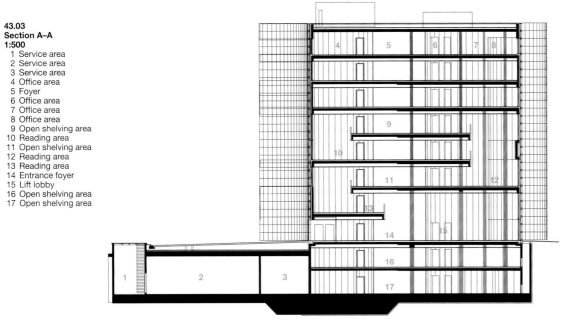

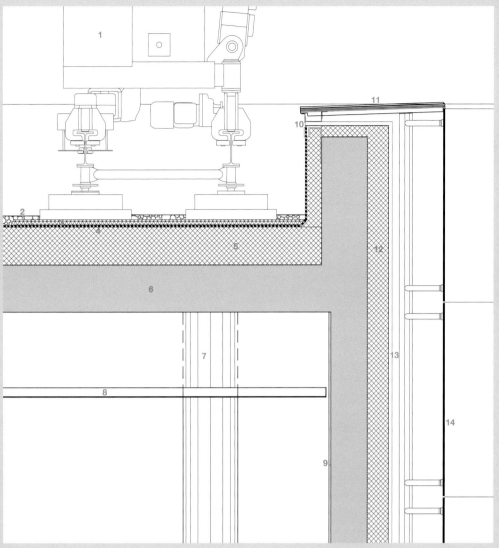

43.04
Roof Parapet Detail
1:20
1 Building
maintenance cradle
2 50 mm (2 inch)
gravel layer over roof
sealing layer
3 30 mm (1 1/5 inch)
protection mat
4 Vapour barrier
5 200 mm (8 inch)
thick insulation
comprised of bitumen
with inlaid cellular
glass and mineral fibre
6 250 to 300 mm
(9 4/5 to 11 4/5 inch)
reinforced concrete
roof slab
7 Cylindrical concrete
column
8 50 mm (2 inch)
suspended ceiling
9 Skim render finish
to internal wall
10 Metal grille over
facade ventilation void
11 Glass parapet
cover
12 Insulation
13 70 mm (2 3/4 inch)
vertical tube
14 Glass cladding cut
according to geometry
of exterior wall

43.05
Glazing Plan Detail
1:10
1 External double
glazing comprised of 6
mm (1/4 inch) float
glass, 16 mm (2/3 inch)
cavity and 8 mm (1/3
inch) toughened glass
partially screen printed
with white pattern
2 Aluminium
extrusion glazing
framing
3 127 mm (5 inch)
vertical galvanized
steel tube structure
4 70 mm (2 3/4 inch)
diameter horizontal
steel tube structure
5 70 mm (2 3/4 inch)
diameter vertical steel
tube structure
6 Aluminium glazing
fixing with stainless
steel countersunk
point fixing
7 Aluminium disc
between internal glass
and point fixing
8 8 mm (1/3 inch)
toughened glass
internal glazing layer,
screen printed in white
with open joints

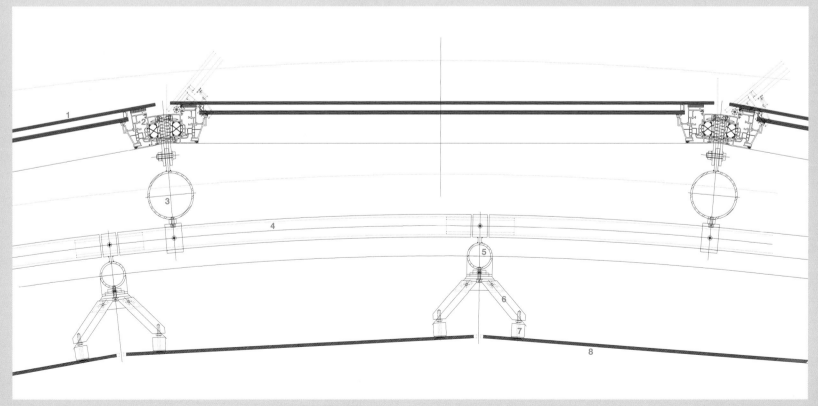

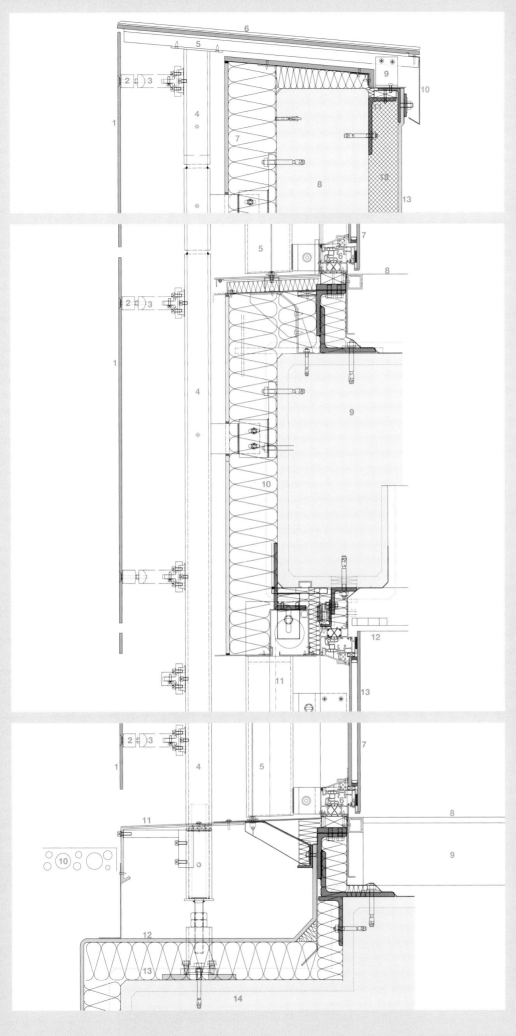

43.06
Facade Glazing at Roof Level Section Detail
1:10
1 8 mm ($1/3$ inch) toughened glass internal glazing layer, screen printed in white with open joints
2 Aluminium disc between internal glass and point fixing
3 Aluminium glazing fixing with stainless steel countersunk point fixing
4 70 mm ($2^3/4$ inch) diameter vertical steel tube structure
5 Steel fixing plate
6 Glass parapet cover
7 140 mm ($5^1/2$ inch) Rockwool thermal insulation
8 250 mm ($9^4/5$ inch) concrete column
9 Galvanized steel connection plate
10 Folded aluminium edge capping
11 Steel angle
12 80 mm ($3^1/8$ inch) rigid thermal insulation
13 Cladding

43.07
Facade Glazing at Wall Section Detail
1:10
1 8 mm ($1/3$ inch) toughened glass internal glazing layer, screen printed in white with open joints
2 Aluminium disc between internal glass and point fixing
3 Aluminium glazing fixing with stainless steel countersunk point fixing
4 70 mm ($2^3/4$ inch) diameter vertical steel tube structure
5 127 mm (5 inch) vertical galvanized steel tube structure
6 Aluminium extrusion glazing framing
7 Double glazing comprised of 6 mm ($1/4$ inch) float glass, 16 mm ($2/3$ inch) cavity and 8 mm ($1/3$ inch) toughened glass partially screen printed with white pattern
8 Raised floor
9 350 mm ($13^3/4$ inch) reinforced floor slab with 270 mm ($10^2/3$ inch) deep reinforced downstand beam
10 140 mm ($5^1/2$ inch) Rockwool thermal insulation
11 Sun protection roller blind
12 Steel grille suspended ceiling
13 Double glazing comprised of 6 mm ($1/4$ inch) float glass, 16 mm ($2/3$ inch) cavity and 8 mm ($1/3$ inch) toughened glass partially screen printed with white pattern

43.08
Facade Glazing at Ground Level Section Detail
1:10
1 8 mm ($1/3$ inch) toughened glass internal glazing layer, screen printed in white with open joints
2 Aluminium disc between internal glass and point fixing
3 Aluminium glazing fixing with stainless steel countersunk point fixing
4 70 mm ($2^3/4$ inch) diameter vertical steel tube structure
5 127 mm (5 inch) vertical galvanized steel tube structure
6 Aluminium extrusion glazing framing
7 Double glazing comprised of 6 mm ($1/4$ inch) float glass, 16 mm ($2/3$ inch) cavity and 8 mm ($1/3$ inch) toughened glass partially screen printed with white pattern
8 Raised floor
9 210 mm ($8^1/4$ inch) floor cavity
10 Exterior concrete paving slabs
11 Aluminium profile sloped for drainage
12 Waterproof membrane
13 100 mm (4 inch) thick insulation
14 Reinforced concrete floor slab

Central Law Library, University of Hamburg
Hamburg, Germany

Client
Freie und Hansestadt Hamburg,
Behörde für Wissenschaft
und Forschung

Project Team
Peer Hillmann, Till Kindsvater,
Katharina Kreiss, Uwe Schicker, Julia
Strunk

Structural Engineer
Assmann Beraten und Planen

The new library stands confidently beside the existing Faculty of Law Building, defining a new entrance square for the campus. The existing function of the Faculty of Law Building as the main entrance is preserved, with the entrance to the new library being through the foyer of the existing building. Both premises are connected to each other by a glass atrium. The library building is conceived as a compact book storage depot. The glazed facade, studded with glass panes of different colours, changes its appearance depending on the light falling on it, the time of day or the season. The three glazed facades are furnished with four different yellow and amber tones. The south facade includes six different green tones symbolizing a mixed forest scenery. In addition, opaque yellow stripes of glass symbolize autumn and transience. A cube of books whose colour is perceived in the interior space by day transforms itself at night into a beaming object of yellow light. Access to both the old and the new building is via a staircase and an elevator in the atrium. The controlled library areas start on the mezzanine level of the new building. From here, information and research systems are located in the galleries opening onto the atrium. Naturally-lit reading areas are located against the glass facades. All of the shelving is concentrated in the inner areas in front of the security fire-wall. Once completed, the Central Law Library will house 700,000 volumes with 1,200 reading places and will be open 24 hours a day.

1 Together with the existing Law Faculty building, the library forms a new square which is popular with students who use it as a gathering place.
2 By night, the variegated coloured glass facade glows like a beacon, an important function of a building that operates 24 hours a day.
3 The atrium is the most important aspect of the passive energy concept of the building, acting as a buffer space to retard the loss of heat, as well as acting as a thermal flue to drive natural ventilation of the library floors.
4 Glazing to the reading areas is treated with a sun protection foil and together with sand blasting, appropriate levels of sun protection, natural lighting and privacy are achieved.

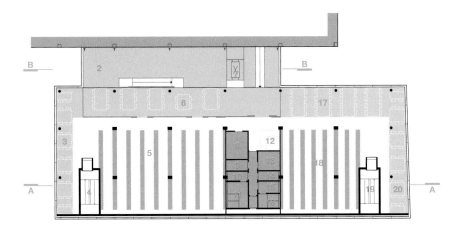

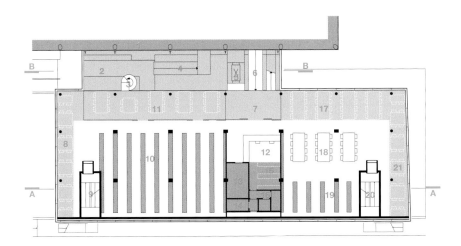

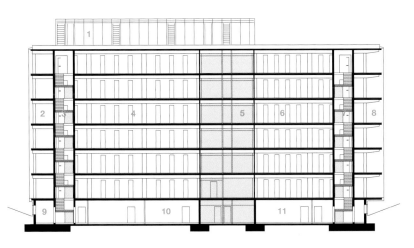

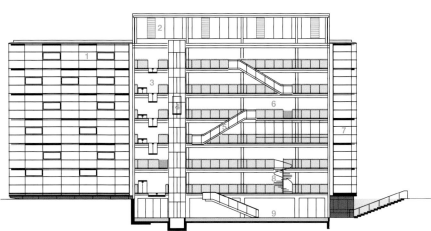

44.01
First Floor Plan
1:500
1 Existing Law
   Faculty building
2 Atrium
3 Reading area
4 Fire stair
5 Book stacks
6 Reading area
7 Atrium lift
8 Copier room
9 Store
10 Male WC lobby
11 Male WCs
12 Librarian's desk
13 Server room
14 Store
15 Female WC lobby
16 Female WCs
17 Group study area
18 Book stacks
19 Fire stair
20 Reading area

44.03
Ground Floor Plan
1:500
1 Existing Law
   Faculty building
2 Atrium
3 Circular stair
   between ground
   and first floor
4 Ramp
5 Atrium lift
6 Entrance ramp
7 Entrance lobby
8 Reading area
9 Fire stair
10 Book stacks
11 Reading area
12 Librarian's desk
13 Audio visual store
14 Store
15 Audio visual stacks
16 Disabled WC and
   cleaners store
17 Group study area
18 Group study area
19 Book stacks
20 Fire stair
21 Reading area

44.02
Section A–A
1:500
1 Lift motor room
   and services plant
2 Reading area
3 Fire stair
4 Book stacks
5 Librarian's area
   and services core
6 Book stacks
7 Fire stair
8 Reading area
9 Pressure aeration
   room
10 Seminar room
11 Computer work
   room

44.04
Section B–B
1:500
1 Glazed facade of
   law library
2 Lift motor room
   and services plant
3 Atrium ramp
   circulation
4 Atrium lift
5 Atrium stair
6 Atrium balustrade
   to reading areas
7 Reading area
8 Circular stair
   between ground
   and first floor
9 Basement

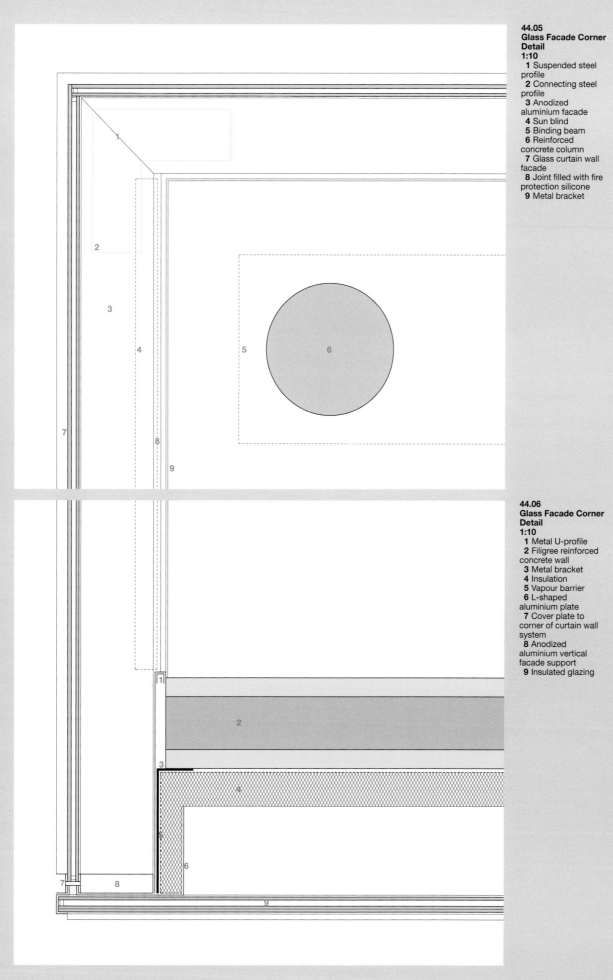

44.05
Glass Facade Corner Detail
1:10
  1 Suspended steel profile
  2 Connecting steel profile
  3 Anodized aluminium facade
  4 Sun blind
  5 Binding beam
  6 Reinforced concrete column
  7 Glass curtain wall facade
  8 Joint filled with fire protection silicone
  9 Metal bracket

44.06
Glass Facade Corner Detail
1:10
  1 Metal U-profile
  2 Filigree reinforced concrete wall
  3 Metal bracket
  4 Insulation
  5 Vapour barrier
  6 L-shaped aluminium plate
  7 Cover plate to corner of curtain wall system
  8 Anodized aluminium vertical facade support
  9 Insulated glazing

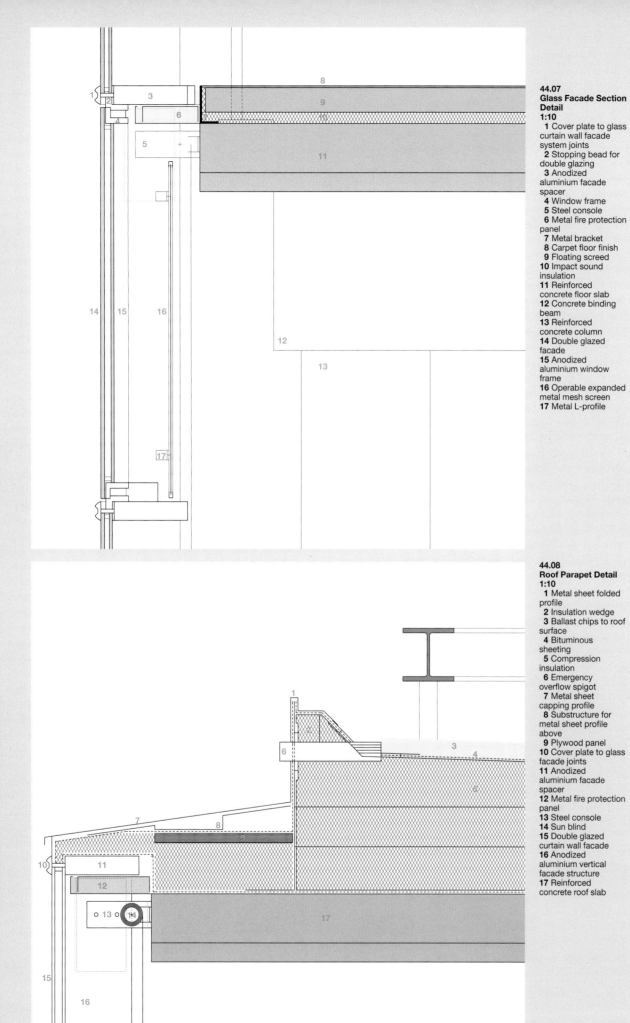

44.07
**Glass Facade Section
Detail**
1:10
 1 Cover plate to glass
curtain wall facade
system joints
 2 Stopping bead for
double glazing
 3 Anodized
aluminium facade
spacer
 4 Window frame
 5 Steel console
 6 Metal fire protection
panel
 7 Metal bracket
 8 Carpet floor finish
 9 Floating screed
10 Impact sound
insulation
11 Reinforced
concrete floor slab
12 Concrete binding
beam
13 Reinforced
concrete column
14 Double glazed
facade
15 Anodized
aluminium window
frame
16 Operable expanded
metal mesh screen
17 Metal L-profile

44.08
Roof Parapet Detail
1:10
 1 Metal sheet folded
profile
 2 Insulation wedge
 3 Ballast chips to roof
surface
 4 Bituminous
sheeting
 5 Compression
insulation
 6 Emergency
overflow spigot
 7 Metal sheet
capping profile
 8 Substructure for
metal sheet profile
above
 9 Plywood panel
10 Cover plate to glass
facade joints
11 Anodized
aluminium facade
spacer
12 Metal fire protection
panel
13 Steel console
14 Sun blind
15 Double glazed
curtain wall facade
16 Anodized
aluminium vertical
facade structure
17 Reinforced
concrete roof slab

**The Active Learning Lab, University
of Liverpool
Liverpool, England, UK**

Client
University of Liverpool

Project Team
Rod McAllister, Ian Butler, Tony
O'Brien, Dan Burr, Michael Raithby,
Anthony Furlong, Rick Bowlby, Paul
Frondella, Simone Ridyard, Leo Harris,
Anna Hinde

Structural Engineer
Arup

Main Contractor
BAM Construction

The Active Learning Lab (ALL) was
conceived as a studio-based teaching
environment for engineers that would
regenerate the run-down laboratory
building complex within the campus
and provide a beacon for teaching
and learning at the university, visible
from the city centre and even from at
sea. Existing laboratories and the
boiler house were demolished to
accommodate a new glazed
circulation element, or street, to link
together all the existing buildings,
including the differing floor levels. The
street was designed as the heart of
the department with clearly visible
circulation routes combined with
display and break-out facilities. At the
same time the design included a new
single entrance into the department
that leads directly from the main
historic University Quadrangle into
the street.

The Active Learning Lab has been
developed as a glass faced cube,
floating above the existing podium.
This has been achieved by the use of
a bespoke glass rainscreen cladding
system on the outside face of the
external wall. The external wall itself is
of lightweight insulated cladding, with
a liquid-applied membrane facing, and
incorporates separate windows. This
combines the need for restricted
window space in lab areas with the
landmark appearance of a glass box.
The glass rainscreen panels alternate
clear glass and fritted glass with
adjoining panels offset in plan and
section to introduce a rhythm to each
facade. An external lighting scheme
uses LED based luminaires, allowing
the possibility of programmable colour
designs, and positioned so that the
glass frit pattern picks up the light to
give the effect of a glowing facade.

1 The base of the
tower, placed above
the existing podium,
contains services,
while the glazed floors
above house two
levels of laboratories.
2 At night the building
is transformed by the
ever-changing and
programmable light
emitting diodes (LEDs)
that are housed within
the maintenance zone
of the double facade.
3 The veiled
transparency of the
glass facade is
achieved by three
panes of glass. The
outer two panes form
an unsealed rainscreen
while the inner layer is
formed of double
glazed windows set
between insulated
cladding. This layered
composition is thus
responsibly detailed
in its thermal
performance.

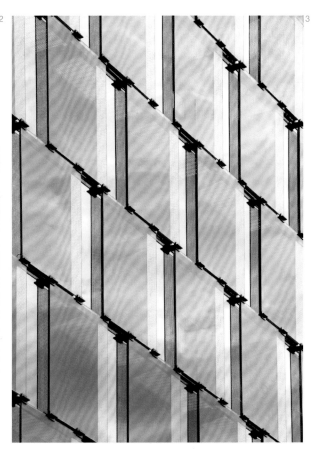

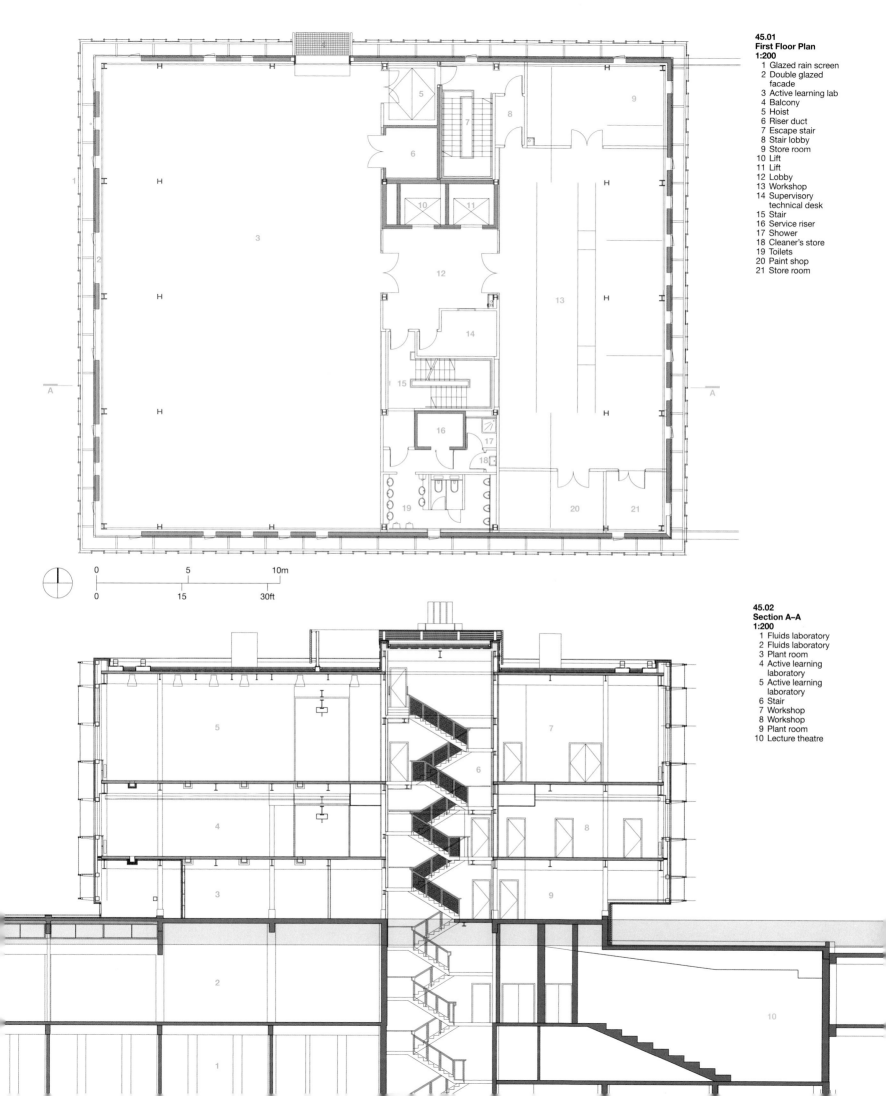

1 Glazed rain screen
2 Double glazed facade
3 Active learning lab
4 Balcony
5 Hoist
6 Riser duct
7 Escape stair
8 Stair lobby
9 Store room
10 Lift
11 Lift
12 Lobby
13 Workshop
14 Supervisory technical desk
15 Stair
16 Service riser
17 Shower
18 Cleaner's store
19 Toilets
20 Paint shop
21 Store room

0   5   10m
0   15   30ft

1 Fluids laboratory
2 Fluids laboratory
3 Plant room
4 Active learning laboratory
5 Active learning laboratory
6 Stair
7 Workshop
8 Workshop
9 Plant room
10 Lecture theatre

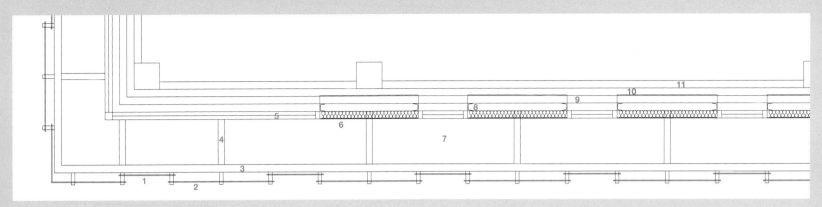

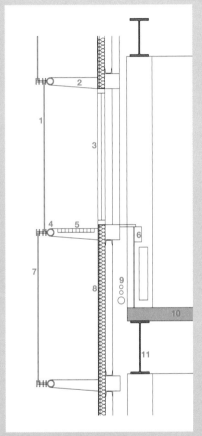

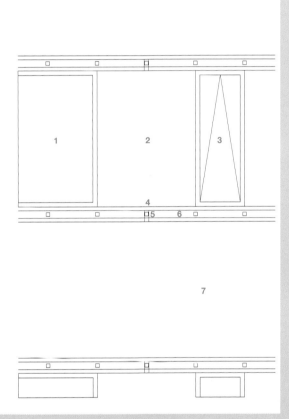

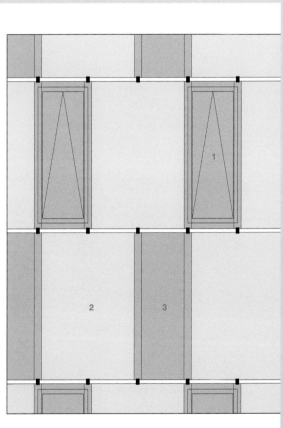

45.03
Glass Facade Plan Detail
1:50
 1 770 mm (30^1/$_3$ inch) wide by 2000 mm (78^3/$_4$ inch) high mirrored glass panel
 2 1465 mm (57^2/$_3$ inch) wide by 2000 mm (78^3/$_4$ inch) high fritted glass panel
 3 Steel tube spanning between brackets
 4 Steel brackets at 2032 mm (80 inch) centres
 5 Double glazed corner window
 6 1365 mm (53^3/$_4$ inch) Decothone membrane on cement based board
 7 Maintenance walkway
 8 100 mm (4 inch) light steel framing to support cladding and windows
 9 200 mm (8 inch) main secondary steel support brackets
 10 Line of internal

lining
 11 Line of window sill

45.04
Glass Facade Section Detail
1:50
 1 770 mm (30^1/$_3$ inch) wide by 2000 mm (78^3/$_4$ inch) high mirrored glass panel
 2 Steel bracket
 3 Double glazed window
 4 Steel tube spanning between brackets
 5 Maintenance walkway
 6 Trunking for small power and communications
 7 1465 mm (57^2/$_3$ inch) wide by 2000 mm (78^3/$_4$ inch) high fritted glass panel
 8 Decothone membrane on cement based board
 9 150 mm (6 inch) services route
 10 Concrete floor slab
 11 Primary steel structure

45.05
Internal Layer of Glass Facade Elevation Detail
1:50
 1 Fixed double glazed window
 2 Decothone membrane on cement based board
 3 677 x 1800 mm (26^2/$_3$ x 70^9/$_{10}$ inch) double glazed openable window
 4 Maintenance walkway
 5 Steel brackets at 2032 mm (80 inch) centres
 6 Steel tube spanning between brackets
 7 Decothone membrane on cement based board

45.06
External Layer of Glass Facade Elevation Detail
1:50
 1 Window behind mirrored glass panel
 2 1465 mm (57^2/$_3$

inch) wide by 2000 mm (78^3/$_4$ inch) high fritted glass panel
 3 770 mm (30^1/$_3$ inch) wide by 2000 mm (78^3/$_4$ inch) high mirrored glass panel

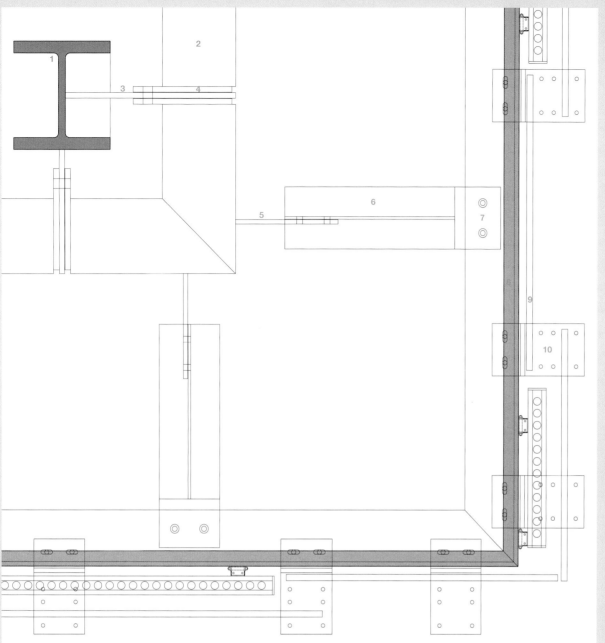

45.07
Glass Facade
Mounting Bracket
Plan Detail
1:10
  1 Steel universal
beam stanchion
  2 200 x 200 mm (8 x
8 inch) rectangular
hollow section steel
rails
  3 Steel bracket
connection to
stanchion
  4 Steel end plates to
rectangular hollow
section rails
  5 Steel bracket
welded to rectangular
hollow section rail
  6 Walkway and glass
support bracket
  7 Walkway and glass
support bracket
  8 Galvanized steel
electrical cable
trunking
  9 Clear glass panel
16.8 mm (²/₃ inch)
laminated glass with
mirror finish
  10 Extruded aluminium

45.08
Glass Facade
Mounting Bracket
Section Detail
1:2
  1 Extruded aluminium
carrier bracket
  2 Stainless steel
fixing sets
  3 33 x 50 x 5 mm
(1¹/₄ x 2 x ¹/₅ inch)
aluminium locking
angles
  4 24 x 125 x 11 mm
(1 x 5 x ²/₅ inch) setting
block
  5 30 x 120 x 4 mm
(1¹/₅ x 4³/₄ x ¹/₈ inch)
pack gasket
  6 16.8 mm (²/₃ inch)
laminated glass with
dot matrix ceramic frit
  7 LED luminaire
  8 Galvanized steel
electrical cable
trunking
  9 150 x 90 x 12 mm
(6 x 3¹/₂ x ¹/₂ inch)
steel angle rail
  10 Walkway and glass
support bracket
fabricated from 356 x
171 x 51 mm (14 x 6³/₄
x 2 inch) universal
beam cut to form a
T-section
carrier bracket
  11 Fritted glass panel
16.8 mm (²/₃ inch)
laminated with dot
matrix

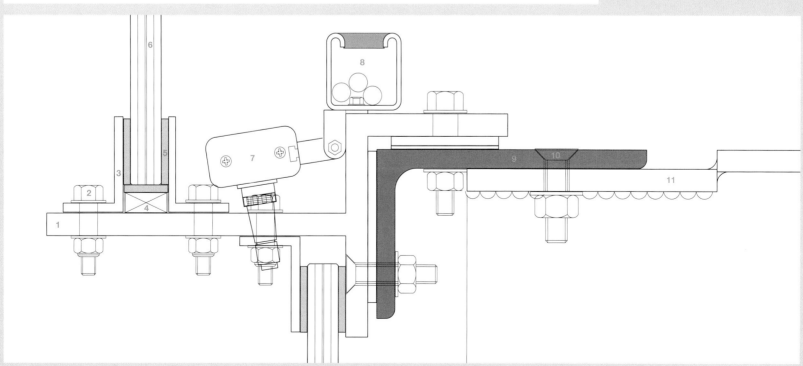

**New Biochemistry Building,
University of Oxford
Oxford, England, UK**

Client
Oxford University Estates

Project Team
Russell Brown, Oliver Milton, Louisa
Bowles, Hazel York, Morag Morrison,
Chloe Sharpe

Structural Engineer
Peter Brett Associates

Main Contractor
Laing O'Rourke

The Biochemistry Department at Oxford University is the largest in the UK and is internationally renowned for its research in the understanding of DNA, cell growth and immunity. Previously the department suffered from being accommodated in six different outmoded buildings. As well as consolidating the department, the brief for the new building was to achieve a new ethos of interdisciplinary working where the exchange of ideas is promoted in a large collaborative environment. At the same time, space was required to enable the research groups to focus on their cutting-edge work in state-of-the-art laboratories. The new facility, with its glass facades and coloured glass fins, brings together over 300 researchers and post-graduate students working in bioinformatics, chromosome biology, molecular biophysics and biochemistry.

The building was conceived as four blocks of laboratories bisected by perpendicular routes and cut backs to create external spaces for arrival and entrance. All of the external surfaces are transparent, making the laboratories visible from the outside. Here, the traditional research building model where laboratories are buried in a highly serviced core with write-up areas dispersed around the periphery of the building has been inverted. Instead the laboratories have been deliberately placed at the edges of the building with write-up areas integrated into the open plan spaces of the central atrium. In addition to transparency, the curtain walling incorporates the principles of rhythm, unity, control and reflection. The facades are enriched by a series of laminated glass fins which frame views in and out of the building, creating complex patterns of colour as the light changes.

1 In the central courtyard, the regular rhythm of the glass fins breaks to frame an artwork created by Nicky Hirst in which a series of images explores the repetition of experimentation and analysis of information. 2 The new Biochemistry Building was conceived as a group of laboratory blocks linked by a central top lit atrium. 3 The glass fins create a vertical rhythm that reflects the character of the historic buildings in Oxford. A palette of warm ochres and burnt siennas makes reference to the surrounding historic building materials of Coral Rag limestones, rubble stones, and Taynton and Headington stones.

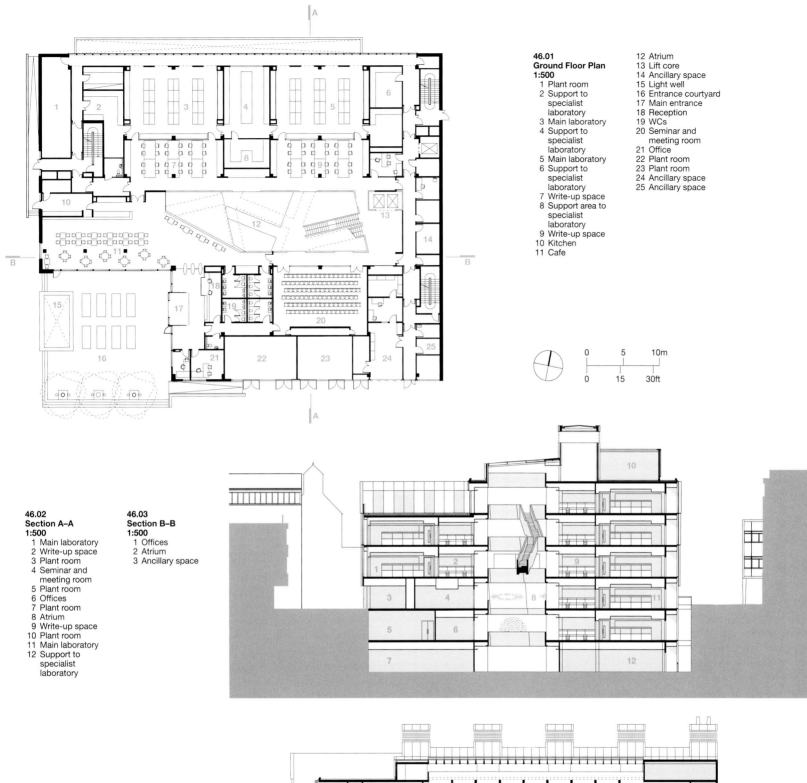

46.01
Ground Floor Plan
1:500
1 Plant room
2 Support to specialist laboratory
3 Main laboratory
4 Support to specialist laboratory
5 Main laboratory
6 Support to specialist laboratory
7 Write-up space
8 Support area to specialist laboratory
9 Write-up space
10 Kitchen
11 Cafe
12 Atrium
13 Lift core
14 Ancillary space
15 Light well
16 Entrance courtyard
17 Main entrance
18 Reception
19 WCs
20 Seminar and meeting room
21 Office
22 Plant room
23 Plant room
24 Ancillary space
25 Ancillary space

0 5 10m
0 15 30ft

46.02
Section A–A
1:500
1 Main laboratory
2 Write-up space
3 Plant room
4 Seminar and meeting room
5 Plant room
6 Offices
7 Plant room
8 Atrium
9 Write-up space
10 Plant room
11 Main laboratory
12 Support to specialist laboratory

46.03
Section B–B
1:500
1 Offices
2 Atrium
3 Ancillary space

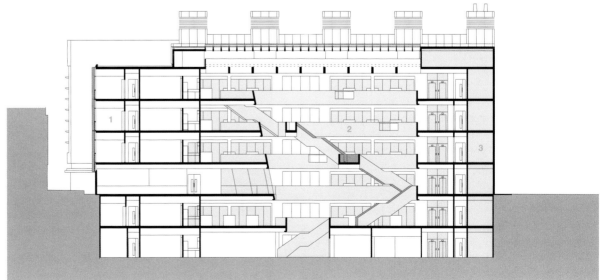

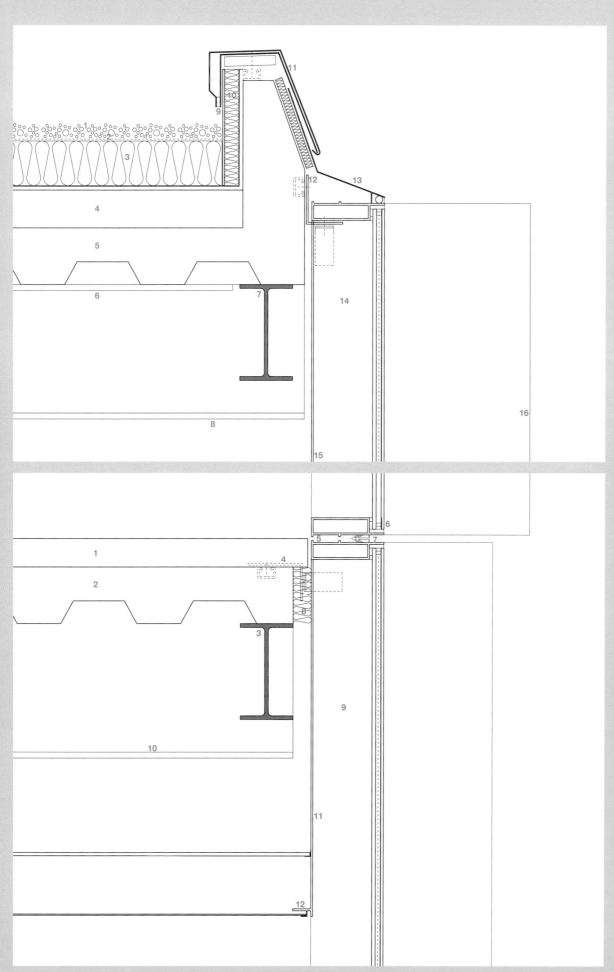

46.04
Section Detail at
Curtain Wall and Roof
Interface at
Laboratory Corridor
1:10
1 Paving and ballast
2 Protective
membrane
3 Insulation
4 Screed and liquid
applied waterproofing
membrane
5 Composite
concrete slab
6 Structural steelwork
7 Structural steelwork
8 Structural steelwork
9 Concealed fixing
detail to coping
10 Insulation to
upstand
11 Extruded
powder-coated
aluminium coping to
parapet set back from
curtain walling so as
not to be visible from
ground level
12 Bracket and
channel fixing for
curtain walling
13 Butt jointed
extruded powder-
coated aluminium
flashing

14 Cavity between
glass and aluminium
designed to control
heat build up
15 Powder-coated
aluminium downstand
as part of curtain wall
system designed to
incorporate perforated
sections for air supply
and extract
16 Outline of glass fin
beyond

46.05
Section Detail at
Curtain Wall and
Floor Interface
1:10
1 Screed
2 Composite
concrete slab
3 Structural steel
4 Bracket and
channel fixing for
curtain walling
5 Centre line of
aluminium transom to
line up with finished
floor level
6 Border to glazed
units to clear panels to
be translucent glass to
extent of mullions only
7 Gasket in horizontal
joints recessed to
same depth as sealant
on vertical joints
8 Fire stop
9 Cavity between
glass and aluminium
designed to control
heat build up

10 Structural steelwork
11 Powder-coated
aluminium downstand
as part of curtain wall
system designed to
incorporate perforated
sections for air supply
and extract
12 Powder-coated
aluminium downstand
designed to receive
ceiling finishes

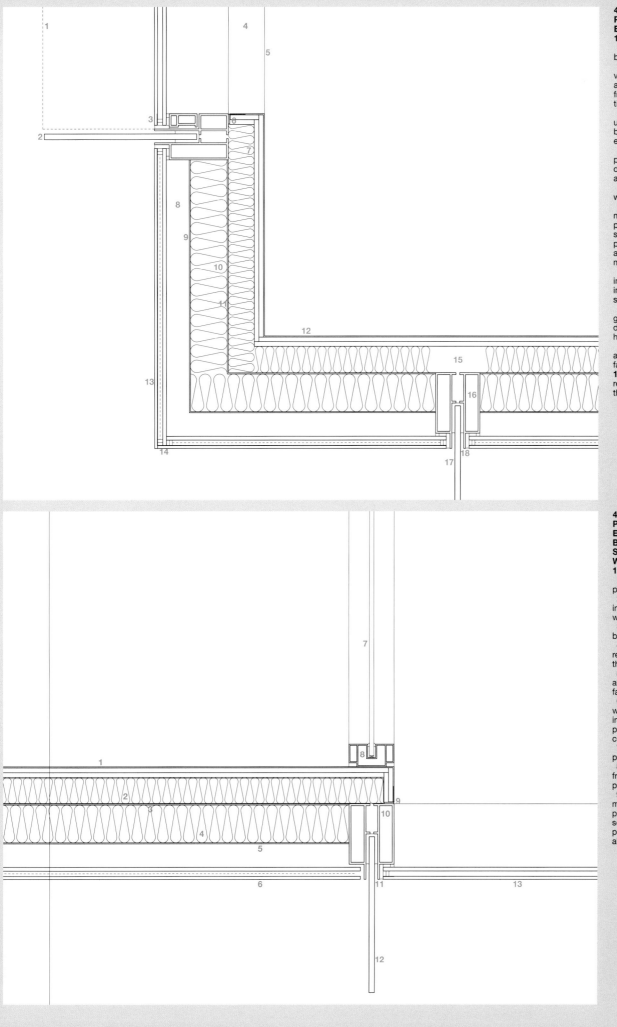

46.06
**Plan Detail of Typical
External Corner**
1:10
1 Outline of glass fin
beyond
2 Fin projection,
varies on each floor
and to be measured
from face of glass to
tip of fin
3 Border to glazed
units to clear panels to
be translucent glass to
extent of mullions only
4 Accessible
pre-formed sill
designed to conceal
actuator
5 Line of plasterboard
wall lining beyond
6 Joints between
mullion and
plasterboard silicone
sealed for acoustic
performance and to
allow for differential
movements
7 Additional
insulation as part of
internal wall lining
system
8 Cavity between
glass and aluminium
designed to control
heat build up
9 Powder-coated
aluminium panel to
face of insulation
10 Insulated panel to
rear of unit to provide
thermal performance

11 Aluminium panel to
back of curtain walling
12 Severe duty
plasterboard wall lining
13 Double glazed
window unit with argon
infill and high
performance solar
control coating
14 Glass to glass
junction at corners
15 Structural steel
column
16 122 mm (4⁴/5 inch)
overall mullion width to
line up with internal
partitions
17 Fin projection,
varies on each floor
and to be measured
from face of glass to
tip of fin
18 Sealant to either
side of fin recessed 20
mm (³/4 inch)

46.07
**Plan Detail of South
Elevation Junction
Between Office
Screen and Curtain
Walling**
1:10
1 Severe duty
plasterboard wall lining
2 Additional
insulation to internal
wall lining system
3 Aluminium panel to
back of curtain walling
4 Insulated panel to
rear of unit to provide
thermal performance
5 Powder-coated
aluminium panel to
face of insulation
6 Double glazed
window unit with argon
infill and high
performance solar
control coating
7 Internal glazed
partition to office
8 Extruded aluminium
framing to glazed
partitioning system
9 Joints between
mullion and
plasterboard silicone
sealed for acoustic
performance and to
allow for differential

movements
10 122 mm (4⁴/5 inch)
overall mullion width to
line up with internal
partitions
11 Sealant to either
side of fin recessed 20
mm (³/4 inch)
12 Fin projection,
varies on each floor
and to be measured
from face of glass to
tip of fin
13 Double glazed
window unit with argon
infill and high
performance solar
control coating

199

EWHA Womans University
Seoul, South Korea

Client
EWHA Womans University

Project Team
Dominique Perrault Architecture with
Baum Architects, Seoul

Structural Engineer
VP & Green Ingenerie

Local Architect
Baum Architects

The complexity of the immediate site through its relationship to the greater campus and the city of Shinchon to the south demands what the architects refer to as a 'larger than site' response – a global landscaped solution which weaves together the tissue of the EWHA campus with that of the city. This gesture, the 'campus valley', in combination with the 'sports strip', creates a new topography which impacts the surrounding landscape in a number of ways. The sports strip, like the valley, is many things at once. It is a new gateway to the EWHA campus, a place for daily sports activities, a location for the special yearly festivals and celebrations, and an area which truly brings together the university and the city. It is most importantly a place for everyone, animated all year round. Like a horizontal billboard, the sports strip presents the life of the university to the inhabitants of Shinchon, and vice versa.

Once through the sports strip, pedestrian movement and flow through the site is celebrated. A dramatic entry court slices through the topography revealing the interior of the EWHA campus centre. A void is formed in which a variety of activities can unfold. It is a gently descending avenue, controlling the flow of traffic, leading to a monumental stair carrying visitors upwards, inviting the public into the campus and bringing together the different levels of the site. The pastoral nature of the campus is perhaps its most remarkable quality. It is intended that the landscape will grow outwards, or inwards in this case, covering the campus centre with trees, flowers and grass. An idyllic garden will be the result, creating a special place for gathering, conducting informal classes, and simply relaxing.

1 The central piazza, in its scale and sense of place, recalls the Champs Elysées in Paris or the Campidioglio in Rome. Here, a shallow staircase can also be used as an outdoor theatre and informal gathering place. From here, the glazed panels of the facade reveal the interior of the campus centre.
2 The central piazza is flanked by the sports strip, a newly created topography that hosts festivals and celebrations as well as sports activities.
3 At night, the glazed facade of the campus building illuminates the central piazza.
4 Detail view of the glazed facade in which openable panels cool and ventilate the interior of the building.

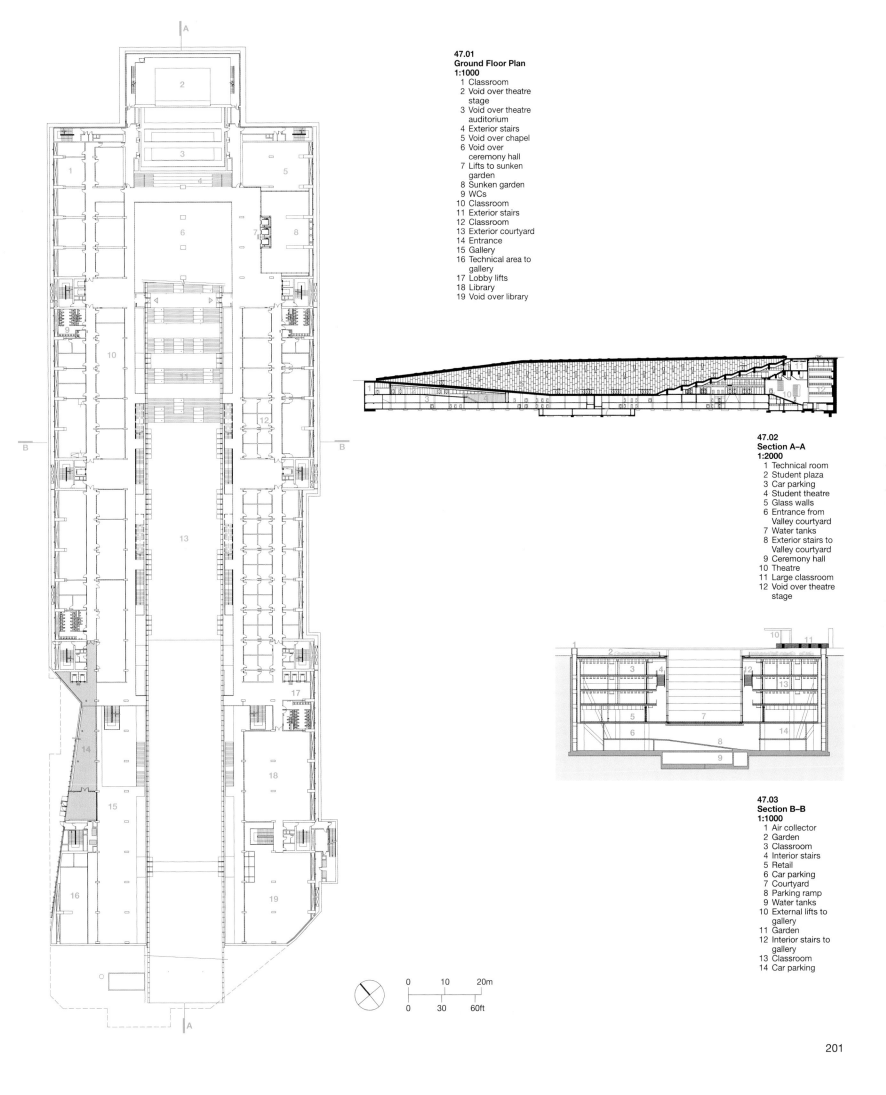

47.01
Ground Floor Plan
1:1000
1 Classroom
2 Void over theatre stage
3 Void over theatre auditorium
4 Exterior stairs
5 Void over chapel
6 Void over ceremony hall
7 Lifts to sunken garden
8 Sunken garden
9 WCs
10 Classroom
11 Exterior stairs
12 Classroom
13 Exterior courtyard
14 Entrance
15 Gallery
16 Technical area to gallery
17 Lobby lifts
18 Library
19 Void over library

47.02
Section A–A
1:2000
1 Technical room
2 Student plaza
3 Car parking
4 Student theatre
5 Glass walls
6 Entrance from Valley courtyard
7 Water tanks
8 Exterior stairs to Valley courtyard
9 Ceremony hall
10 Theatre
11 Large classroom
12 Void over theatre stage

47.03
Section B–B
1:1000
1 Air collector
2 Garden
3 Classroom
4 Interior stairs
5 Retail
6 Car parking
7 Courtyard
8 Parking ramp
9 Water tanks
10 External lifts to gallery
11 Garden
12 Interior stairs to gallery
13 Classroom
14 Car parking

0   10   20m
0   30   60ft

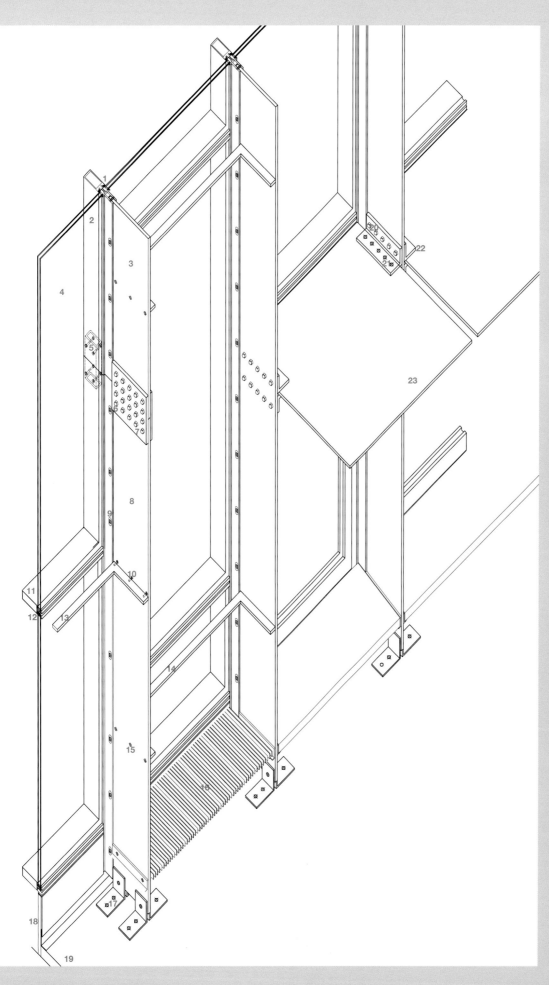

47.04
Curtain Wall Glazing Axonometric Detail 1:20
 1 Dow Corning structural glazing sealant
 2 Aluminium profile
 3 Polished stainless steel fin
 4 Insulated glass unit, tempered on ground floor and heat strengthened on upper floors
 5 Spliced aluminium profile bolted to interior steel reinforcement as required
 6 Polished stainless full threaded rod and cap nut
 7 Polished stainless steel plate
 8 Polished stainless steel fin
 9 Slotted hole in fin for vertical differential movement between aluminium and stainless steel with flush threaded stainless steel bolt every 400 mm (15¾ inches)
 10 Bracket bolted to fin with flush threaded stainless steel bolt
 11 Horizontal aluminium profile
 12 Aluminium cover plate
 13 Polished stainless steel horizontal bracket
 14 Polished stainless steel horizontal bracket
 15 Flush threaded stainless steel bolt to fin and bracket connection
 16 Galvanized steel grill
 17 Galvanized steel angle support
 18 Aluminium flashing
 19 Concrete floor slab
 20 Polished stainless steel full threaded rod and cap nut fin and angle connection
 21 Flush threaded stainless steel bolt to canopy and angle connection
 22 Polished stainless steel angle
 23 Polished stainless steel canopy

47.05
Wall to Sunken Garden Elevation Detail 1:20
 1 Exterior stone paving
 2 Waterproof underlayer to exterior paving
 3 Gutter around sunken garden
 4 Reinforced concrete roof slab with integral downstand beams
 5 Glazed walls
 6 Raised interior floor to classroom
 7 Reinforced concrete floor slab
 8 Batten substructure to stainless steel shingle cladding
 9 Concrete wall
 10 Structure and framing for external cladding of mirror-polished and matt stainless-steel shingles
 11 Base of tracks for sliding glass walls
 12 Sliding glass doors
 13 Gutter
 14 Reflecting pool to sunken garden
 15 Structure and framing for external cladding of mirror-polished and matt stainless-steel shingles
 16 Structure and framing for external cladding of mirror-polished and matt stainless-steel shingles
 17 External cladding of mirror-polished and matt stainless-steel shingles
 18 Air chimney ventilator

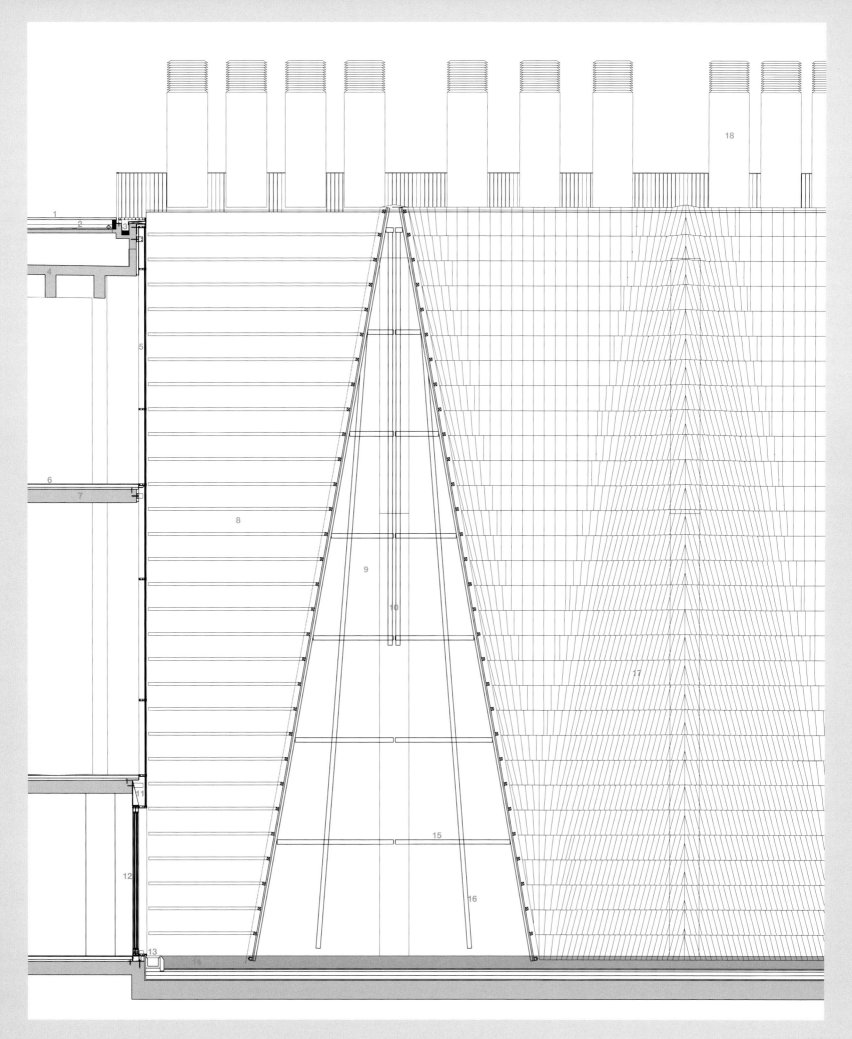

Cocoon Tower
Tokyo, Japan

Client
Mode Gakuen

Project Team
Paul Noritaka Tange, Yoshinori
Takahashi, Tomohiro Kimura, Masaki
Nakayama, Masayoshi Honda, Hitoshi
Watanabe, Masahide Matsuda,
Toshiharu Cho

Structural Engineer
Arup

Main Contractor
Shimizu Corporation

Located in Tokyo's Nishi-Shinjuku
high-rise district, Mode Gakuen
Cocoon Tower contains three
vocational schools with approximately
10,000 students. The 50-storey tower,
the world's second tallest educational
building, received the prestigious
Emporis Skyscraper Award in 2008.
The innovative shape and cutting
edge facade, wrapped in a criss-cross
web of diagonal lines, embodies the
unique 'Cocoon' concept. Tange
Associates' image of the Cocoon as a
nurturing space where students are
embraced and inspired to create,
grow and be transformed, convinced
the client, Mode Gakuen, to select
their scheme from more than 150
competing designs.

The site's limited size posed a
challenge for the development of a
new typology for educational
architecture. Three storey high atrium
lounges, placed between the
classrooms, located every three
floors, offer sweeping views of
the surrounding cityscape and are a
new type of 'schoolyard'. These
innovative lounges, offering students
a comfortable place to relax and
communicate, provide an innovative
solution for educational architecture
in densely populated cities. The
characteristic cocoon pattern on the
facade is composed of extruded
aluminium panels along the grid
column with the diagonal frame.
A special film which consists of
aggregated points has been applied to
the triangular glass panes and avoids
obscuring the view when looked
through from inside the classrooms,
yet appears unified with the aluminium
pressed panels when viewed from a
distance.

1 Located among the giant corporate headquarters of Tokyo's Shinjuku business district, the building houses three vocational schools including its namesake Mode Gakuen, a fashion design school, as well as information technology and medical schools.
2 White aluminum and dark blue glass form the structure's curved shell, which is criss-crossed by a diagonal web.
3 The building's futuristic interior holds a variety of dramatic spaces, providing comfortable gathering places such as the lounge on the 50th floor.
4 Each floor of the tower contains three rectangular classrooms that surround an inner core which consists of an elevator, a staircase and a services shaft.

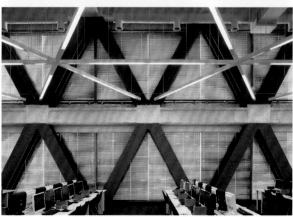

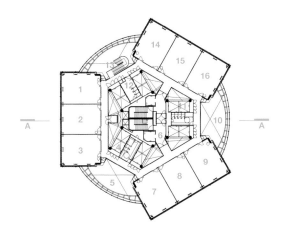

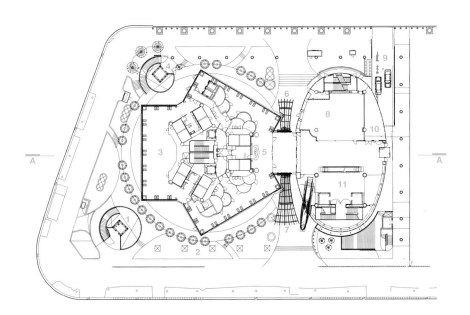

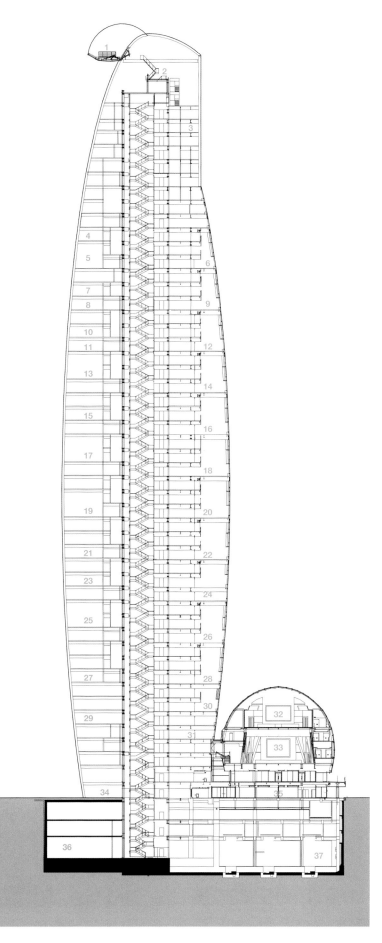

48.01
Level 23 Floor Plan
1:1000
1 Classroom
2 Classroom
3 Classroom
4 Service riser
5 Void over student lounge
6 Vertical circulation zone
7 Classroom
8 Classroom
9 Classroom
10 Void over student lounge
11 Service riser
12 WCs
13 Open stair between student lounge and classrooms above
14 Classroom
15 Classroom
16 Classroom

48.02
Ground Floor Plan
1:1000
1 Circulation from basement car park
2 Public plaza
3 Offices and administration area
4 Circulation from basement car park
5 Reception counter
6 Entrance
7 Entrance
8 Retail space
9 Car park entrance and exit
10 Facility machine room
11 Vertical circulation to low rise building

48.03
Section A–A
1:1000
1 Fold out maintenance platform
2 Maintenance access stair
3 Penthouse floors
4 Single level classroom
5 Two level classroom
6 Student lounge
7 Single level classroom
8 Single level classroom
9 Student lounge
10 Single level classroom
11 Single level classroom
12 Student lounge
13 Two level classroom
14 Student lounge
15 Single level classroom
16 Student lounge
17 Two level classroom
18 Student lounge
19 Two level classroom
20 Student lounge
21 Single level classroom
22 Student lounge
23 Single level classroom
24 Student lounge
25 Two level classroom
26 Student lounge
27 Single level classroom
28 Student lounge
29 Single level classroom
30 Student lounge
31 Library
32 Hall A
33 Hall B
34 Entrance lobby
35 Retail
36 Retail
37 Car park

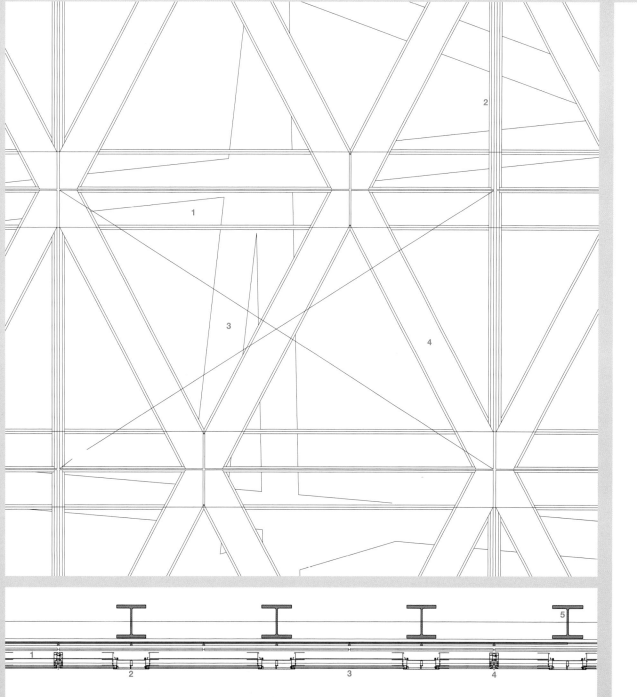

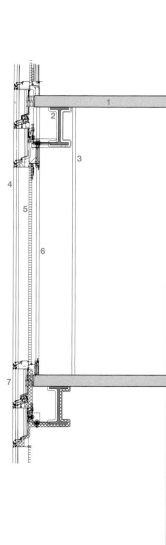

48.04
Facade Elevation Detail
1:50
1 Spandrel panel with aluminium sash and float glass plate comprised of 10 mm (²/5 inch) glass, 12 mm (¹/2 inch) air gap and 15 mm (³/5 inch) glass
2 Gondola rail for facade maintenance from aluminium profile with fluoroplastic baked finish
3 Glass banderole with special film with fritted dot pattern
4 Diagonal section of aluminium curtain wall system comprised of aluminium profile with fluoroplastic baked finish and float glass

plate comprised of 10 mm (²/5 inch) glass, 12 mm (¹/2 inch) air gap and 15 mm (³/5 inch) glass

48.05
Facade Plan Detail
1:50
1 Spandrel panel with aluminium sash and float glass plate comprised of 10 mm (²/5 inch) glass, 12 mm (¹/2 inch) air gap and 15 mm (³/5 inch) glass
2 Gondola rail for facade maintenance from aluminium profile with fluoroplastic baked finish
3 Glass banderole with special film with fritted dot pattern
4 Diagonal section of

aluminium curtain wall system comprised of aluminium profile with fluoroplastic baked finish and float glass plate comprised of 10 mm (²/5 inch) glass, 12 mm (¹/2 inch) air gap and 15 mm (³/5 inch) glass
5 Primary steel facade structure

48.06
Facade Section Detail
1:50
1 Reinforced concrete floor slab
2 Primary steel facade structure
3 Plasterboard partition
4 Glass banderole with special film with fritted dot pattern
5 Blind
6 Inner sash
7 Spandrel panel with aluminium sash and float glass plate comprised of 10 mm (²/5 inch) glass, 12 mm (¹/2 inch) air gap and 15 mm (³/5 inch) glass

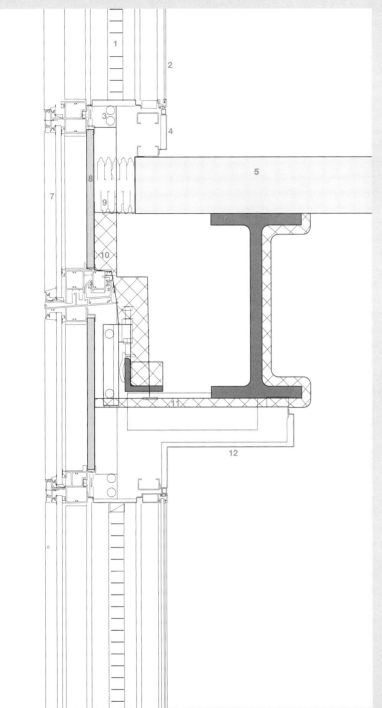

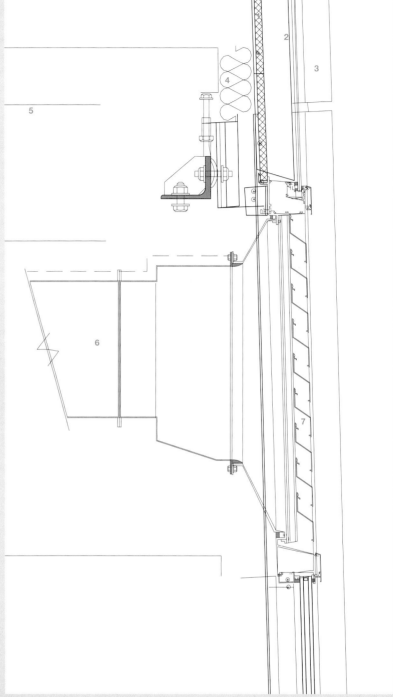

48.07
Curtain Wall Section
Detail 1
1:10
  1 Blind
  2 Inner sash
  3 Electrical conduits
  4 Removable
aluminium skirting
plate
  5 Reinforced
concrete floor slab
  6 Steel facade
structure
  7 Aluminium curtain
wall system comprised
of aluminium profile
with fluoroplastic
baked finish and float
glass plate comprised
of 10 mm (²/5 inch)
glass, 12 mm (¹/2 inch)
air gap and 15 mm (³/5
inch) glass
  8 1.6 mm (¹/16 inch)

thick steel spandrel
panel over Rockwool
spray fill
  9 Rockwool acoustic
panel
  10 Fire rated insulation
  11 Rockwool spray
insulation with one
hour fire rating
  12 Plasterboard wall
and ceiling fill panel

48.08
Curtain Wall Section
Detail 2
1:10
  1 1.6 mm (¹/16 inch)
thick steel spandrel
panel over Rockwool
spray fill
  2 Aluminium curtain
wall system comprised
of aluminium profile
with fluoroplastic
baked finish
  3 Float glass plate
comprised of 10 mm
(²/5 inch) glass, 12 mm
(¹/2 inch) air gap and
15 mm (³/5 inch) glass
  4 Rockwool acoustic
board
  5 Ventilation duct in
ceiling void
  6 900 x 350 mm
(35²/5 x 13³/4 inch)
galvanized sheet

exhaust air duct
finished with
moisture-proof spray
  7 Anodized
aluminium louvre panel

University Library Utrecht
Utrecht, The Netherlands

Client
University Utrecht

Project Team
Wiel Arets, Harold Aspers, Dominic
Papa, René Thijssen, Frederik Vaes,
Henrik Vuust

Structural Engineer
ABT Adviseurs in Bouwtechniek

Landscape Architect
West 8

The Utrecht University Library, comparable to a data recorder, is more than a place to consult books. It is a place where people can work in a dedicated environment, but also a place where they can meet and communicate without the need for any stimulation other than the atmosphere that the building creates. The book depots, built in black figured concrete, divide the space into zones and are interconnected by stairs and ramps. A partly double-glazed facade to which a silk-screened figurative pattern has been applied, encases the reading rooms. The same glass facade encloses the car park like a smooth skin to ensure that it reads as an integral part of the complex. From one side of the library building is a view of the university campus and the open countryside beyond.

Based on the idea that silent communication is important in a library, the atmosphere emphasizes a sense of security which is expressed in the choice of black for the interior. A light, reflective floor provides enough reflected natural or artificial light to illuminate some of the 42 million books that are on open shelves, while the long white tables make it possible to read a book or to consult electronic information comfortably. The individual workplaces have been positioned in such a way that the user's choice of workplace determines the degree of communication with other users. Routes through the building also facilitate choices and opportunities for meeting and communicating with others. The bar, lounge area, reception corner, auditorium and shops, add an extra dimension to the pedestrian routes, thereby breaking down the mono-functionality of the library programme.

1 The glazing is covered in a printed dot pattern, which forms the image of a papyrus plant which was the main material used in paper production in ancient Egypt.
2 The papyrus design is printed on glass panels with the pattern running vertically, and with each panel bearing the same design. The printed dots allow light to filter into the library in a highly controlled manner, protecting the books within from the damaging effects of light. Some of the panels fold out from the facade to act as light control devices.
3 White tables and other work surfaces sit in the otherwise all black interior.

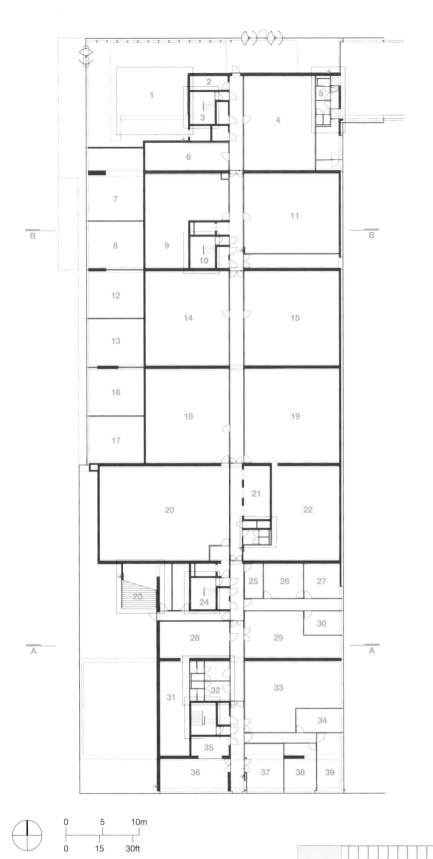

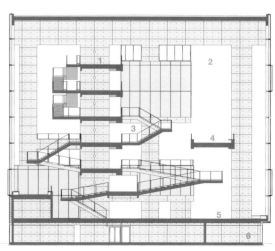

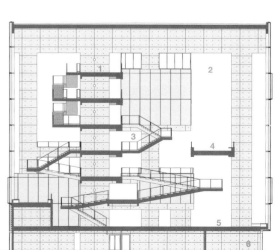

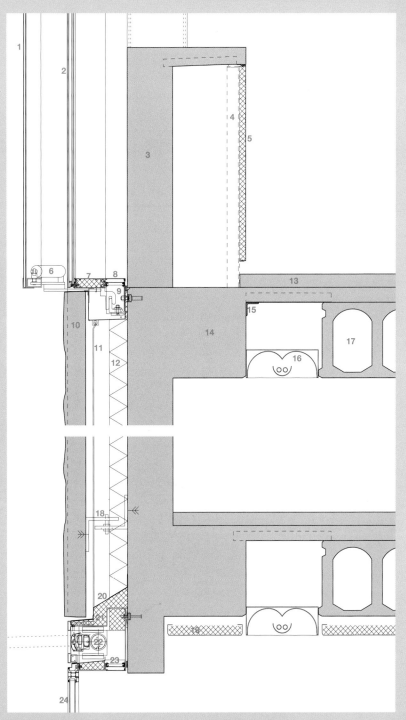

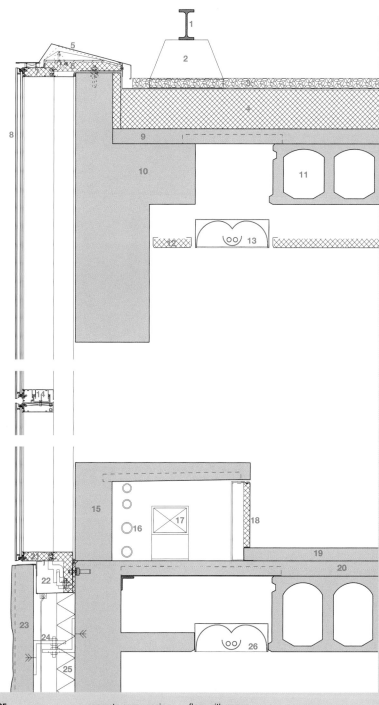

49.04
Glass and Concrete Panel Facade Detail
1:20
1 Automatic operable glass blade
2 Aluminium framework with adhesive-fixed structural fixed glass
3 250 mm (9⁴/5 inch) in-situ concrete wall with black coating
4 Timber framing shown dotted
5 Painted MDF infill panel
6 Exterior light fixture
7 Painted MDF infill sill panel
8 Ventilation grille isolated with high quality insulation
9 Ventilation duct assembly

10 100 mm (4 inch) prefabricated concrete panel with maximum 25 mm (1 inch) thick irregularly patterned surface with black coating
11 Vertical ventilation shaft
12 Minimum 100 mm (4 inch) thick insulation
13 70 mm (2³/4 inch) thick concrete floor with epoxy coating
14 Concrete beam with black coating
15 Steel angle support bracket
16 Light fixture fitted flush with concrete structure on either side
17 400 mm (15³/4 inch) concrete hollow core concrete slab with black coating

18 Bolted steel angle support for hanging concrete facade panel
19 Acoustic ceiling
20 Folded drip profile
21 Insulation
22 Prefabricated easel frame for cantilevered shade canopy (shown dotted)
23 Insulated steel cassette with aluminium coating
24 Insulated aluminium window frame with thermally insulated glass

49.05
Glass and Concrete Panel Facade Detail at Roof Parapet
1:20
1 Steel rail for glass cleaning and maintenance
2 Concrete mounting block for steel rail
3 Gravel roof ballast
4 Two layers of 100 mm (4 inch) thick double sided roofing with vapour retarder
5 Aluminium parapet cover
6 Foil-backed insulation
7 Insulation
8 Aluminium framework with adhesive-fixed structural fixed glass
9 80 mm (3¹/8 inch)

concrete compression slab
10 Concrete beam with black coating
11 320 mm (12³/5 inch) hollow-core concrete slab
12 Acoustic ceiling
13 Light fixture fitted flush between acoustic ceiling on either side
14 Secret fixed metal plate facade framing
15 200 mm (8 inch) in-situ poured concrete wall and seat with black coating
16 Electrical conduit concealed under concrete seat
17 Air supply vent
18 Painted MDF infill panel
19 70 mm (2³/4 inch) monolithic concrete

floor with epoxy coating
20 80 mm (3¹/8 inch) thick concrete slab
21 Painted MDF infill sill panel
22 Ventilation duct assembly
23 100 mm (4 inch) prefabricated concrete panel with maximum 25 mm (1 inch) thick irregularly patterned surface with black coating
24 Bolted steel angle support for hanging concrete facade panel
25 Minimum 100 mm (4 inch) thick insulation
26 Light fixture fitted flush between acoustic ceiling on either side

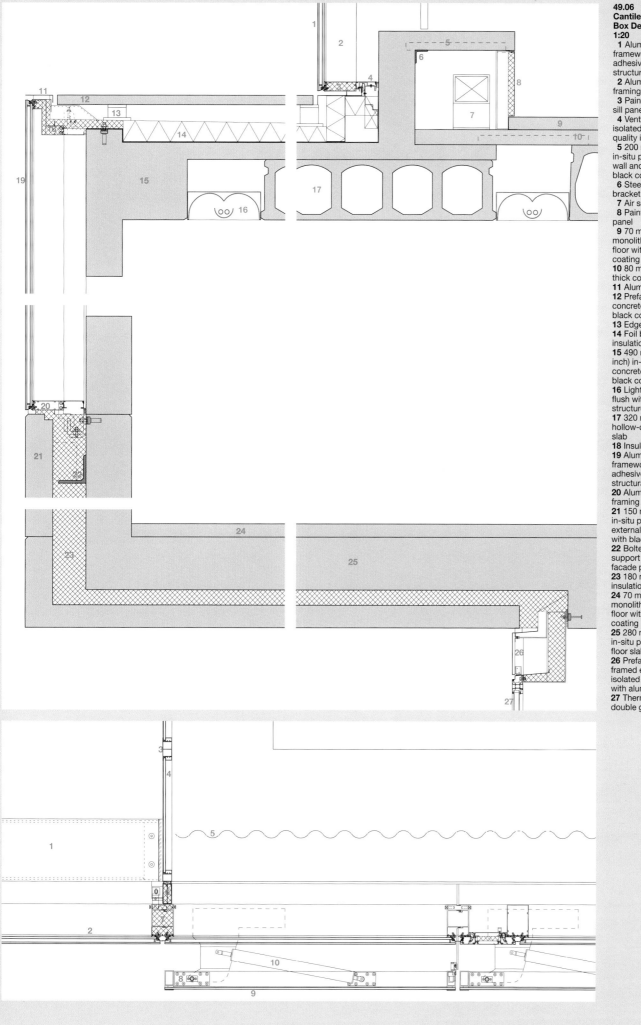

**Clapham Manor Primary School
London, England, UK**

Client
London Borough of Lambeth

Project Team
Philip Marsh, Satoshi Isono, Michael Spooner, Mirko Immendoefer, Junko Yanagisawa, Jonas Lencer, Russ Edwards

Structural Engineer
Michael Hadi Associates

Main Contractor
The Construction Partnership

dRMM's intervention into a Victorian school features a polychromatic extension inserted into a tight urban context which offers the school a new identity, much-needed learning spaces and an organizational hub, while maximizing play space. The new intervention is pulled away from the flank wall to sit parallel with the neighbouring Odd Fellows Hall. The resultant interstitial space establishes a formal entrance into the school in the form of a triple height transparent atrium. A glazed lift and stairs that scissor overhead reconcile four contemporary storeys within the height of three existing levels.

The formal grid that typically defines glazed curtain walling is replaced here by a random grid to provide an expression appropriate for a primary school. The facade is a polychromatic loop of colour that shifts as it moves around the building. The contextual brick colours inform the rich reds and yellows along Stonhouse Street. The colour spectrum shifts into greens as the building emerges on the playground side, echoing the landscaping, and finally into vibrant sky blues. In addition to new classrooms, pupils benefit from spaces for performance, music, breakout learning and a medical room. Staff share a resource room, copy facilities, administration and offices. The informal, social spaces that connect the classrooms are vibrant and stimulating, eliminating corridors and offering visual transparency. The vibrant coloured glass panels of the exterior are upholstered on the inside allowing opportunities for the display of pupils' work, while elsewhere, solid, fritted and clear panels at varying heights create vistas towards the urban landscape.

1 View of both the new building and the existing Victorian board school building from Stonhouse Street.
2 The new glass structure is angled away from the neighbouring building to create an interstitial exterior space that now defines a glazed atrium entrance structure.
3 In the new classrooms, a random pattern of solid, clear and fritted glazed panels frame views of the surrounding context.
4 The internal facades incorporate felt pinboard panels within the glazing system to provide space to exhibit the children's work.

50.01
Ground Floor Plan
1:500
1 Ramp and stair access from Belmont Road
2 Playground
3 Playground entrance
4 Premise manager
5 Medical room
6 WC
7 Staff room
8 Staff kitchenette
9 Meeting room
10 Administration
11 Reception area
12 Parents and visitors entrance
13 Main pupil

14 Entrance lobby
15 Existing Victorian board school
16 Existing Grade II Listed Odd Fellows Hall

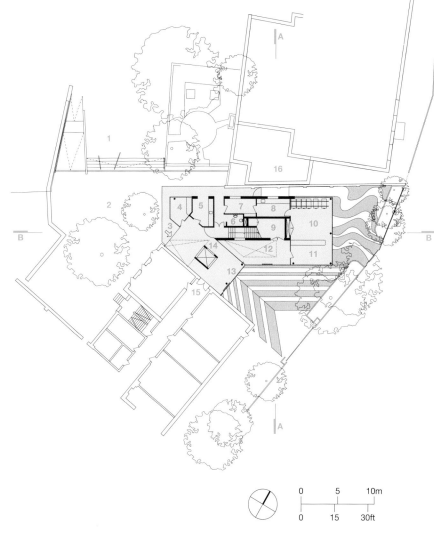

50.02
Section A–A
1:200
1 Playground
2 Clear glazed link
3 Waiting area
4 Meeting room
5 Bursar's office
6 Walkway
7 Staff work area
8 Walkway
9 Breakout space
10 Lobby
11 Stair
12 Breakout space
13 Plant room

50.03
Section B–B
1:200
1 Lobby
2 Meeting room
3 Administration
4 Staff room
5 Staff kitchen
6 Classroom
7 Performance space
8 Stair
9 Classroom
10 Classroom
11 Conference room

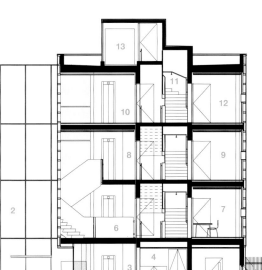

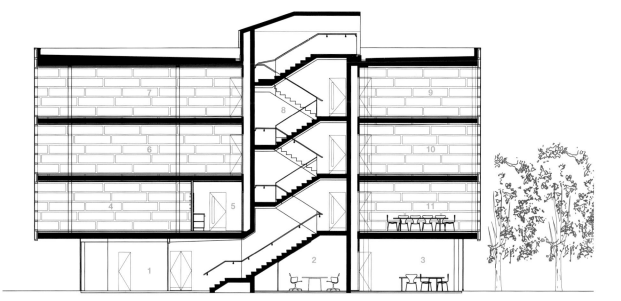

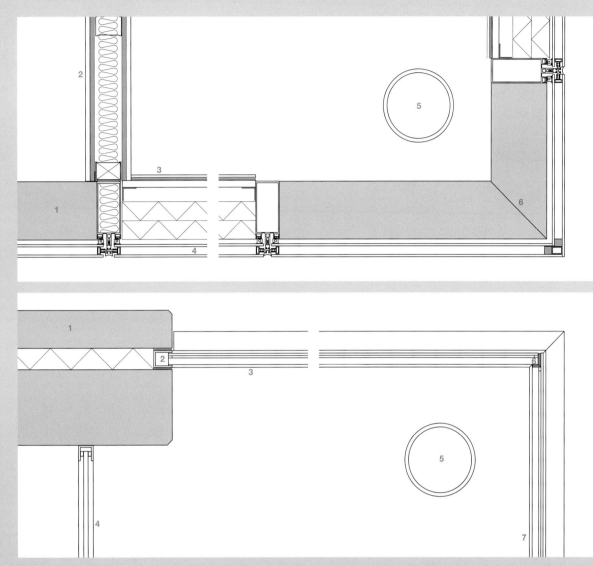

50.04
Upper Level Curtain
Walling Plan Detail
1:10
  1 Schuco curtain wall
system
  2 Internal partition
aligned with centre of
curtain wall primary
mullion
  3 Felt pinboard
panels
  4 Schuco structural
double glazed curtain
walling system
  5 Circular hollow
section steel column
  6 Frameless corner
structural support and
hanger

50.05
Ground Level Double
Glazing Plan Detail
1:10
  1 Fair-faced
reinforced concrete
outer leaf cast in self
compacting concrete
  2 Steel U-section
facade fixing
  3 Fully toughened
double glazing, fire
rated to 60 minutes
  4 Toughened glass
panel fixed within satin
anodized aluminium
channel with silicone
pointing
  5 Circular hollow
section steel column
  6 Mastic joint
  7 Fully toughened
double glazing

50.06
Cross Section
Through East Facade
1:50
  1 Flat roof waterproof
membrane
  2 Tapered rigid
insulation
  3 Reinforced roof
slab and parapet
upstand
  4 Suspended
acoustic ceiling
  5 Folded metal-
backed single ply
membrane coping
  6 Double glazed
curtain walling system
  7 Two layers of 50
mm (2 inch) thick rigid
thermal insulation
installed behind
coloured glass
  8 Primary curtain wall
transom
  9 Rubber flooring on
18 mm (7/10 inch)
waterproof exterior
grade plywood tongue
and groove sheeting,
over underfloor
heating, polyethylene
damp proof membrane
over 275 mm (104/5
inch) cast in-situ
reinforced concrete
floor slab
  10 Clear glazed panel
in curtain wall system
  11 Openable double
glazed window
  12 Powder-coated
aluminium sill profile
  13 275 mm (104/5 inch)
cast in-situ reinforced
concrete floor slab
  14 Suspended ceiling
system
  15 Prefabricated 12
mm (1/2 inch) plywood
box-blind pocket and
roller blind
  16 External soffit lining
to ground floor
overhang comprised of
two layers of 12.5 mm
(1/2 inch) multiboard
  17 Full height double
glazed units to ground
floor plinth fixed with
thermally broken
stainless steel head
and base channels
  18 Resin flooring on 65
mm (21/2 inch)
minimum thickness
screed over 35 mm
(11/3 inch) underfloor
heating system
  19 Concrete paving on
sand and cement
levelling layer on
granular sub-base

50.07
Parapet Wall Detail
1:10
  1 Flat roof waterproof
membrane
  2 Tapered rigid
insulation
  3 Waterproof
single-ply roof
membrane
  4 40 mm (11/2 inch)
rigid insulation board
  5 Vapour shield
  6 18 mm (7/10 inch)
waterproof exterior
grade plywood
sheeting fixed to
concrete upstand
  7 Folded metal-
backed single ply
membrane coping
  8 Reinforced
concrete roof slab and
parapet upstand
  9 Primary curtain wall
transom
  10 Two layers of 50

mm (2 inch) thick rigid
thermal insulation
installed behind
coloured glass
  11 Double glazed
curtain walling system
  12 Perforated acoustic
suspended ceiling
  13 Roller blind
  14 Circular hollow
section steel column

50.08
Typical Slab Edge
and Curtain Wall
Detail at Upper Level
Classrooms
1:10
  1 275 mm (104/5 inch)
cast in-situ reinforced
concrete floor slab
  2 Loose laid
polyethylene damp
proof membrane
  3 Underfloor heating
system
  4 18 mm (3/4 inch)
waterproof exterior
grade plywood tongue
and groove sheeting
from 1220 x 2440 mm
(48 x 96 inch) full
sheets
  5 Elastomeric poured
sports floor
  6 Mastic joint
  7 Plywood to
maintain 20 mm (3/4
inch) expansion joint
around perimeter of
continuous floor finish
  8 Two layers of 12.5
mm (1/2 inch) of
moisture resistant
plasterboard acoustic
cavity closer
  9 Acoustic mastic to
all edges of acoustic
cavity closer
  10 Schuco curtain wall
system with aluminium
profile frameless joint
  11 Two layers of 50
mm (2 inch) thick rigid
thermal insulation
installed behind
coloured glass
  12 Felt pinboard
panels to classrooms
  13 Tightly packed
mineral wool insulation
  14 Prefabricated 12
mm (1/2 inch) plywood
box-blind pocket
  15 Roller blind
  16 Suspended ceiling
system
  17 Full height double
glazed units to ground
floor plinth fixed with
thermally broken
stainless steel head
and base channels
  18 Mild steel
galvanized Z-section
mechanically fixed to
underside of concrete
slab at intervals for
head restraint to
glazed wall
  19 Rigid insulation to
underside of concrete
slab
  20 External soffit lining
to ground floor
overhang comprised of
two layers of 12.5 mm
(1/2 inch) multiboard
  21 25 mm (1 inch) rigid
insulation
  22 Timber packer
  23 Spacer to fit curtain
wall system
  24 Powder-coated
aluminium sill profile

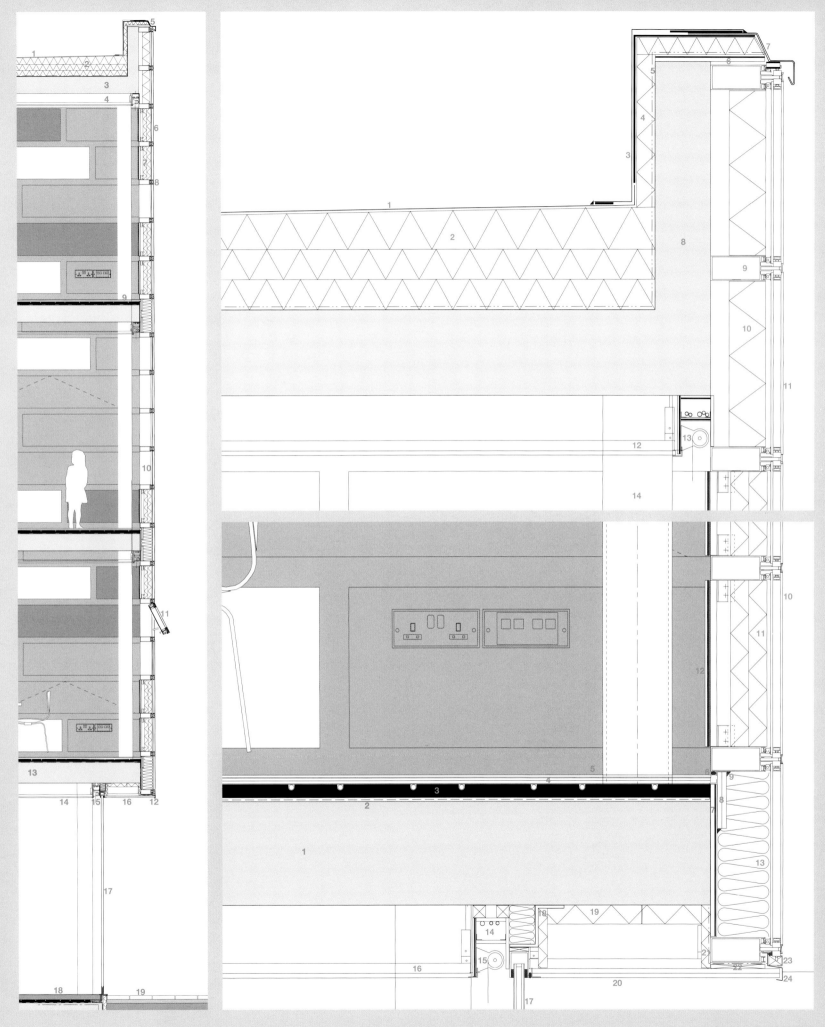

Directories
of Details and
Architects

Directory of Details

Australia

LAB architecture studio
Level 4, 325 Flinders Lane
Melbourne, Victoria 3000
info@labarchitecture.com
T +61 3 9612 1026
F +61 3 9620 3088
www.labarchitecture.com
32 SOHO Shangdu

Peter Elliott Architecture + Urban Design
Level 11 / 180 Russell Street
Melbourne, Victoria 3000
office@peterelliott.com.au
T +61 3 9654 0015
F +61 3 9654 0094
www.peterelliott.com.au
02 Latrobe University Visual Arts Centre

The Buchan Group
133 Rosslyn Street
West Melbourne, Victoria 3003
tbg@melbourne.buchan.com.au
T +61 3 9329 1077
F +61 3 9329 0481
www.buchan.com.au
05 Christchurch Art Gallery

Wood Marsh Architects
30 Beaconsfield Parade
Port Melbourne, Victoria 3207
wm@woodmarsh.com.au
T +61 3 9676 2600
F +61 3 9676 2811
www.woodmarsh.com.au
23 YVE Apartments

Austria

Baumschlager Eberle
Lindauer Strasse 31, 6911 Lochau
office@be-lochau.com
T +43 5574 430790
F +43 5574 43079 30
www.baumschlager-eberle.com
31 CUBE Biberwier-Lermoos Hotel

COOP HIMMELB(L)AU
Spengergasse 37, 1050 Vienna
office@coop-himmelblau.at
T +43 1 546 60
F +43 1 546 60 600
www.coop-himmelblau.at
27 BMW Welt

Delugan Meissl Associated Architects
Mittersteig 13 / 4, 1040 Vienna
office@deluganmeissl.at
T +43 1 585 3690
F +43 1 585 3690 11
www.deluganmeissl.at
25 House Ray 1

Denmark

Dorte Mandrup Arkitekter
Nørrebrogade 66D, 1.SAL, DK-2200, Copenhagen
info@dortemandrup.dk
T +45 3393 7350
www.dortemandrup.dk
06 Sport and Culture Centre

France

Dominique Perrault Architecture
6, rue Bouvier, 75011 Paris
dpa@d-p-a.fr
T +33 1 44 06 00 00
F +33 1 44 06 00 01
www.perraultarchitecte.com
47 EWHA Womans University

Jakob + MacFarlane
13-15 rue des petites écuries
75010, Paris
info@jakobmacfarlane.com
T +33 1 44 79 05 72
F +33 1 48 00 97 93
www.jakobmacfarlane.com
14 Institut Français de la Mode

Manuelle Gautrand Architecture
36 bd de la Bastille, 75012 Paris
contact@manuelle-gautrand.com
T +33 156 950 646
F +33 156 950 647
www.manuelle-gautrand.com
28 Citroën Flagship Showroom

Germany

Barkow Leibinger Architects
Schillerstrasse 94, 10625 Berlin
info@barkowleibinger.com
T +49 30 3157 120
F +49 30 3157 1229
www.barkowleibinger.com
35 TRUTEC Building

Medium Architects
Oberstrasse 14 b, 20144 Hamburg
office@medium-architekten.de
T +49 40 420 50 24
F +49 40 420 90 98
www.medium-architekten.de
44 Central Law Library, University of Hamburg

Ireland

Heneghan Peng Architects in association with Arthur Gibney & Partners
14-16 Lord Edward Street
Dublin 2
hparc@hparc.com
T +353 1 633 9000
F +353 1 633 9010
www.hparc.com
41 Áras Chill Dara

Japan

Kazuyo Sejima + Ryue Nishizawa / SANAA
1-5-27, Tatsumi, Koto-ku
Tokyo 135-0053
press@sanaa.co.jp
T +81 3 5534 1780
F +81 3 5534 1757
sanaa.co.jp
17 Toledo Museum of Art Glass Pavilion

Tange Associates
7–15–7 Roppongi, Minato-ku
Tokyo 106-0032
ichikawa@tangeassociates.com
T +81 3 5413 2811
F +81 3 5413 2211
www.tangeweb.com
48 Cocoon Tower

TNA Architects
5-10-19-3F Yagummo Meguro-ku
Tokyo 152-0023
mail@tna-arch.com
T +81 3 5701 1901
F +81 3 5701 1902
www.arch.webaddress
21 Ring House

Toyo Ito & Associates
Fujiya Bldg., 1-19-4, Shibuya
Shibuya-ku,Tokyo,150-0002
T +81 3 3409 5822
F +81 3 3409 5969
www.toyo-ito.co.jp
08 Municipal Funeral Hall

Norway

Snøhetta
Skur 39, Vippetangen, 0150 Oslo
contact@snohetta.com
T +47 24 15 60 60
F +47 24 15 60 61
www.snohetta.com
13 Norwegian National Opera and Ballet

Portugal

João Luís Carrilho da Graça, Architect
Calçada Marquês de Abrantes 48 2dtº
1200-719 Lisbon
arquitectos@jlcg.pt
T +351 213 920 200
F +351 213 950 232
www.jlcg.pt
15 Poitiers Theatre and Auditorium

Spain

Coll-Barreu Arquitectos
Pol. Ind. Axpe, Edificio B, Dpto. 104, 48950 Erandio, Vizcaya
info@coll-barreu-arquitectos.com
T +34 946 569 775
F +34 946 569 776
www.arch.webaddress
39 Basque Health Department Headquarters

FAM Arquitectura y Urbanismo
Carretas 19, 3º 28012, Madrid
correo@estudiofam.com
T +34 915314732
www.estudiofam.com
11 11 March Memorial

Lluís Clotet Ballús, Ignacio Paricio Ansuatégui, Abeba arquitectes
Carrer Pujades 63, 3ªpl.
08005 Barcelona
abeba@coac.net
T +34 93 485 36 25
F +34 93 309 05 67
01 Alicia Foundation

Miralles Tagliabue – EMBT
Passatge de la Pau, 10 bis, pral.
08002 Barcelona
info@mirallestagliabue.com
T +34 93 412 53 42
F +34 93 412 37 18
www.mirallestagliabue.com
33 Natural Gas Headquarters

QVE Arquitectos
San Gregorio 19, 3º Izquierda, Madrid 28004
estudio@qve-arquitectos.com
T +91 308 2497
F +91 1412818
www.qve-arquitectos.com
18 Salburúa Nature Interpretation Centre

Switzerland

Camenzind Evolution
Samariterstrasse 5
8032 Zürich
info@camenzindevolution.com
T +41 44 253 95 00
F +41 44 253 95 10
www.camenzindevolution.com
37 Cocoon

Diener & Diener Architects
Henric Petri-Strasse 22
4010 Basel
buero.basel@dienerdiener.ch
T +41 61 270 41 41
F +41 61 270 41 00
www.dienerdiener.ch
42 Westkaai Apartment Towers

Herzog & de Meuron
Rheinschanze 6, 4056 Basel
communications@herzogdemeuron.com
T +41 61 385 57 57
F +41 61 385 57 58
43 Information, Communications and Media Center, Brandenburg Technical University

The Netherlands

Erick van Egeraat
Calandstraat 23
3016 CA Rotterdam
edkwaasteniet@erickvanegeraat.com
T +31 10 436 9686
F +31 10 436 9573
www.erickvanegeraat.com
38 INHolland University of Applied Sciences

Powerhouse Company
Westplein 9, 3016 BM Rotterdam
rieke@powerhouse-company.com
T +31 10 404 67 89
www.powerhouse-company.com
20 Villa 1

UNStudio
Stadhouderskade 113
1070 AJ Amsterdam
info@unstudio.com
T +31 20 570 20 40
F +31 20 570 20 41
www.unstudio.com
30 Galleria Department Store

Wiel Arets Architects
D'Artagnanlaan 29
6213 CH Maastricht
info@wielarets.nl
T +31 43 351 2200
F +31 43 321 2192
www.wielaretsarchitects.nl
49 University Library Utrecht

UK

Carpenter Lowings Architecture & Design
198 Blackstock Road
London N5 1EN
info@carpenterlowings.com
T +44 20 7704 8102
www.carpenterlowings.com
10 International Chapel, Salvation Army International Headquarters

Cecil Balmond
13 Fitzroy Street
London W1T 4BQ
london@arup.com
T +44 20 7636 1531
www.arup.com
40 Coimbra Foot and Cycle Bridge

**dRMM
de Rijke Marsh Morgan Architects**
1 Centaur Street
London SE1 7EG
ciara@drmm.co.uk
T +44 20 7803 0777
F +44 20 7803 0666
www.drmm.co.uk
50 Clapham Manor Primary School

Foreign Office Architects
55 Curtain Road
London EC2A 3PT
kate.kilalea@f-o-a.net
T +44 20 7033 9800
F +44 20 7033 9801
www.f-o-a.net
26 John Lewis Department Store, Cineplex and Footbridges

Hawkins \ Brown
60 Bastwick Street
London EC1V 3TN
mail@hawkinsbrown.co.uk
T +44 20 7336 8030
F +44 20 7336 8851
www.hawkinsbrown.co.uk
46 New Biochemistry Building, University of Oxford

Niall McLaughlin Architects
39-51 Highgate Road
London NW5 1RS
info@niallmclaughlin.com
T +44 20 7485 9170
F +44 20 7485 9171
www.niallmclaughlin.com
22 Peabody Trust Housing

Sheppard Robson
77 Parkway
London NW1 7PU
Sr.mail@sheppardrobson.com
T +44 20 7504 1700
F +44 20 7504 1701
www.sheppardrobson.com
45 The Active Learning Lab, University of Liverpool

Terry Pawson Architects
12 Great Titchfield Street
London W1W 8BZ
tpa@terrypawson.com
T +44 20 7462 5730
www.terrypawson.com
04 VISUAL and the George Bernard Shaw Theatre

Tony Fretton Architects
109-123 Clifton Street
London EC2A 4LD
admin@tonyfretton.com
T +44 20 7729 2030
F +44 20 7729 2050
www.tonyfretton.com
19 New British Embassy

USA

Brand + Allen Architects
601 California Street, Suite 1200
San Francisco, CA 94108
k.wong@brandallen.com
T +1 415 441 0789
F +1 415 441 1089
www.brandallen.com
29 185 Post Street

Kohn Pedersen Fox Associates
11 West 42nd Street
New York, NY 10036
info@kpf.com
T +1 212 977 6500
F +1 212 956 2526
www.kpf.com
36 Shanghai World Financial Center

Murphy / Jahn
35 East Wacker Drive
Chicago, IL 60601
info@murphyjahn.com
T +1 312 427 7300
F +1 312 332 0274
www.murphyjahn.com
34 Merck-Serono Headquarters

Neil M. Denari Architects
12615 Washington Boulevard,
Los Angeles, CA 90066
info@nmda-inc.com
T +1 310 390 3033
F +1 310 390 9810
www.nmda-inc.com
24 HL23

Randall Stout Architects
12964 Washington Boulevard
Los Angeles, CA 90066
info@stoutarc.com
T +1 310 827 6876
F +1 310 827 6879
www.stoutarc.com
16 Taubman Museum of Art

Skidmore, Owings & Merrill
14 Wall Street
New York, NY 10005
somny@som.com
T +1 212 298 9300
F +1 212 298 9500
www.som.com
12 The Cathedral of Christ the Light

Steven Holl Architects
450 West 31st Street, 11th floor
New York, NY 10001
nyc@stevenholl.com
T +1 212 629 7262
F +1 212 629 7312
www.stevenholl.com
09 Nelson-Atkins Museum of Art

Studio Daniel Libeskind
2 Rector Street, 19th Floor
New York, NY 10006
info@daniel-libeskind.com
T +1 212 497 9100
F +1 212 285 2130
www.daniel-libeskind.com
03 Jewish Museum Glass Courtyard

Thomas Phifer and Partners
180 Varick Street, 11th Floor
New York, NY 10014
t.phifer@tphifer.com
T +1 212 337 0334
F +1 212 337 0603
www.tphifer.com
07 Brochstein Pavilion and Central Quadrangle, Rice University

Picture Credits

All architectural drawings are supplied courtesy, and copyright of, the respective architects, unless otherwise specified.

Photographic credits:
In all cases every effort has been made to credit the copyright holders, but should there be any omissions or errors, the publisher will be pleased to insert the appropriate acknowledgment in any subsequent editions of the book.

Front cover: drawings by featured architects, including Perrault Projets / © ADAGP, Paris and DACS, London 2010

10 © Lluis Casals Fotografia scp
14 © Trevor Mein
18 © Jewish Museum Berlin, Photo: Jens Ziehe **1, 3, 4**
     © Jan Bitter **2**
22 Helene Binet **1, 2**
     © Ros Kavanagh / VIEW **3, 4**
26 Murray Hedwig / Hedwig Photography and Imaging
30 © Torben Eskerod **1, 2, 4**
     © Michael Reisch **3**
34 scottfrances.com
38 © Courtesy Toyo Ito & Associates, Architects
42 © Andy Ryan
46 © Robert Mehl **1**
     © Dennis Gilbert / VIEW **2, 3**
50 © Esaú Acosta Pérez
54 © Tim Hursley
58 Jens Passoth / Snøhetta **1**
     Jiri Havran / Snøhetta **2, 4**
     © Gerald Zugmann / www.zugmann.com **3**
62 © Paul Raftery / VIEW **1, 2, 4**
     © Nicolas Borel **3**
66 © Fernando Guerra
70 © Timothy Hursley
74 © Iwan Baan
78 Eduardo Moratinos / www.eduardomoratinos.info
82 © Peter Cook / VIEW
88 © Jeroen Musch
92 © Edmund Sumner / VIEW
96 © Nick Kane
100 Peter Bennetts **1, 2**
     John Gollings **3**
104 © Hayes Davidson
108 © Rupert Steiner **1, 4**
     © Hertha Hurnaus **2, 3**
114 © Hufton+Crow / VIEW
118 © Marcus Buck **1**
118 © Nick Guttridge / VIEW **2, 3**
     © 2007 Ari Marcopoulos **4**
122 © Grant Smith / VIEW
126 © Mariko Reed
130 © Christian Richters
134 © Eduard Hueber / archphoto.com / CUBE Hotels

138 Minoru Iwasaki/Yanqi Ren (Japan) **1, 2, 3**
     Courtesy LAB Architecture Studio **4**
142 © Duccio Malagamba
146 © Rainer Viertlböck
150 © Christian Richters / VIEW
154 © Shinkenchiku-sha **1, 2**
     © Tim Griffith **3**
158 Courtesy Camenzind Evolution
162 © Christian Richters
166 © Inigo Bujedo Aguirre / VIEW
170 © Christian Richters **1, 2**
170 Cecil Balmond **3**
     John Balmond **4**
174 © Dennis Gilbert / VIEW
178 Drawings by architects featured in chapter, including Perrault Projets / © ADAGP, Paris and DACS, London 2010
179 Drawings by architects featured in chapter, including Perrault Projets / © ADAGP, Paris and DACS, London 2010
180 © Christian Richters
184 © Margherita Spillutini
188 © Klaus Frahm / ARTUR Images
192 © Hufton+ Crow / VIEW
196 © Keith Collie **1, 2**
196 © Tim Crocker **3**
200 © André Morin / DPA / © ADAGP, Paris and DACS, London 2010
201 Perrault Projets / © ADAGP, Paris and DACS, London 2010
202 Perrault Projets / © ADAGP, Paris and DACS, London 2010
203 Perrault Projets / © ADAGP, Paris and DACS, London 2010
204 © Edmund Sumner / VIEW
208 © Jan Bitter
212 Courtesy dRMM de Rijke Marsh Morgan Architects / © Jonas Lencer

About the CD

The attached CD can be read on both Windows and Macintosh computers. All the material on the CD is copyright protected and is for private use only. All drawings in the book and on the CD were specially created for this publication and are based on the architects' original designs.

The CD includes files for all of the drawings included in the book. The drawings for each building are contained in a numbered folder. They are supplied in two versions: the files with the suffix '.eps' are 'vector' Illustrator EPS files but can be opened using other graphics programs such as Photoshop; all the files with the suffix '.dwg' are generic CAD format files and can be opened in a variety of CAD programs.

Each file is numbered according to its original location in the book: project number, followed by the drawing number(s), followed by the scale. Hence, '01_01_200.eps' would be the eps version of the first drawing in the first project and has a scale of 1:200.

The generic '.dwg' file format does not support 'solid fill' utilized by many architectural CAD programs. All the information is embedded within the file and can be reinstated within supporting CAD programs. Select the polygon required and change the 'Attributes' to 'Solid', and the colour information should be automatically retrieved. To reinstate the 'Walls'; select all objects within the 'Walls' layer/class and amend their 'Attributes' to 'Solid'.

Acknowledgments

Thanks above all to the architects who submitted material for this book. Special thanks to Hamish Muir, the designer of this book, and to Sophia Gibb for researching the pictures. Sincere thanks to Philip Cooper and Gaynor Sermon at Laurence King, to Justin Fletcher for editing the drawings, to Vic Brand for his technical expertise and to Vimbai Shire for her patient research. And finally, special thanks to my husband Vishwa Kaushal.